Supplement to the

DICTIONARY
OF
AMERICAN LIBRARY
BIOGRAPHY

ADVISORY BOARD

Edward G. Holley, Professor
School of Information and Library Science
University of North Carolina
Chapel Hill, North Carolina

Jean E. Lowrie, Director Emeritus
School of Librarianship
Western Michigan University
Kalamazoo, Michigan

Peggy Sullivan, Dean
College of Professional Studies
Northern Illinois University
De Kalb, Illinois

Robert Wedgeworth, Dean
School of Library Service
Columbia University
New York, New York

Herbert S. White, Dean
School of Library and Information Science
Indiana University
Bloomington, Indiana

Wayne A. Wiegand, Professor
School of Library and Information Studies
University of Wisconsin
Madison, Wisconsin

SUPPLEMENT TO THE
DICTIONARY OF AMERICAN LIBRARY BIOGRAPHY

Edited by Wayne A. Wiegand

1990
Libraries Unlimited, Inc., Englewood, Colorado

Copyright © 1990 Libraries Unlimited, Inc.
Supplement to the Dictionary of American Library Biography
Copyright © 1978 Libraries Unlimited, Inc.
Dictionary of American Library Biography
All Rights Reserved
Printed in the United States of America

No part of this publication may be reproduced, stored in a retrieval system, or transmitted, in any form or by any means, electronic, mechanical, photocopying, recording, or otherwise, without the prior written permission of the publisher.

LIBRARIES UNLIMITED, INC.
P.O. Box 3988
Englewood, CO 80155-3988

Library of Congress Cataloging-in-Publication Data

Supplement to the Dictionary of American library biography / edited by
  Wayne A. Wiegand.
    xix, 184 p. 22x28 cm.
    ISBN 0-87287-586-5
    1. Librarians--United States--Biography--Dictionaries.
  I. Wiegand, Wayne A. II. Dictionary of American library biography.
  Z720.A4D5 1990
  [Suppl.]
  020'.92'2--dc20
  [B]   90-5755
                                                  CIP

Dedicated to the memory of
JESSE HAUK SHERA
(1903-1982)

Table of Contents

Preface xi

Contributors xv

About the Editor xix

Scott Adams (1909-1982) 1
by Estelle Brodman

James Tinkham Babb (1899-1968) 3
by Arthur P. Young

Tommie Dora Barker (1888-1978) 5
by James V. Carmichael, Jr.

Lillian Lewis Batchelor (1907-1977) 11
by Jacqueline C. Mancall

Bernard Reuben Berelson (1912-1979) 12
by Lester Asheim

Edwin Castagna (1909-1983) 15
by Ronald Blazek and Theresa Griffin Maggio

William Shepherd Dix (1910-1978) 19
by Michael H. Harris and Mary Ann Tourjee

Luther Harris Evans (1902-1981) 22
by John Y. Cole

Ruth Gagliardo (1895-1980) 27
by Marilyn L. Miller

Wayne Clayton Grover (1906-1970) 29
by Faye Phillips

Daniel Nash Handy (1875-1948) 32
by William Fisher

Frances Elizabeth Henne (1906-1985) 36
by Peggy Sullivan

John Phillip Immroth (1939-1976) 40
   by Blanche E. Woolls

Virginia Lacy Jones (1912-1984) 42
   by William Caynon and Rosemary Ruhig Du Mont

Augustus Frederick Kuhlman (1889-1986) 46
   by David Kaser

Harold Adlore Lancour (1908-1981) 50
   by Peter J. Gilbert

Milton Edward Lord (1898-1985) 52
   by Donald G. Davis, Jr.

Edmon Horton Low (1902-1983) 56
   by David Kaser

Archibald MacLeish (1892-1982) 59
   by Frederick J. Stielow

Guy Elwood Marion (1882-1969) 63
   by Robert V. Williams

Blanche Prichard McCrum (1887-1969) 66
   by Betty Ruth Kondayan

Francis Eugene McKenna (1921-1978) 68
   by Herbert S. White

David Chambers Mearns (1899-1981) 71
   by John C. Broderick

Daniel Melcher (1912-1985) 75
   by Gordon B. Neavill

Keyes DeWitt Metcalf (1889-1983) 78
   by Peter Hernon

Jack Cassius Morris (1911-1954) 84
   by Robert V. Williams

L. Quincy Mumford (1903-1982) 87
   by John Y. Cole

Elizabeth Nesbitt (1897-1977) 91
   by Margaret Hodges

Eli Martin Oboler (1915-1983) 94
   by Frederick J. Stielow

Benjamin Edward Powell (1905-1981) 95
   by Mattie U. Russell

Derek de Solla Price (1922-1983) 98
   by Saul Herner

Ernest James Reece (1881-1976) 101
   by Larry E. Sullivan

Sarah Rebecca Reed (1914-1978)..104
by Mary Biggs

John Stewart Richards (1892-1979)...108
by Marion Casey

Charlemae Hill Rollins (1897-1979)..111
by Holly G. Willett

Jean Carolyn Roos (1891-1982)..115
by Susan Steinfirst

Jesse Hauk Shera (1903-1982)..119
by Howard W. Winger

Louis Shores (1904-1981)...123
by Lee Shiflett

Harold Spivacke (1904-1977)..129
by D. W. Krummel

Kathleen Brown Stebbins (1905-1962).......................................131
by Miriam Tees

Maurice Falcolm Tauber (1908-1980).......................................133
by Doris Cruger Dale

Carolyn Farquhar Ulrich (1880-1969)......................................136
by Charles D. Patterson

Ralph Adrian Ulveling (1902-1980)..138
by Daniel Ring

Carl Peter Paul Vitz (1883-1981)...144
by John Mark Tucker

Douglas Waples (1893-1978)...148
by John V. Richardson, Jr.

Israel Albert Warheit (1912-1973)..151
by Gordon E. Randall

Carl Milton White (1903-1983)...153
by Larry E. Sullivan

Louis Round Wilson (1876-1979)..156
by Jesse H. Shera

Constance Mabel Winchell (1896-1983)..................................163
by Pamela Spence Richards

George Alan Works (1877-1957)..166
by John V. Richardson, Jr.

Wyllis Eaton Wright (1903-1979)..168
by Margaret Maxwell

Name Index...173

Preface

Libraries Unlimited filled a huge gap in the literature of American library history when it published the *Dictionary of American Library Biography* (*DALB*) in 1978. This work contained original biographical sketches of 302 people who made significant contributions to the development of libraries and the library profession in the United States. It also marked the culmination of a five-year cooperative effort by members of the American library history community, which was carefully coordinated and monitored by an editorial board consisting of George S. Bobinski, Jesse Hauk Shera, and Libraries Unlimited President Bohdan S. Wynar. In a short time *DALB* became the standard reference work for biography in American library history, and for the past decade it has provided valuable information.

This *Supplement to the Dictionary of American Library Biography* reflects a similar cooperative effort among members of the American library history community, many of whom contributed to the original *DALB*. It also marks Libraries Unlimited's continuing commitment to adding reliable information on the library leaders who have crafted the foundation for contemporary theory and practice in school, special, public, and academic libraries. The *Supplement* extends the coverage of its predecessor by adding biographical sketches of 51 library leaders.

In most cases, *Supplement* sketches constitute the initial or most extensive studies yet made of the biographee. A majority of these individuals died between June 30, 1976 (*DALB*'s cut-off date) and June 30, 1987 (the *Supplement*'s cut-off date). Some, however, cover individuals who died before June 30, 1976, but who were missed in the original *Dictionary* because original and basic historical research published since 1978 has revealed their quiet yet formidable contributions. All contributions offer a fresh perspective on their protagonists; most offer new information. Several are based upon research into previously unexplored primary source materials.

Like those in its predecessor, entries in the *Supplement* are arranged alphabetically by surname. With a few exceptions, the biographical sketches begin with information on the subject's family background and education. The remainder of each sketch covers professional career and contributions. Each sketch concludes with a bibliography consisting of biographical listings and obituaries, books and articles by and about the biographee, and primary source collections, if known.

HISTORY

At the January 1985 ALA midwinter conference, Bohdan Wynar asked Wayne A. Wiegand to become Editor of the *Supplement* and invited him to assemble an Advisory Board of Editors. Wiegand requested assistance from five people knowledgeable about recent library history, especially in the areas of school and special librarianship and minority contributions. These five included Edward G. Holley, now William Rand Kenan Professor at the School of Information and Library Science at the University of North Carolina at Chapel Hill; Jean E. Lowrie, Director Emeritus of the Western Michigan University School of Librarianship;

Peggy Sullivan, Dean of the Northern Illinois University College of Professional Studies; Robert Wedgeworth, Dean of the Columbia University School of Library Service; and Herbert S. White, Dean of the Indiana University School of Library and Information Science. Each member of the Advisory Board assisted the Editor not only by evaluating candidates for inclusion in the *Supplement*, but also by helping to identify potential authors for each biographee. In addition, the editor also relied upon the membership lists of the American Library Association Library History Round Table, an organization whose early interest in the original *DALB* continues to the present. Several of the authors selected were also personal friends and colleagues of their protagonists and had an extensive set of experiences from which to draw observations of their subjects.

SELECTION CRITERIA

The *Supplement* follows the practice of the original *DALB* by slighting coverage of book dealers, book collectors, and founders of large and unique libraries, but including all Librarians of Congress and presidents of the American Library Association (nine of whom died between June 30, 1976, and June 30, 1987). Forty-two others made the final list by weathering an editorial review process that began with a pool of 75. Nineteen of those 75 had been inherited from the files of previous *DALB* editors, who had worked for several years beyond the publication of the original *DALB* to identify individuals worthy of consideration for inclusion in a supplement or new edition.

During that period, coverage of several of the 19 individuals had been assigned to authors, who by previous arrangement, published their sketches in the pages of the *Journal of Library History* (now *Libraries and Culture*). These are reprinted here by permission. They include sketches of Douglas Waples and George Works by John V. Richardson, Jr., and Louis Round Wilson by Jesse Shera. All other decisions for inclusion were made by the current *Supplement* Advisory Board of Editors, which sought to identify deceased individuals who made contributions of national significance to library development, who wrote influential professional publications, or who could claim major accomplishments in special areas of librarianship. The *Supplement* had an added mission, however. It also sought to rescue several special librarians missed in the original *DALB* and to review the history of women and minorities in American libraries. The contributions of these individuals have often been circumscribed—and regularly buried—by forces in the sociocultural environment in which they performed their professional duties. Future generations of library historians also need to be aware of these historical biases.

Editors of the *Supplement* readily admit that the selection process is not perfect. Just as the original *DALB* missed people like Blanche Prichard McCrum and Daniel Nash Handy because published research had not yet identified their contributions, this *Supplement* has undoubtedly missed several people for whom future research will justify the need for coverage in coming supplements or new editions of *DALB*. We commend them to their efforts and encourage them to correct our shortsightedness. The process of writing history is always one of discovery and rediscovery.

ACKNOWLEDGMENTS

The Editor would like to thank the Advisory Board of Editors who contributed freely of their time, their expertise, and extensive talents. He would also like to thank all contributors for their patience throughout the project, and above all to congratulate them on their scholarship. Special thanks are due to Deanne Holzberlein, Northern Illinois University, who volunteered to compile an index for the *Supplement*, which also serves the original *DALB*. The Editor would also like to thank all the librarians and archivists who assisted contributors in their research, and especially the librarians at the universities of Kentucky and Wisconsin, where quality collections built over the decades enabled him to track down scores of details and expand the bibliographies.

The editorial staff of Libraries Unlimited deserves much praise, and especially Rebecca Morris, In-House Editor, whose patience and promptness are refreshing. Judy Gay Matthews was responsible for the book design and typesetting. Bohdan Wynar's continued support of biographical coverage of library leaders of the past is unique among publishers of library literature. The American library history community continues in his debt.

Finally, a note about the dedicatory page. The *Supplement* is dedicated to the memory of Jesse Hauk Shera (1903-1982), a pioneer in American library history whose *Foundations of the Public Library: The Origins of the Public Library Movement in New England, 1629-1855* (Chicago: University of Chicago Press, 1949), remains a seminal work, and who served so willingly and ably on the original *DALB* editorial board. All royalties from this *Supplement* will be donated to an endowed fund set up for the Jesse Shera Award, offered annually by the American Library Association Library Research Round Table for an outstanding and original contribution to library research.

Wayne A. Wiegand
Editor

Contributors

LESTER ASHEIM, Professor Emeritus, School of Information and Library Science, University of North Carolina, Chapel Hill, North Carolina

MARY BIGGS, Director of Libraries, Mercy College, Dobbs Ferry, New York

RONALD BLAZEK, Professor, School of Library and Information Studies, Florida State University, Tallahassee, Florida

JOHN C. BRODERICK, Assistant Librarian for Research Services, Library of Congress, Washington, D.C.

ESTELLE BRODMAN, Librarian and Professor of Medical History Emerita, Washington University School of Medicine, St. Louis, Missouri

MARION CASEY, Professor, Department of History, University of San Francisco, San Francisco, California

JAMES V. CARMICHAEL, JR., Assistant Professor, Department of Library and Information Studies, University of North Carolina at Greensboro, Greensboro, North Carolina

WILLIAM A. CAYNON, Assistant Professor, School of Library Science, Kent State University, Kent, Ohio

JOHN Y. COLE, Director, Center for the Book, Library of Congress, Washington, D.C.

DORIS CRUGER DALE, Professor, Department of Curriculum and Instruction, Southern Illinois University, Carbondale, Illinois

DONALD G. DAVIS, JR., Professor, Graduate School of Library and Information Science, University of Texas at Austin, Austin, Texas

ROSEMARY RUHIG DU MONT, Professor and Dean, School of Library Science, Kent State University, Kent, Ohio

WILLIAM FISHER, Associate Professor, Division of Library and Information Science, San Jose State University, San Jose, California

PETER J. GILBERT, Graduate Student, School of Library and Information Studies, University of Wisconsin-Madison, Madison, Wisconsin

MICHAEL H. HARRIS, Professor, College of Library and Information Science, University of Kentucky, Lexington, Kentucky

SAUL HERNER, Chairman, Herner and Company, Arlington, Virginia

PETER HERNON, Professor, Graduate School of Library and Information Science, Simmons College, Boston, Massachusetts

MARGARET HODGES, Professor Emerita, School of Library and Information Science, University of Pittsburgh, Pittsburgh, Pennsylvania

DAVID KASER, Distinguished Professor, School of Library and Information Science, Indiana University, Bloomington, Indiana

BETTY RUTH KONDAYAN, Lexington, Virginia

D. W. KRUMMEL, Professor, Graduate School of Library and Information Science, University of Illinois, Urbana, Illinois

THERESA GRIFFIN MAGGIO, Head of Reference and Technical Services, Southwest Georgia Regional Library, Bainbridge, Georgia

JACQUELINE C. MANCALL, Professor, College of Information Studies, Drexel University, Philadelphia, Pennsylvania

MARGARET F. MAXWELL, Professor, Graduate Library School, University of Arizona, Tucson, Arizona

MARILYN L. MILLER, Chair, Department of Library and Information Studies, University of North Carolina at Greensboro, Greensboro, North Carolina

GORDON B. NEAVILL, Associate Professor, Graduate School of Library Service, University of Alabama, Tuscaloosa, Alabama

CHARLES D. PATTERSON, Professor, School of Library and Information Science, Louisiana State University, Baton Rouge, Louisiana

FAYE PHILLIPS, Head, Louisiana and Lower Mississippi Valley Collections, Louisiana State University, Baton Rouge, Louisiana

GORDON RANDALL, Banner Elk, North Carolina

PAMELA SPENCE RICHARDS, Associate Professor, School of Communication, Information and Library Studies, Rutgers University, New Brunswick, New Jersey

JOHN V. RICHARDSON, JR., Associate Professor, Graduate School of Library and Information Science, University of California at Los Angeles, Los Angeles, California

DANIEL F. RING, Reference Librarian, Kresge Library, Oakland University, Rochester, Michigan

MATTIE U. RUSSELL, Curator of Manuscripts Emerita, William R. Perkins Library, Duke University, Durham, North Carolina

JESSE HAUK SHERA, Professor and Director Emeritus (Deceased), School of Library Science, Case Western Reserve University, Cleveland, Ohio

LEE SHIFLETT, Associate Professor, School of Library and Information Science, Louisiana State University, Baton Rouge, Louisiana

SUSAN STEINFIRST, Associate Professor, School of Information and Library Science, University of North Carolina, Chapel Hill, North Carolina

FREDERICK J. STIELOW, Associate Professor, School of Library and Information Science, Catholic University of America, Washington, D.C.

LARRY SULLIVAN, Chief, Rare Books and Special Collections Division, Library of Congress, Washington, D.C.

PEGGY SULLIVAN, Dean and Professor, College of Professional Studies, Northern Illinois University, DeKalb, Illinois

MIRIAM H. TEES, Associate Professor Emerita, Graduate School of Library and Information Studies, McGill University, Montreal, Quebec, Canada

MARY ANN TOURJEE, North Adams, Massachusetts

JOHN MARK TUCKER, Senior Reference Librarian and Professor of Library Science, Humanities, Social Science and Education Library, Purdue University, West Lafayette, Indiana

HERBERT S. WHITE, Dean and Professor, School of Library and Information Science, Indiana University, Bloomington, Indiana

HOLLY G. WILLETT, Assistant Professor, School of Library and Information Studies, University of Wisconsin-Madison, Madison, Wisconsin

ROBERT V. WILLIAMS, Associate Professor, College of Library and Information Science, University of South Carolina, Columbia, South Carolina

HOWARD W. WINGER, Professor Emeritus, Graduate Library School, University of Chicago, Chicago, Illinois

BLANCHE E. WOOLLS, Professor, School of Library and Information Science, University of Pittsburgh, Pittsburgh, Pennsylvania

ARTHUR P. YOUNG, Dean of Libraries, Thomas Cooper Library, University of South Carolina, Columbia, South Carolina

About the Editor

Wayne E. Wiegand is Professor in the School of Library and Information Studies, University of Wisconsin-Madison. He has authored and edited scores of articles and books on the library profession and American library history, including *Leaders in American Academic Librarianship, 1925-1975* (1983), *"An Active Instrument for Propaganda": The American Public Library during World War I* (1989), and *Politics of an Emerging Profession: The American Library Association, 1876-1917* (1986), which won the 1988 G. K. Hall Award for Outstanding Contribution to Library Literature. He is currently working on a biography of Melvil Dewey.

ADAMS, SCOTT (1909-1982)

Scott Adams, a descendant of the *Mayflower*'s William Bradford, was born to Scott and Edith Fisher Adams in Agawam, Massachusetts, on November 20, 1909. Educated in the elementary and high schools of Springfield, Massachusetts, he took his undergraduate degree at Yale University in 1930 and his library school degree from Columbia University in 1940. Between degrees he taught English and Latin for one year at a private school in Wynnewood, Pennsylvania; worked as a seaman; and, in the depths of the Great Depression, spent six years as a book distribution salesman for a Springfield commercial distribution company. It was the latter experience, with its 40,000 miles of driving the back roads of several midwestern states, that introduced him to many librarians and taught him about the book trade, especially about out-of-print materials. These experiences—and his added responsibilities after marriage to Barbara Winn in 1935—convinced him that he should become a librarian. He often said that Emerson Greenaway, then at Pittsburgh's Carnegie Free Public Library, finally persuaded him to go to library school in 1939.

With his background in book distribution it seemed natural that Adams should be appointed head of the order department of the Teachers College Library of Columbia University immediately after graduation from library school. He remained at that post through 1942 when the need to provide for a growing family induced him to accept the position of head of the order and catalog department at the Providence, Rhode Island, Public Library. Somehow he also managed that year to write and have published his first book, *The O.P. Market* (New York: Bowker, 1943), based on the knowledge he had amassed as a book salesman. The book went into a second edition in 1945.

Adams was appointed head of the acquisitions division at the Army Medical Library in Washington, D.C. (now the National Library of Medicine) in 1945. The Army Medical Library was undergoing a major revitalization and reorganization. When he arrived at the Library in 1943 he found piles of unrecorded serials, uncataloged books, gaps in the collection, and only a few systematic programs for overcoming these shortcomings. Modern cataloging was just beginning there. A shelflist was under development, and a classification scheme was being tried out. Adams quickly compiled "want-lists," set up exchanges to fill gaps in receipts created by the war and to assure receipt of on-going publications; and he negotiated with the American Medical Association to acquire some missed publications from the 1930s. He remained with the Army Medical Library/National Library of Medicine from 1945 to 1950 except for an eight-month absence (1945-1946) to take part in a Library of Congress Mission to Germany to help reestablish the German publishing system and to fill in gaps in wartime receipts for American university libraries. He returned to the Army Medical Library in 1946, and for the next four years he was officially acting librarian, first under Colonel Joseph McNinch and then under Frank B. Rogers.

In 1950, Adams became librarian at the National Institutes of Health (NIH), another institution undergoing great changes in size, groups of people served, and purposes. He found there only the beginnings of a library suitable for the new establishment. He set about to bring together three libraries, each with different classification and bibliographic schemes and differing acquisitions policies and methods. The three libraries had come under NIH from the merger of several different Health Department institutions forming the new National Institutes of Health being built in Bethesda, Maryland. He supervised the physical consolidation of the three libraries, moved them into a new building, and oversaw the formation of a single bibliographic record to encompass all their holdings. He reorganized the acquisitions policies and methods of procurement, and he promulgated service requirements for the new institution. Sensing scientists' need for more personalized service in the larger field of librarianship, he devised a forerunner of what later became known as the *clinical librarian*.

During a period from 1959 to 1960 he served as director of the Foreign Science Program of the National Science Foundation—a logical position in light of his background and personal interests. When Frank B. Rogers asked him to return in 1960 as deputy director of the National Library of Medicine (NLM), Adams accepted. Here he planned (with Estelle Brodman) the extramural program which was later embodied in the Medical Library Assistance Act of 1965. He described the ideas and background of this plan in his Janet Doe lecture to the Medical Library Association (MLA) in 1972 and in the association's Oral History Project tapes in 1980.

Adams made a major contribution to the development of the MEDLARS system (the first successful computer-based program for storage and retrieval of published information) by centralizing bibliographic storage while decentralizing (and therefore repackaging on the local level) the retrieval process. For that purpose, medical school libraries and later hospital libraries were incorporated into MEDLARS and later into its MEDLINE system. This made local libraries distribution points for a system larger than each could have produced individually and enhanced the status of their librarians. Many of these same ideas were also incorporated in a five-year plan for NLM that Adams produced, which was adopted in 1966 by its Board of Regents. Adams remained at NLM until his retirement from government service in 1970.

Throughout his career Adams acted on other professional interests. Shortly after he returned from Europe in 1946, he began to suggest changes in the handling of scientific information that he felt were mandated by the fundamental changes in the pursuit of scientific knowledge occurring in the mid-20th century. These changes included the substitution of mission-oriented research for previously discipline-oriented science, the entrance of governments into scientific funding, and the sudden explosion of scientific literature emanating from war experiences—overwhelming to scientists and enhancing the value of secondary and tertiary tools. Adams wanted such tools as selective abstracting and reviewing (*Proceedings Translation Supplement*, for example), recurring bibliographies in particular fields (such as Parkinson's disease or diabetes), specialized translations, as well as the later *clinical librarian* to help the practitioner at his point of need. In one form or another all his subsequent work was based on a new vision of modern science and an examination of the modern techniques available to solve its communication problems. These he described in a number of his speeches and articles finally culminating in his well-received book, *Medical Bibliography in an Age of Discontinuity* (Chicago: Medical Library Association, 1981).

Although originally planned as a sequel to Estelle Brodman's *Development of Medical Bibliography* (Chicago: Medical Library Association, 1954) but entirely different in plan and outlook, Adams's book contended that violent deflections ("discontinuities") in the pursuit of science are brought about by changes in the ambient social, economic, and technical world (somewhat like a ray of light refracted by a lens) and that changes in the handling of scientific information must follow. The bulk of the book is a description of the changes in science and scientific information handling from the end of World War II to about 1970. Among these are (1) the change from scientific and bibliographic control by professional organizations to control by governmental and commercial entities and (2) the selective repackaging of the same scientific information to meet the needs of different groups of users.

To reach these conclusions Adams called on past experience. He had edited with Frank B. Rogers a *Guide to Russian Medical Literature* (Washington, D.C.: Government Printing Office, 1958), and at the National Institutes of Health in 1950 he was in charge of its Russian Scientific Translations Program under Public Law 480. This experience led him to conclude that scientists were better served by translations of selected and evaluated publications or by reviews of the literature by specialists in the field rather than by cover-to-cover translations. He brought this idea with him when he became director of the Foreign Science Information Program of the National Science Foundation in 1959. Later as consultant for the World Health Organization and as *rapporteur* for and an important participant in the meetings of the Universal System for Information in Science and Technology (UNISIST) Program devised by the International Council of Scientific Unions (ICSU) and UNESCO in the 1970s for worldwide bibliographical control in the sciences, Adams enlarged the scope of each to encompass Third World countries. Moreover, as co-chairman of the Third International Congress on Medical Librarianship in Brussels in 1969, he enrolled medical librarians throughout the world in the process.

A "joiner" who took his responsibilities seriously, Scott Adams served many professional organizations. He was at different times president of the District of Columbia Library Association, director of the Washington, D.C. Special Libraries Association, secretary of the U.S. Book Exchange, president of the American Documentation Institute (now the American Society for Information Science), secretary of the Council of National Library Associations, chairman of a screening panel for the Fulbright Awards, chairman of the Joint Committee for the Protection of

Cultural and Scientific Resources, and president of the Medical Library Association, among others. He helped establish a chapter of the Medical Library Association in Maryland, Virginia, and the District of Columbia. He was 1973 Phineas T. Windsor Lecturer at the University of Illinois Library School and the 1972 Janet Doe Lecturer for the MLA. He was also the recipient of many honors—the Noyes Award in 1969 and the newly created MLA President's Award as well as a posthumous award from the American Society for Information Science in 1983 for *Medical Bibliography in an Age of Discontinuity*.

Even in retirement Adams remained active. The 1970s saw him accepting a series of assignments related to international science information, which sent him traveling to many different parts of the world, often with deleterious effects on his health. At various times he was advisor to the Foreign Secretary of the National Academy of Sciences, head of an Exchange Mission to the Soviet Union to study its information programs, and *rapporteur* to no fewer than three UNISIST conferences. During this time he wrote *UNISIST: Synopsis of a Feasibility Study of a World Science Information System* (UNESCO, 1971). After the death of his first wife, Barbara, he married Joan Titley of Louisville in 1974. In that same year, he became director of the University of Louisville's Center for International Education and director of its Urban Studies Center.

Everyone who worked near Scott Adams recognized his modesty, his sweet disposition, his loyalty, his discretion, his patience, and his ability to put people at ease; all admired his facile mind. He was highly skilled at elegant communication; his knowledge of English was impressive. A courteous man, he always learned a few words of the language of countries in which he worked.

Scott Adams was quick with new and innovative ideas—sometimes pursuing some unworthy ones uselessly. His tendency to procrastinate and leave large quantities of work to be done quickly irritated his assistants and lost him secretaries. His published articles ranged from pragmatic "how-to" descriptions to some searchingly theoretical and philosophical. His best are excellent. He could talk better extemporaneously than most people could after drafting a talk several times. In the future, as his writings are studied more closely, the force of his mind will undoubtedly influence the field he illuminated. After several years of increasing medical difficulties he died in Louisville on October 3, 1982, of chronic obstructive pulmonary disorder.

Biographical listings and obituaries—Rogers, Frank B. "Scott Adams." *Bulletin of the Medical Library Association* 55:343-4 (July 1967); Rogers, Frank B. "Scott Adams, 1909-1983." *Bulletin of the Medical Library Association* 71:245-8 (April 1983). **Books and articles about the biographee**—Garfield, Eugene. "Scott Adams and *Medical Bibliography in an Age of Discontinuity*—A Tribute to a Visionary Leader in the Field of Medical Information." *Current Contents* 26:5-11 (June 27, 1983); Rogers, Frank B. "Adams, Scott." In *Encyclopedia of Library and Information Science*. New York: Marcel Dekker, 1983. Vol. 38, Supp. 3, pp. 1-7. **Primary sources and archival materials**—Biographical interview with Scott Adams by Wyndham Miles in July 1979 at National Library of Medicine (2 tapes); biographical interview with Scott Adams by Carol Fenichel in March 1980 in Archives of Medical Library Association (9 tapes), housed at the National Library of Medicine.

—ESTELLE BRODMAN

BABB, JAMES TINKHAM (1899-1968)

The only child of James Elisha and Daisy (Tinkham) Babb, James Tinkham Babb was born August 23, 1899, in Lewiston, Idaho. Babb moved to the east coast in 1917 and enrolled in Phillips Exeter Academy. Following a brief period of military training at Cornell University in 1918, he graduated in 1920. That fall Babb entered Yale University where he earned respectable grades, enjoyed social activities, and trounced every tennis opponent. Only much later would his early exposure to such scholars and collectors as Chauncey B. Tinker, Wilmarth S. Lewis, and Harvey Cushing surface in the form of bibliophilic pursuits and a library career.

Intending to become a lawyer, his father's profession, Babb enrolled in the Yale Law School. By 1926 he left law school, married Margaret Bradley, and joined his father-in-law's New Haven investment firm of Edward M. Bradley and Company, Inc. Their son, James Bradley, was born in 1933, and their daughter Barbara arrived in 1937. During this period Babb became an avid reader of fiction and a collector of books and manuscripts by William Beckford, Joseph Conrad, Ernest Hemingway, William McFee, L. A. G. Strong, and H. M. Tomlinson. Babb's bibliography of the works of nautical author William McFee was published in 1931. Reviewer Gilbert Troxell in the *Saturday Review of Literature* complimented Babb for the "clearness and finality" of his treatment. Later Babb began to acquire a substantial collection of American fiction published before 1850. This penchant naturally took Babb to the Yale Library on numerous occasions and to a leadership role in the Yale Library Associates, a fledgling support group. His special commitment was recognized in 1938 by appointment as assistant librarian. Elevated to associate librarian in 1941, Babb succeeded Bernhard Knollenberg as university librarian in 1945.

For the next two decades Babb presided over the dramatic growth of Yale's collections and solidified its position as a premier scholarly library. Babb had a natural affinity with book collectors, quickly earning a reputation as a "collector of collectors." His western affability, reinforced by his eastern sophistication, proved to be compelling attributes to potential donors. Longtime Yale rare book specialist Marjorie G. Wynne observed that Babb "could ... charm unsuspecting collectors into thinking Yale was the only place for their collections. The tall, handsome, graceful librarian, as transparent and guileless as the day he came out of the west, had a way with donors that was the despair of rivals."

During Babb's stewardship the collection increased by 1.3 million volumes to a total of 4.7 million volumes. Noteworthy additions were made to rare books and archival holdings. A selective enumeration of the more significant acquisitions might include the *Bay Psalm Book*, the William Robertson Coe collection of Western Americana and ornithology, the Boswell Papers, the many donations of Hebrew manuscripts by Louis M. Rabinowitz, the John J. Slocum collection of James Joyce, the Thomas E. Marston medieval manuscripts, the Curt von Faber du Faur Collection of German baroque literature, the David Wagstaff Collection of Sporting Books, the Pacific Northwest Collection of Winlock Miller, and the Robert Louis Stevenson collection donated by Edwin J. Beinecke. These and other collections came to Yale, in large measure through Babb's cultivation of donors with and without a Yale connection. By his retirement in 1965, the Yale Library Associates provided more than $200,000 annually for enhancement of the collections. Insatiable in his quest for new Yale collections, Babb nevertheless respected the territorial claims of peer libraries. Everyone knew Byron went to Yale and Keats resided at Harvard.

Although devoted to the building of distinctive collections, Babb was concerned with all facets of library administration. In staff recruitment, a constant activity, he often added persons who did not possess library degrees, a practice not always approved by others. Many nonlibrarians were employed as curators of special collections. When Babb was asked if all those curators were not a "damned nuisance and headache," he replied: "Yes, and the moment they stop being so I will get rid of them." Librarians managed the technical operations, public services, and many department/school libraries, but did not attain a level of professional authority throughout the Yale Library. Babb's appointments in the professional ranks included such distinguished associate librarians as David W. Clift and John H. Ottemiller; and Frederick G. Kilgour, librarian of the medical library. Babb detested the bureaucratic regimen and consequently eschewed regular staff meetings and other organizational trappings. Viewed by some as aloof, he was approachable to those who penetrated the cool exterior. Administrators reported ample freedom to manage their units and a standing offer from Babb to assist whenever needed. Improving staff salaries was a continuing concern, and Babb made considerable gains for Yale library personnel during his tenure.

Two issues pervaded Babb's term: the organization of the many school and department libraries and the perennial lack of adequate space. Long a decentralized library system, the Yale departmental and school libraries were incrementally placed under the central library beginning in the 1950s. Within a decade all of Yale's 50 separate libraries were brought under the authority of the university librarian. Together these libraries held more than 1.5 million volumes. Centralization did not retard the proliferation of libraries; 13 new libraries were established during Babb's directorship. A second, persistent concern was the lack of adequate space to house the burgeoning collection, a concern that led to a systematic plan for selective book retirement.

In his annual report of 1952-1953 Babb noted that before World War II Yale was ambitious to be a library of record, a "... questionable ambition in an educational institution, impossible of attainment and based on lack of, or fear to use, judgment in book selection on the part of the librarians." Yale must take "drastic steps," Babb concluded, and not "wait for the millennium." By

1959 slightly over 100,000 volumes had been transferred to compact storage. And in 1962 Yale completed a three-year project supported by the Council on Library Resources known as the Selective Book Retirement Program. Babb's commitment to discard and storage was often tested by fractious scholars from several departments. Even storage would not save research libraries from the consequences of exponential growth. Cooperative acquisitions and mutually agreed upon areas of collection emphases, a venerable concept, remained Babb's first choice as the long-term solution. Yale's analytical approach to solving the problems of rapid growth and constricted space punctured the myth of self-sufficiency and ushered in a new era of resource evaluation.

Babb surely had the Midas touch with donors. He is credited with raising more than $30 million in monetary funds and $20 million more in donated books, collections, and papers. Two donations bracket the Babb years and confirm his special talent for attracting donors to Yale. William Robertson Coe's Collection of Western Americana, donated in 1945, and the numerous gifts of the Beinecke family, culminating in the magnificent Beinecke Rare Book Library, dedicated in 1963, testify to the quality and magnitude of Babb's acquisition efforts for Yale. Librarian Raymond P. Morris of the Yale Divinity School saluted Babb's acquisitive genius which is "... destined to make Yale distinctive and great, a place of superlatives in the world of books."

Considering the extent of Babb's immersion in the world of scholarship and early bibliographical contribution, his own record of publication is modest. Recurrent themes in his library-related writing included the call for selective acquisitions and simplified processing, the need to plan adequate facilities, and the importance of cooperative arrangements with other libraries. His writing style is sparse and direct with little evidence of substantial research.

Active in professional associations, Babb was president of the Bibliographical Society of America (1950-1952) and the Connecticut Library Association (1945-1946). He was also a member of the Grolier Club, the Century Association, the New Haven Colony Historical Society, and the governing board of the Yale University Press. In 1962 Jacqueline Kennedy asked Babb to oversee selecting books for the White House library, a list which numbered 2,600 volumes in 32 categories.

Politically, Babb was a Republican. His favorite hobby was fishing, a sport at which he was more persistent than proficient.

Undeniably "bold for Yale," Babb retired in 1965 after nearly three decades of exceptional service. The library staff created a book fund in honor of his retirement. He died three years later on July 21, 1968. Perhaps the best distillation of Babb's career was penned by book collector and newspaper columnist Bradford F. Swan in the *Providence Journal*. Babb was a man of "taste and drive" who in his quest for excellence at Yale became "one of the great librarians of modern times." His enduring legacy, shared with such contemporaries as Robert Bingham Downs and Lawrence Clark Powell, was that of master collector and proponent of the research library.

Biographical listings and obituaries—*National Cyclopaedia of American Biography* 54; [Obituary]. *AB Bookman's Weekly* 42:410 (August 5-12, 1968); [Obituary]. *Yale University Gazette* 43:165-70 (January 1969); *Who Was Who in America* V (1966-1973); Wynne, Marjorie G. "In Memoriam: James Tinkham Babb, 1899-1968." [Obituary]. *Bibliographical Society of America, Papers* 63:1-3 (January 1969). **Books and articles about the biographee**—Liebert, Herman W. "James T. Babb." *Bulletin of Bibliography* 23:217-19 (January-April 1963); *The White House Library: A Short Title List*. Washington, D.C.: White House Historical Association, 1967. **Primary sources and archival materials**—Personal interview with Herman W. Liebert (January 29, 1987); telephone interview with Frederick G. Kilgour (March 13, 1987). Material by and about James Tinkham Babb is held in the Division of Manuscripts and Archives, Sterling Memorial Library, Yale University.

—ARTHUR P. YOUNG

BARKER, TOMMIE DORA (1888-1978)

Tommie Dora Barker was born on November 15, 1888, in Rockmart, Georgia, to Thomas Nathanial and Medora Elizabeth Lovejoy Barker. Her father had immigrated to the United States from Abaco, Bahama Islands, in 1868 and taught in Atlanta and Rockmart schools. Her mother, a Georgia native, was the daughter of a Methodist minister. Barker received her education at Atlanta Girls' High, Agnes Scott College, and the Carnegie Library School of Atlanta, from which she was graduated in 1909.

Throughout her long career, Barker was involved in major national and regional planning and coordinating efforts. Her professional life can be divided into three phases: her years as public librarian (1909-1930) and as director of the Carnegie Library School of Atlanta (1915-1930); her years as American Library Association (ALA) regional field agent for the South (1930-1936); and her long tenure as dean (1936-1947) and later director (1948-1954) of the Division of Librarianship at Emory University.

Barker's career began inauspiciously when Thomas M. Owen of the Alabama Department of Archives and History reluctantly hired the unassuming young woman as assistant in charge of library extension. The position entailed management of Alabama's system of traveling libraries, but also included, in 1909 and 1910, responsibility for a training course in library work, routine reference work, reorganization of the department's library, and the position of Secretary for the Alabama Library Association. Despite this great workload, Owen assured her in 1910 that her work had given him "entire satisfaction."

Barker returned to Atlanta in 1911 as assistant, then head of the reference department. She also taught reference in the Carnegie Library School of Atlanta, which was housed in the library from 1905 until 1930. After librarian Katherine H. Wooten resigned over a salary dispute in 1914, Barker became assistant librarian under Delia Foreacre Sneed. When Sneed resigned in 1915 to marry, Barker succeeded her. She stayed in this position for 15 years. She never married and lived throughout her career with her mother and two of her sisters. One of her sisters, Mary Cornelia Barker, a labor activist in the Atlanta teachers' union and president of the American Federation of Teachers (1926-1931), profoundly influenced Barker's political and social philosophy.

Unlike most of her predecessors as director of Atlanta's public library, Barker did not belong to the social elite of the city. The selection of Barker as librarian represented a departure from the slightly oligarchic patterns of appointment that had prevailed in the Gilded Age. Her values reflected the professional ethic of the 1920s, which stressed efficiency, self-discipline, and scientific management.

Until at least 1930, southern librarianship was controlled by women. Only larger southern cities and universities offered the higher salaries commanded by men. Barker never seemed to doubt that women would occupy positions of leadership commensurate with their abilities, but she rarely spoke on women's issues. She implied, however, that if women were dissatisfied with disproportionate male representation in elective offices, it was their responsibility to change the situation with their votes.

Atlanta's Carnegie Library, like most other public libraries, suffered drastic budget cuts in the years immediately during and following World War I. Dual teaching and staffing appointments, crowded quarters, and the tenor of stricture and retrenchment in the city's government, particularly during the mayoralty of Walter A. Sims, created a climate inhospitable to expansion. In spite of these difficulties, circulation of books nearly tripled during Barker's administration. Of all her early achievements, however, she was most proud of opening the city's first black branch library in 1921.

Barker's administrative style consisted of understated, dignified, and businesslike solutions to problems. She usually based her decisions and recommendations on statistical evidence. She was not noted for her beauty or even her "southern charm," and some people found her personality forbidding. Her supporters, however, judged her competent, uniquely knowledgeable about southern library conditions, and possessed of a fine sense of dry wit. Although not usually well liked, she was universally respected.

The Carnegie Library School of Atlanta which Barker headed was the South's only fully accredited library school until 1932. In 1921 C. C. Williamson had recommended to the Board of Education for Librarianship (BEL) of the American Library Association (ALA) that all schools affiliated with public libraries be terminated, and he specifically mentioned Atlanta. He found no evidence of a demand for highly trained public librarians in the South and felt that well-established northern schools such as Pratt could satisfy southern library training needs for more demanding positions.

Although she apparently never read Williamson's specific recommendations, Barker worked closely with the BEL to upgrade her school over the next several years. Through her efforts, the school became loosely affiliated with Emory University in 1925, the curriculum was gradually expanded, and the faculty was enlarged. In 1926, the BEL granted the school junior undergraduate status, followed by designation as a graduate library school only two years later.

Barker was instrumental in convincing the Carnegie Corporation and the Rosenwald Fund to contribute $50,000 each over a five-year period beginning in 1930 to ease financial burdens during the school's most intense period of transition. In 1930, the school was physically moved to the Emory campus and became a professional school within the university. In recognition of these achievements, Emory awarded Barker an honorary doctorate in 1930. She was the first woman to receive such a degree from that school. Convinced of the school's soundness, the Carnegie Corporation permanently endowed it with an additional $100,000 in 1940.

Tommie Dora Barker identified herself with the South throughout her career. Like fellow southern librarians Mary Utopia Rothrock, Louis Round Wilson, and Charlotte Templeton, she advocated solutions to southern library problems formulated by the region's leaders rather than by the ALA. This attitude, necessitated by the region's biracial system, large rural population, high illiteracy rate, and general poverty, led to the creation in 1920 of an informal association of southern librarians. Known after 1922 as the Southeastern Library Association (SELA), the association became the instrument for regional policy making.

As one of the pioneers of SELA, Barker became its third president during the 1926-1928 biennium. In her home state, she had headed the Georgia Library Association (GLA) in 1920-1921. She also served continuously on the Georgia Library Commission from 1916 until 1937. Through SELA, however, she focused her energies on commonalities of library problems in the southern states.

Barker distinguished herself from some of her southern contemporaries in seeking cooperation from ALA for the promotion of southern library development. She joined ALA in 1909, served on the Membership Committee in 1921-1922, and on the ALA Council from 1923 to 1928. Her nomination to the honorary post of first vice-president of ALA in 1927 was a major event among southern librarians of the era since it was only the second time a southerner—excluding the librarians of the Washington, D.C., area—had been nominated to any "executive" post, honorary or otherwise. Her loss in the election to the better-known Charles Rodan of St. Louis in part reflected the South's lack of voting strength in the ALA. Though she never held an elective office within the ALA, she did much to bring southerners into the fold of the national association.

Sensitive to the feeling of sectionalism that prevailed among southern librarians throughout the 1920s, Barker represented a moderate voice within ALA. She and Lila M. Chapman of Birmingham told the ALA Membership Committee in 1922 that many southern librarians felt that "all [ALA] care[s] about us is our membership fee." They suggested biennial regional meetings alternating with national ones as a means of quelling the spirit of separatism and disenchantment among southern librarians. Barker realized that a unified approach to regional problems would be necessary to generate the outside support necessary for southern library development.

Barker also spoke out firmly on the racial situation in Atlanta during the meetings of the Library Work with Negroes Roundtable in 1922-1923, reporting with aplomb that a black library advisory committee in Atlanta had been disbanded "because they did not confine their activities to advice." At the same time, she defended the rights of blacks to read books about race relations or, in fact, any books they chose regardless of subject matter. Her opinions on race were liberal for a southerner of her time.

In 1923, Barker claimed that library schools were "sailing an unchartered course" in the 1920s, but the same might have been said about southern librarianship in general. The South, because of its primitive state of development, became a testing ground for accelerated professional growth in the 1920s and 1930s. Standards were promoted by SELA for school, high school, and college libraries. Her sister's teaching experience gave Barker an insider's view of educational problems in the public schools, and Barker became particularly interested in the emerging patterns of relationship between the public library and the school.

The Rosenwald Fund's announcement of a $500,000 grant for county library demonstrations in May 1929 served to mobilize SELA's leaders into action. At an interfoundation meeting in January 1930, a policy committee, on which Barker served, presented through ALA officials a recommended program for southern library development. The program called for an ALA survey of southern library schools, a library school supervisor in every state, the strengthening of state agencies through field workers, aid to black public library service, better graduate book collections, scholarships in southern library schools, and an ALA Library Extension Division regional field agent whose headquarters would be in the South.

The recommendations of the policy committee were adopted as read by the foundations. Barker was appointed to assist Sarah Bogle with the library school survey. She was also unanimously elected regional field agent for the South, even though several members of the policy committee expressed a preference for Charlotte Templeton because of her broader experience in extension work, and because they felt Barker's reserved personality was not suited to library work of a promotional nature.

From 1930 to 1936, the years Barker served as regional field agent, her horizons broadened, her personality loosened, and she became a national public figure. In many ways, these years represented the pinnacle of her career. Her extensive field notes document her activities, which, according to her own count, included 737 days in the field, 6,088 letters written, 72 talks to professional groups, 54 library and 57 lay meetings attended, and 41 talks before lay groups. Publicity work bolstered her modest publication record.

The intervention of the depression blunted some of the effectiveness of her work. The economic disaster meant that some southern state governments were unable or unwilling to fund new library projects. Barker admitted frankly that the depression had "thwarted many high hopes of library planners." Several of the Rosenwald demonstration projects faltered for lack of local support. Moreover, the Rosenwald Fund itself had to stretch several of its obligations over a longer period of time because of the stock market decline and eventually had to be assisted by the Carnegie Corporation to meet its obligations.

Barker proved an invaluable expert on library organization for the Rosenwald demonstration libraries. Her suggestions so benefited state extension workers, librarians, and citizens' groups that they bombarded ALA with requests to continue her in office after funds ran out. Particularly notable among her accomplishments was the organization of a Conference of Southern Leaders in Chapel Hill, North Carolina, in 1933, a Citizens' Library Conference at Clemson, South Carolina, in 1934, and drafting of successful county library legislation in Arkansas and Georgia in 1934 and 1935. The completed five-year report of her work, *Libraries of the South: A Report on Developments, 1930-1935* (Chicago: American Library Association, 1936), was the first extensive qualitative survey of southern library conditions and Barker's only book.

Ultimately, the position of regional field agent was discontinued because of ALA's precarious financial condition and the Carnegie Corporation's view that the work was of a demonstration nature only. But the experience had been useful. Southern library leaders formed a better understanding of southern library problems. People such as Barker, Rothrock, and Wilson gradually came to realize that areas larger than counties were needed as units of library service in the rural South. Most counties, as Barker emphasized more and more in her speeches, were too small, too poor, and too sparsely populated to support suggested minimum standards of public library service.

Alternative forms of library development began to emerge after 1934 when the Tennessee Valley Authority (TVA) organized libraries under the direction of Barker's colleague, Mary Utopia Rothrock. The TVA plan and, to a lesser extent programs of the Works Progress Administration (WPA), successfully stimulated long-sought-after state support, which the more diffuse efforts of the regional field agent could not.

Barker's work had established necessary intermediate precedents in many areas of the South. The TVA and WPA could build on the networks of lay support, legislation, state library plans, and groundwork for the cooperation between state departments of education and librarians that Barker had created. And considering southern librarians' mistrust of the ALA, it is doubtful that the national association alone could have attained these objectives without the benefit of Barker's knowledge of southern conditions and her ability to activate library consciousness.

As Barker finished her last year's work for the ALA, Clara Howard, who had headed Emory's library school since Barker's resignation, died suddenly. Barker returned as director of the school in 1936, and she remained there until her retirement in 1954. In some respects, she would never regain the prominence and visibility she had enjoyed during her years as regional field agent. Nonetheless, she continued to be a major force in southern librarianship.

Barker was among the leading proponents of education for librarianship in the South throughout her tenure at Emory. Her major achievements came as an educational administrator rather than as a teacher. She upgraded Emory's curriculum to a master's degree program in 1947 and saw that the school became a division within the graduate school in 1948. Although she was not known as a scintillating classroom lecturer, she was a tireless counselor, and she advised and found positions for the alumnae of the school throughout their careers. She was a virtual employment agency, advocate, and occasionally, surrogate mother. Her efforts on behalf of her graduates and her keen interest in their lives—whether or not they left the profession for marriage or other careers—fostered a remarkable tradition of loyalty toward the school.

She also recognized and developed teaching talent in the school. Most notable among her faculty were Evalene Parsons Jackson (Emory 1929), who succeeded her as director of the Emory Library School in 1954, and Agnes L. Reagan (Emory 1939), who became executive secretary of the Library Education Division of the ALA in 1967. Another of her students from the class of 1950, A. Venable Lawson, became director of the Division of Librarianship in 1965, as well as a trusted friend in Barker's later life. Although she possessed only an informal college education and a library certificate, Barker recognized the value of higher education and was quick to adapt Emory's program to meet new professional criteria. She temporarily squelched the idea of a "cheap" doctoral program by southern schools in 1956, in part because she was skeptical of mere credentialism, in part because she felt that no southern library school had the resources to support one at that time.

Barker remained the primary leader and figurehead of GLA, and her involvement extended far past her official retirement. She secured passage of legislation necessary for the creation of a Board of Certification for Librarians in the state, which she chaired from its inception in 1938 to 1949. When the all-white state library association lost membership in the national association in 1964, Barker chaired the committee that worked out a desegregation plan. By the time GLA nominated her to honorary life membership in 1971, she had chaired more committees than any other GLA member.

In the course of her continued involvement with the national association, Barker served a second term on the ALA Council (1937-1942) and became a director of the Library Education Division of the ALA (1950-1953). She was elected president of the Association of American Library Schools for 1939-1940. Though Barker was identified exclusively with Emory Library School after 1936, her activities and appointments in the national association accelerated during this time. She served on the Library Extension Board (1940-1943), the Nominating Committee (1938-1939 and 1948-1949), the Committee on Honorary Memberships (1938-1939 and 1950-1951), the Membership Committee (Chair, 1946-1951), and the Special Committee on the Correlation and Development of Citizen Interest (1940). Her increased involvement in the national association reflected a growing national and professional awareness of the South as (to use Franklin D. Roosevelt's phrase) "the nation's number one economic problem." While the spotlight helped raise fellow southerners Louis Round Wilson and Mary Utopia Rothrock to the presidency of the association, Barker's relatively low profile robbed her of higher elective posts. Some of her contemporaries discounted her as a teetotaler and blue-stocking, though evidence attests to her humor, her disgust with sham and hypocrisy, and her thoughtful, rather than merely enthusiastic, love of her profession.

In 1952, the same year that Flora B. Luddington was elected first vice-president and president-elect of ALA, and two years before she retired, Barker lost an ALA election for the second and last time, in this instance for the post of second vice-president. Lucile M. Morsch won the contest by a narrow margin of 207 (out of 7,311) votes, but considering Barker's philosophical nature, it is doubtful that she was bitter about the outcome. She believed that leadership entailed responsibility, and that responsibility engendered action. For her, at least, this responsibility lay primarily in her native region.

As for the "essence" of librarianship, Barker was fond of paraphrasing a thought she had first heard expressed by Melvil Dewey: "the librarian is the mediator between the book and reader. This implies that the librarian must know books and their contents, and must show unremitting zeal to see that the necessary connection is made between the book and the individual seeker…. It is not as simple an operation as it appears to be."

With several other prominent southern librarians, notably Louis Round Wilson, she was an early advocate of "regionalism," a concept developed by sociologist Howard Odum that sought to preserve regional strengths and identities while integrating them into a harmonious and productive national framework. Long after she had ceased to be a representative for the ALA in the South, and the South in the ALA, she continued to seek ways of coordinating and measuring the South's library growth. She was a member of the Tennessee Valley Library Council and served on the Executive Committee of the Southeastern States Cooperative Library Survey from 1946 to 1949.

She was also a member of the American Association of University Professors and was active in various current awareness groups in Atlanta. In recognition of her many civic and professional accomplishments, Atlanta named her Woman of the Year in Education in 1954.

Although she was the daughter of a charter member of the Home Mission Society of the Methodist Episcopal Church South, Barker never displayed strong religious feelings. It is said that she kept Austen's *Pride and Prejudice* next to her bed the way that some people keep a Bible. Her progressive conscience, which she shared in common with her sisters, was born of her mother's concern for social justice.

Her social viewpoint extended to librarianship also, for during the heyday of the Ku Klux Klan in the 1920s she did what she could to place southern Catholics on the staff of her own library when they could not find employment in other southern cities. Although she remained aloof from sensationalism of any kind, she was moved to sign a controversial petition protesting the infringement of civil liberties in the arrest of communist Angelo Herndon in 1930 and joined another group of concerned Atlanta citizens to voice dissent over the Scottsboro trial in 1931.

Unremarkable as Barker's brand of political and social liberalism now seems, it was important in shaping a progressive image of the library in the South that was congruent with local custom. On the state and regional levels, she translated the national professional agenda into terms suited to southern conditions. Working quietly behind the scenes rather than in debates from the floor, she was an advocate of gradual change on every front.

Resentments toward the Atlanta Director of Libraries, John Settlemayer (1949-1960), embittered part of her retirement years. This brash midwesterner with new ideas clashed with the slower-paced personnel of the library, and Barker viewed his influence as destructive. She became obsessed with a campaign to oust him from office, wrote indignant letters to the press and the mayor, and would attend no GLA meeting at which he was present. Barker had never let go completely of her control of the library where she maintained surveillance through former associates. The city eventually discharged Settlemayer for technical illegalities in 1960, but the more impersonal, less provincial style of administration presaged by Settlemayer remained.

Her final years were sad. The death of Mary Cornelia Barker in 1962 and the declining health of her sister Meta and her lifelong friend Fannie D. Hinton (Atlanta librarian, 1939-1949) circumscribed Barker's activities. She suffered a stroke in November 1977 and died on February 6, 1978.

For over forty years, Tommie Dora Barker was one of the major links between the national association and the underdeveloped libraries of the South. When she received the Atlanta Woman of the Year Award in 1954, she stated, "I realize that the recipient is a symbol more than an individual ... and so I should like to express my gratitude to those ... for whom I am for a brief moment, a symbol of their achievement, also." In spite of these characteristically dry, self-effacing sentiments, however, her role in southern librarianship was only remotely symbolic. Southern librarianship owes much of its progress in this century to her counsel and leadership, and to the balanced perspective she applied to southern and national, professional and lay viewpoints. She consistently emphasized librarians' obligation to know their constituencies well, and she epitomized this philosophy in the service she rendered both to the profession and her native region.

Biographical listings and obituaries—Cummings, Cynthia S., comp. *A Biographical-Bibliographical Directory of Women Librarians.* Madison: University of Wisconsin-Madison, Library School Women's Group, 1976; [Obituary]. *ALA Yearbook 1979* (1980); [Obituary]. "Death of Miss Tommie Dora Barker, Library Leader." *Georgia Librarian* 15:77 (May 1978); *Who's Who in Library Service*, 1st ed., 2nd ed., 3rd ed. **Books and articles by the biographee**—"In Reply to 'The Weaker Sex?'." *Library Journal* 63:294-5 (April 15, 1938); "Libraries in the South." *Library Journal* 56: 165-69 (February 15, 1931); "Library Progress in the South, 1936-42." *Library Quarterly* 12:353-62 (July 1942); "Patterns of Education for Librarianship in the

Southeast." *Southeastern Librarian* 4:5-13 (Spring 1954). **Books and articles about the biographee** — Hinton, Fannie D. "Our Frontispiece: Tommie Dora Barker." *Bulletin of Bibliography* 17:41-2 (September-December 1940); Nix, Lucille, and Fanny Hinton. "Tommie Dora Barker: A Tribute." *Southeastern Librarian* 4:45-7 (Summer 1954); "Retirements." *College & Research Libraries* 15:463-4 (October 1954). **Primary sources and archival materials** — The Tommie Dora Barker Papers, the Mary Cornelia Barker Papers, and the records of the Georgia Library Association and the Southeastern Library Association are held in Special Collections, Robert W. Woodruff Library, Emory University, Atlanta, Georgia. Additional primary source materials about Barker's career can be found in the ALA Archives, University of Illinois Library, Urbana, Illinois; the Alabama Department of Archives and History, Montgomery, Alabama; the Julius Rosenwald Fund Archives, Fisk University, Nashville, Tennessee; the Carnegie Corporation Archives, New York, New York; the Lillian Baker Griggs Papers, Duke University, Durham, North Carolina; the Mary Utopia Rothrock Papers, Lawson McGhee Library, Knoxville, Tennessee; the Louis Round Wilson Papers and the Frank Porter Graham Papers, University of North Carolina, Chapel Hill, North Carolina; and at the repositories for most southern state library association archives, where such records exist.

— JAMES V. CARMICHAEL, JR.

BATCHELOR, LILLIAN LEWIS (1907-1977)

Lillian Lewis Batchelor, born November 17, 1907, in Camden, New Jersey, was the only daughter of Albert Kirk and Estella May Lewis and was the wife of Dr. Howard I. Batchelor. Although little is known about her early life, her interest in librarianship can be traced from her high school days in Camden, where she was recruited for library work by the staff of the Camden Public Library. Her early working career was quite varied. She worked as an assistant librarian for the Camden Free Library for six years, then as librarian at Ogontz Junior College in Pennsylvania, and as a librarian and teacher in the Prospect Park, Pennsylvania school system. In 1937 she joined the Philadelphia School District as a librarian and teacher at Vaux Junior High School. Two years later she became librarian and English head at Bok Technical High School and then supervisor of high school libraries for the Board of Education from 1948 to 1966. In 1966 she assumed the title she held until her retirement — Assistant Director of Libraries for the School District of Philadelphia — a position in which she served as the senior administrative officer of library services for the district. In addition to her responsibilities for the district, she became an adjunct professor at the Graduate School of Library Science at Drexel University and taught on school library services for many years.

Her educational preparation in school library media services was extensive. She received her initial library science degree from Drexel Institute of Technology in 1930, the same year she completed work on a bachelor of science degree at the University of Pennsylvania. Later she pursued studies at Columbia University in both library science and education, earning a master of arts degree in 1946 and a doctorate in education in 1952, with an emphasis on curriculum and supervision.

Lillian Batchelor was active in the development of one of the major documents advancing the school library field: the 1960 *Standards for School Library Programs*, published by the American Library Association. The concepts developed in these standards shed light on Batchelor's philosophy toward her profession and showed how she believed it should be practiced. The *Standards* advocated cooperation among all types of libraries, suggested the introduction of children to community library services at a young age, emphasized the teaching role of the school librarian, and defended the use of all types of materials in school collections. The philosophy behind these standards was also evident in Batchelor's advocacy of instructional materials centers (IMCs) for the school district she served and in the advice she offered graduate students at Drexel.

It was during her tenure with the School District of Philadelphia that she made many of her major professional contributions. She is credited with the creation in the mid-1960s of approximately 166 new elementary school libraries for Philadelphia, all in a period of about two years. (The funding for these libraries resulted from passage of the Title I Elementary and Secondary Education Act.) This major development had both positive and negative features. Although libraries were put into schools that had not formerly had them, it was impossible to locate enough trained librarians to staff them. As a result, a new position was created — Library Instructional Materials Specialist (LIMS).

Elementary schools got libraries, but they were staffed by individuals not prepared or permitted to engage in real instructional activities with students.

As budgets began to tighten in the early 1970s, Batchelor realized that a program was needed to prepare professional school librarians. Under her leadership, an internship program was developed with Drexel to address the growing demand for trained professionals. This innovative program was aimed at attracting college graduates who already held teacher certification and at practicing teachers interested in moving into library positions. The School District of Philadelphia provided financial support for the coursework of selected individuals who divided their time working in a school library and pursuing graduate study in school librarianship at Drexel. One colleague recalls that books for the earliest of these new libraries came initially from another of Batchelor's cooperative efforts wherein The Free Library of Philadelphia provided a basic starter collection, on loan, to an elementary school.

Batchelor made her mark both inside and outside of the Philadelphia area. She was a leader in many professional organizations—national, state, and local, and organized many institutes, innovative training programs and in-service opportunities for educators. Two examples of the breadth of her work and influence involved institutes to make educators more aware of the potential role of IMCs and school librarians in education. As part of her campaign to develop IMCs in Philadelphia, she organized a conference for school administrators, co-sponsored by Drexel's Graduate School of Library Science. Its intent was to demonstrate the relationship of a functional IMC to reading programs, facilities development, and instructional programs within schools. She was also the active force in developing an institute on reading guidance for gifted students at Immaculate Heart College in Los Angeles, California. She urged librarians to think of books as "the gunpowder of the mind," and believed that "librarians should know how to use them to fire the imagination and ambition of young people."

Batchelor's charismatic leadership was recognized by the many professional organizations in which she worked. National positions included service to the American Library Association, as president of the American Association of School Librarians, and as an ALA councilor, as well as membership on many committees over the years. She was also active in the National Education Association and served as a member of the Board of Directors of the Pennsylvania School Librarians Association and as a member of the Executive Board of the Association of Supervision and Curriculum Development. In addition she was a member of the Executive Board of the Philadelphia YMCA and was on the Board of Directors of the University of Pennsylvania Alumnae.

Lillian Batchelor received a number of awards recognizing her achievements: the Outstanding Alumna Award of the Drexel Alumni Association in 1967; the Award of Distinction of the Alumni Association of the University of Pennsylvania in 1966; and in 1971, citations of merit from the Pennsylvania School Library Association and the Pennsylvania Library Association colleagues, who remembered that Batchelor "never backed down from a fight," "was wonderful in cooperating in anything that went on in the city," "had so much spark," and "pepped everything up." She was a woman with a strong personality and great dedication to her profession. She was also a woman with a superb education and the wherewithall and luck to put it to good use. She died on June 28, 1977 in Morristown, New Jersey.

Biographical listings and obituaries—[Obituary]. *American Libraries* 8:518 (October 1977); *A Biographical Directory of Libraries in the United States and Canada*, 5th ed.; *Who's Who in Library Service*, 4th ed.; *Who's Who of American Women* 1st-4th eds., 8th ed. **Books and articles about the biographee**—"Co-chairman of the AASL Program in Philadelphia." *School Libraries* 4:6-7 (March 1955); "Pennsylvania Librarians—Retirement." *Pennsylvania Library Association Bulletin* 30:62 (May 1975). **Primary sources and archival materials**—Batchelor's official papers are part of the institutional archives of the School District of Philadelphia.

—JACQUELINE C. MANCALL

BERELSON, BERNARD REUBEN (1912-1979)

Bernard Berelson was born on June 2, 1912, in Spokane, Washington, to Max and Bessie Shapiro Berelson. One of five children (two brothers, William and Louis, and two sisters, Sarah and Esther), he grew up in Spokane and was graduated from Lewis and Clark High School, where he edited the school newspaper. He then pursued an English major at Whitman College in Walla Walla, Washington, where he received his bachelor's degree in 1934 and was a member of Phi Beta Kappa. While his career to that point gave no hint of the direction he would eventually take in social science research, the seed for his library interests was sown in an undergraduate job in the college library, which interested him sufficiently to lead him to seek a degree in librarianship at the University of Washington (Seattle). He received the bachelor of library science degree from the University of Washington Library School in 1936, and the master's degree in English in 1937. His master's thesis, "A Bibliography of Chaucer, 1908-1935," was completed under the direction of Dudley David Griffith. Griffith's own *Bibliography of Chaucer, 1908-1953* (1955) incorporated the entries in Berelson's thesis ("a careful and accurate study") and made note of some additional items through 1938 contributed by Berelson.

From 1936 to 1938, Berelson served on the staff of the University of Washington Library in acquisitions work, which combined his already demonstrated interests in bibliography and scholarship. But a new turn in his career interests was on the horizon. He left Seattle to pursue doctoral study in the Graduate Library School at the University of Chicago, where he was introduced to the social science orientation of the Chicago school, and the new ground broken by Douglas Waples's research in communication. His broadening interests were reflected in his participation in a study of reading effects (with Douglas Waples and Frances Bradshaw), entitled "What Reading Does to People" (Chicago: University of Chicago Press, 1941); and by his own doctoral study, "Content Emphasis, Recognition and Agreements: An Analysis of the Role of Communication in Determining Public Opinion," which was completed in 1941. From this time forward, although he kept one foot in the field of library-related research, he would be most widely recognized as a sociologist, researcher, and educator rather than as a practicing librarian.

Berelson was a fellow on a special project for the Rockefeller Foundation in 1941, but with the entry of the United States into World War II, he became a special analyst with the Foreign Broadcast Intelligence Service of the Federal Communications Commission, which employed his content analysis expertise in scrutinizing general broadcasts from the totalitarian countries to help the country improve its ability to predict the enemy's military plans and actions. He joined the Bureau of Applied Social Research at Columbia University in 1944; in the same year his study (with Paul Lazarsfeld and Helen Gaudet), *The People's Choice: How the Voter Makes up His Mind in a Presidential Campaign*, was published.

He left Columbia in 1946 to return to the University of Chicago, where he began a meteoric rise through several ranks and different subject areas: first as an assistant professor in both the Graduate Library School (GLS) and the Division of Social Science in 1946; then, in 1947, as professor in the Library School, and then its dean, while serving also as chair of the University's Committee on Communication; and thereafter (1949-1951) as professor of Library Science and Social Sciences. During this period he continued to produce articles in books and journals related to both librarianship and social sciences. He served as editor of *Education for Librarianship* (1949), the proceedings of a conference sponsored by the Graduate Library School, and he contributed papers to other GLS conferences during his tenure on its faculty. In 1949, he edited, with Lester Asheim, *The Library's Public* (New York: Columbia University Press), a comprehensive survey of all published research up to that time on where people get their reading materials. This book was part of the Public Library Inquiry, a comprehensive series of studies about the American free public library, sponsored by the Social Research Council and supported by a grant from the Carnegie Corporation. In 1950, with Morris Janowitz, Berelson edited *Reader in Public Opinion and Communication* (New York: The Free Press), which became a basic textbook in those fields of study.

In 1951, Berelson became director of the Behavioral Sciences Division of the Ford Foundation, and in 1952 the foundation established, under his guidance, the Center for Advanced Study in the Behavioral Sciences in Stanford, California. During the period of his affiliation with the Ford Foundation, Berelson's *Content Analysis in Communication Research* (New York: The Free Press, 1952) was published: the first full-scale textbook on content analysis as a scholarly research methodology and still a leading textbook in this field. In 1954, he was senior editor of the book *Voting: A Study of Opinion Formation in a Presidential Campaign* (Chicago: University of Chicago Press), which David L. Sills of the Social Science Research Council has called "a milestone in the development of both panel and election studies." In 1956 he contributed "The Study of

Public Opinion" to *The State of the Social Sciences* (Chicago: University of Chicago Press), edited by Leonard D. White.

Berelson left the Ford Foundation in 1957 to return to the University of Chicago as a professor of behavioral sciences, and as director of a two-year study of graduate education sponsored by the Carnegie Corporation. *Graduate Education in the United States* (New York: McGraw-Hill, 1960) was the outcome of this project. In 1960-1961, he returned to Columbia University as director of the Bureau of Applied Social Research, and as professor of sociology. In 1962 he joined the Population Council as director of their Communication Research Program, was appointed vice-president of the council (1963-1968), became its president (1968-1974), and from 1974 to 1979 was a senior fellow and president emeritus of the council. During this period, he was even more prolific in publishing in the social sciences: *The Social Studies and the Social Sciences* (New York: Harcourt, 1962); *The Behavioral Sciences Today* (Boston: Basic Books, 1963); "Graduate Education" (*Collier's Encyclopedia*, 1963, 1979, and 1984); *Human Behavior: An Inventory of Scientific Findings* (with Gary Steiner. New York: Harcourt, 1964); "Voting Behavior" (*Encyclopaedia Britannica*, 1964, 1965); *Family Planning and Population Programs* (1966); *Beyond Family Planning* (1969); *Population: Challenging World Crisis* (1969); *Family Planning Programs: An International Survey* (Boston: Basic Books, 1969); *The Present State of Family Planning Programs* (1970); *Population Policy: Personal Notes* (1971); *Population Policy in Developed Countries* (New York: McGraw-Hill, 1974); and *World Population: Status Report* (1974).

Following his long affiliation with the Population Council, Berelson served in 1976-1977 as visiting senior research demographer and visiting lecturer in Public and International Affairs at Princeton University. He died on September 25, 1979 in North Tarrytown, New York.

Berelson's contributions to scholarly research were acknowledged by several major awards: he received an honorary doctor of laws degree from the University of North Carolina in 1972; an honorary doctor of laws degree from Whitman College in 1973; an American Association for Public Opinion Research Award for "exceptionally distinguished achievement" in 1974; an honorary doctor of science degree from the University of Rochester in 1977; and the University of Chicago Professional Award in 1979.

Berelson's personal life was as eventful as his professional one. He was married in 1941 to Elizabeth Duran and had one son, David. The marriage ended in divorce in 1945. He married Rosalind Kean in 1948, but this marriage also ended in divorce in 1953. He then married Ruth Rappaport in 1953, a union that lasted until his death in 1979 and from which there were three children: Lois, William, and Jenny. He also had a stepdaughter, Alice. He was interested in sports: tennis as a participant from his college days; and baseball, as an avid rooter. The *New York Times* once ran a picture of fans in the bleachers scrambling for a homer heading their way; Berelson was in the center of the scramble. But not all the pictures of Berelson show him that active; there is also a picture, taken in 1940, in which he is sound asleep on a couch with the book, *What Reading Does to People*, lying across his chest. Knowing his sense of humor and lack of pretension, one suspects Berelson's collusion in the creation of this document.

His interests were wide and he retained his love of books, music, and the theater throughout his lifetime. The shifting areas of interest reflected in his educational and professional experiences do not represent an erratic pattern but a cumulative one; he continued his interest in each of the areas of his experience, but simply enlarged each one by enriching it with new perspectives and tools for further analysis. As can be seen from the bare bones of his biography, he excelled in whatever he did. He rose to the top of each of his several professions, using in each all that he had learned before, employing new angles of vision that expanded rather than departed from what he had already mastered. This breadth of vision is graphically reflected in an ingenious and witty essay, "The Great Debate on Cultural Democracy" in Donald Barrett's *Values in America* (Notre Dame, Indiana: University of Notre Dame Press, 1961), in which he persuasively argued each of the three different points of view of "Academicus," "Empiricus," and "Practicus" before summarizing with his own synthesis. In an appreciation of Bernard Berelson printed in *Library Quarterly* after his death, it was pointed out that those who knew him at a certain point in his life were likely to think of him in the narrower terms of his current interest: his obvious leadership in whatever field he happened to be active at the time made those who knew him in that context overlook the many other areas in which he also excelled. The "Bibliography of Chaucer" is likely to come as a surprise to those who know only his studies of voting behavior in the United States; those who worked with him during the war in the analyses that uncovered military implications in apparently innocuous broadcasts could not foresee the contributions he would make to the field of family planning; his coworkers in the Acquisitions Department of the University of Washington Library might have anticipated the possibility of his rising to the deanship of a library school, but not his directorship of the Ford Foundation's Behavioral Sciences Division. It is significant, in this connection, to note that the *Encyclopedia of Library and Information Sciences* contains no biographical article about Bernard Berelson as a librarian but does cite him as an authority sixteen different times in twelve different articles: on censorship; communication science; content analysis; educational media and technology; floating librarians; group dynamics; homebound handicapped; instructional media centers; labor relations in the library; instructions in library use; staff associations; and union activities in U.S. libraries.

When Berelson's death was announced in the *New York Times*, the paper carried a statement from his colleagues on the Population Council that could be applied without alteration to his contribution in each of the fields in which he had been active: "his wisdom, vision and dedication serve as a continuing inspiration.... At once a humanist and a pragmatist, Bernard Berelson leaves ... his ... colleagues richer not only in his accomplishment but in the standards of excellence he set for the rest of us."

Biographical listings and obituaries—*American Men and Women of Science: The Social and Behavioral Sciences* I. New York: R. R. Bowker, 1978; Asheim, Lester. [Obituary]. *Library Quarterly* 50:407-9 (October 1980); *Contemporary Authors*, New Revision Series, Vol. 3. Detroit: Gale, 1981; Ebert, Robert H., and George Zeidenstein. [Obituary]. *New York Times*, September 28, 1979, D15; *New York Times Biographical Service* (University Microfilms International) September 10, 1979; Sills, David L. "In Memoriam." *Public Opinion Quarterly* 44:274-75 (Summer 1980); *Who's Who in America 1* (1980-1981); *Who's Who in World Jewry* (1955, 1972, 1980). **Primary sources and archival materials**—The disposition of the Berelson papers is not known at this time. Some correspondence can be found in collections of individuals with whom Berelson corresponded, e.g., the Paul F. Lazarsfeld Papers, Columbia University Libraries, New York, New York; and the Jesse Hauk Shera Papers, Case Western Reserve University Archives, Cleveland, Ohio.

—LESTER ASHEIM

CASTAGNA, EDWIN (1909-1983)

Edwin Castagna was born May 1, 1909, in Petaluma, California, one of six children of Eugenia Burgle and Frank Castagna, farmer, butcher, and chicken rancher. Both parents were foreign born, his mother emigrating from Alsace-Lorraine and his father from Germany (although he was of Spanish stock with an Italian surname). Petaluma was known as the "World's Egg Basket," and the rugged poultry farm environment must have imbued Castagna with the adventurous spirit that characterized the man throughout his life. Following graduation from Petaluma High School, he served as a merchant seaman, lumber camp worker, and construction worker (or, as he described it, "cook tent flunkey and road builder") on the Coolidge Dam on the Gila River in central Arizona. He also did a "little cotton picking and other miscellaneous but elevating jobs."

Crediting his parents' respect for education and his mother's encouragement for making him a reader and lover of books, Castagna continued to pursue his formal education and earned a junior certificate in English from Santa Rosa Junior College in 1930, followed by an A.B. in English from the University of California at Berkeley in 1935. During this period he worked as a trainman between Oakland and San Francisco, as supervisor of delivery boys for the Oakland *Post-Inquirer*, and finally as a soda jerk in Berkeley.

Following his graduation, he entered the librarianship certification program at Berkeley, receiving the certificate in 1936. When questioned later about his choice of careers, he acknowledged that the proximity of the library school, his major in English, his inclination toward books and reading under the early influence of his mother, and his frequent use of the Petaluma Public Library all played a part. While attending library school, he met Rachel Davida Dent, who was to become his wife seven years later. He admitted that he was not a great student, but suggested that just meeting Rachel would have justified his attending library school.

Castagna began his library career in 1937 with a brief stint as a professional assistant in Alameda County Library in Oakland, California. Later in the same year he became city librarian at Ukiah Public Library, California. He first encountered censorship during this time and took a firm stand supporting the library's obligation to serve all its readers. This experience helped shape his lifelong interest in intellectual freedom and prepared him for the future when he would carry this message on behalf of all libraries in the nation. The experience also taught him that librarians must become active in community affairs since such involvement strengthened their ability to resolve controversial issues.

In 1940 he was appointed director of the Washoe County Public Library in Reno, Nevada, where he lived until the outbreak of World War II, when he voluntarily joined the U.S. Army. By war's end he had become company commander of the 771st Tank Battalion and served with distinction in the Rhineland, Ardennes, and Central European Campaign. Having suffered a slight wound in the Rhineland, he was awarded the Purple Heart and the Bronze Star for heroism. He left the service with the rank of captain in 1946 after eight months of occupation duty in Germany. During his army tenure he had married Rachel, who continued to serve as a military librarian in California posts until his return. At the request of his battalion commander he wrote *The History of the 771st Tank Battalion* (1946).

Upon his return to the United States, Castagna resumed his position in Washoe County and directed his energies within the profession of his choice. He soon became interested in legal aspects of library service. After serving as president of the Nevada Library Association from 1946 to 1947, he produced a report in 1949 codifying Nevada library laws. The previous year he had been elected to the Council of the American Library Association (ALA).

In 1949, Castagna returned to California as the city librarian in Glendale, where he stayed for only one year before he was offered and accepted the directorship of Long Beach Public Library. During his ten years there, he demonstrated his capability as a fund raiser, directing a successful bond election campaign in 1956, which produced four branch buildings. He also organized the city's library system by creating two new branches and planning another, while providing new quarters for four existing branches. Judson Voyles, who served as a branch librarian at the time, recalled the only adverse comment he ever heard about Castagna came from the head of another city department who liked him personally but groaned about his ability "to get anything he wanted" (letter from Judson Voyles, November 1, 1986).

The key to Castagna's success appears to have been his willingness to become involved in the community. According to Voyles, "he belonged to an incredible number of business and service clubs and not only attended meetings but served on their committees." Organizations that received his attention and support included the Welfare Council, the Community Chest, and the Kiwanis Club. Always a liberal politically, he served as president of the Long Beach Chapter of the American Association for the United Nations.

Service to the profession included a term as president of the California Library Association in 1954, only a year after serving as president of the Public Library Executives' Association of Southern California. He was also elected to his second term on the ALA Council and served from 1956 to 1959. Between 1956 and 1960, he served as a building consultant for eight different California communities and developed a national reputation, which was enhanced by his frequent articles in both state and national journals dealing primarily with administrative issues such as planning, building, and service.

He also had become involved in library education, working as visiting lecturer at the School of Library Science at the University of Southern California for three successive years. In addition, he served on the advisory council of the library schools at the University of Southern California, the University of California at Berkeley, and the University of California at Los Angeles.

Castagna's greatest challenge (and therefore his greatest opportunity) lay ahead of him at the age of 51, when he became director of the Enoch Pratt Free Library in Baltimore in 1960. Baltimore faced the same dilemma as most American cities in 1960—a greater demand for library services but fewer resources with which to respond. In Castagna, the city leaders hoped they had an individual who could make some progress despite financial constraints. They were evidently attracted by his reputation as an expert in planning and improving library operations and organizational structures.

While Castagna was director of the Pratt Library, Baltimore experienced drastic social and economic changes. The library's public altered in balance from white to black, from comfortable middle class with a high educational and cultural level to an increasing number of lower-income, less-educated residents with fewer reading skills. Many new projects were launched, especially in the field of statewide library service. A major development was the inauguration of Pratt as the State Resource Center and the extension of interlibrary loan service throughout Maryland. Pratt had taken responsibility for the administration of the priceless collections of the Peabody Library and had regionalized its branch system.

Castagna felt that one of the main tasks of librarians was to explore all avenues, public and private, and all levels of the government for resources needed to expand and improve library service. He believed that libraries generally face two crucial problems: finding enough space and recruiting sufficient personnel. Libraries needed to double in size every few decades.

For the most part, Castagna believed that human beings and books would always be the most important factors in the world of libraries. One of his proudest accomplishments was leading the Pratt Library "into the streets" to serve inner-city residents as part of an attempt to give intensive service. This outreach program made use of multipurpose centers, storefronts, and vans to provide practical help to the community. Castagna felt that this program brought people to the library and gave them some idea that books and printed materials might be more important than they had thought. One of his strongest beliefs was that the right to read should be protected at all costs. In 1964 he told *Current Biography*, "The value of our libraries as democratic institutions will depend on how bold we are as librarians in shouldering the responsibility our fellow citizens place upon us. The degree of courage we display in the face of cowardly tendencies outside and within us will be the measure of our worth as librarians." This sentiment was exhibited in his letter to the editor of the *Baltimore Sun* on March 28, 1967, commending the mayor on his determination to uphold the rights of a radical bookstore to operate in Baltimore.

Continuing his interest in library education, Castagna championed the drive for an accredited library school through his work as chair of the Cooperating Metropolitan Libraries of the Baltimore area. He served as chair of the group's special committee, whose work resulted in the establishment of the library school at the University of Maryland. In addition, he found time to teach a summer term at the UCLA Graduate Library School in 1962.

It was during his tenure as director of the Pratt Library that Edwin Castagna became one of the important names in the field of librarianship. He had served on the International Relations Committee of ALA for five years and represented ALA on two joint committees with the Council of National Library Associations. He then was elected president of ALA and held office from 1964 to 1965. During this period his name became indelibly associated with intellectual freedom through his numerous articles in the library press and his speeches and testimony to government bodies and various professional groups. His ongoing struggle against censorship brought him nationwide attention and helped shape the identity of the progressive librarian.

In addition to his work on intellectual freedom, Castagna considered one of his most important activities as ALA president his initial effort in shaping the report "The National Inventory of Library Needs," which was started during his tenure. Later he continued to serve the organization in many ways, the most important being his chair of the Legislation Committee from 1966 to 1968 and of the Intellectual Freedom Committee from 1968 to 1970. His efforts with the latter committee led to the development of a "Program for Action," serving as the basis for a policy statement implemented later.

Castagna naturally continued to be active on civic, educational, and cultural fronts, participating in such organizations as the Maryland Academy of Sciences, the Adult Education Association, the United Nations Association of Maryland, the Maryland Historical Society, the Baltimore Museum of Art, the Walters Art Gallery, the Citizens Planning and Housing Association, Baltimore Bibliographies, the Rotary Club, and the Hamilton Street Club. Although a member of the Maryland Library Association, he never held elective office. Rachel shared his enthusiasm and membership in many of these bodies and belonged to the Hamilton Street Women's Club. The Castagnas always appreciated the city of Baltimore for their acceptance and, indeed, felt it to be their home.

Never a scholar or researcher, Castagna wrote widely on issues facing the library administrator and published more than 60 articles between 1940 and 1984. These contained practical advice concerning governance, description of current conditions, or analysis of professional responsibility. One of these articles, "Why Is It Always So Bad in California?" (*California Librarian* 26:20-27 [January 1965]) won the Edna H. Yelland Award in 1965. Also in 1965 he co-edited *The Library Reaches Out* (Dobbs Ferry, N.Y.: Oceana Publications, 1965), a reader on library work, with Kate Coplan, a former chief of exhibits and publicity at Pratt.

During this period, two of his booklets were published by Peacock Press in Berkeley, California. *Long, Warm Friendship: H. L. Mencken and the Enoch Pratt Free Library* (1966) was based on an earlier article published in *D.C. Libraries* (July 1963). This work described the relationship of Mencken to the staff and revealed him to be, among other things, generous and thoughtful, a new and refreshing view of the "Bad Boy of Baltimore." The other publication, *Three Who Met the Challenge: Joseph L. Wheeler, Lawrence Clark Powell, Frances Clarke Sayers* (1965), was a warm and affectionate tribute to three contemporary librarians whom he considered to be inspirational.

Castagna originally announced his retirement from the Pratt to occur at the end of the fiscal year 1974, following his sixty-fifth birthday. Instead, it was exactly one year later when he left the post. He had spoken earlier of the opportunity to catch up on his reading, do some writing, and participate in various activities. Evidently his adventurous spirit was dictating the need for a change, because mandatory retirement for city employees was still four years away. Before he left Pratt he was already inquiring about a faculty position in Shiras, Iran, with the Pahlavi University.

Instead, the Castagnas found themselves back in California, where he had accepted an appointment for the spring term at USC. Following this term there was yet one more opportunity to manage a large city library: his six-month interim appointment in San Francisco began in the summer of 1976. Former City Librarian Kevin Owen Starr had resigned to write history, leaving what was termed by the *San Francisco Chronicle* as an "ailing library system." It was Castagna's responsibility to review the organization, operation, and services and to recommend solutions and remedies for the system's problems. He finished this assignment by the beginning of the new year.

His remaining years were spent in Baltimore and enjoying leisurely pursuits and travel. His last major work, *Caught in the Act: The Decisive Reading of Notable Men and Women and Its Influence on Their Actions and Attitudes* (Metuchen, N.J.: Scarecrow Press) was published in 1982. This book explored the possibility that ideas from books could change the course of people's lives.

Castagna's death was tragic: on November 26, 1983 the Castagnas were found dead in their Baltimore apartment, side by side in bed holding hands. There was an empty bottle of sleeping pills nearby and a package of personal records with wills, legal papers, and instructions to their doctor and lawyer. The reason for this apparent double suicide was Castagna's dramatic loss of health. Always a vigorous individual, he had contracted encephalitis in Spain the previous year. The disease had left him debilitated and requiring twenty-four-hour nursing care. In a December 23, 1986, letter, Lawrence Clark Powell described their death as a "brave act of deep mutual devotion."

According to George Parkhurst, their lawyer and personal friend, "this was just their way of leaving, rather than becoming old people in a nursing home." Half the estate of the childless couple went to the Pratt Free Library, the other half to the library school of the University of California at Berkeley, where they had first met.

The most remarkable feature of Edwin Castagna's professional existence is the degree to which he was liked, as well as respected, by those who knew him at any level. It is virtually impossible to find an individual who would cast aspersions on his administrative style or effectiveness or even damn him with faint praise. Instead, he is warmly remembered by those who knew him and has been described as radiating goodwill and sweetness of spirit. Evidently he always listened to people and treated them with respect. Staff morale where he worked was exceedingly high.

One of his few weaknesses, if one could call it that, was his distaste of popular fiction (a characteristic of many pragmatic managers). Judson Voyles recalls trying to convince him that as the major form of artistic expression of the time, fiction deserved the major representation in public libraries. He provided Castagna with a copy of Thomas De Quincy's essay "The Literature of Knowledge and the Literature of Power," first published in 1848. The argument of the essay stated that the meanest, shoddiest example of literature directed at the emotions is superior in kind to literature which aims merely to teach. Castagna read it and later told Voyles that he was "more resigned to the inevitability of fiction."

Castagna's interests were varied, including travel, world peace, the history of the West, abstract art, and baseball. (Both Castagnas switched their allegiance from the Los Angeles Dodgers and became avid fans of the Baltimore Orioles.) Least defensible in the mind of the urbane Baltimore dweller was his lifelong interest in bullfighting, in which he had an extensive personal library. He was never able to reconcile this passion with his humanitarian outlook and accepted the paradox with the idea that Hemingway was partly responsible.

Edwin Castagna was the consummate administrator, who would have succeeded regardless of the type of organization he managed. His ability to earn the respect and admiration of those he governed as well as those who were his peers and employers was uncommon. Fortunately, he was imbued with a progressive spirit that operated on behalf of those who most needed the services of government.

In times of austerity he was able to pursue goals in keeping with his liberal social philosophy, while supervising the technical changes necessary to large urban libraries in the 1960s. These changes included the reclassification of the entire collection from Dewey to Library of Congress System and the replacement of the card catalog by a book catalog. Ever the pragmatist with a social conscience, his writings in the library press, reports of his numerous consulting activities, and countless speeches were designed to make the library a more effective and responsive organization. His successes in these areas were extraordinary.

Biographical listings and obituaries — *Contemporary Authors*, Permanent Series, Vol. 2. Detroit: Gale, 1978; *Current Biography Yearbook*. New York: H. W. Wilson, 1964; *Directory of Library Consultants*. New York: R. R. Bowker, 1969; [Obituary]. *ALA Yearbook 1984* (1985); [Obituary]. *American Libraries* 15:10-11 (January 1984); [Obituary]. (Baltimore) *Evening Sun*, November 28, 1983, p. 1D; [Obituary]. *Contemporary Authors*, Vol. 111. Detroit: Gale, 1984; [Obituary]. *Library Journal* 109:135 (February 1984); *Who's Who in America* 38, 39, 40 (1974-1978); *Who's Who in the East* 13, 14, 15 (1972-1976); *Who's Who in Library and Information Services*. Chicago: American Library Association, 1982; *Who's Who in Library Service*. 2nd ed., 3rd ed., 4th ed. **Books and articles about the biographee** — "ALA President-Elect." *Wilson Library Bulletin* 38:9 (September 1963); (Baltimore) *Evening Sun* April 15, 1960, June 28, 1960, July 3, 1960, March 14, 1974; "California Librarian Named New Enoch Pratt Director." *Library Journal* 85:1884 (May 15, 1960); Henderson, John D. "The New ALA Officers." *ALA Bulletin* 57:660-63 (July/August 1963); Powell, Lawrence Clark. "Profile — Edwin Castagna." *Library Journal* 87:3390-91 (October 1, 1962); Powell, Lawrence Clark. *Remembering Ed Castagna*. San Francisco: R. J. Hoffman, 1984; "Retirements." *Wilson Library Bulletin* 48: 707 (May 1974). **Primary sources and archival materials** — Material by and about Edwin Castagna is held in the director's office and in the Maryland department of the Enoch Pratt Free Library. These consist mainly of newspaper clippings, biographical information, and correspondence related to his publications and his tenure as president of the American Library Association. A more extensive file of personal papers is in the care of his executor and awaits disposition. Very small files are held by the Long Beach Public Library in Long Beach, California, and by the Washoe County Library, Reno, Nevada.

—RONALD BLAZEK
—THERESA GRIFFEN MAGGIO

DIX, WILLIAM SHEPHERD (1910-1978)

William Shepherd Dix was born in Winchester, Virginia, on November 19, 1910. His parents, William S. and Loula Henson Dix, liberal and educated people dedicated to a quiet but humanistic religious faith, inculcated in him a consistent and thorough liberal commitment. He was a precocious young man with voracious and wide-ranging intellectual interests, and he gravitated increasingly to the study of literature, broadly defined, as his life's work. He received a B.A. and M.A. at the University of Virginia in 1931 and 1932, respectively.

Upon graduation Dix assumed a position with the Darlington School for Boys and remained in that post for seven years (1932-1939). In 1935 he married Darlington teacher, Jane Griffin. However, his life as a teacher to precocious but intellectually immature boys soon grew unsatisfactory, and Dix began work on a Ph.D. in English at the University of Chicago. In 1940 he became an instructor of English and director of Western Reserve University's unique Committee on Private Research.

William Dix left Western Reserve in 1942, but not before he completed research for his dissertation on the theater in early Cleveland. During the next four years he moved from Cleveland to Williams College, Williamstown, Massachusetts, as instructor of English from 1942 to 1944, and then on to the Radio Research Laboratory and an instructorship in English at Harvard from 1944 to 1946. In the latter year he received his doctorate and happily accepted a position as assistant professor of English at Rice University in Houston, Texas.

But his happiness was short-lived, for Dix was ill-suited to the kind of pedantry so common to the English departments of America's elite universities. He was too active, his interests too varied and his writing style too readable and uncluttered by scholarly baggage. Endowed with a gregarious personality and an infectious desire for company and wide-ranging conversation, he was also ill-suited to the long hours of lonely attention necessary to produce the scholarship required for promotion and tenure at a major university. Indeed, Dix's conviction that scholarship must be an integral part of citizenship led him to reject narrow cloistered scholarship, and to disdain its practitioners. He noted in "Scholarship's Closed Circle Opens," in the *Journal of Adult Education*, in 1941:

> If scholarship is to survive, the walls of the cloister must be torn down. To receive the support of the American people, scholarship must be understood. When the scholar is content to remain apart, outside the stream of daily life, he becomes a curiosity, and his destiny is that home of the extinct—the museum.

Dix's pursuit of the professional scholar's life was doomed from the start because of his hostility to the scholarly mode of production. Happily, his awareness of his unsuitability as an academic scholar was paralleled by the emergence of a new career, faintly glimpsed as early as 1941, which would allow him to capitalize upon his intellectual attributes, his gregarious and active personality, and his firmly conceived notions of the role of the academic library. He would become a scholar-librarian.

In 1948, the president of Rice University, recognizing Dix's reluctant scholarship, and yet determined to retain this articulate young professor's services for the university, proposed an alternative. Would Dix accept the position of library director at Rice? Dix's immediate response was unequivocal: he liked the suggestion "not a bit." But in time chance and necessity carried the day. The chance grew out of the president's offer to promote Dix to associate professor with tenure, thus allowing him to retain his affiliation with the English department. Necessity dictated that the father of three young children grasp an opportunity to increase his salary substantially. Thus it was that Dix came to his life's work with no training or experience.

Dix's hesitant and untutored attainment of command of a significant academic library caused some difficulty, for his new colleagues were justifiably skeptical of the untrained newcomer. But he soon overcame these difficulties, as is readily evidenced by his almost immediate and widespread acceptance by librarians. At one time he lamented his lack of a formal library school education, but it was clear Dix felt that *scholarly* credentials were the most essential ingredient of the ideal academic library leader.

William Dix was a humanist, scholar, and liberal activist, and these characteristics, combined with his general disinterest in day-to-day library management, dictated his highly traditional brand of library administration. He believed that libraries—"real" libraries—were large collections of printed materials efficiently arranged for easy use by serious seekers of knowledge. The scholar-librarian had two tasks: acquire the money necessary to buy the books and cultivate the friends who would donate books to the library. In a 1964 *College and Research Libraries* article, "Of the Arrangement of Books," he outlined his philosophy. For Dix the basic test of a quality library was "its ability to get into the hands of the reader the book he wants when he wants it." And it was axiomatic that "the odds of success are obviously better if we have more books." Dix thus concluded that librarians must "raise all the money we can to acquire and house all the books we can." To this end William Shepherd Dix devoted most of his time as librarian at Rice

(1948-1953) and Princeton (1953-1975). An examination of his administrative correspondence clearly demonstrates the special pleasures he derived from work with various friends of the library groups. Above all else, he loved to speak and write, and the Friends of the Library offered him a frequent outlet for his obsession, while at the same time serving as a justifiable expenditure of his time.

Dix's admittedly old-fashioned definition of a library as "an attractive room and a wide-ranging collection of books" paralleled an equally narrow but precise definition of the functions of libraries beyond collection development. In short, he insisted that the large, carefully selected collections of books should be centrally housed, classified by subject, and made accessible in open stacks. From his scholar's perspective, little else seemed necessary to manage a research library.

This extremely conservative, almost reactionary, view of library services was firmly rooted in Dix's identity as a humanist scholar. He felt the serious student needed only access to a large, carefully selected collection, which should be arranged by subject and be conducive to browsing. He called this the "First Law of Bibliodynamics" for the arrangement of books. "One should of course use all the [bibliographic] tools available," Dix noted, but the most important purpose was to "cultivate by practice the marvelous flair of the true bookman and scholar of skimming quickly through a series of volumes and then almost by instinct finding the one which fits exactly his needs of the moment. The library that facilitates this practice is the open-stack, classified collection."

The strength of this conviction is evident in his management of the Fondren Library at Rice and the Firestone Library at Princeton. Throughout his career he insisted on centralization, subject classification, and open stacks. Almost half of his published writings defend this ideal against proposals for closed stacks, space-saving shelving arrangements, or divisional libraries.

Given his definition of librarianship, and his distaste for personal involvement in librarian's work, he naturally left the mechanics of academic library operation to librarians. He devoted the majority of his time to a higher purpose: advocating the significance of libraries to the intellectual and political health of the nation and, ultimately, the world. This advocacy was his passionate interest for the twenty-five years he devoted to librarianship. It was evident in his many professional involvements on behalf of academic libraries, and especially on the question of intellectual freedom and libraries. Dix's lifelong commitment to liberal values, his familiarity with Thomas Jefferson's philosophy on intellectual freedom, and his concern over Senator Joseph McCarthy's red-baiting censorial activities in the early 1950s, led him to project himself into national library affairs through his work with the American Library Association (ALA) Intellectual Freedom Committee, which he chaired from 1951 to 1953. Dix was one of the principal authors of ALA's "Freedom to Read" statement, a daring and influential bulwark for the liberal defense of intellectual freedom during the McCarthy era. Despite his repeated protests that the statement was a collaborative effort, Dix was frequently given sole credit for authoring this document.

As a direct outgrowth of his efforts with ALA's Intellectual Freedom Committee, Dix was appointed a member of the U.S. Commission to UNESCO in 1955 and served as vice-chairman of this prestigious commission from 1958 to 1960. As a result he attended lengthy meetings in Paris, Manila, and Kuala Lumpur, and became one of the nation's most traveled librarians. During this period he also chaired ALA's International Relations Committee (1955-1960), served as Association of College and Research Libraries (ACRL) executive secretary, and was elected chairman of ACRL in 1962. He capped his distinguished service to the field as president of the American Library Association in 1969.

With all of his high-profile professional activity, William Shepherd Dix quickly emerged as an immensely successful professional spokesman. He was particularly well-suited for his chosen role as advocate. A handsome man, he exuded quiet confidence, boundless energy, and an unquenchable zeal for his next assignment. His patient, self-effacing style made him an ideal ALA committeeman. In 1969 he presided over the "lengthy and heated" sessions at the ALA Conference in Atlantic City "with consummate grace and skill." Always "calm, considerate, intelligent, and courageous," Dix emerged from this fray greatly respected for leading the association during this trying year. He was fittingly hailed by fellow New Jersey librarians as "Ambassador for Libraries."

His role as spokesman gained him most fame among fellow librarians, but Dix often admitted embarrassment and puzzlement at the profession's frequent practice of assigning him credit for a series of achievements that were in reality collective efforts. The "Freedom to Read Statement" of 1953 and the so-called "Dix Amendment" to the Higher Education Act of 1965 are two significant examples. Dix himself wrote an articulate and detailed history carefully outlining the role of various individuals in the passage of Title IIC of the Higher Education Act, which provided funds for the Library of Congress's National Program for Acquisition and Cataloging (NPAC). He took great pains to set the record straight, but to no avail. For some reason, the profession had a peculiar need to credit the articulate scholar-librarian with significant but unjustified achievements. In 1970 Guy R. Lyle hailed Dix as "without any doubt" one of the two or three most successful librarians in America. "Of all the academic librarians I have known," said Harvard librarian Douglas W. Bryant, "Bill Dix is the one who became the strongest force in his University." Few other American academic librarians enjoyed such widespread fame and even adulation among the American library community.

Librarians appear to have revered Dix for many reasons, but foremost among them was his unique ability to articulate the profession's unconscious needs in words that were both reassuring and unifying. In 1953 he rallied librarians to the cause of intellectual freedom. In 1965 he managed the NPAC proposal. In 1969 he calmly and magnificently quelled the radical elements within ALA. In these and other instances Dix surfaced as the essential leader, the eloquent word-maker, and the unique symbolic leader.

That Dix was admirably suited for his role as "symbolic leader" is clear from many biographical commentaries, but perhaps the *Princeton Town Topics* which, on July 26, 1959, announced that Dix had been selected as its "Man of the Week," put it best:

> for understanding, and stressing, that "books are among our greatest instruments of freedom"; for seeing that the American library is an invaluable weapon in the arsenal of democracy ... Dix has enabled others to see that the unregimented library is all-important when it comes to promoting the free flow of ideas.

William Shepherd Dix retired from his post at Princeton in 1975 and died on February 21, 1978, shortly after completing a manuscript posthumously published as *The Princeton University Library in the Eighteenth Century* (Princeton: Princeton University Library, 1978).

Biographical listings and obituaries—Bryant, Douglas. "A Tribute to Bill Dix, 1910-1978 [obituary]." *Wilson Library Bulletin* 52:614 (April 1978); *Current Biography* (1969); McDonough, Roger. "William Shepherd Dix, 1910-1978 [obituary]." *American Libraries* 9:190 (April 1978); Rogers, Rutherford David. ["William Shepherd Dix"]. *ALA Bulletin* 62:880, 882 (July-August 1968); Taylor, Robert H. "William S. Dix: A Tribute." *Princeton University Library Chronicle* 36: 225 (Spring 1975). **Books and articles about the biographee**—Harbison, Janet. "More Books for More People." *Presbyterian Life* 21:6-8, 40 (January 15, 1968); Harris, Michael H., and Mary Ann Tourjee. "William Shepherd Dix: Symbolic Leadership and Academic Librarianship." *Journal of Academic Librarianship* 8:221-6 (September 1982); Harris, Michael H., and Mary Ann Tourjee. "William S. Dix." In *Leaders in American Academic Librarianship, 1925-1975*. Wayne A. Wiegand, ed. Pittsburgh: Beta Phi Mu, 1983; Lyle, Guy. "William D. Dix." In *The Librarian Speaking: Interviews with University Libraries*. Guy Lyle, ed. Athens: University of Georgia Press, 1970. **Primary sources and archival materials**—The American Library Association Archives at the University of Illinois are rich with traces of Dix's widespread influence on the association. Dix's official correspondence as Princeton University librarian is located in the Seeley G. Mudd Archives at Princeton University.

—MICHAEL H. HARRIS
—MARY ANN TOURJEE

EVANS, LUTHER HARRIS (1902-1981)

Luther H. Evans, the tenth Librarian of Congress (1945-1953) and the third Director-General of UNESCO (1953-1958), was born on his grandmother's farm near Sayerville, Bastrop County, Texas, on October 13, 1902. His father, a railroad foreman, soon bought land nearby, and young Luther grew up on the family farm. Attendance at a one-teacher school for ten years was followed by one year at Bastrop High School, where he graduated at the head of a class of seven. The topic he chose for his valedictory address, "The League of Nations," became a life-long interest. In 1923 he enrolled at the University of Texas, where he majored in political science and financed his education through teaching and work in local cotton fields. He received a bachelor's degree in 1923, an

M.A. in 1924. Following a summer in Europe, where he studied European governments and the League of Nations firsthand, he began teaching and graduate work at Stanford University. In 1927 he received a Ph.D. in political science from Stanford; his dissertation was on the mandate system of the League of Nations. While at Stanford he married Helen Murphy, who had been a classmate at the University of Texas. Their son, Gill Coffer Evans, later became a political scientist like his father.

From 1927 to 1935, Luther Evans taught at New York University, Dartmouth, and Princeton. During these years he began work on a study of American administration of the Virgin Islands, which was published in 1945 under the title *The Virgin Islands: From Naval Base to New Deal.*

In the summer of 1935 Evans came to Washington, D.C., to develop plans for a national survey of archival records, a project that evolved into the Historical Records Survey (HRS). His teaching contract at Princeton had not been renewed for reasons still not clear today, but probably traceable to disapproval of his involvement in local left-of-center politics. Evans had no experience in archival work. He was also untried as an administrator. But his sponsor, Raymond Moley, professor of public law at Columbia University, and his new supervisor, Works Progress Administration administrator Harry Hopkins, were impressed with his energy and potential. In October 1935 Evans was named "supervisor of historical projects," a title soon changed to director of the HRS. The 33-year-old political scientist-turned-archivist/historian proved to be a skilled administrator. HRS procedures were established in Washington, D.C., but the survey's inventories of records, manuscripts, and imprints were carried out at the state and local level. Evans not only dealt effectively with state administrators and historical agencies, he also kept the Historical Records Survey away from the controversies that plagued other WPA arts projects.

Evans met writer and poet Archibald MacLeish, President Franklin D. Roosevelt's new appointment as Librarian of Congress, as the New Deal arts projects were coming to a close in the fall of 1939. The new Librarian was making plans to reorganize the Library of Congress, and he was attracted by Evans's credentials, self-confidence, and vigor. MacLeish offered Evans the job of director of the Legislative Reference Service, the Library department that served Congress directly. Evans accepted and soon became the Librarian's principal lieutenant, serving as head of the Legislative Reference Service before becoming, in less than a year, chief assistant librarian.

Librarian MacLeish also served as a wartime advisor to President Roosevelt, and during MacLeish's absences Evans served as acting Librarian of Congress. He played a leading role in the administrative reorganization that today is remembered as the hallmark of the MacLeish administration. Staff morale rose sharply during these years, largely because of improved personnel policies and Evans's willingness to involve the staff in decision-making processes. Evans's eventual nomination to succeed MacLeish as Librarian was very popular with the staff. During his term of office, he continued the policies and initiatives that he, MacLeish, and their colleagues had undertaken during the five preceding years.

In 1944 MacLeish resigned as Librarian and joined the Roosevelt administration full-time as Assistant Secretary of State in charge of public and cultural relations. Chief Assistant Librarian Evans was not, however, among President Roosevelt's first choices to be Librarian of Congress. As with MacLeish's appointment as Librarian, Roosevelt paid no attention to the American Library Association's list of possible candidates for the job. Instead he preferred more scholarly candidates, particularly Julian Boyd, editor of the Thomas Jefferson Papers and librarian of Princeton University. Boyd declined the job, however, and Roosevelt died on April 12, 1945, without having nominated MacLeish's successor. Unlike his predecessor, President Harry S. Truman did seek ALA advice on appointing the librarian, and Acting Librarian Evans was among the three candidates ALA recommended. Truman sent Evans's nomination to the Senate on June 18. Confirmation took place, without objection, on June 29, and Luther Evans took the oath of office as the tenth Librarian of Congress on June 30, 1945.

Evans felt President Truman had given him a double mandate: to improve service to Congress and to extend the Library's collections and services to libraries throughout the nation. The Legislative Reorganization Act of 1946 accomplished the first job quickly, establishing the Legislative Reference Service as a separate department to serve the Congress and increasing the Legislative Reference Service's size and independence. The second task became one of Luther Evans's major accomplishments: he renewed and greatly strengthened ties between the Library of Congress and the American library movement. He also extended this partnership to the international scene. In the process he established an international role for the Library of Congress itself, even though his strong international interests met with criticism and some opposition in Congress.

Evans colleague, Verner W. Clapp, once noted that Evans "never lacked an opinion." He was not shy about expressing his opinions either, and he did not particularly care who was listening. As soon as he took office, Evans began emphasizing the importance of the national role of the Library of Congress. He believed that libraries were essential because "the citizenry must be kept at a high level of information and intelligence" if democracy was to work. Thus he felt the Library of Congress had "an inescapable responsibility" to serve the entire country. The Library's resources, he felt, should be considered along with the resources of all other libraries as an "integrated national resource," so that in the postwar era "this nation possesses the printed, the cartographic, and the other material which will be needed by its government and its people." The challenges of the postwar years meant "no spot on the earth's surface is any longer alien to the interest of the American people." In such a world, the Library of Congress could and should become "a powerful instrument of peace and progress."

The first step was for the Library of Congress to expand its services and the scope of its collecting activities. A forthright man who had great confidence in his abilities to persuade, the new Librarian decided to ask Congress to nearly double the Library's budget in fiscal year 1947. He outlined his request in a document he later claimed was "the most important state paper to issue from the Library" since 1802. Asking for the large sum in one budget request was the correct approach, he optimistically explained to a group of librarians in Cleveland in October 1945, because "any failure of the Library of Congress to play its part is due primarily to the fact that we have not seen the large picture ourselves or had the courage to present it."

But Congress did not even come close to sharing Evans's "large picture." His request for a large increase was flatly rejected by an economy-minded Congress, even though small increases were allowed for certain activities, particularly the Legislative Reference Service and the Copyright Office. Furthermore, in its report, the Appropriations Committee challenged the Librarian, questioning not only his expansionist plans but also the Library's authority to serve "as a national and indeed an international library." It also called for "a determination as to what the policy of the Library of Congress is going to be in the way of expansion and service to the public and Congress."

This challenge immediately put Luther Evans on the defensive. He asked David C. Mearns, director of the Reference Department, to prepare a history highlighting the development of the Library's national responsibilities. The result, *The Story Up to Now: The Library of Congress 1800-1946*, was published as part of the Librarian's 1946 annual report. A special Planning Committee, chaired by Keyes D. Metcalf, director of the Harvard University Library, was appointed to consider the Library's functions and future. The committee's report, which emphasized the Library's national role, included a recommendation that the Library be officially designated "The Library of Congress, The National Library of the United States of America." But the report prompted no action or reactions from Congress.

Although Librarian Evans's vision of the Library of Congress as "a national and even an international library" was not spoiled by the economy-minded and querulous Congress, full implementation of his vision became impossible. The Library's appropriation grew during the Evans years, but at a relatively slow pace. Evans's leadership and energy, however, helped compensate for the lack of large budget increases, and many Library of Congress accomplishments between 1945 and 1953 can be traced to his personal initiative and concern.

Important acquisitions and bibliographical achievements included the Library of Congress Mission to Europe to secure multiple copies of European publications for the war period and projects to microfilm priceless manuscript collections on Mount Sinai and in Jerusalem. In response to requests from librarians and researchers, a program was started to publish the Library's card catalogs in book form. With help from an advisory committee of librarians, the Library of Congress developed and published *Rules for Descriptive Cataloging in the Library of Congress* (1949). The number of annual gifts to the Library from private citizens more than quadrupled while Evans was Librarian, a tribute to his forceful personality and his persistence. Over a dozen continuing bibliographies and acquisitions, accessions, and union lists were started. Verner Clapp once asserted that Luther Evans invented the phrase "bibliographic control."

Evans's major concerns included microfilming, copyright, federal libraries, international exchange, intellectual freedom, and international library cooperation. He also believed strongly in cultural reparation: that original source materials belonged in the countries of their creation. As Librarian of Congress he initiated the return of several important manuscripts from the Library to the countries of their origin. In 1948 he personally arranged for the purchase, through private donors, of the original manuscript of Lewis Carroll's *Alice's Adventures in Wonderland* and took great pride in being able to return the manuscript, as a gift, to the British Museum. In 1952 he arranged and presided over the transfer of the Declaration of Independence and the Constitution of the United States from the Library of Congress to the National Archives. Because the documents had been in the Library's possession since 1921 this act was, Evans admitted, "an emotional wrench," but "logic and law require it."

Evans's interest in bibliographical control and in the need for creating uniform cataloging rules reflected his concern for efficient library management. How could libraries serve government and the people effectively if "the cataloging and bibliographical work now done in libraries is not to be relied upon to give the complete and current control of published material which our objective requires?" The problem, he felt, was to strike a balance among "quality, coverage, and timeliness." One solution was a more cooperative approach to cataloging and acquisitions work. Dozens of cooperative projects between the Library of Congress and other libraries were initiated during the Evans administration. In addition to the acquisitions and cataloging projects previously mentioned, Evans organized an advisory committee on the distribution of foreign acquisitions, supported the Library's participation in the Farmington Plan (a cooperative acquisitions effort among research libraries), and established the Documents Expediting Project to ensure that other libraries received copies of government documents promptly.

Luther Evans's management style was itself a positive contribution to the Library of Congress. He believed and practiced "the principle of democratic determination of policy." He consulted frequently with his department directors (the Librarians' Conference was held two full hours a day, three days a week), and his door was open to receive comments and criticism from staff members. He kept the staff well-informed about his activities, even contributing a column to the weekly Library of Congress *Information Bulletin* (itself a MacLeish-Evans innovation). This "open" administrative style, uncommon in the 1940s, was a natural consequence of the Librarian's fervent and optimistic conviction that the free flow of information was a necessity in a democracy. He believed it should be practiced with government institutions such as the Library of Congress and in American society in general, with libraries playing a key role. Moreover, he felt any threat to libraries or to "the freedom to seek and state the truth" must be challenged.

Luther Evans was both the most controversial and most widely liked Librarian of Congress in this century. The controversy was mostly on the Congressional side: many members of Congress opposed Evans's ambitious plans for the Library of Congress, and many disliked his aggressive, boisterous personal style. Committee members who dealt with the Library were unhappy with Evans's reluctance to consult with them about his plans for the Library, and an atmosphere of mutual suspicion prevailed. On the other hand, Evans was genuinely liked and admired by Library of Congress staff members, by Library of Congress colleagues such as Verner W. Clapp, Dan Lacy, and Frederick Wagman, and by librarians around the country.

Evans's unusual personality brought forth strong responses. In a 1965 profile of Evans, Verner W. Clapp, Evans's chief assistant librarian, describes "a voice and manner dogmatic to the point of autocracy," and regrets Evans's "constitutional inability to praise a subordinate to his face." Evans also was a "showman," who deliberately put forth a virile, hard-drinking image which, combined with "a totally uninhibited laugh," tended to intimidate and could cause resentment. Yet it appears that once the staff learned what to expect from Evans, intimidation changed to respect. Clapp also describes Evans's "incredible capacity for work and detail," along with his excellent memory, as reasons for his many achievements. Above all, Clapp, Lacy, and Wagman admired Evans's personal courage. Librarian of Congress Evans openly challenged Senator Joseph McCarthy's allegations about subversives in the government, even hiring a woman who had been dismissed by the State Department after her name had appeared on McCarthy's February 9, 1950, list of "security risks."

Dan Lacy, formerly deputy chief assistant librarian, knew Evans well. In Lacy's opinion, Luther Evans tried to expand the Library of Congress and its "power base" too fast and too soon. The conservative postwar Congress, already trying to cut costs, simply balked. Evans, however, never lost hope and through persistence, hard work, and the force of his strong personality, accomplished much on a relatively meager budget. Lacy also was impressed by Evans's "devoted sense of public service," which was an important factor in the Librarian's resignation in 1953.

Luther Evans's devotion to the United Nations and particularly to UNESCO, its cultural agency, rivaled his devotion to the Library of Congress. In spite of Congressional criticism about his involvement in international activities and his absences from the Library, he served UNESCO while he served the Library of Congress. In June 1953 he permitted his name to be considered for the post of UNESCO Director General. When he was elected, he immediately resigned as Librarian of Congress. He remained with UNESCO until 1958, but then returned to the pursuit of his library and education interests. In 1959 he directed a study of federal libraries for the Brookings Institution. The final report recommended the creation of the Federal Library Council, which was established in 1965. The report also recommended the transfer of the Library of Congress, except for the Legislative Reference Service, to the executive branch of government. Next Evans headed a project for the National Education Association. In 1962 he became a director of International and Legal Collections for Columbia University Libraries and subsequently helped develop a new library for the School of International Affairs. Other activities included the presidency of World Federalists U.S.A. Luther Evans died on December 23, 1981, in San Antonio, Texas, where he had made his home since 1977.

Assessing Evans's career as Librarian of Congress and his overall contribution to the institution is difficult. The picture is clouded by his poor relations with Congress and his failure to make any particular effort to improve the situation. Congress did not trust Evans and was reluctant to accede to his appropriation requests. As a result, the Library's growth during the Evans years was slow and uneven. Congressional unhappiness with Evans and the Library became painfully obvious during the 1954 Senate hearings on the confirmation of Evans's successor, L. Quincy Mumford. In fact, it took Mumford nearly a decade to restore Congressional confidence in the Library of Congress.

Yet Luther Evans made many concrete, lasting contributions to the institution as we know it today. These include an impressive expansion of the collections (nationally and internationally), the strengthening of the Library's relations with the national and international library communities, and his open, staff-oriented management style. Above all Luther Evans is remembered for his remarkable vision of what the Library of Congress could and should become, a vision expressed in his 1947 budget proposal and, in large measure, fulfilled by his immediate successors, L. Quincy Mumford and Daniel J. Boorstin.

Biographical listings and obituaries—[Obituary]. *American Libraries* 13:216 (March 1982); [Obituary]. *Library Journal* 107:935 (May 15, 1982); [Obituary]. *Wilson Library Bulletin* 56:492 (March 1982). **Books and articles by the biographee**—*The Job of the Librarian of Congress*. Washington, D.C.: Library of Congress, 1945. Reprint of a radio address of July 21, 1945; "Library of Congress Records a New Era of World Progress." *The Sunday Star* (Washington, D.C.), December 2, 1945; "Problems Facing the Library of Congress." *Special Libraries* 36:467-70 (December 2, 1945). **Books and articles about the biographee**—Clapp, Verner W. "Luther Evans." *Library Journal* 90:3384-91 (September 1, 1965); *Luther H. Evans, 1902-1981: A Memorial Tribute to the Tenth Librarian of Congress*. Washington, D.C.: Library of Congress, 1982; Sittig, William J. "Luther Evans: Man for a New Age." *Quarterly Journal of the Library of Congress* 33:250-67 (July 1976). **Primary sources and archival materials**—Evans's official and personal papers are in the Library of Congress Archives, Manuscript Division, Library of Congress. A June 25, 1985 interview with Dan Lacy is in the Motion Picture, Broadcasting, and Recorded Sound Division, Library of Congress.

—JOHN Y. COLE

GAGLIARDO, RUTH (1895-1980)

Six months after the death of her father, Elmer H. Garver, a traveling minister, Ruth Jane Garver was born to Mary E. Collier Garver in Hastings, Nebraska, on September 6, 1895. When Ruth was seven, her mother remarried and the family moved to Topeka, Kansas. After completing high school, she taught English from 1915 to 1918 in Kansas rural schools. In 1922 she earned her A.B. degree from the University of Kansas (K.U.) and three years later married Domenico Gagliardo. Ruth and "Dom" reared three children: David, Bettina, and John.

All her adult life Gagliardo devoted herself to the world of writing and authors. Her formal entrance began with her first job as reporter on the Emporia (Kan.) *Gazette* and as part-time secretary to its editor, William Allen White. During most of the two years (1922-1924) she worked for the *Gazette*, she covered art, music, and book events in the "Highbrow Column," so nicknamed by Editor White. She regularly devoted many columns to children's books, making the *Gazette* one of the first small-town newspapers to review children's books on a regular basis. Because White was being discussed nationally as a possible candidate for the presidency, Emporia in those months was a very exciting spot for a beginning reporter. Many touring writers and politicians came through town to talk to White; the editor saw that "R.J.," as he called her, met them all. Many notables later became contacts in Gagliardo's crusade for books and libraries.

In twenty years as a wife and mother of three children, Gagliardo also made time to move into a wide range of cultural and educational activities in her small college town. Most involved books and the promotion of reading. In 1942 she volunteered to write a book review column for the Kansas State Teachers Association (KSTA), headquartered in Topeka. The column, "The Children's Book Shelf," appeared for 25 years in the *Kansas Teacher*, the first children's book review column to be published regularly by any educational journal in the United States. Gagliardo never missed a deadline. She stressed literary quality by focusing the column on the joys of reading and the values of books for children who need access to creative expression.

Gagliardo was concerned with the lack of bookstores in Kansas, an agricultural state with few large cities and towns. At that time more than 40 percent of Kansans were also without library service. Of 286 public libraries, 129 had budgets of less than $1,000, making the state 44th in the nation for state support of libraries. State law required only that schools spend five dollars on books—not per child, but per year.

In 1943 she asked the board of directors of KSTA to provide a traveling children's book exhibit. The request was immediately approved, as was the request for funds to pay the costs incurred by the traveling collection. The first exhibit was held in the Kansas Teachers College at Pittsburg and consisted of 400 books: Gagliardo's personal collection and publishers' review copies with original drawings from the books also contributed by the publishers. The exhibit was an instant success. Attendance demonstrated the immense hunger that Kansans had for access to good children's books. By Gagliardo's own report, 700 farm women came to one particular county institute at which the exhibit was featured.

Throughout the next two decades the exhibit grew to nearly 700 quality books enhanced by a constantly growing and changing collection of original drawings from artists and illustrators. Gagliardo and her exhibit crisscrossed the state year after year to county institutes, state conferences, and school districts. Her exhibit was sponsored by a variety of groups, including teachers' associations, boards of education, library broads, farm bureaus, local youth organizations, the American Association of University Women, the Parent-Teachers Association, and men's service clubs.

Gagliardo highlighted and promoted the exhibit with enthusiastic talks, which resulted in many parents' fund-raisers and commitments by boards of education and principals to allocate money for books in their schools. She always insisted that one public meeting be held in each community the exhibit visited; she wanted to emphasize the need for children's books to prosperous local business owners.

In 1947 Gagliardo accepted a paid position as director of library service for KSTA. She continued to work from her own book-lined study in Lawrence, but because she never drove a car, she had to rely upon taxi and bus drivers and friends and colleagues with cars for all of her state and national travels. In 1947 she also began the University of Kansas radio book program, a monthly feature that lasted eight years.

In both 1950 and 1960 she served as Kansas delegate to the White House Conference on Children and Youth. Legislators, governors, and local government officials corresponded with her about improving the availability of books in schools, libraries, and homes. In 1963 Governor John Anderson appointed her to the State Library Advisory Commission.

In 1952 Gagliardo originated and organized the William Allen White Children's Book Award program, sponsored by the William Allen White Library, Kansas State Teachers College, Emporia. Its premise was simple. Children voted on a favorite book they had read or had read to them from a list selected by Kansas educators and librarians. According to published reports, 40,000 children participated in the first year of the program. The White program grew in popularity and success and spawned other successful book award programs in many other states. It remains a vital state reading program.

Gagliardo worked with many local, national, and international agencies to start reading and book programs, including the Kansas Boys Industrial School (a reform school), the University of Kansas, UNESCO, and the U.S. Department of State. All turned to her for assistance in establishing reading programs, collections of good books, and reading lists. Some of these programs required reading from preselected lists; most issued certificates of award or merit for those who completed specified readings.

When criticized for sponsoring reading programs that confined readers to a list, Gagliardo responded heatedly. In a state with such a paucity of books, she argued, it was best to give as much help as possible in identifying good books. With this method, she predicted a future with more books, more libraries, and more librarians to select the books and give guidance to readers.

Gagliardo was actively involved in the National Education Association (NEA), the National Council of Teachers of English, and the Parent-Teachers Association (PTA) on both the state and national levels. She served the NEA for eight years as a member and chairperson of the NEA-PTA Joint Committee. She was a founder of the National League of Women Voters in Kansas. She worked actively in state library associations. She was also an active member of Theta Sigma Phi, the national journalism fraternity; Delta Kappa Gamma, national fraternity for women members of the teaching profession; and the Women's National Book Association.

Gagliardo targeted two national associations, however, as particularly appropriate for her interest in bringing books and children together: the National PTA and the American Library Association (ALA). From 1956 to 1959, she served the PTA as its vice-president and as its chairperson of the Reading and Library Committee for six years. She also served as director and as assistant editor of the *National Parent-Teacher Magazine* for four years.

She was an active member of ALA, working on many general ALA and divisional boards and committees. Included were the presidency of the Children's Services Division (CSD, now called the Association for Library Service to Children) in 1963. In 1962 she chaired CSD's Newbery-Caldecott Committee. She served on nearly every book evaluation committee administered by CSD. She was also active on the ALA-NEA Joint Committee, serving as member (1952-1958) and chairperson in 1957. She also served in 1959 as a member of the ALA-National Book Publishers Council Reading Development Committee.

Gagliardo wrote steadily for any national magazine that would print lists, reviews, and guidance on the selection of good books for children. *Calling All Girls*, the *NEA Journal*, *Top of the News*, *National Parent-Teacher Magazine*, *Library Journal*, and the *Saturday Review of Literature* all became part of her national forum.

In 1951, she provided "Elementary School Libraries Today" for the 30th Yearbook of the *National Elementary Principal*. She contributed "Parents, Teachers, and Libraries" in *The Wonderful World of Books*, edited by A. Stefferud in 1953. She initiated and assisted in the preparation of *Let's Read Together*, published jointly by ALA and the PTA (1960) and now in its fourth edition (1981). Her own book, *Let's Read Aloud, Stories and Poems*, was published in 1962 by J. B. Lippincott. Characteristically, it celebrates the importance of families reading aloud together.

As Gagliardo neared retirement, state and national organizations and institutions she had served began to recognize her many contributions formally. In 1964 the Kansas Association of School Librarians established the Ruth Garver Gagliardo School Library Scholarship. In 1966 she was the recipient of the first Library Leadership Award presented by the Department of

Librarianship of Kansas State Teachers College, Emporia. In that same year, the year of her retirement from KSTA, the Wichita Public Library founded the Sullivan-Gagliardo gallery. The gallery now houses the extensive Gagliardo collection of original illustrations by children's book artists as well as other collections. In 1967 the University of Kansas presented her with a Distinguished Service Citation. In 1976 she was inducted into the NEA's Hall of Fame for American Women.

Between 1942 and 1966, the name Ruth Garver Gagliardo, "The Kansas Book Lady," was synonymous with good children's books and the rights of citizens young and old to good libraries. Kansas was her home base, but her enthusiasm, book knowledge and skills as writer and speaker pushed her to become a national spokesperson. As a member of many state and national organizations dedicated to libraries, education, parents, and teachers, she worked tirelessly to promote her cause and was one of a pivotal group of laypeople who assisted in the rapid development of libraries in the mid-twentieth century. She died on January 5, 1980, in Wichita, Kansas.

Biographical listings and obituaries—*Contemporary Authors*, Vol. 104 (1982); [Obituary]. *ALA Yearbook 1980* (1981). **Books and articles about the biographee**—Galas, Judith. "A Life of Books." *Kansas History* 11:12-13 (March 1982); Murphy, Anna Mary. "A New Chapter Begins for the Book Lady." *The Kansas Teacher* 53:31-40 (May 1966); Rich Everett. "School Children Judge." *ALA Bulletin* 48:73-4 (February 1954); "Take a Bow." *Publisher's Weekly* 154:1890-3 (October 30, 1948). **Primary sources and archival materials**—Gagliardo's official papers are scattered among the files of the newspapers, magazines, and professional associations for which she worked.

—MARILYN L. MILLER

GROVER, WAYNE CLAYTON (1906-1970)

Wayne Clayton Grover was born September 16, 1906, in Garland, Utah, the son of George Frederick and Mary Clayton Grover. He was educated at the University of Utah, receiving a Bachelor of Arts degree in 1930. He completed a Master of Arts degree in 1937 and a Ph.D. in 1946 in public administration and political science, both from American University in Washington, D.C. His dissertation was entitled "The Records Administration Program of the Department of War." In 1935 he married Esther Thomas, the daughter of U.S. Senator Elbert D. Thomas of Utah.

Before moving to Washington, D.C., Grover worked as an editor on the staff of the Salt Lake City *Deseret News*. He began his career as an archivist at the National Archives in 1935, serving as a War Department Records specialist. For six years Grover served with and learned from the leaders in the field: Solon J. Buck, Robert D. W. Conner, Philip Hamer, Philip C. Brooks, and others. These six years were to be of great significance later in his career. In 1941 Grover left the National Archives to join the Office of Strategic Services, serving as a technical assistant to the Board of Analysts until 1942. From 1943 to 1947 he served as chief of the Records Management Branch of the Adjutant General's Office of the U.S. War Department. In this position Grover served as the Army's leading records management officer and initiated the system of Army records centers. He attained the rank of Lieutenant Colonel and received the Legion of Merit Citation in 1947 for his wartime records management work. Although he returned to civilian status in May 1946, he continued to be in charge of the War Department's records management program.

The National Archives was embroiled in internal squabbles and congressional monetary cutbacks in August 1947 when Archivist of the United States Solon J. Buck appointed Grover assistant archivist. Developing policies to enact congressionally required reductions in staff was Grover's first assignment. His unabrasive style enabled him to carry out such reductions effectively. His time as assistant archivist was short, however, for on May 13, 1948, one day after Archivist Buck announced his retirement, Grover was nominated by President Truman to be the third Archivist of the United States. Confirmation of his appointment was granted by the U.S. Senate on June 3, 1948. He served in that post until 1965. In his history of the National Archives, Donald R. McCoy described Grover as a "man of average height and rotund appearance, which was accentuated by his moonshaped face. More important was Grover's quite different background ... he was neither a teacher nor a writer of history, nor did he have standing in any scholarly association.... He was one of the first trained archivists in the United States and a pioneer in the records management profession. He was, in short, one of the new breed increasingly found in the federal government: a trained administrator."

Grover's seventeen years as Archivist covered some of the most productive and troublesome years for the National Archives. On the troublesome side was the creation of the General Services Administration and the subsequent loss of independent status for the Archives. In 1947 Congress established the Commission on the Organization of the Executive Branch of the Government, better known as the Hoover Commission. Its mission was to find ways in which the federal government could achieve greater economy and efficiency. Archivist Grover suggested to the commission that problems created by federal records were appropriate items for study, arguing that records management could save money for the government. A federal records administration was to be created that would operate records centers and develop standards for the creation, administration, and disposition of federal records. Also proposed was a federal records management bill. Grover sought to capitalize on this proposed legislation and had his staff prepare a draft bill.

Other forces were also at work regarding the role of the National Archives and records management. The Bureau of the Budget pushed for the establishment of a new department of general administration, which would include records management, cultural agencies, and housekeeping functions of the government. Finally, the Hoover Commission submitted to Congress a report which led Congress to authorize an office of general services, which would encompass the National Archives and abolish the office of the Archivist of the United States. Grover gathered his forces to oppose such recommendations, but economy and efficiency based on reorganization were the watchwords of the Truman administration. With almost unprecedented speed for Congress, by June 30, 1949, Congress had passed, and the President had signed, the new Federal Property and Administrative Services Act. This legislation created a new superagency, the General Services Administration (GSA). Under the GSA were five former independent agencies, including the National Archives. Fortunately, the office of the Archivist of the United States was not abolished.

After the creation of GSA, the National Archives became known as the National Archives and Records Service (NARS). Grover saw his agency's responsibilities as fourfold: (1) securing from Congress legislation and regulations that would permit NARS to carry out its functions, (2) the establishment of the Records Management Division within NARS, (3) creation of records centers, and (4) promotion of records administration programs in all federal agencies. Grover pushed for the passage of a new federal records law which would give GSA responsibility for records in all three branches of the government, the authorization of a federal records council, and retention by Congress of the right to approve the destruction of federal records based on recommendations from NARS. Although Grover was not included in GSA discussions regarding the new law, the bill, in a form much as Grover had drafted it, passed Congress in September 1950. The Federal Records Act of 1950 also expanded the membership and functions of the National Historical Publications Commission (NHPC). According to McCoy, "the work of NHPC was just one example of how, under Wayne Grover's leadership, the leading American temple of archives had been plucked from jeopardy during the late 1940s and set on the road to bigger things."

The National Historical Publications Commission had been written into the National Archives Act in 1934 to begin and to carry forward a federal publications program. Congress appropriated no funds for it, however, and the first two Archivists did nothing to advance its program. Between 1940 and 1950 the Commission did not meet. With the support of President Truman, Grover was able to implement programs for the NHPC. The Commission was included in the Federal Records Act of 1950, and Grover designated a small staff to work full time for the NHPC. With Grover's support the Commission published *Writings on American History: A National Program of Historical Documents* (1953), and *A Guide to Archives and Manuscripts in the United States* (1961). The Commission also saw the beginnings of the publication of the papers of the Adams Family, John C. Calhoun, Henry Clay, Benjamin Franklin, Alexander Hamilton, James Madison, Woodrow Wilson, the Continental Congress, and the presidents. Before he retired in 1965, Grover brought the NHPC to a new level of respect in the scholarly community. While he was Archivist, annual volumes of the *Public Papers of the Presidents* appeared for Truman, Dwight D. Eisenhower, John F. Kennedy, and Lyndon B. Johnson. These were published by the Federal Register Division of the National Archives.

Presidents' papers got a further boost under Grover's administration. A system of presidential libraries was begun with the Truman Library because Truman had asked Grover to include in the Federal Records Act of 1950 a section that would give the National Archives the right to receive the papers of presidents. This section became part of the law. Grover encouraged the prompt opening of presidential papers for research and supervised the development of the Truman, Eisenhower, and Herbert Hoover libraries. He also directed the initial planning of the Kennedy and Johnson libraries and continued to serve as a consultant to the Johnson Library after his retirement.

Grover's leadership qualities were evident in his work with the Society of American Archivists (SAA) and the International Council on Archives (ICA). Two of his greatest contributions to the archival profession were the "Archivists' Code" and the Committee on the Education of Archivists. Throughout his career Grover was concerned about the education of archivists and their professional status. Many of his writings reflect that concern. As early as 1955 Grover wrote in "Archives: Society and Profession" (*The American Archivist* 18:3-10 [January 1955]) that the place of archivists in the professional world must be improved and that archivists would have to initiate that improvement. As President of the Society of American Archivists (1953-1954), Grover also attempted to improve education for those wishing to become archivists and to gain recognition for archivists' achievements. In 1953, he established a Committee on Professional Standards and Training that would evolve into the Committee on Education of Archivists. This committee, under the chair of Solon J. Buck, originated the concept of SAA Fellows. Grover became chair of the committee in 1954 and worked to carry forward the SAA Fellows program.

Access for scholars to archival and manuscript sources also concerned Grover. In 1964, his last year as Archivist of the United States, he began to pursue an Extraordinary Congress for the International Council on Archives. He proposed to ICA that its 1968 congress be held in Washington, D.C., and hosted by the National Archives and the Society of American Archivists. The congress was to discuss the problems scholars faced when attempting to use archives and manuscripts, particularly excessive restrictions and the limited use of microcopying. Because of previous commitments the ICA could not meet in Washington in 1968, but instead proposed an Extraordinary Congress for 1966. A grant from the Council on Library Resources made it possible for international participants to attend.

Grover began the planning of the congress and served as chair of the Organizing Committee until his 1965 retirement. The result of this event was the development of initiatives in the lessening of restrictions, equal access to all despite nationality, microfilming of complete series, the recognition of microfilm as a legitimate publication medium, the need for increased finding aid production, and the promotion of international bibliographical and guide projects. Finally, for the first time, ICA established a special committee to oversee the initiatives and to report on progress at the ICA Congress in Madrid in 1968. Certainly, Grover could be proud of the ICA's response to his concerns.

During his tenure as Archivist, Grover was a popular speaker at state and local archival agencies, historical societies, and scholarly organizations. He was awarded honorary degrees from Brown University (1956), Bucknell University (1960), and Belmont Abbey College (1964). In 1958 he was made a Fellow of the Society of American Archivists and in 1959 received the Distinguished Service Award of the General Services Administration. Even greater recognition came in 1962 when Grover was awarded one of the ten Career Service Awards by the National Civil Service League. He served as vice-president of the Western Hemisphere of the International Council on Archives and as a member of its board (1953-1970). Grover also served as a member of the United States National Committee for UNESCO (1961-1970).

Despite his numerous responsibilities and activities Grover found time to be a prolific writer in the archival field. His annual reports of the Archivist of the United States (1948-1965) are excellent, scholarly, state-of-the-art discourses. Subjects of his articles included the archival profession's role in society, the history of the National Archives and its programs, records management, preservation of scientific records, and the use of government records in scholarly research.

On November 2, 1965, Grover sent a letter announcing his retirement to President Johnson. Because President Truman had appointed Grover, Grover determined to resign to a president, not to an administrator of the General Services Administration. In his letter to Johnson, Grover recommended the re-creation of the National Archives as an independent agency under a board of governors. He emphasized that because the Archives had achieved the Hoover Commission's goal to create a functioning federal records management program, it could be returned to cultural and educational activities. Unfortunately, Grover would not live to see the restoration of the independence of the National Archives in 1985, but he did play a vital role in the movement for independence. Grover died on June 8, 1970, in Silver Spring, Maryland, and is buried in Rock Creek Cemetery, Washington, D.C.

Wayne C. Grover will be remembered for many things, but the accomplishment he cherished most was the placement of original copies of the Declaration of Independence and the Constitution in the National Archives. Grover had worked closely with Librarian of Congress Luther H. Evans to move the documents from the Library into a specially designed vault area built into the National Archives building. The vault had existed since the building was completed in 1937, but the documents did not arrive until 1952. Through the cooperative efforts of Evans and Grover, and with the consent of the president and Congress, the precious documents were ordered transferred to the National Archives by the Congressional Joint Committee on the Library of Congress. Grover stated to Evans in a letter dated May 5, 1952, that "Jefferson wanted on his tombstone that he wrote the Declaration. I want on mine that I saw it safely enshrined in the Archives of the United States."

Biographical listings and obituaries — [Obituary]. *The American Archivist* 33:282-84 (July 1970); [Obituary]. *Newsweek* 75:61 (June 22, 1970); [Obituary]. *New York Times*, June 9, 1970, p. 41; *Who Was Who in America* V (1969-1973). **Books and articles about the biographee** — Coggin, Jacquelin. "That We Shall Truly Deserve the Title of 'Profession': The Training and Education of Archivists, 1930-1960," *The American Archivist* 47:243-54 (Summer 1984); Lethbridge, Mary C., ed. "News Notes: National Archives," *The American Archivist* 11:272-74 (July 1948); McCoy, Donald R. *The National Archives: America's Ministry of Documents, 1934-1968.* Chapel Hill: University of North Carolina Press, 1978; Rieger, Morris. "Archives for Scholarship: The Washington Extraordinary Congress of the International Council on Archives." *The American Archivist* 30:81-89 (January 1967). **Primary sources and archival materials** — Material by and about Wayne C. Grover is held in the National Archives, Record Group 200, Wayne C. Grover Papers; in the Manuscripts Division, Library of Congress, Solon J. Buck Papers, and in the Records of the Society of American Archivists, Special Collections Division, University Library, University of Wisconsin-Madison.

—FAYE PHILLIPS

HANDY, DANIEL NASH (1875-1948)

Daniel Nash Handy was born in Prospect Harbor, Maine, on June 11, 1875, to Marcus and Linda Handy. His father was a sea captain who owned his own ship. Handy began his education at the local public school and later attended the East Maine Conference Seminary in Bucksport, Maine. He continued his education at Ohio Wesleyan and Boston University, leaving the latter institution in 1900 to embark upon a career as a journalist. After brief stints with the *Boston Transcript* and the *Boston Post*, Handy joined the Insurance Library Association of Boston in 1901, beginning a career of over 40 years in librarianship.

Handy's professional career is noteworthy on two levels. First, he was a "pioneer" in business librarianship in general and in insurance librarianship in particular. Second, he was very influential in the early activities of the Special Libraries Association (SLA); he was instrumental in helping to "save" SLA from disbanding and from becoming a division of the American Library Association (ALA) in 1924.

When Handy began working at the Insurance Library Association of Boston (ILAB) in 1901, the collection consisted of some 2,800 volumes, a few hundred periodicals, and over 500 pamphlets. But the heart of the library was the collection of Sanborn-Perris Company fire insurance maps of New England. The ILAB made little progress over the next nine years, especially during a five-year period (1903-1908) when Handy was in Puerto Rico. He went to Puerto Rico in 1903 to become the Secretary-Treasurer and, later, Librarian at the University of Puerto Rico. Upon Handy's return from the Caribbean he found things much as he had left them, with the librarian responsible for everything from answering questions to typing catalog cards to dusting the shelves.

By 1910, however, two events occurred that radically changed the situation. First, Gayle Forbush was elected president of the ILAB's Board of Trustees, and chief among Forbush's goals was improvement of the library's facilities and expansion of the staff. Second, several members of the insurance industry established the Insurance Institute of America to further insurance education in the United States. The ILAB supported the ideas of the institute and saw this as an opportunity to bring its own educational goals to fruition. The institute was located in Boston in its early years, and Handy served as its Secretary-Treasurer from 1909 to 1911 and as Chair from 1912 to 1914.

In 1911, the ILAB authorized the establishment of a course in fire insurance, and Daniel Handy's involvement with insurance education began. Handy was tireless in his efforts involving the educational programs of the ILAB. He recruited lecturers for the courses in fire insurance, gave a number of lectures himself, and kept the library open until the last student had left for the night. This commitment to service to the students in the evenings carried over into the daytime operation of the library, as Handy led the transformation of his library from its static, custodial character to that of a dynamic information provider.

In setting up the library as an integral part of the ILAB, Handy first had to tackle the problem of an inadequate classification system, which resulted in haphazard shelving and retrieval of the material in the collection. At the turn of the century, three major classification schemes dominated library collections: the Dewey Decimal Classification, the Cutter Expansive Classification, and the Library of Congress Classification. Handy found that none of these systems suited his needs, so he developed his own, using Dewey's decimal notation as a model. Major divisions were: 000 General Works; 100 Systems of Fire Insurance; 200 Company Organization and Management; 300 Agency—Brokerage; 400 Law of Fire Insurance—Policy Contract—Modifiers of Policy; 500 Rates—Theory and Practice—Statistical Data; 600 Fire Loss Settlements (Adjustments); 700 Government Supervision—Legislation—Statutory Laws; 800 Fires and Fire Waste—Fire Protection and Prevention; and 900 Periodicals. Like Dewey, Handy also expanded each major division into ten subdivisions, such as 500 Rates—Theory and Practice—Statistical Data; 510 Systems of Ratings—Comparative Methods; 520 Classification of Fire Hazards; 530 Rate Investigation; 540 State Rate-Making and Supervision; and so forth.

But Handy was not entirely content with developing his own classification scheme: in 1909 he started the *ILAB Bulletin*. This publication served as an index to current fire insurance and fire protection/prevention literature from all available sources. Because this was the only index of its type, the demand for it was heavy and kept Handy busy for many years. Although he had to discontinue the *Bulletin* in 1924, many of the insurance periodicals covered were incorporated into the *Industrial Arts Index*.

In addition to these projects, Handy worked hard to open the ILAB library to broader use. Membership in the ILAB and use of the library were restricted to members of the New England Fire Insurance Exchange and to financial supporters of the ILAB. However, when the ILAB became involved with insurance education, the focus of the library expanded to serve the needs of students. As other schools in the area began to offer insurance courses, library privileges were extended to these students as well. Soon students from Harvard, Boston University, Tufts, Northeastern University, and the insurance courses offered through the local YMCA were using the collection and services of the ILAB library.

Even while carrying out this pioneering work, Handy found the time to write. He prepared some eighty pages of historical and chronological material that formed the appendixes of Harry Brearley's *History of the National Board of Fire Underwriters* (1916). He also wrote a number of articles that appeared in contemporary professional journals. Several were written from Handy's perspective as an SLA officer, while others provided general descriptions of insurance libraries around the country. Two articles in *Special Libraries* stand out: "The Library as a Business Asset: When and How" (1912) and "How Business and Technical Executives Obtain Information and What It Means to the Special Librarian" (1921). Both are still relevant to the special librarian in a business setting. They summarize Handy's vision of the business library as a functional information center considered essential by its institutional sponsor.

While Handy's efforts as a business librarian were certainly noteworthy, his involvement in the early years of the Special Libraries Association was perhaps even more significant. In his own quiet way, Handy was instrumental in organizing the SLA around both geographic and subject-oriented divisions and keeping SLA an independent association.

In 1909, the American Library Association was the dominant professional library association in the United States. Some librarians, however, felt ALA was not responsive enough to the "specialized" needs of many librarians, especially those in the business community. During the 1909 ALA conference held in Bretton Woods, New Hampshire, a group of these dissatisfied members, led by John Cotton Dana, met to form their own organization, and thus the Special Libraries Association was born. Although Handy did not attend the Bretton Woods conference, George Lee, the librarian at Stone & Webster (a Boston engineering firm) did. Lee returned home and talked about the new association with Handy and another Boston colleague, Guy Marion, who ran the library at the Arthur D. Little Company. When the first SLA conference was held in New York in November 1909, Handy, Lee, and Marion attended and became charter members of the SLA.

Handy began his service in SLA through committee work, chairing the Insurance Libraries Committee and also serving on the Membership Committee. In March 1910, Handy helped form a Boston Branch of the SLA. From the beginning, Handy saw the benefit of special library cooperation, both on a geographic and a subject-oriented basis. So strongly did he hold to this belief that he pushed it before the entire association at its 1912 conference in Ottawa, where he was the third person elected President of the association. In his presidential address, Handy advocated the creation of a system of association "responsibility districts." He divided the United States and Canada into fourteen districts to foster cooperation and communication on a regional level. Each district would elect a head, and the district heads constituted a national advisory board to the executive officers.

Despite the obvious merit of his plan, Handy's efforts were initially unsuccessful. Two districts were organized: an Eastern District, which frequently met in Boston, and a Manhattan District. Both represented large concentrations of special librarians where cooperative efforts were already underway. Elsewhere Handy's ideas fell on deaf ears.

In 1913, Handy was reelected to a second term as SLA President, during which he emphasized cooperation of a more subject-oriented nature. Projects that were begun and encouraged during Handy's tenure eventually resulted in such publications as *P.A.I.S.* (Public Affairs Information Service) and the *Industrial Arts Index* (ancestor of the current *Business Periodicals Index*). These efforts and other similar projects led the members at the 1914 SLA conference held in Washington, D.C., to adopt a theme of cooperation, with programs and meetings addressing existing cooperative efforts and the possibilities for the future. At the end of Handy's second term the SLA took stock of its first five years; membership had grown from the original 40 members to 350, and there was a clear shift in perspective from simply identifying existing special libraries to tackling some specific problems of concern to all members.

During the next ten years (1915-1924), Handy served SLA in a number of ways. First, he was appointed to the SLA Committee on War Service, established in 1917 to cooperate with ALA activities in support of U.S. efforts in World War I. ALA was trying to raise funds to establish "camp libraries" at military camps in the United States and abroad, as well as furnish information to higher levels of the military as needed. The SLA committee urged cooperation with ALA's efforts and offered its technical and specialized expertise in areas such as book selection. But ALA rejected the offer and proposed to put the SLA committee with the camp libraries committee. SLA responded by disbanding its committee. Special librarians, as individuals, did what they could for the war effort, but SLA did not soon forget ALA's heavy-handed actions. Handy himself not only helped raise funds in the Boston area for ALA's efforts, but in 1918 also took a two-month leave of absence to run the camp library at Fort Dix, New Jersey.

In 1921, Handy welcomed a Commerce Department request for SLA assistance to make the department more responsive to the needs of businesses. SLA responded by creating a Committee on Cooperation with the Department of Commerce, and made Handy a member. Over the next two years, the committee made a number of recommendations, which the Department subsequently implemented, on how special librarians could help in the dissemination of business information.

Handy's work on the Committee on Cooperation coincided with other major committee appointments. In 1922, Handy was asked to chair SLA's Committee on Certification. This group was organized to respond to an ALA proposal for certification of librarians. The committee reviewed the available literature and prepared a summary of the proposal. By the time it finished, however, ALA itself was beginning to have doubts about the idea, mostly because the profession still lacked enough adequate training programs. Ultimately the proposal was dropped. Handy began work on another important committee in 1922, which set about to revise the SLA constitution, a document that had been amended three times since 1909, but only to increase the number of officers and members of the Executive Board. The committee worked for two years, and in 1924 presented a new constitution and bylaws to the members. Handy's presence on the committee is evident: one of the major revisions was the provision for formal affiliation between SLA and the geographic and subject-oriented groups.

Throughout SLA's first fifteen years, its relationship with ALA was anything but calm. Things came to a head in 1924, and Daniel Handy was right in the middle of the controversy. For the first few years of its existence SLA held its annual meeting at the same time and place as ALA; joint sessions were common. Many SLA members retained their ALA memberships, and despite the major rebuff by ALA during World War I, most SLA members wanted to retain cordial relations. But problems arose during the early 1920s, as SLA membership began to stagnate and even decline, the costs of producing publications such as *Special Libraries* and the *Handbook of Commercial Information Services* were exceeding income, and the relationship between the association and the local groups was still unclear. And because there were no permanent headquarters or staff, all association business was left to the individual members. SLA Past President Rebecca Rankin detailed these problems for the SLA members attending the 1924 conference in Saratoga Springs, New York. She said SLA had two alternatives: take its place as a full-fledged professional association with a full-time staff, separate meetings, and the like; or dissolve and become a section of ALA. While Rankin supported strengthening SLA, the nominee for President, Alice Rose, felt that SLA had accomplished its purpose and should dissolve. She felt a Business Libraries Section should be created within ALA so SLA members could join that group or whatever existing ALA section was appropriate.

The regular business of the conference was quickly forgotten as the debate over the fate of the association ensued. Handy quickly became a vocal supporter of an independent SLA, and because of his affiliation with the proposed new constitution, he became a pivotal force at the conference even though he had to return to Boston on July 2 before the conference was over. In his absence the revised constitution and bylaws won association approval, a clear signal that the membership wanted to keep the association functioning. In response, Alice Rose withdrew her nomination for president. Nominations from the floor were accepted, and even though he was not in attendance at the time, Daniel Handy was elected president of SLA for a third term.

The association's independence had been preserved, but the challenges facing Handy in 1924-1925 were as monumental as those facing John Cotton Dana during his first term as president. Saving the association was one thing, keeping it alive and growing was another. Slow but continual growth and change were recommended—a recommendation SLA ultimately chose to follow. The geographic and subject groups recognized in the new constitution started to take shape as Boston, New York, Pittsburgh, San Francisco, and Southern California chapters affiliated, as did the advertising-commercial-industrial, financial, insurance, newspaper, and technology groups. The content of *Special Libraries* improved and a series of special issues was planned. Membership grew and a small dues increase coupled with greater advertising revenue helped SLA's financial situation.

In 1925 SLA held its conference in Swampscott, Massachusetts; ALA met in Seattle, Washington. The unrest and apprehension of the previous year were gone, and the 225 attendees (a record attendance for a SLA conference) were optimistic about the future of the association. The idea of slow, steady growth was continued, and Handy was reelected as president to an unprecedented fourth term.

Conditions continued to improve for SLA during Handy's 1925-1926 term of office. Handy did what he could to maintain relations with ALA, although the question of an ALA Business Section persisted. This issue was not fully resolved until Handy was out of office. ALA eventually approved the creation of a Business Libraries Section, but at the section's first conference it held its elections at a secret meeting. The ALA Council ruled the election illegal, and the Business Libraries Section never materialized as a threat to SLA.

Daniel Nash Handy continued his career in librarianship for another 20 years. He never held a major SLA office again, but he continued to be involved through committees, the Insurance Group, and as a contributing editor of *Special*

Libraries. Handy also used this part of his career to turn some of his attention and energy once again to insurance education and the ILAB. New courses were being added and Handy continued his lectures throughout the 1930s. Although classes were suspended during World War II, Handy estimated that some 6,400 people had registered for courses since their inception in 1911.

Although Handy officially retired from ILAB in March, 1945, his involvement continued. He began gathering data to write a history of the ILAB and spent the first two years of his retirement engaged in this effort, which culminated in the publication of his most extensive work, a history of the ILAB entitled *The First Sixty Years* (1947). This work chronicled ILAB's establishment and growth, and the library's role in its development. The chapter on the services of the library is the best available description of Handy's activities and the operating philosophy on which they were based.

Daniel Nash Handy died at the age of 73 on October 17, 1948, leaving behind his wife, Sara, and their two daughters. In 1959, when SLA introduced its Hall of Fame, Handy was recognized in a first group of inductees that included John Cotton Dana, Anna Sears, and Guy Marion. Handy's place in this select group is well deserved after a very active and involved career.

Biographical listings and obituaries—[Obituary]. "An Appreciation." *Special Libraries* 39:325 (November 1948); [Obituary]. "Late D. N. Handy, Father of Insurance Education Courses in Boston." *Eastern Underwriter* 49:21 (November 12, 1948); [Obituary]. *New York Times*. October 18, 1948, p. 23. **Books and articles by the biographee**—*Creation and Development of an Insurance Library*, 2nd and rev. ed. New York: Special Libraries Association, 1941; *The First Sixty Years: The Story of the Insurance Library Association of Boston*. Boston: Insurance Library Association of Boston, 1947; "How Business and Technical Executives Obtain Information and What It Means to the Special Librarian." *Special Libraries* 12:162-64 (September-October 1921); "The Library as a Business Asset: When and How." *Special Libraries* 3:162-66 (October 1912); "The President's Address, Annual Conference, Atlantic City." *Special Libraries* 16:220-23 (July 1925); "Special Libraries Have Earning Power." *Special Libraries* 2:5-6 (January 1911); "The Year with Special Libraries Association." *Special Libraries* 16:220-23. **Books about the biographee**—Christianson, Elin B. *Daniel Nash Handy and the Special Library Movement*. New York: Insurance Division, Special Libraries Association, 1979. **Primary sources and archival materials**—Material relating to the life and career of Daniel Handy can be found in the archives of the Special Libraries Association and the archives of the Insurance Library Association of Boston.

—WILLIAM FISHER

HENNE, FRANCES ELIZABETH (1906-1985)

Frances Henne's career spanned five decades of the twentieth century and several aspects of librarianship. She was a faculty member in the School of Library Service at Columbia University and in the Graduate Library School of the University of Chicago. Although recognized nationally as a caring teacher and adviser, her major contribution to librarianship was the imaginative leadership she gave to the school library field. Her early championing of school libraries as centers for instructional media in various formats, her leadership in the development of school library standards, and her advocacy as writer and speaker on behalf of school library development are major examples of her contributions.

Henne's early life was spent in the Midwest. She was born to J. Z. and Laura (Taylor) Henne in Springfield, Illinois, on October 11, 1906. She earned an A.B. degree from the University of Illinois in 1929, and, five years later, a master of arts degree from the same university. From 1930 to 1934, she worked in circulation and reference at the Lincoln Library of Springfield. Martha Wilson, director of this public library, encouraged Henne to go to Columbia University, where she earned a B.S. degree in librarianship. While at Columbia, she worked at the New York Public Library and at New York State Teachers College at Albany from 1935 to 1938. She was invited by Louis Round Wilson, dean of the developing Graduate Library School (GLS) at the University of Chicago, to serve as an instructor there and to be responsible for the library in the University High School. Her return to the Midwest and her association with GLS gave her opportunity to undertake doctoral study even as she moved from instructor (1939 to 1946) to assistant professor (1946 to 1949) to associate professor (1949 to 1954). In 1949 she received the Ph.D. degree from Chicago while also serving as associate dean and dean of students. She was acting dean in the interim between the resignation of Bernard Berelson and the appointment of Lester E. Asheim.

Henne's years at Chicago were significant; she established her own interests and leadership, sponsored others who were embarking on library careers, and left some significant contributions to the Graduate Library School. She encouraged Alice Brooks McGuire to come to Chicago to start the Children's Book Center at the university and to develop the distinctive and distinguished publication of children's book reviews that continues as *The Bulletin of the Center for Children's Books.* At that time, many of the best and brightest people in librarianship were converging on GLS as its dynamic faculty developed a doctoral program and established patterns for library research that were to have major impact on librarianship. As the first woman faculty member at GLS, Henne was recognized early as a leader and as a gifted faculty member with interests and abilities in many areas of library education.

In 1954 Henne made an important career move that proved to be permanent. She became associate professor at the School of Library Service at Columbia University. She remained there until her retirement as professor in 1975. Although she taught at the University of Minnesota in the summer of 1950 and at Rutgers in the summer of 1954, Columbia became her base of operations, and her New York City and New England residences were among her joys.

Frances Henne knew how to use scholarship and its dissemination for political purposes. Although she allied herself with shrewd practitioners who were leaders in school librarianship—such as Mary Peacock Douglas of North Carolina, Ruth Ersted of Minnesota, and Margaret Walraven of Texas—it was she who provided university sponsorship for many of their efforts to reshape school librarianship into a dynamic force in education and librarianship.

Mary Peacock Douglas chaired the committee that produced the 1945 ALA standards for school libraries, and Henne was a member of that committee. ALA and the library profession were in a period of culmination and planning, building on the leadership that had developed in the 1930s in Works Progress Administration (WPA) programs and emerging library schools and on the euphoria of the post-World War II period. It was a time when a growing population and veterans empowered with educational benefits were dramatically increasing both the demands and the support for library service.

Leaders like Douglas recognized that national guidelines were needed to establish best practice and to encourage nationwide measures of effort and achievement. Since school libraries were customarily part of the evaluation process of regional accrediting associations, it was especially important to have reasonable standards and to get them adopted by the accrediting agencies. Henne understood these needs and threw herself into the effort with enthusiasm and know-how.

In 1947 Henne directed the Chicago Graduate Library School conference, "Youth, Communication, and Libraries." The conference papers, published in 1949 by ALA, are still cited as a landmark in development of library service to youth. Among the issues the conference raised was a controversy about the appropriate location of library services to youth. Henne championed the idea that school libraries should be the source for all library service to elementary school children. She continued to hold that position some twenty years later, when she used her membership on the New York State Regents Advisory Council on Libraries (1964-1974) to obtain that group's recommendation of the same concept. In the post-World War II years there were well-established leaders in public library service to children, while the proponents of greater power and more resources for elementary school libraries had few examples of good practice to cite. It is possible that Henne was knowingly overstating her position to attract the support and attention that elementary school libraries needed. In any case, she angered the powers of public library children's services with her pronouncements in *Youth, Communication, and Libraries*, and there was more to come.

Ruth Ersted, a longtime friend and ally, served on ALA's Fourth Activities Committee and preceded Henne as chair of the American Association of School Librarians (AASL) in 1947-1948. Henne was a member of the ALA Council when the Fourth Activities Committee report was considered. Consistent with actions of other professional associations in that post-war period, the committee challenged the leadership of ALA, and its critical report was instrumental in Carl H. Milam's resignation as ALA executive secretary in 1948. AASL was pressing for a full-time executive secretary of its own, and Henne was a leader in that move, initially proposing autonomy for AASL as a division within ALA when she chaired AASL in 1949. Although Mildred L. Batchelder was an experienced school librarian who served as ALA's staff person with the Division of Libraries for Children and Young People (DLCYP), she was not accepted by school librarian leaders as the logical person for AASL executive secretary. Frances Henne has, probably appropriately, received much of the credit and blame for these leadership positions.

The need for information on how school librarians and others might implement the 1945 standards prompted Henne, with Ersted and Alice Lohrer, to write *A Planning Guide for the High School Library Program*, which ALA published in 1951. Many of its suggestions are still relevant nearly forty years later, and Henne may be credited with providing much of the sound theory on which the highly practical guide was based.

When it came time to revise the standards for school libraries, Henne was the logical choice to chair the committee. Eleven librarians represented AASL on the committee, but twenty-eight representatives of organizations such as the National Council of Teachers of English, the American Association of School Administrators, and the National Education Association's Department of Audio-Visual Instruction (DAVI) provided information and comments based on their special expertise and interests. Chairing these discussions required political savvy and effective coordination, but the resulting document still had to be written by one person—that person was Frances Henne.

In an assignment that Ruth Ersted once compared to that of the heroine in "Rumpelstiltskin," Henne traveled to Chicago by train, carrying her copious notes, and was greeted and virtually locked in a hotel room by Eleanor Ahlers, AASL's executive secretary. Thus did Henne give style and significance to the work of the committee, producing *Standards for School Library Programs* (American Library Association, 1960), a publication that remains a landmark in the story of school library development in the United States.

> A school library does not have to change its name to embrace new materials and new uses of all types of materials any more than a school has to call itself by some other name to indicate that it is a continuously growing social institution. Services, not words, portray the image of the school library. The *school library* is a *materials center*, an *instructional materials center*, an *instructional resource center*, or any of the equivalent terms now springing into existence. In like manner, the *school librarian* is a *materials specialist* or an *instructional resources consultant*.... For the school library, through books, films, recordings, and other materials, goes beyond the requirements of the instructional program, and unfolds for the many private quests of children and young people the imagination of mankind.

Henne's report gave school library programs a new breadth of vision that was more likely to become reality because of the support the AASL standards commanded. Henne also realized the subsequent need for a dissemination project to inform educators and other leaders about the standards. A $100,000 grant from the Council on Library Resources funded the eighteen-month School Library Development Project in 1961-1962. Another grant of $1,130,000 from the Knapp Foundation provided for the five-year Knapp School Libraries Project, which was designed to demonstrate what could be achieved by school libraries that measured up to the 1960 standards. To both of these projects Henne contributed generously as advisory committee member, speaker, writer—becoming a champion in more than one sense of that word. During the Knapp Project, when ALA protocols required that some of the original committee members leave to provide for new appointments, one colleague commented, "You always need Frances for her brain." Henne stayed.

In 1965, with the passage of the Elementary and Secondary Education Act, school libraries were targeted for significant federal support for the first time. Difficulties were minimized by the standards and the projects based on them and by the qualified school library personnel who selected the media and developed the programs made possible by the funding. Henne was already a believer in the value of summer institutes for school librarians when National Defense Education Act funding provided for them. Some of the colleagues she respected did not share her views. During the ALA conference in New York in 1966, Jesse Shera, dean of the library school at Western Reserve University and Henne's friend from their student days at Chicago, railed about the problems of creating "instant librarians" in short-term institutes. He urged respectable library schools to ignore the possibilities the institutes offered. Frances Henne rose to speak after Shera. She remembered directional signs for several trade groups unrelated to the ALA in the corridor outside the meeting room and began by saying, "You're in the wrong place, Jess. The meat cutters are down the hall."

Henne knew how to use humor as effectively as scholarship and other communication skills, but she also followed up with open investigation and criticism. In May 1966, she reported in *Library Journal/School Library Journal* on the design, content, and evaluation of the first summer institutes offered for school librarians. She clearly wanted them to be successful and staunchly defended the concept of the institutes, but she recognized the problems of haste in their planning. She was one of four people who participated in selecting institutions to be funded in the summers of 1965 and 1966, and she had helped to design the idea for them, so she was scarcely an unbiased observer. But she did not overlook their shortcomings or special problems. In time, the most prestigious library schools, including Western Reserve, sought and got the opportunity to offer them.

The cycle of standards development began again in the 1960s, and Frances Henne was asked to coordinate the drafting of revised standards. These were to be based on the 1960 standards, so the publication would be less monumental, but Henne boldly demanded that these should be joint standards, cooperatively developed by AASL and DAVI. This was philosophically reasonable, but it complicated the process considerably. Although the 1969 standards are sound and clear, they lack the drama and elegance of the 1960 standards. There is no doubt that the 1969 standards are the work of a joint committee with members representing a spectrum of views.

While Frances Henne's contributions to librarianship through her many ALA and related national activities are significant, she had a full and active role as a faculty member. Her doctoral students at Columbia alone constitute an impressive array of leadership in library service to youth. Henne had also begun at Chicago to provide the questions, the insights, the challenges that an astute doctoral program adviser must raise to stimulate students engaged in research, but she was aware that her many personal and professional commitments, as well as the demand for her as an academic adviser, limited her accessibility to students. When one of her doctoral advisees was frustrated in trying to see her, Henne joked that there surely would be times when the student would want to shoot the adviser and other times when the student would want to shoot herself, but when the student wanted to shoot herself and her adviser, *that* was serious and Henne would be available to help.

While the doctoral students who completed degrees under her guidance are significant in number and quality, even more students in master's programs found Henne a stimulating, refreshing teacher. She also made herself available to speak to local groups of school librarians, to encourage interest in school library programs in colleagues at Teachers College, and to represent librarianship in New York's publishing world.

One of Henne's strong links with the world of publishing was her friendship with Velma Varner, children's editor for World Publishing Company and, later, Viking Press. The two women shared a home in New York until Varner's death by cancer in November 1972. Henne admired Varner for her mix of imagination, appreciation of creative enterprise, and business acumen. Their personalities complemented each other, and Henne, nearing the end of her own active career, was deeply saddened by the younger woman's illness and death.

Jane Carstens, one of Henne's former students, contributed to the festschrift *Frontiers of Library Service for Youth*, published in Henne's honor by Columbia's School of Library Service in 1979. Carstens's contribution was a sixty-item annotated bibliography of Henne's publications, preceded by a brief but graceful and perceptive statement:

> A consistency of thought cuts across the bulk of Dr. Henne's writing. In some cases one can pursue an idea from its conception in her early writing, through its various stages of development, to its fruition in her later work. At the same time, there is a flexibility in her thinking, and one finds her exploring, testing and in some cases, advocating a particular premise or approach, only to discard it when she becomes

convinced that it is false, or when other factors necessitate change.

Henne was active in a period when doctorally prepared library educators were in limited supply. She did not have to maintain an extensive publication record to achieve the tenured faculty positions she held. Although she wrote well, she did not enjoy writing enough to do it for its own sake. Indeed, her reluctance and her procrastination in preparing articles were legendary. On one occasion in the mid-1960s, when she went past the deadline on an article for *School Libraries*, she paid the one-day, round-trip expenses for her graduate assistant to take it to AASL headquarters in Chicago. These considerations make the extent and quality of her writing more impressive.

Toward the end of her career, Henne received numerous recognitions. She was the 1963 recipient of ALA's Joseph W. Lippincott Award, one of ten people who received special centennial citations from ALA in 1976, recipient of the Beta Phi Mu award in 1978, and of AASL's President's Award in 1979.

Henne's clarity of vision and her legacy of publications may make her notable as a librarian and library educator, but they scarcely hint at the warm humanity she exemplified in numerous personal relationships or the charisma that distinguished her as a speaker. On the speaker's platform, Henne's high tone of voice sometimes surprised those who had not heard her before. Her diction was clear and virtually without regional accent, and her gestures and occasional pauses or increases in volume emphasized what she had to say. She loved hats and usually wore one when she spoke. At a Frances Henne "love-in" reception at the ALA conference in Kansas City in 1968, she was presented with a hat that bore the flags of the fifty states. She was delighted with it and wore it with pride.

In the ten years after her 1975 retirement from the Columbia faculty, Henne enjoyed her favorite hobbies and interests: cats, opera, politics, gardening, and gourmet cooking. She kept in touch with events and people in librarianship and occasionally visited the library school at Columbia, but she enjoyed retirement and the freedom it brought.

Frances Henne died on December 21, 1985, in the Buckley Nursing Home in Greenfield, Massachusetts, as a result of amyotrophic lateral sclerosis. Dorothy Broderick, a student of Henne's who considered her "the most important person in my adult life," wrote of a last visit with her: "She is, and always has been, a rare person, so of course, when her body decided to betray her, it did so with a very rare disease."

Henne was an idea person in librarianship. Her reputation is based not on any direct service she provided to readers or library users, but on her written words and the stimulation and support she gave to students and colleagues with practical advice and sound theory.

Biographical listings and obituaries—[Obituary]. *American Libraries* 17:224 (March 1986); [Obituary]. "Frances E. Henne, 1906-1985." *School Library Journal* 32:12-13 (February 1986); *Who's Who in America* (1984-1985). **Books and articles about the biographee**—Broderick, Dorothy. "On My Mind." *Voice of Youth Advocates* 8:358-60 (February 1986); *Frontiers of Library Service to Youth: Essays Honoring Frances E. Henne, Professor Emeritus, Columbia University School of Library Service.* New York: Columbia University, 1979. **Primary sources and archival materials**—Very helpful insights and items of information were provided by Patricia B. Pond, historian of American school library organizations.

—PEGGY SULLIVAN

IMMROTH, JOHN PHILLIP (1939-1976)

John Phillip Immroth was born in LaJunta, Colorado, on September 30, 1936, the only child of Phillip Andreas and Margaret Boyd Immroth. His childhood was spent in Pueblo, Colorado, where his father, a Santa Fe railroad official, was employed. He began playing the flute at age eight, becoming an accomplished flautist and later joining school and municipal music groups. During his primary school years he contracted poliomyelitis, for which he was nursed at home by his mother and family friends. He recovered without defects and graduated from Centennial High School in 1954.

Immroth received his Associate of Arts degree in liberal arts at Pueblo Junior College in 1956. He continued his education at the University of Colorado where he completed his B.A. degree in speech and drama in 1959 and received an M.A. in English literature in 1962. His master's thesis, "An Analytical Synthesis of Bernard Shaw's Interpretation of Shakespeare's Plays," was written in 1961.

From 1955 to 1964 Immroth was actively involved in college and community theater groups as an actor and a playwright. He wrote unpublished dramatizations of several children's classics and a privately printed play, *Kremhilde*.

He served as music librarian for the Pueblo Municipal Band in Pueblo, Colorado, in the summers from 1960 to 1964. For two summers of this period, 1961 and 1962, he also served as senior library clerk and bibliographer in English literature and drama at the McClelland Public Library there.

After receiving his first M.A. degree, he moved to Stephenville, Texas, taking a position as an instructor of speech at the Tarleton State College. For two years he taught undergraduates at this institution.

Deciding that a career in librarianship more closely suited his interests and abilities, Immroth enrolled in the University of Denver Graduate School of Librarianship in 1964. It was during this year that his close friendship with Bohdan S. Wynar, a faculty member, was established. He also met and married Barbara Froling, who was a fellow student in the master's program. He completed his M.A. in librarianship in 1965 and served as cataloger on the Technical Services staff at the University of Denver Libraries in 1965. His first son, Christopher James, was born on September 21, 1965. Immroth became an instructor in librarianship at the Graduate School of Librarianship at the University of Denver the following year.

In 1966, when Wynar moved to become Dean of the School of Library Science, State University College, Geneseo, New York, he offered Immroth a position as his assistant at the rank of assistant professor. Immroth accepted the position and remained there until 1968. His second son, Andrew Stephen, was born on November 8, 1967.

In 1968, the Immroths moved to Pittsburgh where Immroth accepted a position as instructor in library and information science at the Graduate School of Library and Information Science (GSLIS) at the University of Pittsburgh. There he published *A Guide to Library of Congress Classification* (1969) the first of his seven major works.

In 1969, he completed his advanced certificate and wrote *Library Cataloging: A Guide to the Basic Course* with Jay E. Daily. A preliminary edition of the guide was placed at the University of Pittsburgh Book Center and used by students in the beginning cataloging course. Also that year, his *Classification Library of Congress, Manuel Pratique d'Utilisation* was published by the College de Sainte-Anne-de-la-Pocatiere, La Pocatiere, Quebec.

Immroth was awarded the Ph.D. from the University of Pittsburgh in 1970. His dissertation topic was "An Analysis of Vocabulary Control in the Library of Congress Classification, Indexes, and Subject Headings and the Formulation of Rules for Chain Indexing of L.C. Classification." At this time he was promoted to assistant professor and placed in the tenure stream at Pittsburgh. He was also named coordinator of Library Research Projects in the Office of Communication Programs.

In 1971, *Library Cataloging: A Guide to a Basic Course*, with Jay E. Daily, and *An Analysis of Vocabulary Control in Library of Congress Classification and Subject Headings* were published. That same year, Immroth was awarded the Esther J. Piercy Award from the Resources and Technical Services Division of the American Library Association (ALA) to honor his contributions in the area of technical services. In recognition of his accomplishments, Immroth was granted tenure and promoted to associate professor at Pittsburgh.

Immroth contributed to many professional periodicals, including reviews for "Professional Reading" in *Library Journal*, reviews for *American Reference Books Annual*, and articles for the *Encyclopedia of Library and Information Science*. While Immroth was primarily recognized as a cataloger, he was expert in a number of other areas. He served as assistant dean of the Graduate School of Library and Information Sciences from 1971 through 1973. In 1973 he taught in the areas of collection development, resources in the humanities, and history of books and libraries. In addition, he was area coordinator in resources and bibliography.

Immroth was also an international consultant. In Spring 1973, the Immroths went to England and Wales where Immroth made a lecture tour of library schools in Great Britain, including North London Polytechnic, Sheffield, Liverpool, Glasgow, Aberdeen, and Aberystwyth. In March 1976, Immroth led a panel of experts commissioned to plan a new central library building for King Abdulaziz University in Saudi Arabia.

Immroth was a family man who accompanied his sons to their Little League softball games and watched them play ice hockey. An active churchman, he was director of the Acolytes Guild for the Episcopal Church of the Redeemer of Pittsburgh.

Throughout his career, Immroth was an active participant in professional associations. When he was in Colorado he was active in the Colorado Library Association. He joined the ALA in the mid-1960s and became an early member of the Social Responsibilities Round Table. In 1969 Immroth joined with several University of Pittsburgh colleagues in supporting the Congress for Change. This was a meeting of library science students who expressed their serious concerns about librarianship as a profession and library education in particular. The meeting was a major impetus for the movement for reform within ALA and library practice. Immroth was one of many activists in this effort. Immroth chaired the ALA Scholarship Committee from 1970 to 1971 and served on the ALA Council from 1972 to 1974. He was a nominee for election to Council when he died in 1976.

Immroth's greatest interest was intellectual freedom. He was a member of the ALA Intellectual Freedom Committee from 1972 to 1974 and was instrumental in the organization of the Intellectual Freedom Round Table in 1973, serving as its first chair. With Immroth as its leader, this round table became one of the most active in ALA. The John Phillip Immroth Memorial Award for Intellectual Freedom, sponsored by the Intellectual Freedom Round Table, is now awarded "to honor notable contributions to intellectual freedom and demonstrations of personal courage in defense of freedom of expression."

As a member of ALA and the Pennsylvania Library Association, Immroth edited several papers for both groups. He was also a member of several other associations and societies including the Association of American Library Schools, the American Association of University Professors, the Bliss Classification Society, the Printing Historical Society, the Pittsburgh Bibliophiles, and various regional library associations.

Immroth was a popular teacher and an excellent researcher, both characteristics recognized by students, particularly international students, many of whom chose him as their major advisor for doctoral dissertations. Concerned with the educational progress of students, he was readily available for consultation and assistance.

Immroth died of accidental asphyxiation on April 2, 1976. He had recently been named editor of the Pennsylvania Library Association's periodical, the *PLA Bulletin*, and was attending his first board of directors meeting in Scranton. He died as a result of choking at dinner in a local restaurant. At the memorial service, GSLIS Dean Thomas J. Galvin characterized Immroth as "a brilliant teacher, a dedicated, highly productive scholar, a national leader in his profession, as well as a tireless advocate of free access to information, which is a cornerstone of our democratic way of life."

Immroth contributed some two dozen scholarly papers and research reports to various monographs and journals, including eight major articles for the *Encyclopedia of Library and Information Science*. "A Lexical Essay Towards the Development of the Theory of Indexes to Classification Schemes," presented at the Third International Study Conference on Classification Research at Bangalore, India, in 1975, was published late in 1976.

Immroth's last publication, written with Bohdan Wynar, *Introduction to Cataloging and Classification*, was issued in 1976. At the time of his death, he was also in the process of revising the *ALA Glossary of Library Terms* and the third edition of his *Guide to the Library of Congress Classification*. The death of this creative man at the age of thirty-seven was a true loss to librarianship.

Biographical listings and obituaries — [Obituary]. *ALA Yearbook 1976* (1977); [Obituary]. *American Libraries* 7:243 (May 1976); [Obituary]. *Library Journal* 101:101 (May 15, 1976); [Obituary]. *Wilson Library Bulletin* 50:685 (May 1976). **Primary sources and archival materials** — Immroth's personal papers are in the possession of Barbara Immroth, Austin, Texas.

—BLANCHE E. WOOLLS

JONES, VIRGINIA LACY (1912-1984)

Virginia Lacy Jones, a black library educator, was born in Cincinnati, Ohio, on June 25, 1912, to Edward and Ellen Parker Lacy. She grew up in Clarksburg, West Virginia, which she described as "a town of about 35,000 people with approximately 1,200 Afro-Americans." She attended Sumner High School in St. Louis, Missouri, and was graduated in 1929.

Books were always a part of Jones's home. Although her mother often read to her and she had access to and used the integrated public library in Clarksburg, it was an experience at the St. Louis Public Library, while she was in high school, that led her to decide to become a librarian. Seeking information to write an essay on the values of attending Sunday school, Jones encountered a reference librarian who was warm and friendly. She recalls:

> This experience was a thrilling one to me, and my imagination ran wild at the magic of the St. Louis Public Library, a great storehouse of information, ideas and inspiration. I was fascinated by the systematic organization of the material and how specific lists of information could be made available according to the needs and interest of users. I thought that to be a librarian like that reference librarian who helped me in the St. Louis Public Library would be the greatest thing in the world. I decided then and there that I wanted to be a librarian. ["A Dean's Career," in *The Black Librarian in America*, ed. E. J. Josey. Metuchen, N.J.: Scarecrow, 1970, p. 24.]

Jones received a bachelor's degree in library science from Hampton Institute, Hampton, Virginia, in 1933. Here she met Florence Rising Curtis, a white woman, who was the director of the library school and who quickly became Jones's mentor. In the fall of 1933 Jones became the assistant librarian of the Louisville Municipal College, the Negro branch of the University of Louisville. Inspired by the young faculty, most of whom were pursuing their doctoral degrees, Jones realized that if she wanted to advance professionally, she would need to finish her bachelor's degree in education before she could study for the master's degree in library science. With Curtis's encouragement, Jones got her bachelor's degree in education from Hampton in 1926. She was then granted a fellowship by the General Education Board to study for an advanced degree at the University of Illinois. Curtis had recommended her because she was convinced Jones would make a general contribution to the library development for blacks in the South.

Jones's year of study was plagued by negative racial experiences. In "A Dean's Career," pp. 28-29, Jones related how black students at the university encountered numerous incidents of discrimination. In the library school, black students were not invited to a tea party given for the students at the home of Dean Phineas Windsor; Jones was denied an "A" grade in a course because the instructor had a policy of "never giving an 'A' to a student who had not worked in a library that had 100,000 volumes"; she was questioned as to why she had not chosen to analyze subject headings dealing with blacks for a class project. But she persisted! "I had to make good because Miss Curtis had demonstrated her faith in me, and I was determined to show the faculty that a Negro could do the quality of work required." She received her master's degree in library science from the university in 1938.

Another General Education Board fellowship helped Jones to pursue a doctorate in library science at the University of Chicago. She liked Chicago much more than the University of Illinois:

> The association with the faculty and students of the Graduate Library School was marked with mutual respect. There was an atmosphere in which students of minority groups could work in a relaxed atmosphere conducive to independent study at a high level. Working with Leon Carnovsky, Carleton B. Joeckel, Maurice Tauber, Ralph Beale, and Frances Henne provided the greatest challenge and the most pleasant and rewarding academic experience. ["A Dean's Career," p. 36.]

In 1945 Jones became the second black American to receive the doctoral degree in library science.

Jones's entire professional career was devoted to libraries and library education. From 1933 to 1935 she was employed as the assistant librarian and instructor in library science at the Louisville Municipal College. Rufus E. Clement was dean of the college and Eliza Atkins Gleason, the first black to earn a doctorate in library science, was head librarian. For four summers (1936-1939) Jones taught in a program in Prairie View, Texas, training blacks to work as school librarians. From 1936 to 1939 she was employed as the Louisville Municipal College's head librarian. In 1939, Rufus E. Clement, who had become president of Atlanta University, hired her as the university's catalog librarian and asked her to help organize a library education program for the university. In 1941 she married Edward Allen Jones, chairman of the Department of Languages at Morehouse College. That same year, with financial support from the Carnegie Corporation of New York, the library school opened at Atlanta University with Eliza Atkins Gleason as dean. This school replaced the library science school at Hampton Institute, which had closed in 1938. In 1945 Dean Gleason resigned, and Jones succeeded her.

The Atlanta School of Library Service was committed to provide leadership for the development of library service in the South—particularly for black Americans. During Jones's thirty-six-year tenure, the university trained over 1,800 black librarians, more than any other school in the country. The successful placement of graduates from the school can be attributed at least in part to Jones's determination to provide a quality curriculum. Jones noted that "while the curriculum was so designed as to place special emphasis on the professional library needs of the Negro minority group in the South, it was definitely slanted toward general library development on a national scale and an understanding of the place of libraries in a democratic society" ("Training for Library Service," *Fundamental Education* 3:19-23 [January 1951]).

In serving black students, Jones recognized that some of the students coming into the school's program were ill-prepared and needed special attention from the faculty. This often meant that some students in the program had to spend a longer time to meet the degree requirements than they would have had to spend at other library schools. In defense of this policy Jones stated: "Traditionally, our policy has been to admit some high-risk students and to give them as much individual assistance as possible. If they cannot measure up to our standards we drop them from the program." She lamented that "some accredited library schools ... have taken such students and within an academic year they have been awarded master's degrees. This has been a clear indication of double standards which are detrimental both to the Negro students and the library profession, and I have been outspoken about my resentment of this situation" ("A Dean's Career," p. 40).

In the 1960s, as the Civil Rights movement began to influence hiring practices, Jones became annoyed by requests to recommend the "instant" black to fill a position of responsibility. She said she would help fill positions only if she could recommend a candidate without reservation. She was opposed to the practice of libraries which, in her opinion, would hire blacks regardless of their qualifications to ease the pressure on them and to show that they had an integrated staff. She believed that if blacks employed under these conditions did not measure up to or surpass the performance of their white colleagues, the process of integration would not be advanced.

After retiring as dean in 1981, Jones was named the first director of the new Robert W. Woodruff Library, Atlanta University Center, where she remained until shortly before her death in 1984.

Throughout her career Jones was an active member in many professional organizations. She was a member of the American Library Association (ALA) and was elected to its Council for three terms (1946-1950, 1955-1959, 1967-1969). She served as a member of the association's Executive Board from 1970 to 1976 and was an active member of ALA's Association of College and Research Libraries. She helped to organize ALA's Black Caucus and was chair of the ALA Committee on Opportunities for Negroes in the Library Profession (1966). A member of the Association of American Library Schools (the forerunner of the Association of Library and Information Science Education), Jones served as its secretary-treasurer from 1948 to 1954, as a member of its board of directors from 1960 to 1964, and as its president in 1967. She was a charter member of the Georgia chapter of the Special Libraries Association and a member of the Southern Association of Colleges and Schools. Additionally, President Lyndon B. Johnson appointed her to the President's Advisory Committee on Library Research and Training Projects (1967-1970).

Jones valued her memberships and service to the community, even though she experienced racial discrimination in many. Her initial attempt to join the Georgia Library Association was met with refusal. Instead she became active in the Southeastern Library Association (SELA), which accepted black members. At her first ALA meeting in Richmond, Virginia, in 1936, Jones and other Hampton Institute students and faculty were required to sit together on one side or in the back of the room and were not permitted to see the exhibits. Hampton Director Curtis invited Jones to stay overnight at the John Marshall Hotel as her guest. Probably because of her light complexion, Jones evidently experienced no problems as a guest in the hotel and was able to see the exhibits. She later wrote:

I never liked the idea of passing for white, but I did it, nevertheless, at times when it was to my advantage. This was one of those times. I had mixed feelings about doing so, felt a sense of shame for being where I was not wanted. On the other hand, I felt a sense of triumph in outsmarting the blatant and cruel racial discrimination of whites ["A Dean's Career," p. 26].

Jones was also instrumental in the establishment of the Library Section of the Kentucky Negro Library Association. Following her move to Atlanta, she worked in concert with Mollie Huston Lee of Raleigh, North Carolina, Charlemae Rollins of the Chicago Public Library, and others, to raise the awareness of publishers about the negative images of blacks that appeared in many children's books. She also assisted in the establishment of a Field Services Program under the sponsorship of the Carnegie Corporation of New York that brought consultant services to libraries serving blacks in several southeastern states.

Throughout her professional career Jones wrote a modest amount on issues that concerned her. She addressed the problems and challenges facing libraries in the South as well as issues related to library education for black Americans. In two articles written in the 1940s, she described the opportunities available for black librarians. But most of her writing was done in the 1960s. As an early supporter of the American Library Association's Bill of Rights statement, approved in 1961, she wrote a brief but candid article entitled "Segregation in Libraries: Negro Librarians Give Their Views," in which she outlined ways in which the Association "might help in the desegregation of Southern libraries" (*Wilson Library Bulletin* 35: 707-8 [May 1961]). One of her outstanding characteristics, as reflected in her writing in this decade of civil rights activism, was the consistent belief that good library service for blacks would develop through reliance on the democratic process. She espoused a basic democratic ideology, manifested a firm belief in the equality of all people, insisted upon an integrated society, and expressed a strong faith that the "power of knowledge" and the promise of the "Great Society" could be made to work for all, black and white ("The Library in the South: Educational Problems," *Wilson Library Bulletin* 39:879-84 [June 1965]).

Her strongest statement on the racial situation in libraries came out in 1962, when in a review of the development of segregated library service, she wrote plaintively:

How long, oh how long, does the South have to remain out of step with the nation and the world and continue to waste time, energy, money, and human resources in a futile struggle ... to deny their own citizens, black and white, full opportunities for growth and development? ["How Long? Oh, How Long?" *Library Journal* 87:4504-5 (December 15, 1962).]

Jones was sensitive to the perceptions non-librarians had of librarianship. In 1962 she lamented the lack of recognition given by the President's Commission on National Goals to the value of libraries in its report, *Goals for Americans* ("Goals for Libraries," *Library Journal* 87: 728-9 [February 15, 1962]). In another instance she suggested that students from other disciplines would better appreciate the values of library services if they were encouraged to broaden their educational background by taking basic courses in library science ("Educational Exchange," *Library Journal* 88:3178ff [September 15, 1963]).

As an educator, Jones wrote passionately on the challenges facing the library and library education in the South, and on the need for library systems as a way to improve the availability and delivery of information. She identified areas of concern that should have priority in regional planning for library education in the Southeast: the proliferation of library education programs; generalization versus specialization in library school curricula; continuing education; and higher education and library education for black students.

Over the years Jones received numerous awards and honors. The Savannah (Georgia) State College Library presented her an award for distinguished service to librarianship in 1966. In 1973 she was elected to honorary membership in ALA and was awarded ALA's prestigious Melvil Dewey Award "for creative professional achievement of high order." In 1977 she received the Joseph W. Lippincott Award for distinguished service as a librarian. In 1980 she received the Mary Rothrock Award and the Beta Phi Mu Award for distinguished service to education in librarianship. In

1979 she received the Honorary Doctor of Humane Letters degree from Bishop College and the Honorary Degree Doctor of Letters from the University of Michigan. She was also cited by the Southeastern Library Association in 1981 for her contributions to that organization and to the South. The Southeastern Library Association elected her to honorary membership in 1984.

Virginia Lacy Jones was a leading library science educator when segregation was an integral part of American life, and thus for a significant part of her career, she faced it almost daily. That she and her school were able to flourish during that time is a testimony to her ability as a skilled racial diplomat. In addition, her school functioned as a watchdog over racial developments in libraries. Twenty-six historical studies relating to the development and current status of public library service to blacks in various communities in the South were completed by students at Atlanta during her tenure there. The findings, some of which were published in national library journals, served as a reminder to the profession that segregated conditions needed to be changed.

Jones occupied a sensitive, yet strategic, position insofar as black library interests and outlook were concerned. She had significant opportunity to be of influence, especially as president of the Association of American Library Schools and as a member of the ALA Executive Board. Yet most of her writing and her activities reflect concern with library service and library education in general; race is not a dimension discussed in many of her writings. This reflects the dilemma faced by Jones throughout her career. To be successful, she had to forge relationships with established whites in power and make arrangements to enhance and secure her own position. The library conferences she arranged with the support of the General Education Board and the Carnegie Corporation of New York in the late 1940s and early 1950s attest to this relationship. Reliance on such connections possibly diminished her potential to influence the black library community at large, since these organizations did not speak out on civil rights issues, and in fact, through their grant-making processes, perpetuated segregated conditions in many places.

Virginia Lacy Jones's major contribution to the profession can be found in her leadership at the School of Library Service in Atlanta. Its graduates pushed racial issues and forced the profession to confront discrimination. In a very functional sense, then, Jones was a leader; through her students, she promoted library development for blacks and better library service for all.

Jones died on December 3, 1984, three years after the death of her husband.

Biographical listings and obituaries—*ALA World Encyclopedia of Library and Information Services*, 2nd ed.; [Obituary]. *ALA Yearbook 1984* (1985); [Obituary]. *American Libraries* 16:11 (January 1985); [Obituary]. *Atlanta Constitution*, December 5, 1984, p. A-14; [Obituary]. *Library Journal* 110:94 (February 15, 1985); *The Negro Almanac: A Reference Work of the Afro-American*, 4th ed.; *Who's Who among Black Americans*, 3rd, 4th eds.; *Who's Who in Library Service*, 3rd, 4th eds.; *Who's Who of American Women*, 1st, 2nd, 3rd, 4th, 5th, 6th, 7th eds. **Books and articles by the biographee**—"Changing Concepts of Librarianship." *Kentucky Library Association Bulletin* 33:5-15 (January 1969); "A Delicate Area for Research." *Wilson Library Bulletin* 42:913-14 (May 1967); "Negro School Library Service in the South." *Top of the News* 4:3-4 (December 1947); *Reminiscences in Librarianship and Library Education*. Ann Arbor: University of Michigan, School of Library and Information Science, 1979; "Response to Library Education in the Southeast since World War II." In *Louis Round Wilson Centennial Day*. Chapel Hill: University of North Carolina School of Library Science, 1977; "Wanted—18,000 Librarians." *Opportunity* 25:215-17 (October-December 1947). **Primary sources and archival materials**—Material by and about Virginia Lacy Jones is held in the Special Collections and Archives of the Atlanta University Center, Robert W. Woodruff Library.

—WILLIAM CAYNON
—ROSEMARY RUHIG DU MONT

KUHLMAN, AUGUSTUS FREDERICK (1889-1986)

A. Frederick Kuhlman was born to Henry and Anna Wickman Kuhlman in Hubbard, Iowa, on September 3, 1889, and grew up on a farm nearby. Even as a lad he preferred his middle name: "Not Fred," he would say, "Frederick!" Frederick graduated from Northwestern Academy in Naperville, Illinois, in 1910 and earned his baccalaureate degree from North Central College in 1916. He went into recreation work with the YMCA War Service at the Great Lakes Naval Station in 1917 and soon became assistant secretary of the Illinois War Recreation Board. He entered the United States Army in 1918, and after his discharge the following year, he became director of social surveys for the Southern Division of the American Red Cross.

In 1920 Kuhlman accepted an assistant professorship of sociology at the University of Missouri and upon receipt of his M.A. from the University of Chicago in 1924 was promoted to associate professor. In addition to his teaching and study, he was extensively involved during this period in professional social work activities, serving as president of the Missouri Conference for Social Work in 1923, as assistant director of the Missouri Crime Survey in 1925, and in 1927 and 1928 as director of the Survey of Research on Crime and Criminal Justice for the Social Science Research Council (SSRC). In 1922 he married Katharine Edmonstone Jones of Columbia, a vivacious and intelligent young woman who had earned both her B.A. and M.A. at the university there.

While working for the SSRC Kuhlman began to sense the great challenges for scholar/librarians in the broad field of bibliographical control and the provision of scholarly materials. In 1929 he received his Ph.D. degree in sociology from the University of Chicago, submitting as his dissertation a treatise entitled "A Guide to Material on Crime and Criminal Justice." In that same year he resigned his professorship at Missouri to become the new associate director of libraries at the Chicago institution. That was the same fall that Robert Maynard Hutchins first proposed his "new plan" for the University of Chicago; Kuhlman found himself wholly supportive of the library implications in Hutchins's vision of the university. In fact, he published a paper entitled, "Some Implications in the New Plan of the University of Chicago for College Libraries," in the fledgling *Library Quarterly* (3:21-35 [January 1933]).

Kuhlman remained as associate director of libraries at the University of Chicago for seven years, learning under the watchful tutelage of director M. Llewellyn Raney to apply his extensive administrative experience and bibliographical acumen to a research library. Raney has been described as a forthright and outspoken man, who made no effort to conceal his views, no matter how unpopular—qualities that were greatly admired and well learned by his new deputy. The two men appear to have been an effective team, and Kuhlman often spoke of the high esteem in which he held the older man. Kuhlman also had a high regard during these years, higher than did Raney, for the university's new Graduate Library School. He worked closely with its faculty members and doctoral students, developing there many friendships that lasted throughout his career.

It is not surprising that Kuhlman's early labors at Chicago focused largely on the need for universities to improve their library resources and services. In another early piece, "The Need for a Comprehensive Check-list Bibliography of American State Publications," *Library Quarterly* (5:31-58 [January 1935]) he reported surveying the views of the profession's leaders regarding the microfilming of newspapers, and he pleaded in the interests of scholarship for research libraries to pool their energies to bring this very new technology to bear upon newspaper bibliography. This was also a major concern of Director Raney at that time. No doubt because of his earlier frustrations with social work bibliography, Kuhlman also sought to elicit better distribution and control of state and local documents, in the Harper Library at Chicago specifically as well as cooperatively in the larger national ambit ("Public Document Problems That Confront Large Research Libraries," *ALA Bulletin* 25:513-4 [June 1931]; "Next Step in the Organization of State Document Centers," *ALA Bulletin* 26:555-8 [April 1932]).

In fact, Kuhlman's first prominence in the academic library community came from this concern for state and local documents. During the 1930s he published several pieces on the subject of government publications, spoke of them frequently at American Library Association (ALA) gatherings, and served as member and chair of a number of influential ALA bodies charged with improving their availability. From 1932 until 1936 he chaired ALA's Committee on Public Documents and from the latter year until 1939 he chaired its Committee on Libraries and Archives. He also served as a member of ALA Council from 1932 to 1936, and in 1939-1940 he was nominated for ALA's second vice-presidency, but he lost the election to Donald Coney of the University of Texas.

Kuhlman was especially active in ALA's Association of College and Reference Libraries (ACRL). He worked diligently with others to gain the establishment of an ACRL journal. When *College and Research Libraries* (*C&RL*) was ultimately authorized in 1939, he served as its founding editor-in-chief, a responsibility he sustained through its first two and one-half years. For the most part, he shaped its policies, crafted its practices, and determined its direction. The eight purposes that he enumerated for *C&RL* in the opening pages of its first issue have changed little in the subsequent half-century and bespeak the clarity of his vision and the depth of his faith in the academic library field.

Meanwhile, a drama that was to affect the balance of Kuhlman's life was unfolding in Nashville, Tennessee, where two institutions on adjacent campuses were suffering from gross library inadequacies. Both Vanderbilt University and George Peabody College for Teachers (the latter a leading institution for teacher education in the South), were attempting to serve large and growing graduate, research, and professional programs with very limited library resources. From 1931 on the presiding officers of both institutions had sought financial support to remedy these deficiencies, but their solicitations had been uniformly rejected by foundation officials who felt that they should submit a single cooperative proposal rather than two independent appeals. Multiple efforts to develop such a single scheme were made by faculty and administration representatives of the two institutions, sometimes in concert with Scarritt College and the YMCA Graduate School, which were also situated on contiguous tracts in the same campus center. An outside survey team comprised of William Warner Bishop and Louis Round Wilson was brought to Nashville to study the situation; they too recommended a cooperative approach. Nonetheless, whether because of interinstitutional oversensitivity or simple inertia, four years later no such cooperative proposal existed.

By 1935 the principal philanthropic foundations were losing patience with Nashville's inaction and were threatening to withdraw their interest entirely. As a result the four institutions commissioned a new joint survey of prospects for broader cooperation, to include but not be limited to library services. In November of that year A. Frederick Kuhlman was invited to make the study. During the next seven months he came to the Tennessee capital on four occasions to gather data and to hold conferences, and on March 24, 1936, his proposed plan was signed by the presidents of all four institutions. Among his other recommendations were agreements to eliminate duplicate course offerings and to accept cross-registration of students (280 quarter hours of duplicate course work were deleted from their curricula), to adopt a common academic calendar, and to develop a single, jointly owned and operated library system.

On September 1, 1936, Kuhlman contracted to serve as the first director of the Joint University Libraries (JUL), and he moved his family from Chicago to Nashville. He was also given courtesy appointments as full professor at Vanderbilt, Peabody, and Scarritt, and for the next quarter-century prided himself on practically never missing a faculty meeting on any one of the three campuses. Red-haired, energetic, poised, and self-confident, he was soon a well-known person in the Tennessee city, a member of the Rotary Club and communicant at Christ Episcopal Church. His wife Katharine was also active in civic and sorority affairs until she developed a lingering illness to which she succumbed in 1944. Their two daughters, Clara Ann and Clementina, were a solace to him, however, as was his second wife Virginia Wood Walker, whom he married late in 1946.

Thoroughly knowledgeable about the situation in the Nashville University Center when he arrived, Kuhlman needed no time for orientation. Instead he "hit the ground running," and his presence galvanized a wide range of groups and interests into vigorous action. A Nashville regional union catalog was commenced. A legal document in the form of a "Trust Indenture," setting out the rights and responsibilities of the Joint University Libraries, was drawn up and signed. Formulae by which the joint libraries would be funded by the participating institutions were explored and ultimately agreed upon. Several large foundation grants were sought and received, including $1 million from the General Education Board and $250,000 from the Carnegie Corporation. In addition, a local fund-raising campaign was mounted, and some 5,000 individual donors in the Nashville area contributed more than $500,000 dollars to the library cause. Collections, totaling 274,538 volumes on May 1, 1936, were rationalized, integrated as needed, in many cases re-cataloged, and programs for their future strengthening were prepared. Kuhlman planned, negotiated, and led the implementation of all of these activities on the three cooperating campuses, the YMCA Graduate School having since closed down.

Last but not least, an appropriate building had to be developed to house the suddenly burgeoning JUL resources. Peabody College's library building was good, having been designed by Edward L. Tilton and Alfred M. Githens and built with Carnegie support in 1919. It was much too small, however, to meet the new joint need, and it could not be enlarged easily. Neither Vanderbilt nor Scarritt had free-standing library buildings at all, so planning for a completely new structure occupied much of the new director's time. Between 1936 and 1939 he visited more than twenty of the largest new library buildings in the nation, a feat that was more difficult in an age when they were fewer in number and when travel could be done only by railroad.

At that time textbooks on library building design were nonexistent. Also, many innovative building techniques were beginning to come into use in other kinds of buildings, and Kuhlman found it necessary to evaluate them for libraries. Should the building be air-conditioned? Should it be lighted with fluorescent ceiling lamps? Both were still considered experimental, but he decided each in the affirmative. Retaining as consultants Phineas L. Windsor of the University of Illinois, which had completed a good library building in 1926, and Theodore Koch of Northwestern, which had opened the Deering Library in 1932, he set about to prepare the best building program document that contemporary expertise could conceptualize. He also got Vanderbilt University to deed over to the JUL a tract of land at the juncture point of the tri-campus area to be used for construction of the new building. Alfred M. Githens of New York and Henry C. Hibbs of Nashville were selected to design the building, and construction was begun late in 1939. Dedicated the night before the attack on Pearl Harbor, it was the last major fixed-function university library with a multi-tiered structural stack to be built in the United States. It represented all of the style's qualities while minimizing its weaknesses. Enlarged in 1969, the building still serves as the central library for Vanderbilt University.

Although no college library buildings were constructed for the next five years because of the disruptions of World War II, such construction commenced again in the late 1940s and gained momentum in the subsequent two decades. Because of the knowledge he had gained in the planning of the JUL, Kuhlman found himself called upon with increasing frequency during this period to consult in the planning of academic libraries on other campuses. Of the more than a dozen institutions availing themselves of his building expertise, most were in the South, including Texas Christian University (1949), Mississippi State University (1949), Southwestern at Memphis (now Rhodes College, 1950), Jackson State University (1957), Florence State University and Auburn University (1959), and East Tennessee State University (1966). In 1963 he was sent by UNESCO to the Middle East Technical University in Ankara, Turkey, where he prepared a program for a library building of 1,000 seats and a capacity of 170,000 volumes.

An experienced surveyor from his early days in sociology and social work, Kuhlman was also frequently called upon to conduct or participate in library or institutional studies of broader purpose than just buildings. He made library surveys of the University of Mississippi and the University of Florida in 1940, of North Texas regional libraries in 1943, of cooperative graduate centers in the South in 1944, of four St. Paul college libraries in 1952, of seven libraries of the Arkansas Foundation of Associated Colleges in 1958, and of six libraries in the Atlanta University Center in 1966 and 1968. He also conducted a *Consumer Survey of "New Serial Titles"* for ALA in 1967, published as *A Report on the Consumer Survey of New Serial Titles* (Washington, D.C.: Council on Library Resources, 1967). In these ways he placed the indelible impress of his expertise upon library practice in the South for more than three decades.

During Kuhlman's entire career in Nashville, including a long period after his retirement as director of the JUL on June 30, 1960, he influenced young librarians by teaching in the library school at George Peabody College for Teachers. His favorite course, and that of his students, was "The Library in the College and University Curriculum," and hundreds, if not thousands, of academic librarians in the South were first introduced to their careers in his popular classes. He took great personal interest in his students and always made a point to interview each one in depth in the course of a term. Kuhlman also left his mark on the profession in many other ways. His extensive record of published works spanned more than half a century. A bibliography of his many printed papers, reports, and reviews, containing 111 items was published in the Winter 1961 issue of *Southeastern Librarian*, and he published at least a dozen more after that time. He was widely read, quoted, and cited.

Like his early mentor, M. Llewellyn Raney, Kuhlman also spoke his mind no matter how unpopular his views might have been to his listeners. He expressed his views in faculty councils in Nashville, in the ALA, in the Association of Research Libraries (following JUL's admission to it in 1946), in the Tennessee Library Association (which he served as president in 1954-1955), in the Association of Southeastern Research Libraries (which he was largely personally responsible for establishing), and in the Southeastern Library Association. He often spoke his mind when everyone else had long since decided it was time to leave. But he never spoke until after he had done his homework, and those who stayed to hear him out soon learned that the things he said deserved always to be heard, even if it *was* past time to go home. President Henry Hill of George Peabody College once said of Kuhlman that the only thing that could make his pronouncements more annoying was for them to be right 100 percent of the time instead of only 98 percent.

Yet Kuhlman was selfless regarding libraries and scholarship, and with other people he was generous to a fault. One librarian in the South says that Kuhlman once bought him an automobile so that he could remain in the Peabody Library School, even though the student had no visible prospect of repayment. Kuhlman reportedly waited five years for reimbursement. He generated fierce but not undeserved loyalty in his staff, and he scrupulously gave credit where credit was due. He was dynamic, forceful, and tireless in his professional service and in his dedication to the three institutions in the Nashville University Center. He had high regard for those of his colleagues in the research library community who deserved his esteem, and he kept his mouth shut about those who did not. Most important perhaps, he never carried a grudge.

Kuhlman received some plaudits. He was elected a fellow of the American Library Institute, and he was a member of Phi Beta Kappa. He served a number of elective offices. Upon his retirement, first as director of the JUL and later as professor in the Peabody Library School, he was honored by appropriate resolutions. He was always appreciated most by those who took the trouble to know him best, but he deserved more recognition than he got. A. Frederick Kuhlman died in Nashville, Tennessee, on December 27, 1986, in the ninety-eighth year of his life.

Biographical listings and obituaries—[Obituary]. *Nashville Tennesseean.* December 27, 1986. *Who's Who in America* 31 (1960-1961). Matthews, Jim P. "A. F. Kuhlman—A Bibliographic View." *Southeastern Librarian* 11:313-8 (Winter 1961); Matthews, Jim P. "A Pioneer in Cooperation." *Tennessee Librarian* 12:70-73 (July 1960); Jesse, William H. "Retirement." *College & Research Libraries* 21:307-8 (July 1960); Hoole, William S. "Tribute to Augustus Frederick Kuhlman." *Southeastern Librarian* 10:5-6 (Spring 1960); *Library Quarterly* 3:95-96 (January 1933); 34:192-3 (April 1964). **Primary sources and archival materials**—Two Hollinger boxes and several separate files of unpublished papers, reports, documents and pictures, as well as clipping files about A. Frederick Kuhlman, are held in the Vanderbilt University Archives.

—DAVID KASER

LANCOUR, HAROLD ADLORE (1908-1981)

Harold Adlore Lancour was born in Duluth, Minnesota on June 27, 1908, the only son of Adlore and Mary Hofer Lancour. Details about Lancour's early life are sketchy, but we know he grew up in Seattle, Washington, where the family had moved when he was three.

Lancour was accepted into the University of Washington in 1927. While in college he took various jobs to finance his education, including managing a dance band and working as a park ranger. In 1930 he took advantage of a fellowship to attend the Institute Universitaire de Hautes Etudes Internationale in Geneva, Switzerland. His experiences there seem to have started him on a life-long path of international activities. He returned to the United States in 1931 to finish his studies, receiving his A.B. from the University of Washington in International Relations.

After graduation Lancour established a bookshop in Seattle, which he managed until 1935 when his love of books led him to enroll in the School of Library Service at Columbia. In 1936 he received his B.S. in Library Science and began work as a reference assistant in the genealogy room at the New York Public Library. While working there Lancour met Marie McClellan, a librarian in the Music Department, whom he married in September 1936. Lancour soon started work towards a master's degree. At this same time he took a job as music librarian at Cooper Union for the Advancement of Science and Art in New York City. He held the position until 1940, the same year he received his M.S. in library science from Columbia. During this very busy time in his life, Lancour was also able to produce two notable reference works: *Heraldry: A Guide to Reference Books* (1938) and *Passenger Lists of Ships Coming to North America, 1607-1825* (1938).

Upon graduation Lancour worked for a year as acting librarian at Cooper Union, then became librarian and assistant professor of bibliography. At Cooper Union he inherited a library staffed by five librarians with an annual budget of $29,000. He left it six years later as a lively and vital organization, with several departmental libraries under a strong central organization, staffed by eleven librarians with faculty status, 22 clericals, and an annual budget of $75,000.

Lancour liked library work. His professional interests were challenged by the practical problems of library administration, while his avocational interests gravitated towards bibliographical work. While in New York he became an active member of the Grolier Club; he also joined the American Antiquarian Society. In 1943 he published *American Art Catalogues, 1785-1942*, which a reviewer for *College and Research Libraries* called "the standard work in the field." Lancour was also involved in professional association work. In 1941 he founded and for the next six years served as chair of the Engineering School Libraries section of the Association of College and Research Libraries. He also served on its board of directors from 1946 to 1949.

In 1943 Lancour was inducted into the U.S. Army, and for the next year and a half, he served as instructor in the Army's School for Unit Librarians in Paris and later in Oberammergau. There he met and became friends with LeRoy Merritt and Herbert Goldhor. After the war Lancour was appointed national chair in the field of engineering literature for the American Book Center for War Devastated Libraries, and from that position he directed American assistance in restocking and rebuilding Europe's engineering libraries. Lancour returned to the United States in 1945 to resume his position at Cooper Union and also to complete studies on an Ed.D. degree in education administration.

In September 1947, Lancour was appointed associate director of the University of Illinois Library School at Urbana, with the academic rank of professor of bibliography. He served there under Robert B. Downs, who was also director of the library. The experience fitted Lancour's interests well; he enjoyed his work in teaching, administration, publishing, associational matters and international activities. For a period of time he served as editor of the University of Illinois Occasional Papers Series, and in 1952 helped found *Library Trends*, serving as managing editor until 1962. In 1960 he helped found the American Association of Library Schools's *Journal of Education for Librarianship*, serving as its editor from 1962 to 1967. He remained on its editorial board until 1975. Lancour was also the driving force behind the founding of Beta Phi Mu, the international library science honor society, and served as its executive secretary beginning in 1948. In 1954 he became chair of the American Library Association's Board of Education for Librarianship and saw it through its transition into the Committee on Accreditation in 1956. He was also president of the Association of American Library Schools in 1955-1956.

During these years Lancour was able to satisfy and strengthen his interests in international activities. In 1950 he became a Fulbright Scholar (the first librarian to be so honored) and traveled to England to study the British system of training for librarianship. Two years later he accepted an appointment from the State Department Overseas Information program to coordinate a book and library program in France. As United States Information Service (USIS) director, he observed library education on the European continent while directing the main USIS library in Paris. In 1953 he became a member of the UNESCO International Commission for Social Science Documentation, a post he held for four years. He also surveyed libraries in West Africa for the Carnegie Corporation in 1957 and Liberia for the Ford Foundation in 1959. His efforts in 1957 helped to bring about the founding of the Ibadan Library School, which has since then served as a model for library education throughout Africa. Lancour later acted in an advisory capacity for federal government agency activity in Mali, Guatemala, Iran, and Chile.

In 1961 Lancour assumed duties as dean of the newly formed Graduate School of Library Science at the University of Pittsburgh. He spent the first year developing its curriculum and recruiting its faculty from all over the world. The school opened its doors to students in the fall of 1962. For the next decade Lancour presided with pride over a growing and increasingly influential program at Pittsburgh. The doctoral program he began there attracted many talented international students and future library leaders. He also served as joint editor with Allen Kent on the *Encyclopedia of Library and Information Science*, a massive multivolume publication project called by Harold Borko "a monumental undertaking" and "a valuable reference tool." Health problems limited his long-term involvement, but Lancour made a special contribution in the area of international contributors. Lancour retired as dean in 1974.

Lancour's contributions to the library profession are many. Ample testimony to his lasting influence are the professional journals he helped found, professional associations he helped create, basic professional information tools he nurtured and published, and a library school, which continues to reflect a heritage he wove into its origins. Perhaps even greater, however, was his ability to foster dialogue and a spirit of cooperation among the various communities of librarianship in the English-speaking world. Harold Lancour died at his home in Weston, Vermont, on October 23, 1981.

Biographical listings and obituaries — [Obituary]. *American Libraries* 12:662 (December 1981); [Obituary]. *Catholic Library World* 53:271 (February 1982); [Obituary]. *College and Research Library News* 5:184 (May 1982); [Obituary]. Horrocks, Norman. "Harold Lancour." *Library Association Record* 84:162 (April 1982); [Obituary]. *Journal of Education for Librarianship* 22:88 (Summer/Fall 1981); [Obituary]. *Library Journal* 107:137 (January 15, 1982); [Obituary]. *Wilson Library Bulletin* 56:56 (January 1982). **Books and articles about the biographee** — Nasri, William Z. "Lancour, Harold." In *Encyclopedia of Library and Information Science*. New York: Marcel Dekker, Inc., 1984. Vol. 37, Suppl. 2. **Primary sources and archival materials** — Lancour's papers are scattered among the official archives of his employers, including the University of Illinois and the University of Pittsburgh. Useful information on his life can also be found in the archives of the associations and publications he served throughout his life.

—PETER J. GILBERT

LORD, MILTON EDWARD (1898-1985)

Milton Edward Lord was born in Lynn, Massachusetts, on June 12, 1898, to William Delbert and Elizabeth Anne Bishop Lord, of old New England stock. He was one of four children, including an older brother who died as a child and a younger brother and sister. His father was an electrical contractor by trade. Milton Lord attended local schools, frequented the Lynn Public Library, and was graduated from Lynn Classical High School as valedictorian of the senior class. He also managed the track team. Entering Harvard in the fall of 1915, he began a career as an engineer; but U.S. entry into World War I interrupted his studies in 1917.

Lord entered the U.S. Army Heavy Artillery School at Fort Monroe, Virginia, and trained until his discharge in March 1919 with the rank of Second Lieutenant. He maintained his rank in the Coast Artillery Reserve Corps until 1924. Between his discharge and the beginning of the summer term at Harvard, Lord went to work in the Harvard library. William Coolidge Lane, Harvard College librarian since 1898, encouraged him to continue in library work when he resumed his undergraduate work. He served in part-time positions, including librarian of the Harvard Union, until 1924, having been graduated in 1921, and spending three years doing graduate work in history.

During 1925-1926 Lord studied history at the Ecole des Sciences Politiques of the University of Paris. He then served for four years as the librarian of the American Academy in Rome, where he revitalized the library and built up its collections. William Warner Bishop selected him to serve on the team of American librarians (along with J. C. M. Hanson, Charles Martel, and William Randall) to assist in reorganizing the Vatican Library classification and cataloging system. Lord's role was that of a local expert who knew Italian, had library experience, and could foster relationships with the Vatican Library staff. His youth also helped balance the team. Midway through his sojourn in Rome, Lord married Rosamond Lane, daughter of his mentor, William Coolidge Lane. During their marriage the couple had four daughters and one son. While in Europe, Lord spent his summers visiting numerous libraries in nearly every country in Europe.

During his tenure at the American Academy he served (in 1929) as the U.S. delegate to the first International Library Congress meeting in Rome, Naples, Florence, and Venice — a natural appointment. His library experience, study, and travel during the 1920s established Lord's professional credentials for the rest of his life.

In the summer of 1930 the Lords returned to the United States to be near Lane in his final illness. Lord also began a brief tenure as director of the University of Iowa libraries and library school, where he developed skills at directing a large staff and building a research collection. He also designed a comfortably furnished recreational reading room, novel for the times. He made several trips back to Cambridge and Lynn in his few months at Iowa.

In 1931, Lord was approached about the position of assistant librarian of the Boston Public Library (BPL), vacant because of the death of Frank H. Chase, but within three weeks the untimely death of Charles F. D. Belden, BPL director and librarian, on October 24, 1931, opened up another position. Boston newspapers immediately speculated on Lord's chances of succeeding Belden. The November 25 *Boston Post* reported the trustees' formal announcement: they had found someone with "a liberal education, practical knowledge of library administration, and wide experience." Lord began his new post at the BPL, the oldest large-city free public library and the second largest in the nation, on February 1, 1932, at the tender age of thirty-three.

Few appointments to major library positions received the advance publicity accorded Milton Lord. The selection process was followed by numerous news and feature stories in Boston papers. Many mentioned that he was the youngest person ever to fill such a post; most focused on his Boston-area education and connections, his reputation for international experience and scholarship, and his rugged outdoor interests. The *Boston Sunday Globe* (November 22, 1931) showed some disdain for library schools by suggesting that Lord's "lack of academic library training makes him a believer in reading for enjoyment first of all." Lord spent the rest of his professional life at the BPL; he retired from his post in 1965. His efforts in Boston and his service to the profession in his own country and abroad provided the twin focuses for his public life.

Taking over the reins of leadership of the BPL would have been a daunting task in itself at any period. But for a young man looking at a major urban library in the midst of the Great Depression and in desperate need of internal reorganization, the responsibilities must have been formidable. Lord tackled his new job, however, with grace and flair. On his first day, after visiting the trustees, Mayor James M. Curley, and his department heads, he granted an interview to the press in his small office. The session was widely reported and received favorable comment. Among the topics he discussed were the role of libraries in society, free access to books of all kinds, the interrelationship of other cultural institutions with the library, and preservation. He spoke of reintroducing some of the intimacy and "humanizing" touches of smaller libraries, serving the various clienteles of the library appropriately, and the uses of microfilm and photostat technology for making rare materials accessible. "Almost all libraries," he said, "need to have things done to make them far more human institutions. The whole approach to them should be an atmosphere of books, not of architecture or statuary, but of books easily accessible to people in every walk of life" (*Boston Evening Transcript*, February 6, 1932). Speaking to numerous civic groups, Lord used his early months at the library to excellent advantage. All Boston seemed impressed with his urbane, professional manner. One popular example was his widely heralded "Fine Cancellation Week." As an "emergency Depression measure" he canceled all previous book fines and invited citizens to retrieve their library cards and begin using the library again; 78,000 people responded.

The public goodwill toward the library was reflected unevenly. For the decade 1929-1938, circulation peaked markedly in 1932 and 1933. However, city-funded appropriations for books declined from $175,000 in 1931, to $160,000 in 1932, to $75,000 in 1933, and to less than that by 1938. The increase in circulation because of widespread unemployment coupled with a decrease in funds for the purchase of current circulating material produced a crisis in lending stock that continued despite vigorous and eloquent pleas from Lord in his annual reports to the city of Boston. Only in 1950 did the appropriation for books reach $150,000 again, and those appropriations represented inflated dollars.

Despite the times, Lord continued, as well as implemented, reforms that were called for in a 1918 survey of the library, which identified excessive involvement of the trustees in the daily operation of the library and circumvention of the librarian's authority as the chief problem. In the fall of 1932, recognizing that the roles of popular public library and research library deserved distinction, the trustees adopted a reorganization plan based on functions—circulation, reference, and business operations—each becoming a division with an administrator responsible to the director. This organization freed Lord for more general concerns. The plan gradually came into effect by the end of the decade and served the library well.

A second reform provided for an expansion of the Library Training Class (begun in 1927) to include courses for all full-time staff members in 1932. Entirely voluntary and carried out after working hours, the program's goal was to produce a better prepared staff by supplementing other educational opportunities and providing flexibility outside the conventional systems. Lord was somewhat proud of his professional preparation coming at the hands of "men who represented the complete history of the present library system." He therefore pushed for a merit-based advancement program from within the library and training that supported it and opposed appointments made on the basis of politics or simple longevity. Ten steps from general to specialized qualifications were graduated—the first five were probationary and the last five permanent—and represented increasing salary levels. Allowances were made for college and library school graduates; some 200 staff members were enrolled. New appointments were sought first from among the ranks of the qualified. Having gained city approval for this program, Lord saw a steady rise in salaries. The program lasted into the 1960s.

A final development of the early Lord years was the continued growth of endowments and support by bequests for the book funds. The Josiah H. Benton and the Emily L. Ainsley Funds were among the largest monetary gifts and physical collections that enriched the library. In 1947 a gift of several million dollars from John Deferrari—a tribute to the value of the library in the life of a successful fruit vendor—came to the library. Another bequest from the Wilks estate was used for building modernization in the early 1950s. In short, during the Lord years, the BPL experienced sustained growth and a management style unique for its time.

Having begun to set BPL's house in order and to appoint and develop capable leadership in the library, Lord resumed his participation in international and national professional endeavors. He had joined the American Library Association (ALA) in Iowa and chaired the International Relations Committee from 1934 to 1936. During that time he attended the Second International Library Congress in Madrid, Seville, and Barcelona during May 1935, which dealt with international interlibrary loan. His ALA career also included membership on the Council (1935-1940) and on the Executive Board (1940-1944). In 1937 he chaired the Library Administration Committee.

World War II brought new avenues for service. Lord represented ALA to the new Council of National Library Associations and was secretary-treasurer in 1942-1944 and chair in 1944-1945. He became a member of the ALA International Relations Board in 1942. In 1944 he assumed the chair of the ALA Joint Committee on Books for War-Devastated Libraries and continued with the permanent center from 1945 to 1955. From 1948 to 1950 he was chair of the United States Book Exchange (USBE; now Universal Serials and Book Exchange). He also represented ALA at meetings of the International Library Committee in Geneva (1946) and Oslo (1947). In 1947 he began a term as first vice-president of the International Federation of Library Associations. During this busy period Lord represented his profession at the U.S. National Commission for UNESCO (1949-1952) and the World Town Hall Seminar (1949).

A satisfying contribution that complemented his committee assignments was his appointment as Reorganization Director of the American Library in Paris during the first three months of 1945. His report, abridged in *Library Journal*, June 1, 1945, as "Devastated Libraries," described what he had seen and recommended expansion of that institution's role in the interchange of French and American culture. From 1947 on he served as an honorary trustee of the library's American Advisory Committee.

Lord was awarded other state and national leadership positions. In the years following 1947, he chaired the Conference on State Aid for Libraries in Massachusetts, which he later said had made "perhaps the most thorough-going and extensive study of Massachusetts public libraries yet undertaken" [*Current Biography*, 1950, p. 352]. It studied the most effective methods to bring about statewide legislation and coincided with the national *Public Library Inquiry*—proposed by ALA, conducted by the Social Science Research Council, and supported by a grant from the Carnegie Corporation of New York. He was a public advocate of the reorganization of ALA into a federation of member library associations.

Perhaps the crowning experience of Lord's professional life was his term as ALA president in 1949-1950. Four previous BPL librarians had preceded him since ALA was organized in 1876. He assumed office in Fort Worth, Texas, on November 23, 1949, at one of the seven regional meetings held that year. On July 1, 1950, he reported on his presidential year at the Cleveland meeting, and outlined three areas for further work:

> (1) the necessity for doing away with our over-concern with organizational problems and paper programs; (2) the necessity for relating the A.L.A. more closely with other library groups, and they in turn with the A.L.A.; and (3) the necessity for strengthening our state activities and through them our regional programs.

The first area mentioned displayed Lord's impatience with useless meetings and insignificant paper reading. The second derived from his attempts at cooperation in the national and international context. The third came from his own struggles of twenty years in libraries; he reiterated that "what libraries are suffering from chiefly is excessive veneration and insufficient public support." Citing the new conditions of the Cold War, Lord asked his colleagues to "examine what we are doing, with a view to identifying those programs which are not as valuable as they should be, and then to concentrating thereafter upon those which are of pressing and abiding value" ("Unfinished Business," *ALA Bulletin* 44:310-12 [September 1950]).

After the ALA presidency Lord returned his attention to his primary responsibilities at the BPL, which experienced, in his words, a "bright new era" because of a substantial building program and increased city appropriations as the library began its second century ("Boston Public Library," in *ELIS* 3:103 [1970]). In the early fall of 1952 the BPL trustees sustained Lord by a three to two vote in his resistance to pressure from *The Boston Post* to remove "communist" material from the library. *The Boston Herald* supported Lord and the library, as did *The Pilot*, official weekly newspaper of the Roman Catholic Archdiocese of Boston. This was one of the finest hours of the internationally minded director. He continued as director and librarian until he retired in 1965. During the two years following his retirement, he served as special assistant for library regional development and oversaw a program which the library operated under a state contract. He also served as president of the Massachusetts Library Association. His final legacy was to press for better service to the library's public and to shape plans for the new annex that now adjoins the original building on Copley Square. He enjoyed Director Emeritus status until his death nearly twenty years later.

Retirement allowed him to continue his favorite pursuits. Still cherishing his international involvements, Lord served the International Council of Monuments and Sites, Paris, from 1969 onward. Returning to his former haunts, he was librarian-in-residence at the American Academy in Rome in 1971-1972 and 1973-1974; he was director of the library in 1975-1976. As he spent his last years in Boxford, Massachusetts, with his wife, he continued to serve as a trustee of Simmons College and chaired the board of trustees of the Boxford Public Library from 1966 to 1971.

Among his other memberships were Phi Beta Kappa; Chevalier, Legion d'Honneur (France); Massachusetts Historical Society; Fellow, American Academy of Arts and Sciences; Benjamin Franklin Fellow, Royal Society of Arts (London); Club of Odd Volumes; Old Cambridge Shakespeare Association; and the Dante Society of America.

Throughout his life, the youthful-looking Lord was devoted to an active life—recreation, outdoor living, and travel. Known at Harvard as "the hiking fool" by his friends because of his long tramps in fair and foul weather, he also played tennis and enjoyed canoeing. Even in retirement, Lord continued walking and splitting firewood.

Lord died on February 12, 1985 in a Salem, Massachusetts hospital after a short illness at the age of 86. A memorial service was held in the First Congregational Church of Boxford the Sunday following his death.

His general love of life, early cultural experiences, liberal education, personal charm, conspicuous social connections, and knack for being in the right place at the right time—all these factors propelled him quickly into prominence in Boston and the profession at large in the 1930s and 1940s. His greatest contribution to the profession was as an international ambassador for American librarianship. He was, perhaps more than many of his colleagues, a unique product of circumstances.

Biographical listings and obituaries — *Current Biography* (1950); [Obituary]. *Boston Globe*, February 13, 1985; *Who Was Who in America* VIII (1982-1985). *Who's Who in Library Service*, 4th ed. **Books and articles about the biographee** — Briggs, Walter B. "Milton Edward Lord." *Bulletin of Bibliography* 17: 61-62 (January-April 1941); Van Dusen, M. E. "My Grandfather." (unpublished transcript in possession of D. G. Davis, Jr.); Whitehall, Walter Muir. *Boston Public Library: A Centennial History.* Cambridge: Harvard University Press, 1956, pp. 221-57. **Primary sources and archival materials** — No single, consolidated collection of Milton E. Lord Papers exists which is available to the public for research. The Boston Public Library maintains in a scrapbook collection newspaper clippings that deal with Lord's career to early 1933. Other institutions with which he was briefly associated hold isolated pieces.

— DONALD G. DAVIS, JR.

LOW, EDMON HORTON (1902-1983)

Edmon Horton Low, known as the library profession's finest lobbyist, was born in Kiowa, Indian Territory, on January 4, 1902. Following graduation from the public schools of Tishomingo, Oklahoma, he enrolled in the mathematics curriculum at East Central State College in Ada, Oklahoma. One day while studying in the library, he heard that a student assistant had just resigned, so he immediately applied for the newly vacated position and got it. He enjoyed this work so much that he chose to dedicate the balance of his life to librarianship, and following his graduation in 1926 he remained at Ada for more than a decade serving as assistant librarian. He took leave to earn a B.S. in library science in 1930 at the University of Illinois and later went to the University of Michigan for a master's degree in library science, which he completed in 1938. In the following year he was invited back to Michigan to teach in the summer session, and for twenty-four of the next twenty-seven summers he returned to Ann Arbor regularly to renew an experience he always regarded as "fulfilling."

While a student at Michigan Low wrote a seminar paper on teachers' college libraries, and upon graduation he was appropriately appointed head librarian of Bowling Green State University in Ohio, where he remained through the academic years 1938-1940. In 1940 he was invited to return to his native state to direct the Oklahoma State University Library in Stillwater. Elevated to the deanship in 1946, he remained at Stillwater until his first "retirement" in 1967.

One of Low's major administrative challenges at Oklahoma State University was to develop an adequate building for that library's continuing growth, and this matter dominated his attention during his first dozen years at Stillwater. When its new structure (subsequently named for him) was dedicated in 1953, it surprised no one that it was considered one of the pacesetters in the land. Low described this building in articles published in the *Oklahoma Librarian* (Summer 1953) and *Library Journal* (December 1953). Ever the consummate politician, Low even designed a fine special office in the building for the university president, but the president died before he was able to use it.

The OSU library was one of the earliest completely modular, open-stack buildings using the subject divisional concept. Many of the principal features of the new library were frequently copied in the years thereafter, and Low himself was often called upon to consult on library building planning. Among the more than forty buildings on which he subsequently consulted were Miami University, the University of Guelph, Texas Technological College, Park College, Grambling College, and Tarleton State College. In the days when library surveys were popular, he also consulted in this capacity at such institutions as Henderson State College and the University of South Florida.

Immediately after his "retirement" in 1967, Low assumed a full-time professorship at the University of Michigan, where he "retired" for a second time in 1972. Although during his 33-year involvement at Michigan, Low taught a number of different courses in the reference and administration subject areas, but cataloging was uniformly his principal interest. His classes at Michigan were always popular among his students, and for a quarter of a century large numbers of them deferred their cataloging courses until summer so that they could have the privilege of sitting in his classes. Regrettably he wrote little on the subject, but his expertise as well as his even-handed approach to the subject are evident in his contribution "Problems Encountered by the Users of the Seventeenth Edition of DDC," to *Problems in Library Classification* (New York: R. R. Bowker, 1968) wherein he evaluated the seventeenth edition of the Dewey Decimal Classification from the viewpoint of the academic library. He was proud of his service on the Shared Cataloging Committee of the Association of Research Libraries, but he was also careful to balance this aspect of library work with others, writing in *Problems in Library Classification* (1968) that "the importance of classification is often overestimated by classifiers and underestimated by others."

After his second "retirement" in 1972, Low, upon the recommendation of Archie McNeal, was straightaway appointed Librarian of New College in Sarasota, Florida, where he remained for seven years before "retiring" for a third and final time in 1979. When Low arrived in Florida as the librarian of New College, he found that the catalog there was in great need of his attention, and its revision soon became the principal part of his daily activities. His colleagues at Sarasota recall that, when the morning mail was disposed of, he would go to the lobby, sit down with several drawers of the catalog, shelflist, and authority file, and resume rationalizing entries and subject headings. Always gregarious, he especially enjoyed this particular task because it also provided him with the opportunity to exchange pleasantries with the many students and faculty members who passed by, thus contributing to the library's warm personal ambience.

Low's professional interests covered a broad spectrum of library concerns. Certainly central to his successful career was his extensive involvement in university library administration, and he was long viewed by his peers as the "sly old fox" of academic librarianship. He had learned its rudiments well in William Warner Bishop's seminar on university library administration at Michigan, yet he and Bishop were very different personalities. Where Bishop was urbane and cosmopolitan, Low disarmed others by passing himself off as a naive "country boy." Although not at all provincial in his views, he frequently drew upon rural analogies and homespun anecdotes to make very telling points in colloquies. He likened his work in administration to "stomping out the fuse nearest the powder keg," and he was known for his ability to relieve tense moments with folksy, wry humor somewhat in the vein of fellow Oklahoman Will Rogers.

Nonetheless, as with any other task, there were aspects of administration that Low did not enjoy. Although he was especially adept at "reading" people, he particularly disliked holding periodic discussions with staff members on their performance evaluations, and he always put it off as long as he could. He knew it had to be done, however, and when he would finally finish this onerous task, he would clap his hands together and say "I think I'll go home now," as though he had earned a little reward for having completed an unpleasant chore. During his tenure in Sarasota, New College became affiliated with the state higher education system, and Low's extensive administrative experience in state institutions, as well as his political sensitivity, proved to be very helpful in dealing with the bureaucracy in Tallahassee. By this time in his life, however, bouts of phlebitis were making it painful for him to make the requisite frequent trips to the state capital.

As would be expected, Low's wise counsel and extensive experience in library administrative matters were often sought after by others. He was a member of the first advisory committee to the U.S. Office of Education to plan the program authorized by the Library Services Act, was appointed to the advisory committee to the National Agricultural Library, and from 1964 to 1967 chaired the Oklahoma Regents' Council on Libraries. He served as president of the Oklahoma Library Association in 1949-1950, president of the Southwestern Library Association in 1949-1951, and president of the Association of College and Research Libraries in 1960-1961, and was twice (1961 and 1964) elected second vice-president of the American Library Association (ALA).

Understandably, considering his five full years and twenty-three summer sessions of library school teaching, library education was one of Edmon Low's great interests, a fact demonstrated by his occasional participation on reaccreditation teams sent out to library schools by ALA's Committee on Accreditation. His reputation as the profession's Nestor accompanied him from his Oklahoma office to his Michigan classroom, where he was especially appreciated for his willing and prudent guidance to younger faculty members early in their teaching careers. Senior professors and school administrators there, however, also sought and benefited from his sound counsel.

Edmon Low was very astute politically, and without question his greatest contribution to librarianship was made in his very effective role as the profession's leading spokesperson in Congress in support of library legislation during the halcyon years of the 1960s. As a member of ALA's

Committee on Legislation from 1958 to 1962 and from 1964 to 1969 (and as its chair in 1967-1968), he testified before congressional committees more frequently than any other librarian had ever done, and he advised many cabinet panels on shaping national library programs and legislation in accord with the views of librarians. This was a task that he enjoyed, and he did it exceptionally well. His masterful testimony is scattered throughout many committee prints and hearings on the National Defense Education Act, the Library Services Act, the Higher Education Act, and other bills in Congress, and he came to be a well-known and quite popular figure on Capitol Hill.

ALA Washington Office Executive Director Eileen Cooke often called him a "happy warrior," and Roscoe Rouse, Low's successor at Oklahoma State University, said of him that he "walked the corridors and knew how to talk with lawmakers, citing examples successful in Oklahoma City as well as in Washington, D.C." Low himself once remarked that "legislation, like war, always begins in the minds of men—it does not just happen" ("Implications of Federal Programs for College Libraries," *Library Trends* 18:57 [July 1969]), and he always felt that he could be of greatest value testifying for the profession while bills were still in the "talking" stage. Members of Congress viewed him as an eminently sensible man, and they respected his testimony highly. Congressman Tom Sneed of Oklahoma said in 1967 that "Low exhibited a keen knowledge on all library subjects and could answer any question a committee member asked. He was one librarian who could talk turkey to lawmakers when others couldn't." Because of his major role in the conceptualization of the Library Services Act, Low was invited to witness its signing by President Lyndon B. Johnson and was given a pen used for the purpose. Johnson later said he had "nobly served his state and ... broadened the horizons of learning and of life for all Americans."

Edmon Low wrote more for the library press about library legislation than about any other subject; indeed, more than half of his published writings directly address this subject. He visualized clearly the benefits that could derive upon society from Washington's involvement in library affairs. Considering his interest in cataloging, it is not surprising that he believed that the Shared Cataloging title of the Higher Education Act of 1965 could eventually prove to be "the most important legislation enacted ... for libraries in institutions of higher education" ("Two Decisive Decades: Federal Consciousness and Libraries," *American Libraries* 3:723 [July 1972]), if adequate appropriations were forthcoming to permit the accomplishment of its full purpose. That this has not happened would have disappointed him. He felt that the arguments based upon church/state apprehensions that threatened to delay library construction under the Higher Education Facilities Act of 1963 were groundless: "Who ever heard," he snorted, "of a Communist brick or a Catholic column or a subversive door or a pornographic window?" ("Impact of Federal Legislation on Academic Libraries," in *Federal Legislation for Libraries* [Urbana: University of Illinois Graduate School of Library Science, 1967]).

Low could also change his mind when evidence warranted it. When the Higher Education Act was new in 1966, he foresaw no danger of federal aid to libraries leading to federal control. "This oft quoted charge" he felt, was "not borne out by experience" ("Federal Legislation: An Opportunity and a Challenge," *North Carolina Libraries* 24:9 [Spring 1966]). Political winds shifted, however, and three years later he was warning his fellow librarians that the acceptance of funds inevitably involved relinquishing some control, and he admonished that they not let themselves be distracted from their principal goals by the availability of "easy money" in the nation's capital:

> Of course, [he wrote] an institution or library does not have to take [federal] money but, practically, if money is available an effort is usually made if possible to adjust programs to take advantage of it, whether or not the adjustment is really wise.

In 1970 Low animadverted upon the federal government shifting its higher education emphasis from categorical grants, such as for libraries, to block grants, which placed discretion for their expenditure in the institutional administration. It had been inattention on the part of the institutional administration, he argued, that got libraries into their state of need for outside assistance in the first place. He chastised librarians for their unseemly greed in the hasty establishment of many consortia of little value solely in order to qualify for large but ill-conceived cooperative collection development grants under the Higher Education Act.

For all of his varied library activities, Low wrote very little for publication. His entire bibliography comprises fewer than twenty items and those are brief ones, totaling less than 100 printed pages. As would be expected, his most thoughtful writings concern library legislation and the political process. He also created, and preserved, little in the way of official papers or archives relating to his many professional assignments. Perhaps it should be expected of a man who was impatient, even a little suspicious, of too much bureaucratic red tape that he was careful not to create any himself. As was said above about his favorite step in the lobbying process, he preferred working on things while they were still in the "talking" stage.

Edmon Low received many awards and honors from the library profession and higher education community for his long years and varied kinds of meritorious service. In 1970 East Central State University, where he began his career, gave him its first Distinguished Alumnus Award, and the Oklahoma Library Association gave him its fifth Distinguished Service Award in 1958. The American Library Association conferred on him the Joseph W. Lippincott Award in 1967 and Honorary Membership in 1976. He was also granted an honorary doctor of letters degree by Eastern Michigan University at the ceremony dedicating its library building in 1967.

Following his final retirement in 1979, Low lived for four years in Bradenton, Florida. Suffering from cancer late in 1983, he was flown by air ambulance to his son's home in Tulsa, Oklahoma, where he died on December 2 at age 81. He is buried in Stillwater.

Biographical listings and obituaries — *Biographical Directory of Librarians in the United States and Canada*, 5th ed. Chicago: American Library Association, 1970; [Obituary]. "ALA Legislative 'Warrior,' Edmon Low, Dies at 81." *American Libraries* 15:11 (January 1984); [Obituary]. "Edmon Low, Founder of OSU Library, Dies." (Oklahoma State University) *Daily O'Collegian*, December 3, 1983, 5; *Who's Who in America* 41 (1980); *Who's Who in Library and Information Service*. Chicago: American Library Association, 1982. **Books about the biographee** — Orr, Robert W. "The New ALA Officers, Edmon Low." *ALA Bulletin* 56:733-35 (September 1962). **Primary sources and archival materials** — Eight Hollinger boxes of Edmon Low's papers are preserved in the Special Collections Department of the Library at Oklahoma State University. His family holds a few personal papers.

—DAVID KASER

MacLEISH, ARCHIBALD (1892-1982)

Archibald MacLeish was a controversial and multitalented poet, playwright, professor, and American statesman who served for a time as Librarian of Congress. "Archie," as he was known to friends and casual acquaintances alike, was born into affluent circumstances in Glencoe, Illinois, on May 7, 1892, and raised at the family's Craigie Lea estate on the shores of Lake Michigan.

His later writings demonstrate a quiet pride in his Scottish and Yankee Calvinistic heritage. His father, Andrew, was born in Glasgow in 1838 and ran away from home eventually to arrive in the United States as a determined eighteen-year-old. The elder MacLeish developed into a prosperous Chicago retailer and educational leader who helped found the University of Chicago. At the age of fifty, he married his third wife, Archibald's mother, the remarkable Martha Hillard. Hillard, a Connecticut Yankee with seafaring roots back to the *Mayflower*, was a Vassar graduate who became President of Rockford College in her twenties. After her marriage, she retired to family life and work with charities, such as the Woman's Foreign Mission Society and Hull House.

The son of that stalwart pair departed from home for what he termed a dismal educational experience at Hotchkiss preparatory school in Connecticut. He was graduated in 1911 and matriculated at Yale University. While at Yale, his ability to do many things and do them all well clearly emerged. In the era of the gentleman's "C," he was most concerned with athletic success in football, diving, and water polo, but still managed to edit the Yale *Literary Magazine*, deliver the class poem, and earn a Phi Beta Kappa key. MacLeish also fell in love with Ada Hitchcock, a young singer from Farmington, Connecticut. With a typical sense of self-effacing humor, he later related to his friend Mark Van Doren his desire for a quick wedding and "to avoid going to work," which led to law school:

> I wanted to marry Ada. I wanted to marry her fast, and I had the feeling, which turned out to be justified, that my father, who was a Scotsman, who admired scholarship, would probably support me for a while longer if I went to some scholarly institution. So I went to Harvard Law School.

Harvard studies and his marriage, however, were interrupted by World War I. MacLeish enlisted as a private and served with a hospital unit and then with the field artillery in France, rising to the rank of captain before his discharge. The war had cost the life of his brother and helped to kindle his poetic spirit, yet MacLeish returned to Harvard and the somewhat distasteful study of law. There he edited the *Harvard Law Review* and characteristically was graduated at the head of his class with the Fay Diploma in 1919. By 1920, he was teaching part time at Harvard and then working full time at the Boston law firm of Choate, Hall, and Steward. But MacLeish's love of letters and growing dislike of trial duty soon led to what he called "the beginning of my life." He left his law practice in the winter of 1923 and moved with his wife and two children to join the "Lost Generation" in Paris. Living on the Left Bank, he met and joined with other budding authors such as John Dos Passos and Ernest Hemingway. MacLeish had fervently and irrevocably committed himself to poetry; never again would he easily abandon principle for comfort.

The poet returned to the United States after five years in Europe—a recognized author with several published collections. But as he moved to his permanent home and a new career as poet/gentleman farmer in Conway, Massachusetts, the Great Depression intervened. To support his family, MacLeish accepted an invitation from his friend Henry Luce to write for *Fortune* magazine. That job lasted eight years and allowed MacLeish to continue the traveling that had already included a League of Nations mission to Persia and a retracing of the route of Hernando Cortez in Mexico. The latter trip was in preparation for his long narrative poem *Conquistador*, for which he won the 1932 Pulitzer Prize. During his time with Luce, the writer became increasingly well known and also controversial, with outspoken support for liberal, anti-Fascist causes such as the Loyalist campaign in Spain. MacLeish eventually left *Fortune* in 1938 in response to changes in editorial policies and an invitation from Harvard President James Conant to help establish and serve as the first curator of the Nieman Journalism Foundation.

In 1939, Franklin Delano Roosevelt pulled MacLeish away from Boston by nominating him for Library of Congress. The writer had come to Roosevelt's attention early in the president's first term through a laudatory *Fortune* article (December 1933) on the New Deal, and also through ties to presidential advisor Felix Frankfurter. The job at the Library of Congress surfaced in 1938 after Herbert Putnam announced plans to retire after forty years in charge. The president's choice did not come easily. In the spring of 1939, he wrote to Frankfurter: "I have had a bad time picking a Librarian to succeed Putnam. What do you think of Archie MacLeish? He is not a professional Librarian nor is he a special student of incunabula or ancient manuscripts. Nevertheless, he has lots of qualifications that said specialists have not." Frankfurter was more than supportive of his former law school student and the idea that "only a scholarly man of letters can make a great national library." In his response, Frankfurter also noted MacLeish's experience with newer media in regard to the growing world crisis. He called MacLeish "the father of the so-called radio play" and the "moving spirit" behind the "Contemporary History" series in the movies. He also noted that MacLeish was well prepared to deal with a strange new device called television.

The first problem was to convince MacLeish. The poet was more than hesitant to undertake a three- or four-year commitment that would effectively preclude any poetry writing. As he described his impressions at a 1965 library dedication:

> Thirty years ago, when Mr. Roosevelt informed me of my desire to be Librarian of Congress, I thought I knew what a library was: it was the last place a writer ought to be found until he was stone cold on the page in print.

It took the persuasive Roosevelt two sessions to convince MacLeish, but on June 6, 1939 the president announced his new appointment. An outcry erupted immediately. Representative J. Parnell Thomas denounced the nominee as a communist fellow traveler. The American Library Association (ALA) was particularly insistent, with a formal protest against a confirmation that "would be a calamity." Although several major newspapers joined in opposition, Roosevelt easily weathered the criticism. The final sixty-three to eight favorable Senate vote on June 29 revealed a "tempest in a teapot," which was followed by a rapid rapprochement from a suitably chastened ALA.

The forty-seven-year-old appointee underwent somewhat of a metamorphosis during his time at the Library of Congress. An expatriate, who decried the excesses of World War I, emerged as an ardent Jeffersonian nationalist who shocked many by his warlike stance against the Nazis. He awakened quickly to the potential of libraries as part of his new and controversial stance on scholars as a line of defense. In his words at a well-received May 1940 speech before a now-appreciative ALA audience, "if librarians accept a responsibility for the survival of democracy ... they must themselves become active and not passive agents of the democratic process."

Ironically, the poet who became a reluctant librarian also proved an outstanding administrator. To MacLeish, his predecessor had been a great librarian but still a patriarchal and picayunish leader. The Library was organized into more than thirty-five divisions that ran in his "lengthened shadow" like a feudal manor. With a self-proclaimed "constitutional disinclination" to overly personalized management, MacLeish later maintained he turned for "survival" to a more participatory style that used existing expertise at the Library. He also turned to outside experts and the "chill vocabulary of the science of management."

Within three weeks of his arrival, MacLeish initiated a thorough review of the institution. Within nine months, he began a consolidation into the Library's modern departmental structure. Keyes Metcalf, who originally opposed MacLeish's appointment, called this restructuring MacLeish's "greatest triumph"—especially since only MacLeish could have "gotten away" with it. That triumph is perhaps best recounted in another MacLeish success, the revamped and now readable *Annual Report of the Librarian of Congress*. Among other significant administrative advances, MacLeish launched an important inventory of the holdings and helped articulate the Library's first "Statement of Objectives."

MacLeish also paid close attention to the low status of librarians in the federal government. He orchestrated a successful campaign to upgrade the classification and pay for his professionals. Along the way, he also introduced innovative staff discussion groups and in 1942 the Staff Advisory Committee of union and nonunion representatives for employee grievances. Although his tenure was brief and not without some difficulties, MacLeish and his driving personality left a marked impression on those around him. In the words of David Mearns:

The staff sensed at once that the new chief possessed unusual personal qualities.... His drive was tremendous, and the fresh air that he brought with him invigorating. Working with Archibald MacLeish was almost never easy, but it was almost always fun. His spirit of mission was contagious; he gave libraries (and particularly his own Library) a consciousness of new duties and new responsibilities.

MacLeish did follow Putnam's lead in making the Library a major cultural center and was responsible for inaugurating the Library's first series of poetry readings and the *Library of Congress Quarterly Journal*. The latter was edited by Allen Tate, MacLeish's 1943 appointment to the poetry chair, who also organized the Library's advisory group of distinguished academic fellows. In addition, MacLeish himself furthered special collections in the Hispanic and Slavic fields and took great pride for transferring the most important documents of the nation's patrimony to safety during the war.

Despite such contributions, MacLeish's service at the Library was ultimately limited because of the same political ties that facilitated his actions. Not only did he participate in numerous "midnight speechwriting sessions at the White House," but he himself emerged as a major spokesman for American democracy during the war, with radio plays and more than two dozen addresses. In October 1941, Roosevelt even tapped the "poet laureate of the New Deal" for additional duties as director of a new Office of Facts and Figures. OFF was a counter-propaganda agency that involved MacLeish in controversies over the manipulation of the press and the proper role of propaganda in a democracy. His assignment there and then as the assistant director for the newer umbrella Office of War Information seriously detracted from his role as Librarian of Congress and in 1943 even adversely affected congressional appropriations for the Library.

A portion of these additional duties, however, dovetailed nicely with MacLeish's own conception of the Library as a war agency. The day after Pearl Harbor, for example, the Library began a nonstop reference service for defense departments. Its Division for the Study of Wartime Communications participated in the overall propaganda effort, while other sections served up translations, abstracts, and campaign maps. MacLeish worked intimately with leading intelligence experts, including William Donovan of the Office of Strategic Services (OSS). And, lest it be overlooked, the Division of Special Information eventually became the Research and Analysis Branch of the OSS and occupied a whole floor of the annex building during the war.

After two years, MacLeish resigned from his dual duties and concentrated on completing his organizational initiatives at the Library. Although he left the Library in December 1944, MacLeish never abandoned his ties to the library community. Instead he appeared frequently as a speaker at library dedications and a leader in the fight for intellectual freedom.

MacLeish left the Library of Congress after weathering an even "hotter" review process than in 1939, to be named Assistant Secretary of State for Cultural Affairs. From that position, he helped formulate the original charter for the United Nations at the San Francisco Conference. He resigned from that post on April 13, 1945, the day after Roosevelt's death. But before returning to his farm and to poetry, MacLeish held one last government job—head of the American delegations at the 1945 planning and 1946 inaugural session of the United Nations Educational, Scientific and Cultural Organization (UNESCO), as well as the author of the introduction to its charter.

In 1949, MacLeish returned to Harvard for a thirteen-year stint as Boylston Professor of Rhetoric and Oratory. This was followed by five years as the Simpson Lecturer of Amherst College. The intense writer mellowed noticeably during those years, but never lost his sense of social commitment, his willingness to engage in battle over social issues, or even his respect for librarians in such struggles. For example, he was among the rare early opponents of the McCarthy scares of the early 1950s, which he viewed "like the snail's corrosive track on a clean leaf." His position had been made clear in the 1953 Pulitzer, National Book Award, and Bollinger Prize-winning *Collected Poems, 1917-1952*:

> God help that country where informers thrive!
> Where slander flourishes and lies contrive
> To kill with whispers! Where men lie to live!

MacLeish singled out the role of librarians in this struggle in an important address at the dedication of the Carlton College Library in 1956. "The gelded librarian is a sacrifice which only McCarthyian demands and McCarthyism in decay need not now be handed its dearest victim." In the same speech, he expounded again on an activist position for librarians: "No librarian who believes in the freedom guaranteed by the Constitution, and who detests authoritarianism, can avoid taking positions on controversial issues—indeed on the most controversial of all issues ... the issue of the freedom of the mind in America." MacLeish himself would not shrink from his convictions, including the defense of fellow poet Ezra Pound, who had been convicted of treason and committed by the government to a mental asylum. MacLeish would later battle against segregation and be one of the first to go on record against the war in Vietnam.

Despite (or perhaps in partial response to) his outspoken nature, MacLeish received numerous honorary degrees and awards. His prestige was also reflected in his election as President of the American Academy of Arts and Letters from 1953 to 1956. He won his third Pulitzer Prize in 1959 for "J.B.," a play about a modern Job; the award produced another storm of criticism. He also wrote the 1966 Academy Award-winning *Eleanor Roosevelt Story*. Controversies somewhat declined near the close of his life, but not his recognition as a national literary figure. In 1977 he received a Presidential Medal of Freedom and in 1978 the National Medal for Literature.

After his retirement from teaching, MacLeish continued to write, but turned more and more to prose. He also remained a notable figure on the speakers' circuit. But his main recourse was as a gentleman farmer in Concord, with frequent retreats to Paris and Antigua. He died on April 20, 1982 in Boston, survived by his wife of 65 years, 2 of his 4 children, 9 grandchildren, and 5 great-grandchildren. His life had involved a kaleidoscope of the major events and personages of the twentieth century. His legacy for librarianship still remains to be fully plumbed.

Biographical listings and obituaries—Library of Congress. *Librarians of Congress 1802-1974*. Washington, D.C.: Library of Congress, 1977; [Obituary]. *New York Times*, April 21, 1982, Sec. 1,5; [Obituary]. *Washington Post*, April 21, 1982, A-16; *Who Was Who in America* V (1982-1985). **Books and articles by the biographee**—*Champions of a Cause*. Chicago: American Library Association, 1971; *Collected Poems*. Boston: Houghton Mifflin, 1963; *A Continuing Journey*. Boston:

Houghton Mifflin, 1976; *The Dialogues of Archibald MacLeish and Mark Van Doren.* New York: E. P. Dutton, 1964; *Riders on the Earth.* Boston: Houghton Mifflin, 1978; *A Time to Act.* Boston: Houghton Mifflin, 1941. **Books and articles about the biographee** — Cole, John, ed. *The Library of Congress in Perspective.* New York: R. R. Bowker, 1978; Mearns, David C. *The Story Up to Now.* Washington, D.C.: Library of Congress, 1947; Metcalf, Keyes. "Merits, Respect and Gratitude." *Library Journal* 70 (March 1945); Orne, Jerold. "The Annual Reports of the Librarian of Congress." *Library Quarterly* 14:239-45 (July 1944); Thomison, Dennis. "F.D.R., the ALA, and Mr. MacLeish." *Library Quarterly* 42:390-8 (October 1972). **Primary sources and archival materials** — The best primary information sources are the papers of Archibald MacLeish at the Library of Congress, which have their own 34-page finding aid, and the Library of Congress archives for 1939-1944. See also *Annual Report of the Librarian of Congress* (Washington, D.C.: Library of Congress, 1940-1944).

— FREDERICK J. STIELOW

MARION, GUY ELWOOD (1882-1969)

Guy Elwood Marion was born March 25, 1882, in Woburn, Massachusetts. He attended public schools in Woburn, graduating from Woburn High School. He received an A.B. in 1903 and an A.M. in 1904 from Tufts College (later Tufts University). Both degrees were in biology.

Marion began his library career in an accidental fashion and without any type of formal education or training for the field. In 1905 he took a job with the American Brass Company in Waterbury, Connecticut, and was assigned the responsibility for collecting and centralizing information about idle machinery in the five plants of the company. The information was collected, tabulated, and organized on index cards for use by the company. Out of this basic file of information, as Marion would say many years later in an interview, "grew the library."

From these innocent and seemingly happenstance origins began the career of one of the most innovative and influential special librarians in the emerging special libraries movement. Marion's work at American Brass (1905-1909) and later at Arthur D. Little, Inc. (1909-1914) of Boston, was marked by the development of collections of information and the offering of innovative services that differed significantly from traditional libraries of the time. These collections and services were detailed in an influential paper that received wide circulation and attention at the time it was written. Entitled "The Library as an Adjunct to Industrial Laboratories," the paper was originally presented at a 1910 meeting of the American Association for the Advancement of Science, then at a joint American Library Association (ALA) and Special Libraries Association (SLA) meeting. It was later published in the *Journal of Industrial and Engineering Chemistry* (2:3 [March 1910]) and in *Library Journal* (35:400-404 [September 1910]).

The paper detailed the extensive collections and unique services that Marion developed, particularly while he was manager of the Information Department at Arthur D. Little, Inc. These collections included the traditional books, pamphlets, and periodicals organized by the Dewey Decimal Classification system. Equally important, however, were the collections of trade catalogs, specifications issued by the company laboratories and other groups, special data files of news clippings, articles, the results of library staff interviews with scientists, correspondence, and many other data files culled from a variety of internal and external sources. All of these were carefully cataloged or indexed in one giant subject catalog. The library was the clearinghouse for most of the information maintained by the laboratories. A "museum" collection of samples of various materials was also maintained in the library for exhibit purposes as well as for the use of the scientists.

From these collections a variety of services, traditional and nontraditional, was offered to the staff. Marion began one of the first library bulletins to market his collections and services. He also used the library and library staff to keep scientists in the different laboratories of the company informed of each other's work. He culled journals, newspapers, advertisements, company correspondence, and a variety of other sources for potential leads to new business for the company and circulated these in a separate library bulletin. He maintained selective dissemination of information (SDI) files for the laboratory scientists and used this information to build his collections in advance of actual need.

The philosophy of library purpose and service described in Marion's article were strikingly different from that of the traditional libraries of the time. Marion was quick to give credit to others who had helped him develop these ideas. He said that he had gained valuable advice and help from public and academic librarians in the Boston area, but he gave principal credit for his ideas to George W. Lee, librarian at Stone and Webster in Boston, and to other special librarians whom he had met in the newly created Special Libraries Association. Marion also noted that he profited from a trip to Europe in 1909. He visited a number of libraries, including the Institute of Bibliography in Brussels, where he observed their use of the Universal Decimal Classification (UDC) system. Marion later used the UDC to help classify his collections at Arthur D. Little, Inc.

Marion was an enthusiastic supporter of the newly created SLA. Though he had not attended the organizing meeting at Bretton Woods, New Hampshire, in July 1909, he was at the first "annual conference" in November 1909 in New York City and became a charter member of the association. He immediately volunteered to take an active role and became the business manager for the new journal of the association, *Special Libraries*. In March 1910 he became the secretary-treasurer of SLA and held that position until 1915. In July 1918 he became the president of SLA.

The period from 1917 to 1919 was a critical time for SLA. The association was running a deficit, membership was down, leadership was lacking, and there was a strong feeling among some members that it should be disbanded or merged with ALA. By the end of Marion's term as president in 1919 the situation had been reversed, and a solid foundation had been firmly laid that would ably serve the association in the coming years.

Characteristically, Marion gave credit to his fellow executive board members for this dramatic turnaround. While he did have a particularly effective group of board members who worked well together, Marion's knowledge of the affairs of the association and his boundless enthusiasm for the special libraries idea in general and SLA in particular seems to have been the critical determinants. As Robert V. Williams and Martha Jane Zachert said in their review of this period, "Imagination, enthusiasm, and positive leadership gave the Association new life and a vision for the future" ("Crisis and Growth: SLA, 1918-1919," *Special Libraries* 74:262 [July 1983]).

The association had not only been revived during Marion's term as president, but the foundations for future development of the structure of SLA had also been laid. The basis for formation of the geographic chapters and the subject divisions was also established at this time, and these were given official representation in decision-making matters. These developments were critical to the future of SLA because they gave members two avenues of representation and participation in SLA, the local chapter and the subject interest group. Marion, an active member of the unofficial Boston Special Libraries Association and a keen participant in the affairs of scientific and technical librarians, recognized and promoted these two types of participation. They would prove to be the distinctive feature of SLA in the years ahead.

Even though the zenith of Marion's career in SLA was his period as president, he remained an active participant in the affairs of the association until his final retirement in 1964 and an interested follower of its activities until his death. In 1922 he helped organize the Southern California Chapter of SLA and was its president from 1924 to 1925.

Because of his enthusiasm for SLA and his ability to interpret the special libraries movement, Marion was frequently called on to write about them. His lengthy article in an early issue of *Library Journal* (45:295-304 [April 1, 1920]) recounted the story of SLA and the idea of the special library. In it, quoting a Mr. Jacob, librarian of the General Electric Company, Marion gave the definition of the special library that is now considered classic: "A special library consists of a good working collection of information either upon a specific subject or field of activity; ... serving the interests of a special clientele, and preferably in charge of a specialist trained in the use and application of the particular material." In this same article he addressed the continuing and plaguing issue of cooperation with ALA and the possibility of merger with the larger organization. He came down solidly on the side of separate organizations but pleaded for active cooperation in the service of providing Americans with books and information.

Marion's working career was a diverse one. His work with American Brass and Arthur D. Little was exemplary, and through his articles about the work of those libraries he articulated his ideas about the nature of the special library. Anthony Kruzas, in *Business and Industrial Libraries in the United States, 1820-1940* (SLA, 1965), called Marion's library at American Brass the first true information center in the United States. The "Information Department," as Marion called his library at Arthur D. Little, was even more exemplary as the forerunner of genuine information resources management.

Marion resigned his position at Arthur D. Little in 1914 and took a position with Warren H. Manning, landscape designers in Boston, where he established another library. About 1915 he moved to the Bowker Fertilizer Company, where he also set up a library and developed statistical services for the company. He left that job in 1917 to set up a library for the Pilgrim Publicity Associates in Boston. During the period 1918 to 1920, he organized a library for the Community Motion Picture Bureau in New York City. His central job there was the cataloging of a motion picture collection. The catalog contained over 300,000 entries.

Sometime in 1918, Marion established his own library consulting business on a part-time basis. Unfortunately, very little is known of Marion's work as a library consultant during the years 1918-1922. In a 1969 interview he noted that he had begun doing consulting work with other libraries while he was employed with Arthur D. Little. Apparently, Marion performed this early consulting work for a fee and Arthur D. Little billed the client, in keeping with its usual consulting procedures. Marion apparently continued work as a private consultant after he left Arthur D. Little. It is possible that Guy Marion was the first paid special library consultant.

In 1922, Marion moved from his native Massachusetts to Los Angeles, California, where he began work as an assistant librarian in the Science-Technology Department of Los Angeles Public Library. He made this move because his wife was from southern California and wanted their children to be near their grandparents. Marion was at the Los Angeles Public Library, however, for only two years, when he was asked to move to the Los Angeles Chamber of Commerce and develop the Research Department and Library. This position was to occupy his professional attention for the remaining years of his active career.

Marion's work at the Chamber of Commerce reflected the philosophy of service and collection development that he had developed earlier. He stressed the integral relationship between the purposes of the organization and the objectives of the library. As manager of the Research Department and as librarian, he was able to integrate the two functions for efficient and effective management of internally and externally produced information.

Marion again developed nontraditional collections of information and, through the development of thorough indexing and cataloging systems, was able to meet the information needs of researchers within the chamber as well as the business community of Los Angeles.

Marion had gained some experience in working with statistical data in his earlier positions and wrote on the value of this information for research and planning purposes in "The Library: A Necessary Adjunct to Statistical Work," *Special Libraries* 15:104-7 (March 1924). At the Chamber of Commerce he began a model program for the collection and publication of local statistical data that would eventually be adopted across the country by chambers of commerce. These "green sheets" were based on the files of the library, usually from ephemeral sources, and were distributed to various groups and organizations in the city. (See Marion, Guy E. "Information Files of the Los Angeles Chamber of Commerce." *Special Libraries* 19:75-78 [February 1928].) Marion also developed procedures for the first tracting of the city of Los Angeles by the U.S. Bureau of the Census and aided the bureau in completing this work.

Throughout his career, in his writings and in his development of the special libraries he managed, Marion stressed the important role the library could and should play in making the parent agency successful. He saw himself as a special librarian and a businessman and made little distinction between the two aspects. Because of this, and because of what he saw as the failure of traditional librarians to give the kinds of information services needed in business, Marion placed little value on the importance of formal library education. He believed that a classical college education and knowledge of the subject matter of the library were essential for a good special librarian. This conviction did not change much over the years despite the increasing acceptance of special library ideas and practices in library schools and the library world at large. To some extent this idea of distinctiveness was essential to the definition of the special libraries idea and the establishment of SLA. At the same time, however, it may have been partially responsible for long-term problems in the reconciliation of these two groups of librarians.

Marion retired from the Chamber of Commerce in 1952, at age 70. In 1959, on the occasion of the 50th anniversary of SLA, he was inducted into the SLA Hall of Fame. He worked for a short while in 1964 as interim librarian for the Historical Society of Southern California. In 1961 he moved to Atlanta, Georgia, to live with his daughter, Mrs. Charles L. Young, and died there on June 24, 1969.

Marion's accomplishments during his career as a special librarian are significant. He provided leadership to the Special Libraries Association at a critical time in its life and helped lay the foundations of the association's structure and goals for the years ahead. His concepts of the purposes and objectives of the special library and, particularly, his writings about those ideas, gave focus and direction to the special libraries movement. Because he was the first to articulate these ideas, he established the basis for the development of the collections and services of special libraries. Many of these ideas have been incorporated into the collection development and services philosophy of the profession at large.

Biographical listings and obituaries — [Obituary]. *Special Libraries* 60:412 (July 1969). **Books and articles by the biographee** — "The Founding Fathers Recalled." *Special Libraries* 55:353-55 (July/August 1964); "Remembrance of Things Past." *Special Libraries* 40: 134-47 (April 1949). **Primary sources and archival materials** — Some materials (minute books, correspondence, etc.) relating to Marion's administration as president of SLA are in the SLA Archives, SLA Headquarters, Washington, D.C. Unfortunately, however, the SLA Archives are very poor for this early time period. The principal source of primary information on Marion is an oral history interview conducted with him in 1966 by Robert V. Williams; a copy of the transcript and the tape are in the SLA Archives.

— ROBERT V. WILLIAMS

McCRUM, BLANCHE PRICHARD (1887-1969)

Blanche Prichard McCrum was born on November 2, 1887, in Lexington, Virginia, to Rufus Barton and Martha Ann White McCrum. Although she was graduated from Lexington High School in 1904, she entered the working world only in 1910 when she went to nearby Rockbridge Baths to teach high school English for two years. In 1912, McCrum, who at one time acknowledged that she "devoured books with a kind of omnivorous joy" all her life, commenced her struggle toward a formal education, a process that eventually stretched over nearly twenty years, mostly in the form of interruptions in a strenuous career at the Washington and Lee University library. She entered the Drexel Institute library school, from which she earned a certificate in 1913. Although she later attended summer classes at various institutions including McGill, the Universities of Virginia and Wisconsin, and Boston University, it was not until she had spent most of 1925-1926 at Radcliffe and 1927-1928 at Boston University that she was able to complete a Bachelor of Science degree at Boston in 1930, when she was over forty years old. Taking one more leave of absence, this time in 1930-1931, she earned a Master of Arts degree in librarianship at the University of California, Berkeley, where Sydney B. Mitchell, its director, was her chief guide and mentor.

McCrum held posts at four libraries. Following her preparation at Drexel she worked in the Carnegie Library of Pittsburgh from 1913 until 1918, when she was abruptly called back to Lexington to care for her mother. Here she was forced by circumstances to accept the only position available in her small hometown. Years later McCrum wrote to a friend about this difficult time: "To function at all, it was necessary for me to 'hire' myself — I cannot call it by a better name — as a sort of day laborer to the incredibly venial but fascinating kinswoman who was the so-called librarian there at Washington and Lee University." In 1922, when her relative finally retired, McCrum was appointed librarian, a post she held until 1937. From 1937 to 1947 she was librarian at Wellesley College. The final phase of her career was at the Library of Congress, where from 1947 to 1952 she was a bibliographer in the general reference and bibliography division, and from 1952 to 1955 a specialist in documentation. After her retirement in April 1955, she was called back for a brief period in 1957 to assist in the planning of the supplement to *A Guide to the Study of the United States of America*, the monumental bibliography with which she had been intimately involved between 1952 and 1955.

Blanche McCrum's determined efforts to acquire her degrees provides a clue not only to her personality but also to her most significant contributions, all of which are reflections of a unifying philosophy of librarianship developed throughout the four arbitrary divisions of her career. Like Chaucer's gentle clerk of Oxford, and as a genuine heiress of the educational values of her Scotch-Irish forebears, this gentle Virginian led a professional and personal life dedicated to gladly, and intensely, learning and teaching. "In school or out, self-obtained or directed by teachers, the raw material for such education is found in books, to which access may be had, generously and efficiently, only through good libraries," she wrote in 1936, when as president of the state library association she was attempting to upgrade the barren Virginia library scene.

If, then, *education* is one keyword in expressing the structure of her life and career, the other must be *excellence*. "[Libraries]," she wrote, "must be places from whence ideas circulate"—ideas which properly assimilated will result in "a working of the Soul towards Excellence."

As an educator she was an early practitioner and promoter of building library use instruction into course syllabi. While at Washington and Lee, she also developed stringent, structured methods for in-house training of student assistants, whom she groomed for careers as scholar-librarians. "I was permitted ... to slip into my profession under the demanding, but very gentle teaching of this remarkable woman," wrote John Burton Nicholson, Jr., who until his retirement in 1981 was successively the assistant librarian at Dickinson College and director of libraries at Kent State University and the University of Baltimore. At Wellesley McCrum created a new position—research librarian—for the most promising of her professional staff. She then encouraged them by generous vacations, a Book Arts Laboratory, collection development responsibilities, and special research projects to make themselves into librarians worth "interrupting." "It is the librarian's business to be interrupted," McCrum wrote in 1954, "[but] only the conservation of his time for careful, studious work makes him worth interrupting." She taught summer school courses at both the University of California at Los Angeles (1939) and the University of Illinois (1941), and wrote two of her finest articles about how library school students could be better educated ("The Idols of Librarianship," *Wilson Library Bulletin* 21:41-7 [September 1946], and "Education for Librarianship on Trial," *College & Research Libraries* 8:128-31ff [April 1947]).

If the Soul was to achieve excellence through books and libraries, it followed that libraries had to be excellent, full of the best that had been thought and said in the world. McCrum's contemplation and practical explorations of how these goals might be realized were reflected in substantial articles on collection evaluation ("A College Library Makes Its Own Survey Plan," *ALA Bulletin* 31:947-52 [December 1937]) and budgeting ("Groundwork in Budget Making for the College Library" [1935]), but they were best encapsulated in her pioneering book, *An Estimate of Standards for a College Library* (2d ed. rev. Lexington, Va.: Washington and Lee University, 1937), which not only suggested a set of measurable standards but also outlined how they could be implemented. The book was frequently used as a college library administration text in library schools during the 1930s and 1940s. A second edition was issued in 1937 after McCrum was awarded a grant from the Carnegie Corporation to revise and enlarge the book, a task which she accomplished at Columbia with the encouragement of the library school director, C. C. Williamson.

A Guide to the Study of the United States of America (Washington, D.C.: Library of Congress, 1960), which McCrum co-compiled with Donald H. Mugridge under the direction of Roy Basler at the Library of Congress, is a fitting capstone to a career devoted to excellence and education. By listing and annotating the best works for American studies, the *Guide* successfully fulfilled one of its major objectives—to assist librarians who were attempting to develop choice collections, and to lend orientation to "serious students."

The two facets of McCrum's philosophy were reflected also in her contributions as the President of the Virginia Library Association (1934-1936) and of the Association of College and Reference Libraries (1945-1946). Appalled by the lack of quality and quantity of school and public libraries of Virginia, McCrum eloquently wrote and spoke on their behalf, launched a successful campaign for state certification for all future librarians, and assiduously worked for a new state library building where leadership could be concentrated and adequate assistance proffered to all types of libraries.

After serving on the College Library Advisory Board (CLAB) of the American Library Association (ALA) from 1934 to 1939, on numerous ALA and ACRL committees, and on the publication board of *College & Research Libraries* from its inception in 1939, McCrum was elected president of ACRL for the 1945-1946 term. Continuing the impetus begun in the CLAB, she appointed a committee to study the worsening relations between ACRL and ALA. Although this committee, chaired by Charles Harvey Brown, eventually effected a peaceful agreement between the two groups, it is safe to say that ACRL came closer to severing itself from its parent in 1945-1946 than at anytime in its history. McCrum went along with the compromise that resulted in the hiring of ACRL's first executive secretary, N. Orwin Rush. However, it is quite evident from archival materials that she felt ACRL would never achieve excellence until it had autonomy, could promote the research activities of its members, and could publish proceedings as other professional academic associations did.

Blanche McCrum was "diminutive," until old age had reddish-brown hair, spoke softly, dressed neatly and smartly, and by all accounts was "a southern lady." However, those who recall her softness and physical frailness also remember her strength, confidence, and subtle, often astringent wit. A former professor at Washington and Lee summed up this duality in his recollection of a small figure firmly grasping the helm of her tight library ship under a big Carnegie dome. All her life she was an avid theater-goer and collector of first editions of contemporary poets.

In later life, McCrum received two awards, a Drexel Institute alumni citation in 1951, and the Library of Congress Award for Meritorious Service in 1961. She died in Arlington, Virginia, on August 26, 1969, of a brain tumor. That her unfailing devotion to education and excellence has been appreciated is not hard to verify. Mildred H. McAfee Horton, the president of Wellesley during McCrum's years there, stated: "She did a superb job for our college library and I welcome an opportunity to pay tribute to her." Horton specifically noted Blanche McCrum's "clear understanding of the educational objective of the library within the academic community." Henry J. Dubester, McCrum's young supervisor at the Library of Congress, commented on her personal qualities: "She was a lovely person, genteel in the old-fashioned sense of the word.... I felt always the better for having known her and for the knowledge that I enjoyed her regard."

Biographical listings and obituaries—[Obituary]. *LC Information Bulletin* 28:441-2 (August 28, 1969); [Obituary]. (Lexington, Virginia) *News-Gazette*, September 3, 1969, 2B; [Obituary]. Palmer, Foster McCrum. "Blanche Prichard McCrum." *The Wellesley Alumnae Magazine* 54:37 (1969); *Who Was Who in America* 5 (1969-1973); *Who's Who in Library Service*, 1st, 2nd, 3rd, 4th eds. (1933, 1943, 1955, 1966). **Books and articles about the biographee**—Curtis, Edward Ely. "Blanche Prichard McCrum." *The Wellesley Magazine* 31:339-40 (July 1947); Kondayan, Betty Ruth. "Blanche P. McCrum." In *Leaders in American Academic Librarianship, 1925-1975*. ed. by Wayne A. Wiegand. Pittsburgh: Beta Phi Mu, 1983, 184-210; Kondayan, Betty Ruth. "Blanche Prichard McCrum: A Small Giant." *Journal of Academic Librarianship* 8:68-75 (May 1982); Kondayan, Betty Ruth. "Blanche Prichard McCrum: Librarian from 1922 to 1937." In *A Historical Sketch of the Library in Washington and Lee University: From the Beginnings of 1776 through 1937*. Lexington, Va.: Washington and Lee University, 1980, 37-41; Nicholson, John Burton, Jr. "Apologia Pro Vita Sua." 1979, 8-11 (typescript); "Personnel." *LC Information Bulletin* 14:9-10 (April 25, 1955). **Primary sources and archival materials**—Material by and about Blanche McCrum is held in the special collections division of the University Library, Washington and Lee University, principaliy in the presidential and library files; at the Wellesley College Archives, Margaret Clapp Library, Wellesley College; and at the Virginia State Library, Richmond, Virginia, in the Virginia Library Association files.

—BETTY RUTH KONDAYAN

McKENNA, FRANCIS EUGENE (1921-1978)

Francis Eugene (Frank) McKenna was born in Globe, Arizona, on July 29, 1921, the son of Patrick and Eugenia With McKenna. He was an only child. Globe was a center for copper production, an industry which employed his father, an immigrant from Donegal, Ireland. McKenna's mother came from Alsatian stock, and her ancestors had come to pioneer in the Arizona and New Mexico territories.

When Frank McKenna was three his family began a trek across the desert in their Model T Ford, ultimately settling in Oakland, California, in a former orchard area known as Fruitvale, where Patrick McKenna was able to indulge his interests in the development of fruit trees. Young Frank was an early avid reader and writer who received citations from the public library's summer reading club and at the age of twelve won a short story prize offered by a local newspaper. He was particularly interested in the sciences, literature, and music. At the time of his high school graduation in 1937 he was named valedictorian and received special prizes in both science and music.

McKenna enrolled at the University of California in Berkeley as a chemistry major in 1937. He was graduated with honors in 1941, and immediately went on to graduate work in chemistry at the University of Washington in Seattle. He received his doctorate in chemistry in 1943 at the age of 22, at that time the youngest person to earn a doctorate from a university in the western states. His scientific training made him a valuable asset for the war effort. In 1944 he was appointed to the staff of General Leslie Groves, who supervised the Manhattan Project. When the war ended, McKenna returned to academia as a postdoctoral research fellow at the Institute for Nuclear Studies at the University of Chicago, where he worked with Dr. Willard Libby, the noted atomic physicist.

Although he seriously considered teaching as a career, McKenna was also drawn to scientific work in industry, and in 1948 he joined the Air Reduction Company (Airco) as a Senior Research Chemist. This rapidly growing company had its headquarters in Murray Hill, New Jersey, but also operated plants and offices in other states, in Canada, and in Europe. Like many organizations of its kind, Airco had difficulty conceptualizing and developing the information services needed in such a dynamic and growing field, and in 1953 Frank McKenna was asked to establish an information center to provide needed services to all units of this far-flung organization. He once explained that he probably received the assignment because he was the loudest and most vociferous critic of existing information approaches.

Without formal training or education as a librarian, McKenna nevertheless drew on his love of reading and information to conceive of a service that would be "a tool of progress ... standing at the frontier of scientific, technological and sociological know-how." Over the next thirteen years the company's collection increased tenfold, and included the consolidation of so-called non-traditional literature such as drawings and notebooks into a central information source. In this McKenna was a pioneer in developing approaches now generally accepted in industrial information work. From his background as a chemist drawn into information service work, he recognized instinctively that the value of the special library lay in the services it performed for its users and not in the promulgation of policies or even in a concentration on acquisitions unless those were geared to the expectation of specific users. In this regard he was a forerunner in developing the philosophies of pragmatic service emphasis that differentiate special librarians from others.

Frank McKenna threw himself into his new activities with the vigor, energy, enthusiasm, and confidence that characterized everything he did. He became a prolific contributor to the literature of scientific information, publishing both articles and monographic publications. These works, on relatively narrow and specific topics, indicated early on a characteristic that was to mark all of his future activities. McKenna identified what the problem was, then moved to address it with dogged determination, boundless energy, and a concentrated focus that would not allow for distraction. He also immediately joined the Special Libraries Association (SLA) and became prominent in its activities. By 1958 he was chair of the science-technology group of the New York Chapter, and in 1959 he became chair of the Metals/Materials Division. His meteoric rise within the association continued. He became division liaison officer and a member of the board of directors in 1962, and was elected in 1965 to the office of president.

At this point Frank McKenna's career took a strange, and ultimately for the Special Libraries Association, fortunate turn. Tempted throughout his professional career by the lure of the academic community in which he had performed so superbly, McKenna had maintained and cultivated these contacts throughout his work at Airco. He had taught and lectured as the opportunity arose, and served on the Advisory Board of the Graduate School of Library Service of Rutgers University and the New Jersey Council for Research and Development. On completing his term as president of SLA, McKenna decided on a career change. He negotiated a faculty appointment in his beloved Pacific Northwest, resigned his position at Airco, and headed cross-country. For reasons that are not clear, he found that the position was not as he had assumed it to be. He returned, disillusioned and jobless, to his book-lined apartment in the Greenwich Village section of New York City.

A bachelor all of his life, Frank McKenna was considered by many a loner. He was a perfectionist who demanded high standards from himself and from others, and he could appear difficult to those who could not meet his standards of energy and intelligence. Some people were uncomfortable in his presence. He was a large and heavy-set man with a booming voice and laugh, and he smoked almost constantly. His energies were boundless, and suggestions that he slow down were inevitably ignored. Frank McKenna also had a sensitive and caring side, and was interested in and curious about many things. He had a mischievous sense of humor and an unfailing eye for the absurd, and a genuine respect for those he felt merited his esteem. He was an elitist in the most positive sense of that much-maligned term. To the surprise of many who did not really know him, he was also a sentimental person, and he cared deeply about friends and family. Not having been close to other children during his own youth, and having no children of his own, he devoted himself to the love and care of the children of relatives, friends, and coworkers. Children, who sometimes have far better instincts about adults than do other adults, knew him instantly for the caring and warm person he really was.

This individual, proud and conditioned to succeed, then returned to his New York apartment, in his late forties, with his career plans in shambles. He had insisted on living amid the cosmopolitan atmosphere of lower Manhattan even during the many years he worked in New Jersey, stubbornly commuting in what everyone thought was the wrong direction. He had filled his life and his apartment with culture, with literature, and with the fine things he treasured. At this crucial point in his life, McKenna decided that what he needed most was a vacation to help put his priorities in order.

However, he could not be idle for very long. He began to wander down the short distance to the Special Libraries Association headquarters, to see if he could help. There was a huge backlog of work there, and ample opportunities for volunteers, particularly those so energetic and knowledgeable, and with such a flair for memory and detail. Soon this volunteer was working longer hours than the regular staff. In 1968 the executive director offered him the vacant post of editor of *Special Libraries* (he was doing all of the work anyway, and the executive director reasoned he ought to be paid at least something). In 1970, after the executive director resigned, the search committee of the board named Frank McKenna to the post, a position he held until his death eight years later.

This appointment was highly beneficial to both parties. McKenna already knew the association in intimate detail from the variety of posts he had held over the previous seventeen years. He had an impeccable memory and boundless energy and enthusiasm, knew what he wanted to do, and mastered an ability to inspire others with his dreams. Those he could not convince he simply tended to overwhelm. Although he presumably served as an employee of the association between 1970 and 1978, many judged that he really *was* SLA.

Organizational success is frequently measured in growth, and here McKenna's contributions were impressive. The Special Libraries Association doubled its membership; established and maintained a firm financial footing; established new geographic chapters, new subject divisions, and new publications; and began a successful implementation of office automation. During the eight years of Frank McKenna's stewardship SLA consolidated its position as the second largest professional library association, with membership growing at a steady average of 6 percent per year. McKenna implemented an automation process at the association that was remarkably efficient and trouble free, and he established a level of financial stability and a reserve fund that are the envy of professional association executives. He recognized that for many members unable to attend national conferences, the association was only as strong as the activities of local chapters, and he realized that for special librarians close collaboration with others working in the same area of collection specialization was important. During his term in office, the association expanded to fifty-four geographic chapters, including three in Canada and one in Europe, and twenty-nine divisions representing subject interests and types of information approaches and emphases. However, McKenna's greatest contribution was in developing a positive national and international image for special librarianship. He took the lead in making special libraries more important and more visible in the International Federation of Library Associations (IFLA), and in making American special librarians a greater part of the international library community. He served as a member of the U.S. delegation in the 1965 U.S.-U.S.S.R. exchange of special librarians and information center managers. He also taught and lectured about special librarianship in Japan, at the universities of Tokyo and Osaka.

In the Council of National Library Associations (CNLA), McKenna helped shape what had been a rather moribund organization dominated by the shadow of the American Library Association and galvanized it to action. Nowhere was this more clear than in the development of a united front in dealing with copyright legislation before Congress in the mid-1970s. The bill already passed by the Senate would have severely restricted library activities in this area, and it was in large part the work of Frank McKenna that forged a coalition of power and eloquence which changed the Copyright Law to its present form, one far more palatable for librarians.

Frank McKenna not only increased the visibility and activity of special librarians on the international scene through his work within IFLA, but also planned and developed the first international conference of special librarians, a conference held in Hawaii in June 1979 seven months after his death. It represented a fitting monument to his work and dreams. McKenna died in his sleep on November 10, 1978, at the age of 57. At the time he was still full of energy, vigor, plans, and ideas.

Biographical listings and obituaries — *Current Biography* 27:23-25 (1966); [Obituary]. *American Libraries* 9:642 (December 1978); [Obituary]. *Catholic Library World* 50:302 (February 1979); [Obituary]. *Current Biography* (1979); [Obituary]. *IFLA Journal* 5:68 (1979); [Obituary]. *INSPEL* 13:113-5 (1978); [Obituary]. *Library Journal* 104:345 (February 1, 1979); [Obituary]. *Publishers Weekly* 214:29 (December 11, 1978); [Obituary]. *Special Libraries* 69:447-9 (November 1978); [Obituary]. *Wilson Library Bulletin* 53:311 (December 1978); Wasson, Donald. "SLA's New President." *Special Libraries* 57:376 (July 1966); *Who Was Who in America* 7 (1977-1981). **Books and articles by the biographee** — "Pollution of Information: Do Attempts to Systematize the Flow of Information Assist or Impede the Flow?" *Special Libraries* 64:245-50 (May-June 1973); "Readin', Ritin', and Reproducin': Tools for the Special Librarian." *Special Libraries* 53:526-30 (November 1962). **Primary sources and archival materials** — McKenna's official correspondence as an officer of the Special Libraries Association is in the SLA Archives, SLA Headquarters, Washington, D.C.

— HERBERT S. WHITE

MEARNS, DAVID CHAMBERS (1899-1981)

David C. Mearns was born in Washington, D.C., December 31, 1899. He was the son of William Andrew and Mary Beard Chambers Mearns. A quintessential Washingtonian, he spent his 81-plus years almost entirely in the capital city and its environs, more than fifty of these in association with the Library of Congress. He was, in the opinion of Archibald MacLeish, "the rarest treasure in the Library of Congress." He received the Library's Distinguished Service Award in 1958 and, upon his retirement in 1967, was named Honorary Consultant in the Humanities, a title that only he and Robert Frost have borne in the near 200-year history of the Library.

Mearns's father was a lawyer and banker in Washington, D.C., and Mearns was reared in comfortable circumstances, residing in the Kalorama section of the city until 1916, when his family moved into the Q Street home of his late grandfather and namesake, Washington attorney David A. Chambers. He entered the National Cathedral School for Boys (St. Albans) in 1914, five years after its founding, taking the Glover English Medal and graduating in 1916. He always cherished his relationship with the school and the Class of 1916, of which he was class secretary. In 1953 he was elected to the school's governing board.

In 1916-1917 Mearns was a student at George Washington University, where his father had received his law degree. That was to be his last full year of formal education. About that time William Andrew Mearns established a short-lived company called International Sales Corporation, of which Mearns, then eighteen, was listed as secretary-treasurer. (Mearns himself later described his role as that of "typist.") In the fall of 1918 Mearns was enrolled at the University of Virginia, where he was a member of the Student Army Training Corps, from which he was released after the Armistice. He came home for the Christmas holidays in 1918 and never returned to college. In 1961, however, the University of Virginia chapter of Phi Beta Kappa elected him to membership.

His formal education over, Mearns began a lifetime education at the Library of Congress, accepting a temporary position in the Library's Order Division December 16, 1918, ostensibly to earn some Christmas money. That position lasted until March 25, 1920, when he transferred to the Reading Room, where he remained for the next twenty years.

Throughout the 1920s and 1930s Mearns moved to more responsible positions and assignments as his natural curiosity and zest for answers to arcane questions helped him assemble a body of reference lore unmatched by his contemporaries. He has amusingly described one special assignment as that of "bibliographical stable-boy" when he was asked to assist in arranging books at the White House. His first assignment there was in 1923, and he was summoned back in 1927 after a summer of reconstruction at the presidential mansion. On the latter occasion he came perilously close to kicking President Coolidge (by mistake) in the seat of the pants.

The Library of Congress in the 1920s was, in Mearns's words, "an exciting, integrated, homogenized, Waring blended, closely knit institution, afflicted with growing pains, undefined aspirations and a heady sense of thrust and power." And the Reading Room was "the blood stream, the pulse of the Library, making it animate and endowing it with spirit." It was also a fortunate location in another respect. There Mearns met Mildred Sellers Haines, whom he married in 1929. They had one daughter, Anne. After Mildred Mearns's death in 1945, Mearns remarried in 1951 to Mary Richardson, who briefly survived him.

Mearns's later career in the Library of Congress rested on two decades of success in reference librarianship. His longtime Library of Congress cohort and the first president of the Council on Library Resources, Verner Clapp, said of him: "In you we know one of the greatest reference librarians—perhaps the greatest—of all time." Mearns's own assessment of his legendary abilities was more modest. In the closest he came to a credo of reference librarianship, a lecture delivered at Catholic University, April 29, 1948, and published as "Master of Materials: Reference Librarian" in *The Catholic Library World* (19:249-51 [May 1948]), Mearns said that he possessed "conviction rather than competence, familiarity rather than knowledge, experience rather than understanding." Nevertheless, he identified the seven attributes he thought necessary for the reference librarian: (1) literacy, (2) imagination or resourcefulness, (3) enthusiasm, (4) persistence, (5) a sense of media, by which he meant knowing when to go to primary sources, when to secondary, etc., (6) humility, and (7) a love of service. Mearns had all of these in abundance, except possibly the sixth. Certainly no one in his own time rivaled his grasp of the voluminous collections of the Library of Congress. He never lost his zest or his touch in that respect. Mearns regarded the collections as a mighty instrument capable of yielding a complex symphony or a simple jingle. On that instrument he could play any note. And he sometimes seemed as fond of the jingles as of the symphonies.

In September 1937, he became acting superintendent of the Reading Rooms. For the next thirty years he was a principal officer of the Library of Congress, and found himself drawn more and more into central administrative duties. In the 1930s the Reading Rooms Division encompassed the Main and Congressional reading rooms, loan, services to the blind, the U.S. Capitol Station, exhibits, etc., in short, most of the public services of the Library. The MacLeish reorganization of the Library (1940-1942) departmentalized and compartmentalized the Library of Congress as it had not been before. After two years, 1941-1943, as chief reference librarian under the new dispensation, Mearns succeeded Luther Evans as director of the Reference Department, the largest department in the Library, encompassing legislative reference and many administrative services, as well as the public service divisions and collections. He was also gradually assuming a role he never completely relinquished, that of principal interpreter to the general public of the Library's history and services.

The first major product of this type was *The Story Up to Now: The Library of Congress, 1800-1946* (Washington, D.C.: Government Printing Office, 1947), which served as an extensive preamble to the Librarian's *Annual Report* for 1946. The background of this assignment was Luther Evans's request of a virtual doubling of the Library's appropriations for fiscal 1947. The House of Representatives Appropriations Committee, though denying most of the increase, asked for a "determination of policy" about the future of the Library. *The Story Up to Now*, as its title implied, was intended to provide the historical perspective on the Library necessary to understand the need for increased resources for its future. Mearns, always a fast worker, wrote the 227-page "chapter" in three months.

Despite its haste of preparation and Mearns's characteristic over-reliance on long documentary excerpts, *The Story Up to Now* was an impressive achievement. Lyman Butterfield thought it set "a new standard for institutional history." Julian Boyd called it "a classic." And Lawrence Wroth declared Mearns "a straightforward and learned historian," which the Library of Congress family had long known, but which a larger public would soon understand.

The year 1947 was undoubtedly Mearns's *annus mirabilis*, for before the year was out he had produced another major work, one which pivoted on the opening of the Abraham Lincoln papers in July of that year. The opening was an extravaganza, which Mearns had orchestrated and scored, little suspecting perhaps that his own fortunes would soon become so intimately involved with those of the sixteenth president.

The two-volume *Lincoln Papers: The Story of the Collection, with Selections to July 4, 1861* (Garden City: Doubleday, 1948), was Mearns's ticket to eminence among Lincolnians. There had been little evidence of a special affinity for Lincoln in the years before the *Lincoln Papers*. Thereafter, Lincoln was almost his obsession. Once more, he prepared a major publication in great haste, probably at most three months. His preface (dated November 6, 1947) acknowledges the aid of four "transcribers," as well as five other long-time associates, including Percy Powell, who had helped arrange the Lincoln papers in advance of their well-publicized availability to the public July 26, 1947. This compilation, therefore, is not a critical edition. It is, as the subtitle suggests, "the story of the collection," the kind of history at which Mearns excelled, replete with arcane details and systematic deadpan debunking of insubstantial myths. The selections from the papers are well chosen, and the headnotes informative.

In 1949 Mearns was elevated to the position of assistant librarian of Congress, completing an administrative triumvirate of Evans, Clapp, and Mearns, virtually identical in age if not in outlook. Although third in command and called upon to function as acting librarian during the not infrequent absences of both Evans and Clapp, Mearns continued to perform chiefly as the keeper of the Library's public image. Only the Exhibits and Information and Publication officers reported directly to him.

During the Library's sesquicentennial year of 1950, Mearns was almost continually occupied with the documentary history of the Library of Congress and the sesquicentennial celebration. Virtually every issue of the Library's *Information Bulletin* that year led off with one or more of his notes on the Library's history and related topics. Many of the more than fifty pieces were substantial extracts from (sometimes obscure) nineteenth-century books and articles. Altogether, these go far toward a documentary history of the institution or, perhaps more accurately, a heavily annotated set of references. He brought to light facts and impressions of the Library itself, some former Librarians and others, and the interaction of the Library with American national leaders. His lavishly illustrated description in the May 1 issue of the Sesquicentennial Day itself (April 24) is one of the most detailed accounts of any celebration in its history. In addition, throughout the year he spoke often to library and literary groups and, in the fall, participated in no fewer than nine concert intermission broadcasts on Library history and biography. Of mixed merit and sometimes whimsical to the point of triviality, the *Information Bulletin* notes of 1950 were a sustained tour de force, and the entire year took on a Mearnsian hue.

In May 1951, virtually without fanfare, Mearns and Solon J. Buck swapped positions, Buck becoming assistant librarian and Mearns, chief of the Manuscript Division. The Library's *Information Bulletin* called it merely "a major rotation on a permanent basis." Buck, former Archivist of the United States, had come to the Library in 1948, having resigned his position at the National Archives, apparently in mistaken anticipation of the election of Republican Thomas E. Dewey to the presidency. Although the change was officially unexplained, it was generally assumed that Buck would provide more effective central administrative backup to the Librarian and Chief Assistant Librarian than Mearns had.

Whatever the motivation, Mearns had arrived at the right place for him, as congenial for the last third of his Library career as the Reading Room had been for the first. He was in charge of not only the Abraham Lincoln papers, but those of twenty-two other presidents and thousands of collections in American history and culture of almost equal value. He served as chief of the Manuscript Division until his retirement in December 1967. These were not years of repose, of resting on one's laurels. On the contrary, they were years of great achievement and recognition and the initiation of important programs. But first there remained one more major contribution to Library of Congress history.

Herbert Putnam, 1861-1955: A Memorial Tribute (Washington, D.C.: Library of Congress, 1956), although it contains no name on the title page, is almost entirely the work of Mearns. The emphasis in the earlier part of his tribute is on

Putnam's vision and resolve as the new Librarian of Congress in 1899 and for a few years thereafter; in the latter part, on his personal qualities, patrician ways, and paternal sternness in dealing with the staff. There are few personal anecdotes, despite Mearns's long acquaintance and association with Putnam. Instead, Putnam is treated with "an impenetrable dignity," which is said to have characterized his relations with others. The phrase might, with almost equal justice, have been applied to Mearns himself.

Among Mearns's major accomplishments in the Manuscript Division, three may be highlighted: a broader and more aggressive acquisitions program, the initiation of the Presidential Papers Program, and the drive to establish the *National Union Catalog of Manuscript Collections* (*NUCMC*). The acquisitions push occurred in 1954, when hundreds of American leaders in various fields were invited to donate their papers to the Library of Congress. Whereas the Library's manuscript holdings, with a few notable exceptions, had been primarily in political, military, and diplomatic history, Mearns extended its reach into cultural history and, later, the history of science. The results were both immediate and gradual. For nearly thirty years, the 1954 acquisitions push yielded dividends.

Public Law 85-147, approved August 16, 1957, authorized a program "to arrange, index, and microfilm the papers of the Presidents of the United States in collections of the Library of Congress." A processing and indexing section was established in the Manuscript Division in August of the following year, and two years later the first four microfilm editions (including the Lincoln papers) were released. The program was completed in the early 1970s, with some two million presidential manuscripts filmed and indexed. Among other forms of scholarship, the Presidential Papers Program greatly facilitated the documentary editions of the "founding fathers," supported by the National Historical Publications Commission (NHPC) from the 1950s onward. In 1954 Mearns had succeeded Buck as the Library's representative on NHPC and served for thirteen years. He was also on the advisory boards for editions of Benjamin Franklin, Thomas Jefferson, and Woodrow Wilson papers.

Mearns was closely involved in the planning for *NUCMC* and one of its most effective missionaries. He has told the story of its establishment in the September 1959 issue of *College & Research Libraries*. *NUCMC* had a long gestation period and many parents, but not until the Library received a $200,000 grant from the Council on Library Resources in November 1958 was it possible to turn hopes into realities. David Mearns's role in securing that result was decisive.

The "manuscript years" were also marked by active resumption of the Library's foreign manuscript copying program and establishment of the Center for the Coordination of Foreign Manuscript Copying in the 1960s and a significant enhancement of the Manuscript staff to meet its new program responsibilities. Mearns drew around him a stable of remarkable specialists, with one of whom, Lloyd A. Dunlap, he collaborated on several Lincoln projects, including the Library's best-selling *Long Remembered* (1963), facsimiles of the five Gettysburg Address manuscripts, with historical commentary. Another product of these years was his chapter on Lincoln in *Three Presidents and Their Books* (Urbana: University of Illinois Press, 1955).

As Mearns's long career continued, one by one his former associates left the Library. Mearns was invariably called upon for the customary eulogy in florid, pun-filled, witty prose. He never failed to rise to the occasion. When his turn came, two hundred fifty friends gathered at a black-tie dinner in the Willard Hotel to pay him homage. Once again, Mearns was equal to the moment. He adapted Lincoln's "Farewell to Springfield" for his own remarks: "No one, not in my situation, can appreciate my feeling of sadness at this parting. Here I have lived two quarters of a century and have passed from a young to an old man."

He continued to serve the Library for the next nine years as Honorary Consultant in the Humanities, one of many honors that came to him. Others that he particularly prized were honorary degrees from Lincoln College and Lincoln Memorial University and medallions from the Abraham Lincoln Sesquicentennial Commission, the U.S. Civil War Centennial Commission and those of the states of Illinois and New Jersey. He was a member and officer of many professional associations and served as president of both the Manuscript Society and the District of Columbia Library Association and vice-president of the U.S. Grant Association. He was also a Fellow of the Society of American Archivists.

In explaining his own fascination with Abraham Lincoln, Mearns picked up his friend Carl Sandburg's phrase about the sixteenth president: "the son-of-a-gun grows on you." The same may be said of Mearns. Active, energetic, prolific, ambitious, and indefatigable as a younger man, he never lost sight of the strange, the ironic, or the whimsical in human experience. In his later years, that sense may have predominated. Mearns was a fascinating mixture. Never one to suffer fools gladly and blessed with a healthy cynicism about human motives and a sardonic wit to express it, he was nevertheless courtly in manner and publicly polite to all. He was also something of a hero-worshipper, with a pantheon that included Lincoln, Archibald MacLeish, Adlai Stevenson, Sandburg, and Felix Frankfurter, among others. Mearns himself had his own band of hero-worshippers as well. A large man (he is said to have weighed seventeen pounds at birth) with a resonant voice and completely at ease behind a podium, he was always in great demand as an unfailingly witty speaker, but his preference was to sit with two or three professional intimates and exchange historical gossip or delight in his family and old friends. He wrote with facility and admired good writing by others, but he could be guilty of dreadful wordplays (Lincoln was "prodigal of follicle") and cloying whimsicality (that was Lincoln's "hairesy"), along with his great wit and wisdom.

David Mearns's contributions to the Library of Congress were perhaps more qualitative than quantitative. He steeped himself in the Library's history and its collections to know the answers to questions and to make them known to others. He published his own findings but more often encouraged publications by others. He fashioned the Presidential Papers Program and thus spread throughout the American research library system the Library's most treasured original research materials. More than anything else, he represented the Library of Congress to a world of historians, bookpeople, the working press, and the public at large. And within the Library he seemed the beau ideal of integrity, dedication to learning, and wit. Luther Evans called Mearns "the embodiment" of the Library of Congress, "perhaps because you loved it most." If institutions are the "lengthened shadows" of individuals, for a good part of the twentieth century the Library of Congress's silhouette was decidedly Mearnsian. He died on May 27, 1981, in Alexandria, Virginia.

Biographical listings and obituaries — *Current Biography* 22:302-303 (1961); [Obituary]. *LC Information Bulletin* 40:181-3 (June 5, 1981); [Obituary]. *New York Times*, May 30, 1981; *Who Was Who in America* 7 (1977-1981). **Books and articles about the biographee** — Miers, Earl Schenk. "Byways in History: A Scholar's Scholar." *History* 1:122-7 (September 1959). **Primary sources and archival materials** — The basic source is the David C. Mearns Papers in the Manuscript Division, Library of Congress. Also valuable are the papers of Librarians of Congress Herbert Putnam, Luther H. Evans, Archibald MacLeish, and L. Quincy Mumford, and Mearns associates Verner W. Clapp and Roy P. Basler, all of which are part of the Library of Congress Archives, located in the Manuscript Division. Other primary source materials include Mearns's voluminous writings, identified in the text, and tapes of interviews conducted by or with Mearns concerning the history of the Library of Congress and related topics. The latter are located in the Library's Motion Picture, Broadcasting, and Recorded Sound Division.

— JOHN C. BRODERICK

MELCHER, DANIEL (1912-1985)

Daniel Melcher was born on July 10, 1912, in Newton Center, Massachusetts. He was the oldest child of Frederic Gershom and Marguerite Fellows Melcher. He grew up with two younger sisters in a household where books and reading were of central importance. His father began his career as a bookseller, edited *Publishers Weekly* for more than forty years, and served as president of the R. R. Bowker Company for twenty-five years. His mother was a poet, playwright, and author of children's books as well as a scholarly history of the Shakers. Frederic Melcher was an energetic, versatile, influential, and widely respected leader of the American book world. Daniel largely followed in his father's footsteps.

Melcher decided early that he wanted to be a publisher. Book manufacturing, the problems of distribution, and the business side of publishing interested him most. He attended Harvard during the Depression and began his college career as a physics major. He soon changed to economics when he realized that the toughest problems of that era were economic. It was an ideal major for an inveterate problem-solver with a strong social conscience who also appreciated more than most the business side of his intended profession.

After his graduation in 1934 he considered going on to Harvard Business School, but his father, who took a dim view of people who tried to manage work they had never performed, discouraged this idea. Instead they worked out a program that would give him experience in every area of publishing and prepare him to start his own firm in the early 1940s. He pursued this program from 1934 to 1942. It began with an apprenticeship year in London at George Allen and Unwin, followed by several months studying book trade procedures at leading book wholesalers in London and Leipzig. He spent the next six years in New York working for Henry Holt & Company, Oxford University Press, Alliance Book Corporation, and Viking Press. Most of these jobs involved promotion and sales. He also wrote his first book, a novel for high school readers interested in book publishing. *Young Mr. Stone Book Publisher* was issued by Dodd, Mead & Co. in its Career Books series in 1939. It concerns three students, two boys and a girl, who run their high school paper and later embark on publishing careers. The chief protagonist, Bob Stone, is the paper's business manager and appears to be closely modeled on Melcher himself.

Following American entry into World War II, he began a five-year period of public service in Washington, D.C. He spent 1942 to 1945 at the Treasury Department, first as a publishing consultant, then as national director of the war bond campaign in schools. Melcher's success in this position was widely recognized, and in November 1945, he was appointed the first director of the National Committee on Atomic Information (NCAI). The committee was established as part of the atomic scientists' movement to generate public support for international and civilian control of atomic energy. Melcher and his staff created and distributed a fortnightly bulletin, *Atomic Information*, and a wide range of other literature to affiliated religious, labor, professional, and other organizations. The collective memberships of these affiliated organizations, which included the League of Women Voters and the General Federation of Women's Clubs, totaled over ten million people. The work of the committee and its affiliated organizations contributed to the passage of the McMahon Act, which established the Atomic Energy Commission, and Senate confirmation of the commission's first members. Despite these successes, Melcher's tenure as NCAI director was short-lived. He was a forceful and independent administrator in an environment where the lines of administrative responsibility were ambiguous, and personal animosities developed between Melcher and some of the leaders of the scientists' movement. These problems led to his dismissal in late summer 1946. All but one of his fourteen-member staff resigned in protest.

It was probably at this point that Melcher began compiling the *Printing and Promotion Handbook: How to Plan, Produce and Use Printing, Advertising, and Direct Mail*, coauthored with Nancy Larrick (McGraw-Hill, 1949, rev. eds. 1956, 1966). During his years in Washington he had written, produced, and distributed millions of pieces of literature and used virtually every printing process but had been unable to find a source of practical information to help him. The *Printing and Promotion Handbook* was created to fill this need. It served as a standard reference work during the final twenty years of the era in which type cast from hot metal was the basis of printing technology.

Melcher had found public service very satisfying, and at one point he considered making it his career. His father reminded him that publishing was also a form of public service. Then, after his dismissal from NCAI, he offered his son a job. In 1947 Melcher joined the R. R. Bowker Company as publisher of *Library Journal*. He spent the next twenty-two years at Bowker, becoming director and general manager in 1956, vice-president in 1959, president in 1963, and chair in 1968.

Underlying Melcher's contributions were an unusual combination of personal attributes and deeply held principles and beliefs. Among these were a passion for efficiency, a love of technology, and a sound business sense coupled with social and political idealism. Most fundamental of all were his beliefs in cooperation and international understanding, universal education, and the value of books and reading. He was able to harness these disparate attributes and beliefs most fully during his years at Bowker, a service-oriented firm catering to the needs of all branches of the book world. His work at Bowker had a great and enduring impact on the world of books in the United States and around the world.

Melcher helped inform librarians, publishers, and booksellers about current developments in all areas of the book world in a steady stream of articles in *Library Journal, Publishers Weekly,* and other journals. He played an especially important role in promoting mutual understanding between librarians and publishers. He encouraged international contacts among publishers and American participation in the Frankfurt Book Fair. As publisher of *Library Journal* he worked with four successive editors, Karl Brown, Helen E. Wessells, Lee Ash, and Eric Moon, contributing to its emergence as the preeminent professional journal in the field. Like his father, who established the Newbery and Caldecott medals for children's books, he was a strong supporter of children's books and library service for children. In 1954 he founded *Junior Libraries*, renamed *School Library Journal* in 1961. When his father died in 1963, he succeeded him as donor of the Newbery and Caldecott medals. He was an early advocate of standard book numbers and helped introduce International Standard Book Numbers in the United States in the late 1960s.

The development of the Bowker family of trade bibliographies, beginning with *Books in Print*, was probably Melcher's most significant contribution to the book world. He began planning *Books in Print* shortly after he joined Bowker. *Publishers' Trade List Annual*, which listed in-print books by publisher, had been issued by Bowker since 1873, but no one had ever published an annual directory of U.S. books in print arranged by author and title. (The defunct *United States Catalog*, last published by H. W. Wilson in 1928, had never been an annual publication.) Melcher considered the prompt listing of books with prices and sources as the first objective of national bibliography, and he insisted that *Books in Print* had to appear annually with the most up-to-date information possible. There were formidable obstacles against such a venture. Most experts believed that the project would require nine months of editorial work followed by nine months of production. Melcher established editorial procedures that utilized college librarians and faculty members working intensively during the summer months. Rejecting linotype composition, he devised a production system in which entries were typed on separate cards. This allowed new and revised entries to be inserted at the last moment and outdated entries to be deleted. The cards were then shingled on boards for paging and photographed for offset reproduction. Shingle boards, mounting equipment, and cameras were all designed by Melcher himself. The first edition of *Books in Print* appeared in 1948. It was followed by other trade bibliographies, including *Paperbound Books in Print* (1955), *Subject Guide to Books in Print* (1957), *American Book Publishing Record* (1960), and *Forthcoming Books* (1966). His interest in Latin America led in the early 1960s to the establishment of *Fichero Bibliografico*, a book trade periodical that tried to list all new Spanish-language books published in the Americas, and *Libros en Venta*, a books in print volume for Spain and Spanish America.

Developments in automation and the advent of computers engaged Melcher's attention on several levels. His first article on automation, "Primer in Machine Information Storage and Retrieval," appeared in *Library Journal* in March 1960 (85:909-12). He was fascinated by the technological implications of automation and never doubted the ultimate role that computers would play. But as he gained experience with early computerization projects, his fascination with the technology was tempered by his passion for efficiency. He was appalled by inefficiencies such as batch processing, and he deplored the all-too-common automation of inefficient routines. He often argued that the greatest benefit of computerization derived from the analysis of an institution's operations that ideally took place before a computer was installed. He challenged the overblown claims of computer salespeople and some computer enthusiasts; in 1969 he recommended that library trustees take "a hard-nosed, 'show me' attitude when automation is proposed." In some circles he came to be known unfairly as an enemy of computers. But his strongest attacks were reserved for those who prophesized the demise of the book. He liked to use computer terminology in defending books: "Books are the standard we judge computers by. They give us random access, fast forward-and-reverse, hi-density, legibility, portability, freedom from breakdown, easy integration of alphanumeric data, easy handling of analog features such as graphs, drawings, and photos. They handle color easily. They even cost less than any competitor."

Bowker was acquired by Xerox Corporation on December 31, 1967, through an exchange of stock valued at $12,410,000. Melcher and the other stockholders, most of whom were near or over retirement age, became millionaires. The Bowker Company became part of Xerox Educational Division. There was little room for Melcher's brand of idealism under the new regime, and he remained with the company for barely a year. In August 1968 he was replaced as president and transferred to the Xerox Educational Division staff as Director of Venture Planning. He was also named Bowker chair, but he resigned from Bowker and Xerox a few months later. He explained: "The planning group within the Xerox Educational Division had no background in education or publishing, and I had no background in oil, plastics, chemicals, or business machine sales, and we just weren't on the same wavelength."

Melcher was fifty-six when he resigned from Bowker in January 1969. The next few years were devoted to writing and serving on various boards. *Melcher on Acquisition*, written with his second wife, Margaret Saul Melcher, was published by the American Library Association in 1971. He had been impressed with the work of the Institute of Human Potential in Philadelphia in teaching brain-damaged and very young children to read, and he became a member of its board. His work with the institute resulted in several publications, including an article in *Library Journal* (98:3109-17 [October 15, 1973]), "Johnny Still Can't Read: Would Children Learn to Read as Early as They Learn to Talk If We Let Them?," which was reprinted in *Library Lit. 5 — The Best of 1974*. He was board chair of Gale Research Co., 1971-1973; served as trustee of the Montclair, New Jersey, Public Library (another position previously held by his father), 1972-1973; and was elected to the Council of the American Library Association, 1972-1974. He received the American Library Association's highest award, Honorary Membership, during the Centennial Conference in 1976.

Melcher was active in the civil rights, civil liberties, and peace movements. He found time for an astonishing array of hobbies, including optics, electronics, photography, tape recording, skin diving, skiing, sailing, instrumental music, and languages. Nancy Larrick described him as follows: "Quiet, somewhat retiring in a large group, Dan Melcher has a knack of forging deeply loyal friendships in some quarters while raising antagonism in others.... Anyone who has worked with Melcher is soon aware that his mind simply operates in a higher gear than anyone else's, a fact he has never fully accepted." He said of himself: "I enjoy more than many people the excitement of finding out that something I have always known is not so. This leads to a whole series of discoveries as I search the pigeon holes of my mind for notions based on the newly identified misinformation. Often entirely new and intriguing correlations come to light during this mind cleaning process. I like, too, seeing around new corners."

He married Peggy Zimmerman, a children's librarian, in 1937. Their son, Frederic II, was born in 1946. Peggy Melcher developed multiple sclerosis in 1947; as the illness progressed she was confined to the Melcher home in Montclair, New Jersey. She died in 1967. Later that year he married Margaret Saul, a former editor of *School Library Journal*.

Melcher died of drowning on July 22, 1985, after suffering an epileptic seizure in his swimming pool at Glen Echo Farm, his home in Charlottesville, Virginia. He was 73.

Biographical listings and obituaries — "Melcher, Daniel." *ALA Yearbook 1976* (1977); [Obituary]. *Publishers Weekly* 228:22 (August 9, 1985). **Books and articles about the biographee** — Alley, Brian. "A Conversation with Daniel Melcher." *Technicalities* 2:4-5, 7 (September 1982); Larrick, Nancy. "Daniel Melcher." *Bulletin of Bibliography* 24:225-8, 248 (January-April 1966). **Primary sources and archival materials** — Eight to twelve file drawers of material are in the possession of Margaret Saul Melcher, who expects eventually to give them to an institution.

—GORDON B. NEAVILL

METCALF, KEYES DeWITT (1889-1983)

Keyes DeWitt Metcalf, the 17th of 18 children, was born on April 13, 1889 in Elyria, Ohio. Since both his parents died when he was young, neither had a direct impact on his work habits or career choice. An older sister who shared their father's belief in the importance of a college education raised him. With the support of this sister, Metcalf endeavored to overcome a "handicap" in the fifth grade: shifting writing from his left to his right hand. The transition was long and difficult. During his freshman year in high school, Metcalf withdrew from school and lived for a month with another sister, Anna, wife of Oberlin College Librarian Azariah Smith Root.

Metcalf admired Azariah Root and wanted to follow in his footsteps. Since his brother-in-law believed that practical experience was the best way to enter librarianship, he encouraged Metcalf to work as a student page in the Oberlin College library while he completed studies at Oberlin High School (1906) and College (1910). Root exposed him to a wide variety of activities and gave him increased work responsibilities. The young man learned binding and visited community residents who wanted to donate materials to the college library. He assisted Root in deciding what to add to the library's collection, in exchanging duplicates with other libraries, in planning a new library building, and in supervising the relocation of the book collection to a new building.

These experiences shaped Metcalf's belief that library buildings should be functional, flexible, and capable of meeting space needs for the foreseeable future. He realized that money should not be wasted on the design and construction of libraries. Surplus funds would be better spent on collection development. Careful book selection, combined with an active program of attracting gifts and exchanging duplicates, would enable a college library faced with a limited budget to obtain those books that undergraduates most need.

During Metcalf's senior year at Oberlin College, history professor Albert Howe Lybyer encouraged him to advance his budding library career by obtaining a doctoral degree from Harvard University. Root, who disagreed, maintained that librarians should be generalists, not specialists. Although Harvard's history department accepted him and extended a graduate fellowship, Metcalf declined the offer. Instead, following his brother-in-law's advice, he sought systematic training in the fundamental practices of librarianship. He applied to Pratt Institute, where Mary Wright Plummer had built a national reputation for preparing well-trained librarians. Although accepted into the Pratt program, Metcalf instead entered the newly opened New York Public Library School in 1911, after he discovered that Plummer had transferred there.

For the next two years, Metcalf took courses at the library school while working in the library itself. For part of 1912, he returned to Oberlin College library and became executive assistant while Root spent a sabbatical abroad. Metcalf earned his certificate in 1913 and received a diploma two years later.

Harry Miller Lydenberg, then chief reference librarian at the New York Public Library (NYPL), recognized that Metcalf would benefit from administrative opportunities. In 1913, Metcalf became chief of the stacks. In this position, he put the stacks in order, took an inventory of the main stack collection, improved services, and selected books for binding. He handled numerous personnel problems and dealt with the staff of all the library's divisions. The young librarian soon became familiar with the functions and problems of each division.

He refined his interpersonal skills, experience with teenagers, and ability to work with people by serving as a referee for high school football games. As he fondly recalled years later, refereeing taught him to make quick decisions and to cope with agitated people.

Metcalf worked as chief of the stacks until September 1916, when he took another leave of absence to become acting director of the Oberlin College library while Root spent the year at the NYPL library school. In July 1917, he returned to the NYPL, where he remained for the next two decades. During these years, he held various library positions and received numerous administrative assignments.

In 1919, Metcalf became acting chief of the order division, a position that introduced him to foreign booksellers and the collection of international resources. During that same year he served as executive assistant in the office of the director and liaison between the administration and the staff. He also married Martha Gerrish, a high school classmate whom he dated for several years.

From 1927 to 1929, he served as chief of the preparation division and, in 1928, became chief of the reference department. These various positions provided him with an opportunity to evaluate gifts received by the library, to manage part of the library budget, to assist in book selection, and to realize that students and the public are best served by access to a general collection.

Metcalf became increasingly active in professional organizations and in creating a national presence beginning in 1930. He served as chair of the American Library Association's Cooperative Cataloging Committee and a member of the American Library Institute. In 1933, he was appointed to ALA's Board of Education for Librarianship. From 1934 to 1937, he chaired the board and implemented the 1933 minimum requirements that accredited library schools under qualitative rather than quantitative standards.

Metcalf was offered the position of Harvard College librarian in 1936, with the understanding that later he would also become the university library director. Recognizing the problems faced by Harvard's libraries (e.g., low staff morale, a decentralized but not well-coordinated library system, and the need to modernize the library system), he initially declined the offer. Robert P. Blake, the retiring library director, urged him to reconsider. Metcalf did so and accepted the position the following year. He said later that he had changed his mind because he recognized the influential role that Harvard exerted among research libraries, found the position challenging, was offered simultaneously the positions of Director of Harvard University Library and College Librarian, and would be able to influence library policies and procedures immediately. With many senior staff members retiring, he could replace them while still hiring additional personnel.

Metcalf became Harvard's first library director with formal library training, but no degree from that institution. When he assumed his new duties, Widener Library employed few professional staff members and had little unused shelving. Congestion on the bookshelves affected quality of service and threatened to damage book spines. Metcalf immediately began to hire staff and develop a plan for dealing with the space shortage and the large volume of materials added to the collection each year. Since Widener was built with the proviso that it not be added to, there could be no new addition to relieve the space congestion. It had been completed in 1915 and, within twenty years, its stack area was virtually full. As a solution to the space problem, Metcalf renovated Widener and supplemented it with a building for rare books and manuscripts (Houghton Library, 1942), a cooperative storage center for infrequently used titles (New England Deposit Library), new stacks located beneath the southeast corner of Harvard Yard, and a separate undergraduate library (Lamont, 1949). Lamont and Houghton influenced the design of many subsequent library buildings.

Another of his accomplishments was to increase coordination among units of the university library, especially the libraries of the professional schools. Favoring "coordinated decentralization," Metcalf adopted the idea of a union catalog which reflected the holdings of all campus libraries. He regarded space shortages, the shifting of collections to departmental libraries, cooperative arrangements, improved selection policies, and library building design as related problems. His goal was to increase the efficiency of the library and ensure that the library did not consume an ever larger percentage of the institution's resources and annual budget.

His concern about the financial condition of higher education and the inability of institutions to allocate larger percentages of their budgets to libraries helped persuade the Association of Research Libraries (ARL) to plan a conference in 1954 on financial problems facing university libraries. The conference, and the resulting published proceedings, had limited impact, however, because higher education soon entered a period of rapid growth sparked by massive federal support. Nonetheless, the conference reflected Metcalf's approach to problem solving: identify problems with long-range and broad implications, create an awareness of these problems and an opportunity to hear diverse viewpoints, and develop strategies for finding sensible solutions.

During his eighteen years at Harvard, Metcalf participated actively in professional organizations. He served as chair of ALA's Committee on Photographic Reproduction of Library Materials (1939-1941), as ARL executive secretary (1938-1941), as ALA president (1942-1943), and as a founding member and president of the American Documentation Institute (now the American Society for Information Science). He influenced the development of the Farmington Plan of 1949, which attempted to ensure that one copy of every important foreign publication was held in an American library, listed in the *National Union Catalog*, and available for interlibrary loan or photoreproduction. Cooperating libraries collected publications in predetermined subject areas.

By August 31, 1955, Metcalf had accomplished his primary goals at Harvard. He had added over two million volumes to the collections, upgraded the professional staff, recruited staff outside the institution, and overcome low staff morale. He had expanded interinstitutional cooperation, trained administrators for positions within and outside the institution, relieved the critical space shortage problem, and modernized the library. At the age of sixty-six, he retired from Harvard University to pursue interests in interlibrary cooperation, training of librarians for top administrative positions, and library building planning. His wife, "Mart," had died in 1938, and several years later he married Elinor Gregory.

When the Graduate School of Library Service at Rutgers University began operations in 1954,

Dean Lowell Martin offered Metcalf a position as adjunct professor on either a full- or part-time basis. The Harvard Librarian Emeritus accepted a part-time assignment. For three years, he taught administration and building planning to master's-level students and library administrators.

Metcalf strongly believed that teaching librarianship required years of practical and varied experience. Teachers should be generalists, not specialists, and they should *train* students. He did not view librarianship as having a theoretical base. For these reasons, he disliked the emerging trend to place young doctorates or theoreticians on the faculty of library schools. Metcalf also taught library administration at Columbia University and was a Fulbright lecturer in Australia. He became widely known for his lectures and writings on library administration and building planning, and his consulting to more than 600 institutions in the United States and elsewhere.

Several principles governed Metcalf's professional practice. First, he thought library collections should be developed carefully, through better book selection and minimizing unnecessary duplication of little-used material. Second, library service should be improved by the recruiting and training of capable staff; these individuals should receive salaries sufficient to make librarianship an attractive career. Third, new buildings require careful planning, should not waste money, and should invite use. Fourth, research libraries should prepare for the future, cooperate, and view themselves as interdependent parts of a national whole; each library ought to take the policies and collections of other institutions into account when formulating acquisition and retention policies. Fifth, library collections should be cataloged so that they are easy to use; simplified cataloging provides a means to control processing costs. Finally, libraries should provide good service and be housed in functional buildings that are attractive and comfortable to work in. In brief, Metcalf thought the ideal situation for any library administrator is a "good library building, a fine collection which is heavily used, a good catalog, and a smooth running operation." Further, "the best way to avoid trouble was to make difficult management decisions without hesitation and to execute them without delay."

Metcalf's contributions to librarianship were myriad and reveal a pragmatic view of librarianship, one devoid of a "theoretical" or "philosophical" basis. Generally they fall into the areas of library building design; administration; cooperation, collection development, and resource sharing; microforms; and the published literature. He never forgot the building that Root had planned at the turn of the century. It contrasted sharply with its predecessor and made Metcalf realize the benefits of careful planning and avoiding the construction of enduring monuments "to many wasted dollars." His *Planning Academic and Research Library Buildings* (New York: McGraw-Hill, 1965) showed "how a mixture of utility in library buildings can be achieved for the funds available, without sacrificing beauty." By getting the most out of the money expended, more funds would be available for developing a library's collections. Both Houghton and Lamont libraries became the prototypes for their time. Other academic institutions concurred that undergraduate students did not need access to research collections (except in special instances) and that they should not be left to their own devices. Other institutions then developed undergraduate libraries.

Metcalf believed that recruiting good people was a library administrator's most important duty. He wanted to improve the quality of staff and prepare administrators for positions within and beyond their immediate institutions. He strongly believed that training people to assume positions at other institutions was an obligation to the profession, and he advocated mobility among top administrative posts; such a view was not widely shared or practiced at the time. Like Edwin Hatfield Anderson, under whom he had served as an assistant at the NYPL, Metcalf wanted to move librarianship away from its identification as a female profession and to advance qualified and educated men. As he explained to an audience at Eastern Illinois University in April 1981,

> Mr. Anderson made it clear to me that librarians, both males and females, were suffering from the fact that there were few men in the field except for those in charge of the larger libraries and that until there were more men, librarianship would not be recognized as a profession. He said that both men and women would benefit by higher salaries if there were more men in libraries and men began to be added to the staff in large numbers. When I came to Harvard ... I found there were almost no men in the library except the department heads

and the heads of the major graduate school libraries. I tried to change the situation.

He wanted to attract promising individuals, primarily men, to administration and provide them with assignments similar to those he had encountered at the NYPL. He acquainted them with different branches of library operations and exposed them to various problems. Metcalf believed in the value of experience and common sense. These two attributes guided his view of the training of administrators. Some have suggested his preparation of over 100 people for top administrative positions was his most important contribution to research libraries.

In the areas of cooperation, collection development, and resource sharing, Metcalf encouraged libraries to control unit costs (cataloging, storage, service, operations, etc.), to screen the number of potentially little-used titles added to their permanent collections, and to live with limited budgets for the selection of materials. He recognized that Harvard could not collect and store all recorded knowledge. He told the Illinois audience he was

> interested in building up collections, but size in itself is not of first importance. We should not seek acquisitions simply to show that we have more volumes than another library. We should not establish special inclusive collections if similar collections are available elsewhere.

Metcalf encouraged libraries to cooperate in their collecting of materials not essential to specific faculty teaching and research interests. Cooperation, he maintained, "will make it unnecessary [for libraries] to grow at anywhere near the rate at which we have been growing." Still, he recognized that interinstitutional borrowing was a poor substitute for a good collection.

As university librarian, Metcalf took President Charles W. Eliot's plan for cooperative storage, specified in an annual report of 1900-1901, and suggested that it be modified in two areas: storing little-used rather than merely nonused or "dead" books, and reducing storage costs by narrow aisles and cheap construction, rather than shelving books four-deep.

Through his efforts, as well as those of others, the New England Deposit Library opened in 1941. It provided economical storage and helped relieve Harvard, the Massachusetts State Library, and Boston Public Library, and certain other area libraries of shelf congestion. Harvard shifted a quarter of the Widener collection (over 500,000 volumes) to storage. Yet the Deposit Library did not result in the integration of deposit collections or the elimination of duplicate copies. Since the libraries did not have similar holdings, little duplication among lesser-used titles occurred. And because the Deposit Library shelved materials by size and stored numerous new acquisitions, some scholars complained that infrequently used publications were not easily accessible. The project, however, proved financially and administratively successful; the thirty-year mortgage amortized in twenty years.

The success of the Deposit Library persuaded President Robert Hutchins of the University of Chicago to invite Metcalf (in 1940) to study the feasibility of a library deposit center for the Midwest. Because of other commitments, Metcalf asked John Fall of the NYPL to conduct a feasibility study under his supervision. The report, completed the same year, advocated joint storage and cooperative acquisitions; however, the opposition of head librarians of thirteen midwestern institutions delayed the creation of a center. The proposal was finally approved in 1947, after most of the thirteen librarians had retired. The Midwest Inter-Library Center was established in 1949 and renamed the Center for Research Libraries in 1965.

Metcalf supported the Library of Congress Mission to Europe in 1946. He wanted to avoid the practice prevalent following World War I, when Harvard and other large libraries purchased book collections from European professors. He preferred purchases by the Library of Congress as part of the normal book trade because he wanted libraries to cooperate. The success of the mission pointed the way to the Farmington Plan, which was a logical extension of the type of cooperative arrangement Metcalf advocated. It provided for a decentralized collection, a voluntary agreement among some sixty libraries, cooperative acquisitions, storage, and a means for controlling the number of duplicate holdings. The major difference between this plan, on the one hand, and the New England Deposit Library and regional centers on the other, was the geographical base; it would be national rather than local, statewide, or regional. Still, Metcalf thought that other cooperative arrangements not restricted to the national level were viable.

Metcalf also made significant contributions to the profession in the area of microforms. At the NYPL, he experimented with microphotography and its role in collection development. He believed that microforms would save space but realized that many research collections could not be shifted to this format. Further, he reminded the library community that increased reliance on microforms necessitated the purchase of more viewing and reproduction equipment and expanded storage facilities. In 1938, as the new Harvard librarian, Metcalf observed that research libraries in the United States collected few newspapers produced in other countries. To develop a program by which these libraries could obtain needed newspapers, he obtained $5,000 per year from Harvard to purchase the newspapers and a $6,000 revolving fund from the Rockefeller Foundation to handle filming costs. Based on the recommendations of Harvard's history department and interested libraries, fifty newspapers were selected; thirty-seven gave permission to film and sell copies. Harvard produced and retained the microfilm master and a copy; other copies were sold to libraries. By the 1950s, the microfilm program had become so successful that Harvard made a $15,000 profit. Since this presented a possible income tax liability, Harvard turned the operation over to the Midwest Inter-Library Center. The Center greatly increased the number of newspapers available.

Metcalf was also a major contributor to the professional literature. In 1947, he began the *Harvard Library Bulletin*, patterned after the *New York Public Library Bulletin*, to demonstrate the responsibility of a research library to the research, bibliography, and library communities. The journal provided a forum for communicating Harvard's and his views on library matters.

Perhaps he is best known for his *Planning Academic and Research Library Buildings* (1965) and his memoirs, *Random Recollections of an Anachronism or Seventy-five Years of Library Work* (1980). He also wrote *Library Lighting* (Washington, D.C.: Association of Research Libraries, 1970), which linked good lighting to use of a library; "it is pennywise and pound foolish," he said, "to economize [in building a library] at the expense of good lighting."

Metcalf also wrote numerous surveys and reports based on his consulting and committee assignments. As he neared retirement age in the early 1950s, he had a *Report on the Harvard University Library* prepared. It not only assessed the accomplishments under his directorship, but also identified major problems facing his successor. The report is important because it provided the basis for long-term planning by his successor; reflected his view that staff members should participate in the planning process (he had discussed the manuscript with the professional staff so that they could comment on it prior to publication); and provided an example to other institutions on how to determine where they were and planned to go.

His articles on library building planning, policies and planning for Harvard (collection development, administrative structure of the library system, and use of the university library), interlibrary cooperation, library administration and management, microforms, and trends in research and academic libraries have all been acclaimed. Admittedly, many of his ideas and solutions were not original, but he used his position as a noted library leader to publicize major problems and to generate support for practical solutions.

Keyes Metcalf had a long and varied professional career. Three men—Azariah Smith Root, Edwin Hatfield Anderson, and Harry Miller Lydenberg—influenced his career and approach to librarianship. His debts to Root and Lydenberg extended to collection development, interinstitutional cooperation, and library building design. Anderson, on the other hand, emphasized staff development and the preparation of library administrators. Metcalf's views of librarianship, and the importance of utility and economy, were firmly in place prior to his departure from the NYPL in the 1930s.

Metcalf received twelve honorary doctoral degrees. In May 1961, the NYPL's Fiftieth Anniversary Award recognized his "creative contributions to research librarianship." He received the Association of College and Research Libraries Distinguished Service Award in 1978. At his seventieth Oberlin College reunion in 1981, he was inducted into Phi Beta Kappa.

Despite all his achievements, Keyes Metcalf remained modest, approachable, and caring. He enjoyed meeting people and discussing librarianship. Soft spoken, he had a delightful sense of humor and could accurately recount numerous past experiences and encounters with library leaders. Nonetheless, he lived for the present, not the past. Metcalf wanted librarians to understand the historical development of a rapidly changing profession. In this way, the profession could develop sensible solutions to major problems. He worked on the second volume of his memoirs (1987) and consulted with other librarians until his death on November 3, 1983, at the age of 94.

Biographical listings and obituaries — *ALA Yearbook, 1976* (1977); Horner, S. J., "Spotlighting a Nonagenarian Achiever: Keyes DeWitt Metcalf." *Wilson Library Bulletin* 55:353-7 (January 1981); [Obituary]. *American Libraries* 14:696 (December 1983); [Obituary]. *College & Research Libraries News* 11:437-8 (December 1983); [Obituary]. *Library Journal* 108:2293 (December 1983); [Obituary]. *Wilson Library Bulletin* 58:311 (December 1983). **Books and articles about the biographee** — Hernon, Peter. "Keyes DeWitt Metcalf." In *Leaders in American Academic Librarianship: 1925-1975*, ed. Wayne A. Wiegand (Pittsburgh: Beta Phi Mu, 1983), 213-35; Williams, Edwin E. *The Metcalf Administration (1937-1955) and Keyes D. Metcalf*. Cambridge: Harvard University Library, 1969. **Primary sources and archival materials** — The Florida State University School of Library and Information Studies houses Metcalf's architectural papers; Harvard University holds correspondence and administrative files from Metcalf's directorship; the New York Public Library has material from Metcalf's tenure there; Oberlin College has material on the Metcalf family; and the University of Illinois, Urbana, houses the ALA Archives, which include papers covering Metcalf's tenure on the Board of Education and as president.

—PETER HERNON

MORRIS, JACK CASSIUS (1911-1954)

Jack Cassius Morris was born March 3, 1911, in Ten Sleep, Wyoming, the son of Charles Cassius and Cecil Grace Burke Morris, both Wyoming ranchers. Around 1925, the family moved to Lincoln, Nebraska, where Morris's father became a grain broker. Morris completed high school in Lincoln and enrolled in the University of Nebraska. He graduated from the University of Nebraska in 1934 with a B.S. in chemistry. During his years in college and shortly afterwards, from 1930 to 1935, he was manager and half-owner of the Nebraska Book Company in Lincoln. From 1935 to 1938 he was owner/proprietor of the Morris Book Company in Lincoln, a store specializing in rare and second-hand books.

In 1938, Morris gave up his bookstore and enrolled at the University of Illinois Library School, where he received a B.S. in library science in 1939, and an M.S. in library science in 1941. While he was working on his Master's degree, he also worked full time as an assistant reference librarian at the University of Illinois Library. In 1940 he married Lois Mae Lympus, who before their marriage had graduated from the University of Illinois Library School and worked as a public librarian in Lincoln. She had encouraged Morris to become a librarian. A son, Mark, was born in 1943.

Morris intended to be a university librarian. To this end his first job after the Master's program was an librarian at the University of South Dakota Library. He held this position from 1941 to 1943, but national efforts to aid the war intervened. Morris, with his backgrounds in chemistry and librarianship (and ineligibility for military service because of physical disabilities), felt compelled to join in this work. In 1943, he took a position as patent chemist with the Hercules Powder Company in Wilmington, Delaware. During his three years there he held a variety of positions, including a stint in 1946 as patent supervisor. He continued his patent-related work during 1946 and part of 1947 when he worked for the Office of Rubber Reserve of the Reconstruction Finance Corporation and the U.S. Patent Office, as patent advisor, both in Washington, D.C. In 1947, he accepted a position with the Oak Ridge National Laboratory.

Morris's career as a professional librarian was a short but distinguished one, covering a period of only thirteen years. His educational background and his experience as a patent specialist gave him admirable qualifications for the position that he assumed in 1947 as chief librarian for the Oak Ridge National Laboratory (ORNL) at Oak Ridge, Tennessee. At that time it was one of the most desirable jobs in the world of special libraries, since it served as the preeminent library for the Atomic Energy Commission (AEC), a federal agency with great significance in the postwar era and at the beginning of the Cold War. As chief librarian at ORNL, Morris used his abilities as a leader and as a mentor to have a quiet but significant influence on special librarians of his time. He also used his understanding of subject cataloging and indexing, gained through his education and experience in both librarianship and chemistry, to develop an outstanding technical reports control system. His writings on this subject brought him and his ideas in conflict with the newly emerging ideas of the documentation movement as championed by Mortimer Taube.

But Morris's most significant and lasting contribution appears to have been the influence he had on other special librarians of his time. This influence was manifested in two ways: as a result of the development of the ORNL library as a model special library and as a result of his personal influence as mentor and correspondent with other special librarians. Herbert White, dean of the School of Library and Information Science at Indiana University, was just beginning his career as a special librarian in the early 1950s; he later recalled that: "Morris operated a very impressive operation in those days and it was a model for other special librarians." Gordon Randall, another contemporary, gave a similar testimony in his obituary for Morris in 1955, but cast it in a personal framework: "Preeminence in the library profession is not always achieved by those who seek it; sometimes it is acquired unknowingly by a librarian by virtue of his influence on others. Such was the case of Jack C. Morris." According to Randall, Morris carried on an extensive correspondence with special librarians around the country about the nature of subject analysis and the cataloging of technical reports. Morris was also influential with his colleagues within other AEC libraries and was largely responsible for the basic ideas and systems used in the cataloging and handling of the extensive series of reports issued by the AEC.

While Morris was an active participant in professional associations and regularly attended their meetings, he apparently did not actively seek office or committee work in these groups. The sole exception to this seems to be his work in organizing and serving as the first president of the Oak Ridge Chapter of the Special Libraries Association, 1952-1953.

Morris was a reluctant writer and presenter of his ideas about the nature of the profession and his favorite topic within the field, subject analysis. He wrote only two articles on subject analysis and one short manual, *Corporate Entry Guide for Report Literature at Oak Ridge National Laboratory Library* (Oak Ridge, Tenn.: ORNL Library, 1953), during his lifetime. The manual intended only for limited distribution, received high praise from Lucille Morsch of the Library of Congress when it was reviewed in the January 1954 issue of the *Journal of Cataloging and Classification.*

Morsch noted that Morris's suggestions were invaluable for future revisions of the 1949 American Library Association *Cataloging Rules.* There are also indications that Morris's suggestions for the cataloging of technical reports, particularly the handling of corporate body entries, had significant influence on the development of the Committee on Scientific and Technical Information (COSATI) *Rules for Cataloging* a few years later.

The two articles by Morris on subject analysis, however, are more indicative of his expertise and interests in the profession. Had Morris been able to extend this work in the next few years, he doubtless would have gained a considerable reputation as a developer of major concepts in the area of subject analysis. Taken by themselves, however, they are more suggestive of trends in the development of the struggle for professional dominance (particularly in the area of scientific and technical information) between librarians and documentalists than they are major contributions to the theory of subject analysis.

Randall says that Morris had been unwilling to prepare articles for publication because his duties at ORNL precluded use of his time in that way. "Only within the last two years," says Randall, "when his concern with retrieval systems overcame his distaste for personal aggrandizement did he permit publication of his ideas." Morris's concern centered particularly on one system that in 1953-1954 was achieving considerable notoriety—Mortimer Taube's Uniterm information retrieval system. Both of his articles were reactions to Taube's system. The first article, entitled "Evolution or Involution? Notes Critical of the Uniterm System of Indexing," was published in the July 1954 issue of the *Journal of Cataloging and Classification* (10:111-18). It was a direct challenge to the claims made by Taube for his system. The second article, "The Duality Concept in Subject Analysis" (which appears to have been written prior to the first one but actually appeared shortly after Morris's death), was published in *American Documentation* (5:117-46) in August 1954. It was a carefully developed review of the advantages of subject headings in scientific and technical libraries, and it concluded that subject headings when used in a unit card system of application were superior to the Uniterm system developed by Taube. Morris advocated the development of an information retrieval system that would combine the best features of subject-headed unit cards with those of marginal punched cards.

Morris's criticisms of the Uniterm system were precise and to the point. Over the next few years others echoed his complaints, and the system was eventually corrected to reflect those views. Morris was particularly critical of the superficial subject indexing that would take place if the system was implemented as instructed in its accompanying manual. He concluded that it was an ineffective system because of the problems of lack of vocabulary control, inflexibility, "false drops," difficulty in searching, and, particularly, its failure to compare in retrieval effectiveness with current subject heading systems used in libraries.

Taube's response, which appeared immediately following Morris's article in the *Journal of Cataloging and Classification*, was blistering. In general, the Morris article had been restrained and straightforward in its criticism, with an occasional hint of ridicule at the Uniterm system. Taube chose to make his response in terms that were largely personal and directed them, first, at Morris particularly and, secondly, at "traditional librarians" in general. Taube used such phrases as "we are sure that Mr. Morris does not understand the probabilities involved ..." and "has entered a controversy beyond his competence." Taube then went on to attack those who insisted on maintaining obviously inferior but traditional library practices in the face of new challenges in the field of documentary retrieval.

This exchange reflected a disagreement occurring at two levels: a critique and a defense of the Uniterm information retrieval system and a skirmish in the larger battle between librarians and documentalists (later, information scientists). Morris, in a variety of ways, was attempting to bridge the growing gap between these two groups. His two articles on subject analysis and his larger role as leader and mentor in special librarianship were oriented in that way. Through his writings and by the development of the ORNL library, he was attempting to maintain tradition while also gladly accepting advances in the field. But Taube, often known as an acerbic critic to those with whom he disagreed, was not willing to compromise.

Ultimately, both Morris and Taube proved correct in the specifics of their confrontation over the Uniterm system. Morris had anticipated the vocabulary control and searching problems the system would encounter. Even Documentation, Inc., Taube's company, later admitted to these difficulties and noted that they were using a thesaurus in their own work. Indeed, the entire controversy over the use of "links" and "roles" in indexing was foreshadowed in the Morris/Taube exchange. Taube, however, was justified in asserting the value of the coordinate indexing approach that he had developed. In 1954, the manual systems that utilized the Uniterm system were very cumbersome and time consuming, involving the manual matching of several pairs of numbers before a document could be retrieved. Morris hit very hard on this point in his critique, citing studies that showed the difficulties involved. Morris, however, failed to anticipate—and indeed may have been unaware of several trends—use of the coordinate indexing system in machine- and later, computer-based systems. Coordinate indexing, as a concept, would have a bright future as the use of computers in information retrieval became more common.

In 1954, however, the argument was intense and joined on many sides by a variety of writers. Douglas J. Foskett, for example, who observed these arguments from the United Kingdom, commented: "The Co-ordinate Indexing System of Mortimer Taube and his associates in Documentation, Inc., is chiefly remarkable for the violence of the controversy it has set off in the U.S." (*Information Services in Libraries*, London: Crosby, Lockwood and Sons, 1958, p. 47). Nonetheless, the Uniterm system was installed in a number of different special libraries and received both praise and condemnation from users. Morris did not install the system in the ORNL library; he had studied it thoroughly, but was unhappy with what he saw.

Unfortunately, just as the argument between these two innovative and bright leaders of the profession was beginning, it ended. Morris died on September 23, 1954, of lung cancer, at the age of 44. An editor of *American Documentation* lamented in a brief obituary: "That Jack Morris was only at the beginning of a promisingly brilliant career, makes his departure doubly tragic."

In the few short years that he was active in the profession, however, Morris made a substantial contribution to the field. The area in which he made the greatest contribution was his personal influence on the special librarians and documentalists that he came in contact with through professional associations, on-site visits to the ORNL library and by way of his extensive correspondence. His writings on subject analysis, though brief, give evidence of an excellent mind at work in applying the concepts of subject headings to the needs of scientific and technical libraries. In all aspects of his professional life Morris attempted to be a link between the best traditions and ideas of the general library profession and the innovations and developments of special librarians and documentalists. He was eminently successful in doing this during his time and the information profession at large was enriched by his efforts.

Biographical listings and obituaries — [Obituary]. "Jack Cassius Morris, 1911-1954." *American Documentation* 6:1 (January 1955); Randall, Gordon E. "Necrology: Jack Morris," *College & Research Libraries* 16: 105-6 (January 1955); *Who's Who in Library Service*, 1st ed. **Primary sources and archival materials** — Searches made for archival and manuscript collections relating to Morris have not been successful. The libraries of the Department of Energy at Oak Ridge, Tennessee, do not contain materials relating to his work there. And, even though Morris was an extensive correspondent, it has not been possible to locate any persons with a collection of his letters. Mrs. Morris informed the author that a fire a few years ago destroyed materials she might have had that reflected his life and work.

—ROBERT V. WILLIAMS

MUMFORD, LAWRENCE QUINCY (1903-1982)

Lawrence Quincy Mumford, 11th Librarian of Congress (1954-1974), was born on a farm near Ayden in Pitt County, North Carolina, on December 11, 1903. His father Jacob was a successful tobacco farmer who depended on a large family to help cultivate and harvest the crops. Jacob and his wife Emma also were determined that each of their children would have a good education, including college if possible. Young Quincy attended a one-room school in Hanrahan until he went to high school in Grifton, about three miles away.

There Mumford was an excellent student who became an outstanding debater and orator, both at Grifton High School and at Trinity College in Durham, which became Duke University while he was in residence as a student. He received his A.B. from Duke in 1925, graduating magna cum laude and earning membership in Phi Beta Kappa. He received an M.A. degree in English from Duke in 1928.

Mumford's library experience began at Duke, where as an undergraduate he worked as a student assistant in the Duke University Library. He accepted a full-time position in the library in 1926 when he began his graduate studies. His mentor was assistant Duke librarian Louis T. Ibbotsen, a recent graduate of Columbia University's School of Library Service. As a graduate student Mumford considered both teaching and librarianship as possible careers, but with Ibbotsen's encouragement, he enrolled in Columbia's School of Library Service in the fall of 1928. He worked part-time in the school's library while pursuing his B.S. degree in library science, which he received in 1929.

Mumford quickly made the transition from excellent student to excellent librarian. In the spring of 1929 he accepted an offer from Keyes D. Metcalf, who was in charge of the central building of the New York Public Library, to become a reference assistant. Twenty-five years later, during Mumford's confirmation hearing to become Librarian of Congress, Metcalf recalled:

> The quality of his work was such that, four years later when a general administrative assistant was needed in the office, Mumford was selected. Three years later when the largest and most complex division of the library, the catalog division, needed a new chief, he was chosen.... In both positions, Mr. Mumford's success was outstanding.

Metcalf also called Mumford "the best judge of people I have ever known."

L. Quincy Mumford served as executive assistant and chief of New York Public Library's Preparation Division from 1936 to 1943, then as executive assistant coordinator of the General Service Divisions from 1943 to 1945. Soon after he joined the New York Public Library staff, he met Permelia Catherine (Pam) Stevens, a children's librarian. They were married on October 4, 1930, and had one child, Kathryn. Permelia Mumford died in 1961 following a long illness. In 1969 Mumford married Betsy Perrin Fox.

An important interruption in Mumford's New York Public Library career occurred between September 1940 and August 1941. At the request of Librarian of Congress Archibald MacLeish, he was granted a leave of absence to reorganize and coordinate the processing services of the Library of Congress. Keyes Metcalf, by then director of the Harvard University Library, had recommended Mumford for the task. According to Metcalf, Mumford "did this difficult and intricate job with the most conspicuous success." Librarian MacLeish agreed, explaining in his 1941 annual report that Mumford had performed "a miracle in the Processing Department, where he has not only administered the reorganization of the divisions involved, but directed as well the renovation and improvement of many of the basic technical procedures."

Mumford served as assistant director of the Cleveland Public Library from 1945 to 1950 and as director from 1959 until he became Librarian of Congress. In Cleveland he expanded his own administrative experience and his knowledge of all phases of a large library's operations. He improved the Cleveland Public Library's financial status, skillfully dealing with city officials and the board of trustees. He also worked closely with the city's business and social leaders. Simultaneously, he became active and increasingly popular with his professional colleagues, serving as president of the Ohio Library Association (1947-1948) and chairing several important committees of the American Library Association between 1944 and 1953. He was elected president of the American Library Association for 1954-1955, and, while ALA president-elect, was nominated by President Dwight D. Eisenhower to become Librarian of Congress.

Mumford's predecessor, Luther H. Evans, had served as Librarian of Congress from 1945 to 1953, when he resigned to become director-general of UNESCO. Evans's relations with Congress were poor, and obviously a major task for the new Librarian was to restore Congressional confidence in its library. The Eisenhower administration felt that an early favorite for the job, Chief Assistant Librarian Verner W. Clapp, was tied too closely to former Librarian Evans. But Mumford's credentials were impeccable, and the Cleveland librarian had strong support from the Ohio congressional delegation and from the professional library community. Soon after his name was sent to the Senate by President Eisenhower on April 22, 1954, the *Washington Post* praised the nomination as "a merit selection" that deserved "the warmest public approbation." L. Quincy Mumford was confirmed by the Senate on July 29 and was sworn in and assumed his duties on September 1, two months after taking office as president of the American Library Association. He was the first, and remains the only, professionally trained librarian to become Librarian of Congress.

Before he was confirmed by the Senate, however, Mumford had to learn firsthand about Congressional dissatisfaction with the Library. In effect, he bore the brunt of Congressional displeasure with his predecessors, particularly Luther Evans. The tone was polite, but the nominee to be the eleventh Librarian of Congress never forgot the lesson: the Library of Congress belonged, first and foremost, to the Congress of the United States.

Mumford's indoctrination began three weeks after his nomination. At the Library's budget hearings on May 10, 1954, the chair of the House Subcommittee on Appropriations stopped the hearings and expressed his unhappiness with the Library's presentation. He requested that Mumford, the nominee who had not yet been confirmed, appear before the subcommittee on May 12. At this hearing Mumford heard, in detail, about Congressional unhappiness with the Library and its administrators. Moreover, he was told in no uncertain terms: "The new Librarian should be mindful that the Library is the instrument and the creature of Congress." At his own confirmation hearings, on July 26, 1954, Mumford heard more. "It is apparent that too often the Library seems to be submerged by its own good intentions," one congressman opined. "A stopping place—a final line—should be set beyond which its public services and those to the executive agencies cannot go. Indeed, a withdrawal of many of those services or their deemphasis appears to be in order." Mumford promised to be a full-time Librarian, to strengthen the Library's services to Congress, and to consider all of the questions raised by the Appropriations Committee and its staff. But his responses were sensible, and he stood his ground against a diminution of the Library's established national role, maintaining that the vast resources collected by the Library through the years should be available both to Congress and "to the constituents of Members of Congress—the people."

Mumford's first few years as Librarian were difficult, primarily because of the atmosphere of distrust he inherited. Congress continued to be wary of the Library's national activities, which the Librarian carefully explained and cautiously supported. Mumford, however, slowly gained

Congress's confidence. His budget requests increased annually, but they were conservative and never over-dramatized. He treated members of Congress with great respect, consulting frequently with individual members before making new requests. The Library's budget increased, as did its staff and the size of its collections. Further expansion was on the horizon: in 1958 Mumford submitted a proposal to the Architect of the Capitol for a third major Library of Congress building. The James Madison Memorial Building, located across Independence Avenue from the main Library building, was authorized in 1965. Construction was started in 1971 and the 2.5 million square foot structure was completed in 1980. The Madison Building is one of L. Quincy Mumford's major accomplishments. Like much that happened during the Mumford years, however, it is an accomplishment he shared with an important Congressional ally, Senator B. Everett Jordan from Mumford's home state of North Carolina. Senator Jordan, chair of the Joint Committee on the Library, was instrumental in gaining Congressional approval for the Madison Building's initial plans and appropriations.

While Mumford's cautious philosophy worked with Congress, it made some of his fellow librarians impatient. In particular, many university and research librarians felt the Library of Congress was not exercising enough national leadership. At the request of Senator Claiborne Pell of the Joint Library Committee, Director of the Harvard University Library Douglas W. Bryant prepared a memorandum in 1962 on "what the Library of Congress does and ought to do for the Government and the Nation generally." Bryant urged expansion of the Library's national activities and services. He also felt the Library should be recognized as the National Library and that "though it would be desirable, it is not essential to transfer the Library of Congress to the Executive (branch of government)."

Mumford decided to rebut the "Bryant memorandum," and his reply was inserted in the *Congressional Record* of October 2, 1962, by Senator Jordan. The Librarian strongly defended the Library's position in the legislative branch of government and opposed changing or altering the Library's name to reflect its national role: "The Library of Congress is a venerable institution, with a proud history, and to change its name would do unspeakable violence to tradition."

Mumford asserted that "on the question of being the national library the substance is more important than the form," and pointed out that, while fulfilling its responsibilities to the legislature, the Library of Congress also performed "more national functions than any other national library in the world."

The Bryant memorandum and Mumford's reply, both reprinted in the Library's 1962 annual report, stimulated a healthy debate—as Pell hoped it would. Mumford and his senior staff had prepared a forceful statement, one that signaled a new confidence and even aggressiveness on the part of the Library of Congress. Times had changed, and the atmosphere had improved. The Madison Building had been authorized, and promising new overseas acquisitions and cataloging programs were getting underway.

The expansion of the Library's overseas acquisitions and cataloging programs was a Mumford accomplishment built on initiatives taken by Librarian of Congress Evans in the postwar years. In 1958 the Library was authorized to acquire books by using U.S.-owned foreign currency under terms of the Agricultural Trade Development and Assistance Act of 1954 (Public Law 480). The first appropriation for this purpose was made in 1961, enabling the Library to establish acquisitions centers in New Delhi and Cairo to purchase publications and distribute them to research institutions around the United States. In 1965, Title II-C of the Higher Education Act authorized the creation of the National Program for Acquisitions and Cataloging (NPAC), greatly expanding the Library's foreign procurement program and inaugurating, for use by American libraries, a centralized cataloging system for foreign acquisitions. The goal was nothing less than to acquire and provide cataloging information for "all library materials currently published through the world of value to scholarship."

Other expansions of the Library's national role during the Mumford administration included: new automation efforts, particularly the beginning of the MARC (Machine-Readable Cataloging) system for distributing cataloging information in machine-readable form; the establishment of the Cataloging-in-Publication program to provide cataloging information within published books; inauguration of a preservation program intended to serve as the basis of a national preservation effort for books and other materials in library collections; the beginning of projects to publish important multi-volume bibliographic tools such as the *National Union Catalog of Manuscript Collections* and the *Pre-1956 National Union Catalog*; new cooperative arrangements with other federal libraries; the expansion of the National Books for the Blind program to include the physically handicapped.

The remarkable growth of the national services of the Library of Congress during the 1960s can be attributed to several factors, including greater support by the federal government for all library and educational activities, and increased support for the Library from organizations such as the Association of Research Libraries, the Council on Library Resources, Inc., and the American Library Association. The key, however, was increased confidence on the part of Congress in the Library, its programs, and its administration. This was Librarian Mumford's major accomplishment.

The Legislative Reorganization Act of 1970 also helped Mumford immensely. This measure redesignated the Library's Legislative Reference Service, the department which works directly for the Congress, as the Congressional Research Service (CRS). It also broadened the responsibilities of the Congressional Research Service and provided for an extensive and rapid expansion of its staff. Furthermore, it gave the CRS a new independence within the Library's administrative structure, stipulating that "the Librarian of Congress shall grant and accord to the Congressional Research Service complete research independence and the maximum practicable administrative independence consistent with these objectives." The Legislative Reorganization Act of 1970 helped Librarian Mumford by easing the pressure from Congress for priority services, for under the terms of the act, services to Congress would be performed by a department that itself had priority within the institution. There was a cost, however: a split between the Congressional Research Service and the rest of the Library of Congress that caused Mumford and his senior administrators considerable difficulties and strain.

The last years of the Mumford administration were troublesome for other reasons as well. Final approval from Congress for the use of the Madison Building as a Library of Congress building was not easy to obtain and did not occur until the spring of 1971; in the meantime, the Library's other two buildings became badly overcrowded. The Library was accused of "discrimination on racial grounds in recruitment, training, and promotion practices," and the American Library Association called for an investigation. Librarian Mumford, a shy man who dealt primarily with his department heads, became increasingly remote. He was rarely seen by staff members. His health was poor, but he requested, and President Richard M. Nixon approved, an extension of his tenure a year beyond the mandatory retirement age, allowing him to continue in office until December 31, 1974. But his health continued to deteriorate. He died in Washington, D.C., on August 15, 1982.

While the 20-year Mumford administration may have ended unhappily for the Librarian personally, his librarianship constitutes one of the most productive periods in the Library's history. He takes his place with Ainsworth Rand Spofford (1864-1897) and Herbert Putnam (1899-1939) as one of the three "expansionist" Librarians of Congress. Each was responsible for a new Library of Congress building and for the rapid growth of both legislative and national services. The growth of the Library during the Mumford administration was unprecedented. The annual appropriation increased tenfold between fiscal 1955 and 1975 from $9,400,000 to $96,696,000. The collections of the Library of Congress when Mumford took office in 1954 totaled 33,152,852 items and the staff numbered 1,564; collections in 1974 were 73,932,425 and the staff numbered 4,250. It was fitting that on December 13, 1982, he was permanently honored with the dedication of the L. Quincy Mumford Room, a large assembly hall, on the top floor of the Madison Building.

In retrospect, it is easy to see that in the heady days of the mid-1960s, the peak of the growth years during the Mumford administration, the Library of Congress probably promised too much. Mumford's insistence, in response to the Bryant memorandum, that the Library of Congress carried out more national library functions than most officially designated national libraries led to even more extravagant assertions. In 1967, at the conclusion of a meeting of the National Advisory Commission on Libraries, the Library of Congress was asked to provide a statement "of its view of itself as the National Library of the United States." The visionary response, prepared by the Library's staff and published in *Libraries at Large* (R. R. Bowker, 1969), again raised expectations among many librarians about what the Library of Congress might do for them in the future. But budgetary constraints of the early 1970s tempered this vision, and while the Library of Congress has continued to grow, it no longer makes the kinds of claims about national library leadership that were put forth by L. Quincy Mumford and his colleagues.

Those claims of the 1960s are, however, understandable. The achievements in acquisitions, cataloging, and collection development were remarkable, particularly in view of previous budget restrictions. Rutherford D. Rogers, deputy Librarian of Congress under Mumford and subsequently the director of libraries at Stanford and Yale universities, admired Mumford. Like Keyes Metcalf, Rogers believed Mumford's greatest strength was his ability to deal with people. Too few people outside the Library of Congress, Rogers felt, "realized the significance of Mumford's achievement" in reaching a rapprochement with Congress between 1954 and 1960. Once trust between Congress and its Librarian had been reestablished, the way was paved for a remarkable period of expansion and growth that brought the Library of Congress into the ranks of the world's foremost research institutions.

Biographical listings and obituaries—[Obituary]. *American Libraries* 13:563-5 (October 1982); [Obituary]. *Library Journal* 107:1805 (October 1, 1982); [Obituary]. *Wilson Library Bulletin* 57:15 (September 1982). **Books and articles about the biographee**—Powell, Benjamin E. "Lawrence Quincy Mumford: Twenty Years of Progress." *Quarterly Journal of the Library of Congress* 33:239-57 (July 1976); Rogers, Rutherford D. "LQM of LC." *Bulletin of Bibliography* 25:162-5 (September-December 1968); U.S. Congress, Senate. Committee on Rules and Administration. *Nomination of Lawrence Quincy Mumford to Be Librarian of Congress.* 83d Cong., 2d sess., 1954. **Primary sources and archival materials**—Mumford's official papers are in the Central Services Division, Library of Congress. A small collection of his personal papers is in the Manuscripts Division, Library of Congress.

—JOHN Y. COLE

NESBITT, ELIZABETH (1897-1977)

Elizabeth Nesbitt was born on April 15, 1897 in Northumberland, Pennsylvania, north of Harrisburg on the Susquehanna River. Her education began in a small private school run by two spinster sisters in Mt. Airy, a suburb of Philadelphia. From the sixth grade through high school, she attended the Germantown Friends School in Philadelphia. Her brother Robert has said that attendance at the weekly Quaker meeting was required as part of the curriculum, and Elizabeth became imbued with the Quaker philosophy, retaining that influence in later years, although she never abandoned her family's Presbyterianism. She was graduated from high school in 1914 at the top of her class, and in 1918 earned the A.B. degree from Goucher College for women, in Baltimore.

The Nesbitt family moved from Philadelphia to Pittsburgh in 1919. After a year of teaching at a private school in Pittsburgh's Shadyside district, Elizabeth became an assistant in the Central Boys and Girls Division of Carnegie Library of Pittsburgh and held this position while attending Carnegie Library School in the same building; she thought this an advantage for the school. In 1922 she received her certificate as a children's librarian and was appointed in that capacity at the Mt. Washington Branch, moving in 1924 to the East Liberty Branch. At the same time she became supervisor of storytelling for all the branches of Carnegie Library of Pittsburgh, in recognition of her outstanding ability as a storyteller.

In 1926 she left Pittsburgh briefly for Clarion State Teachers' College, north of Pittsburgh, serving there as librarian and lecturing in a New Jersey library school during the summers. By the fall of 1929 she had returned to Pittsburgh as a teacher in the Carnegie Library School. The school was now affiliated with Carnegie Institute of Technology so that students could earn bachelor's degrees in library science. Elizabeth Nesbitt earned this degree in 1931 and went on to earn an M.A. in English at the University of Pittsburgh in 1935. Meanwhile, she was promoted from instructor through successive steps until 1948, when she was named associate dean of the Carnegie Library School. She held this position until her retirement in 1962. During several summers she also taught in the library schools of Columbia University and the University of Illinois. When she retired in 1962, the Carnegie Library School moved to the University of Pittsburgh and became the Graduate School of Library and Information Sciences. The new dean, Harold Lancour, persuaded Nesbitt to continue for three years as lecturer in library work with children. He knew that "Miss Nesbitt" was the one person whose presence and influence would make the new status of the school acceptable to both students and alumni.

Elizabeth Nesbitt was known internationally as an authority on children's literature, as a teacher, a storyteller, and an administrator in library education. She also served as chair or as head of numerous important library associations and committees. All of these accomplishments are evidence of her ability to communicate ideas and to lead and cooperate effectively with other people. She was friendly, approachable, even-tempered, and cheerful. To a few friends, she was "Betty." But to most of those who knew her, friends and students alike, she was "Miss Nesbitt," a name spoken with admiration, love, even with veneration, bearing witness that her teaching, writing, and, above all, her example, had the power to change lives. Elizabeth Nesbitt was so reticent about her inmost thoughts and feelings that few, if any, even among her friends, could claim to know her intimately. She was a very private person, and so modest that her own family seldom heard of the honors that came to her until after the event, yet her name appeared in *Who's Who in America*, in numerous other biographical indexes, and in library publications covering noteworthy accomplishments of the library profession.

From 1921 onward, Elizabeth Nesbitt addressed audiences at major meetings of librarians and teachers, both in the United States and abroad. Many of these speeches were later published in leading periodicals concerned with education for librarianship and with principles of book selection. A few appeared in books along with essays by other writers. The Children's Library Association of ALA tried to persuade her to allow a collection of her essays to be published as a single volume, but in her view all of her work would have to be rewritten to bring it up-to-date; she felt unequal to the task. For this reason she is best remembered as co-author of *A Critical History of Children's Literature* (London: Macmillan, 1969), a landmark publication which has been recognized as a classic in its field.

Nesbitt's essays still retain their freshness and reflect the quality of her reading and thinking. They explain, in part, the impact she had on students and colleagues. For example, in *A Child Went Forth* (Pittsburgh: Carnegie Library School, 1940), she saw the present "machine age" as one that had brought material well-being, but a decrease in idealism, an increase in leisure time but no increase in ability to use leisure, more artificial recreation but less ability to entertain ourselves, more emphasis on education of the individual to think for himself or herself, but increased dependence on predigested thought, demand for more and better books for children but "apparent lessening of faith in the child's ability to appreciate these books." The two great democratic institutions, the public school and the public library, should mean more than acquisition of facts, she argued. Facts should lead to thought and to comprehension of the best traditions of the past, the meaning of the present, the ideal of the future. The public library, offering voluntary education for a lifetime, should feed the child's hunger to find meaning in life. Mediocre books could not answer this need.

In 1941, as America hovered on the brink of war, Elizabeth Nesbitt spoke on "Tomorrow's Shrines of True Virtue," expanding on the theme of the damage done by the welter of mediocre books flooding the market. If children were "the hope of a better world" and literature the fullest expression of ideas underlying the democratic principle, it followed that the foundation for creative reading and constructive thinking must be laid in the elementary grades. Library funds were being curtailed, but this could have beneficial results if it led to more careful and discriminating book selection.

"Storytelling—The Creative Way," a speech given at the Detroit Storytelling Festival in 1964, contradicted the widely held theory that children should read only books that they could understand completely. Nesbitt saw storytelling as a "creative way" to lead young people to apprehend the meanings in books of "true greatness." The interpretive power of storytelling evoked a response from an audience that was in itself an education. Storytelling, Elizabeth Nesbitt said, "penetrates the mind and leaves an indelible impression."

The effect of the stories she told was enhanced by her ability to immerse herself in the telling, and so to carry her audience with her. Her appearance and her voice were not overly dramatic, but compelling, allowing the depth and clarity of her intellect and her intense sincerity to shine through. Her face became even more attractive as age brought out character. Those who knew her at the peak of her career remember her restraint, her conservative dress, her white hair, her quiet, self-controlled but cheerful manner; the total effect added to her power to convince her audience of ultimate truths through storytelling.

Shortly before her retirement she told a series of stories about the heroes of myth and legend on Pittsburgh's educational television station; even the artificial barrier of the electronic medium did not totally block the effect of her telling, but one sensed that she preferred a live audience.

Material from Elizabeth Nesbitt's courses taught in the Library School became the basis for her section in *A Critical History of Children's Literature*. The section, titled "A Rightful Heritage," covered the period 1880-1920, which Nesbitt judged to be a "golden age" in children's literature. This was the time of Howard Pyle, Robert Louis Stevenson, Rudyard Kipling, Kenneth Grahame, Beatrix Potter, and others of like quality. Nesbitt's name, along with the other coauthors (Cornelia Meigs, Anne Thaxter Eaton, and Ruth Hill Viguers) came to the fore when the book appeared. Nesbitt also published *Howard Pyle* (London: Bodley Head, 1966). Here she identified Pyle as "the first truly great American author and illustrator of children's books." The claim has not been disputed.

Elizabeth Nesbitt's speaking, writing, and teaching did not exhaust her energies. Her many contributions to the American Library Association included leadership and membership in the Children's Library Association, the Division of Libraries for Children and Young People, the Children's Services Division, and the Library Education Division. She also belonged to the American Association of Library Schools and the Pennsylvania Library Association. She served as a member of the ALA Executive Board and represented ALA at the International Federation of Library Associations Conference in Sweden in 1960. In 1968 she spoke at a symposium in Frankfurt, West Germany, on training of children's librarians in the United States. She was chair of the Newbery-Caldecott Committee in 1958 when Robert McCloskey was nominated to win the Caldecott Award for a second time. Nesbitt made the landmark decision, in cooperation with award sponsor Frederick Melcher, that an artist could win twice. In every instance, as her colleagues have attested, her presence promoted effective, harmonious action. When Elva S. Smith retired as head of the Children's Room at Carnegie Library of Pittsburgh, the staff unanimously petitioned Ralph Munn, director of the library, to appoint Nesbitt to this position, and he agreed.

Nesbitt received numerous awards and honors. In 1955 she was listed as one of Pittsburgh's "Ten Women of Talent." In 1958 the Governor of Pennsylvania named her a Distinguished Daughter of Pennsylvania. She was the first woman to receive the Pennsylvania Library Association's Distinguished Service Award (1962), and was the recipient of the Beta Phi Mu Award for Distinguished Service to Education for Librarianship. The 1965 Clarence Day Award was given to her by the American Library Association for "serving librarianship with distinction at home and abroad," the citation also noting that her recent writings continued "the notable contribution to the history and appreciation of children's literature made over many years." In 1976 a room housing an invaluable historical collection of children's books in the Graduate School of Library and Information Sciences at the University of Pittsburgh was named in her honor. A plaque next to the entrance door reads: "The Elizabeth Nesbitt Room—A Goodly Heritage." One of the special collections in the room is the library of children's books given by Clifton Fadiman. This would no doubt have delighted Nesbitt, who so greatly admired his literary judgment, but she did not live long enough to know about that gift. Her last public speech was on October 29, 1976, when she returned to Pittsburgh for the dedication of the room. After her retirement in 1965 she had lived in Brigantine, New Jersey, near her brother Robert. She died in Atlantic City on August 17, 1977 of cancer.

Biographical listings and obituaries—[Obituary]. (Pittsburgh) *Post Gazette*, August 20, 1977; [Obituary]. (Atlantic City) *Press*, August 20, 1977; [Obituary]. (Pittsburgh) *Press*, August 20, 1977; [Obituary]. *University of Pittsburgh Carnegie Schools Alumni Association Newsletter* 2:2 (Autumn 1977); *Who's Who in America* 32 (1962); *Who's Who in Library Service*, 1st, 2nd, 3rd eds. **Books and articles about the biographee**—"ALA Awards and Citations for 1965." *Library Journal* 90: 3206 (August 1965); "ALA Awards, Citations and Scholarships for 1965." *Library of Congress Information Bulletin* 24:416 (August 2, 1965); "Elizabeth Nesbitt Hailed as Honored Guest" and "The Elizabeth Nesbitt Room: 'A Goodly Heritage'." *University of Pittsburgh Carnegie Library Schools Alumni Association Newsletter* 1:1-3 (1976); "Elizabeth Nesbitt Named a Distinguished Daughter of Pennsylvania." *Pennsylvania Library Association Bulletin* 14:9 (Fall 1958); "Ex-Library Dean at Tech Honored." (Pittsburgh) *Press*, July 10, 1965; Foster, Joan, ed. *Reader in Children's Librarianship* (Englewood, Colo.: Information Handling

Services, 1978); Hodges, Margaret. *Elizabeth Nesbitt 1897-1977*. Pittsburgh: School of Library and Information Science, University of Pittsburgh, 1987; Hodges, Margaret. "A Laying on of Hands." *Catholic Library World* 47:4-11 (July-August 1975); Kelly, Marion. "Look for a Lovely Thing." *Pennsylvania Library Association Bulletin* 18:7-8 (November 1962); Leslie, Marion. "Work on Children's Books Wins Citation." (Pittsburgh) *Post Gazette*, October 11, 1958; "1965 American Library Association Award Winners." *American Library Association Bulletin* 59:659 (July 1965). **Primary sources and archival materials**—Materials by and about Elizabeth Nesbitt are held in the Elizabeth Nesbitt Room, Graduate School of Library and Information Sciences, University of Pittsburgh. The material includes a full set of class notes taken by Marion M. Haushalter from courses Nesbitt taught at Carnegie Library School.

—MARGARET HODGES

OBOLER, ELI MARTIN (1915-1983)

Eli Martin Oboler is perhaps best known as the idiosyncratic doyen of the intellectual freedom movement in the 1960s and 1970s. To understand Oboler, however, one must begin with his roots. He was born in Chicago on September 26, 1915 into a middle-class Jewish family, headed by his optometrist father, Leo, and his mother Clara. The intellectual fervor of Chicago's Jewish community in the 1920s and 1930s must have affected him, as did the economic conditions of the Great Depression. His 1941 bachelor's degree from the University of Chicago, for example, was delayed until well into his twenty-fifth year, but soon after that he earned a bachelor's degree in library science in 1942 from Columbia University in New York City. The war then intervened. He served as assistant chief of the lend-lease expediting branch in Washington, D.C., from 1942 to 1943, before being called to full-time duty in the U.S. Army in the Canal Zone for the rest of the conflict.

After the war, he returned to the University of Chicago as head of the library's reserve room, yet also managed to pursue graduate work on a part-time basis there until 1949. It was in Chicago that his library career began to blossom. By 1947, Oboler was appointed to direct the University's College Library. In that same year, he began a two-year involvement as consultant to the fledgling Great Books Foundation. This interest in great literature would continue as another major theme throughout his life. It resulted in numerous articles, television appearances, and a twenty-seven year run for his own weekly radio commentary, "Books and You" in Pocatello, Idaho.

Oboler was drawn to Pocatello in 1949 as the new Head Librarian at Idaho State University, a post he held for some thirty-one years until his 1980 retirement. There he was known as a stringent and effective manager. During his tenure, the library increased its holdings from a mere 30,000 to over 300,000 volumes. He twice supervised the creation of new buildings to house the expanding collections. His identification with the Idaho State University library was so complete that the second of those library buildings was named for him on his retirement.

Oboler's private and public life reflected an eclectic nature. He married Marcia Lois Wolf, an art teacher, during the Depression and before earning his degrees. Over the years, the couple had two children—Leon David and Carol Judy. In addition to family matters and great books, Oboler's avocational interests long centered on philately and classical music. Beyond his radio work, the journalistic side of Oboler helped produce more than two hundred columns for the *Idaho State Journal*. His media interests led to avid support and frequent chairmanships of the Pocatello Film Festival. On the political side, Oboler served as a member of the Pocatello Chamber of Commerce from 1966 to 1968 and received a commendation from the Mayor's Committee on Employment of Handicapped in 1968. His fraternal interests included the Kiwanis, where he was a member of the board of directors from 1972 to 1974, and B'nai B'rith, where he was elected president of the city branch from 1951 to 1953.

His professional energy and activities could hardly be contained in Pocatello. He very quickly rose to prominence in the state, the Pacific Northwest, and the entire nation. From 1950 to 1953, Oboler served as president of the Idaho Library Association, and then in 1968 and again in 1973, as chair of the Idaho Council of State Academic Librarians. In 1974, his various efforts earned him the honor of Idaho Librarian of the Year. At the regional level, he served as president of the Pacific Northwest Library Association in 1955-1956 and held a place on the advisory board of the Pacific Northwest Regional Health Sciences Laboratory from 1968 to 1977. He also was a lecturer at Utah State University in 1960 and 1966 and the University of Washington in 1975. On the national scene, he was elected to the council of the American Library Association between 1954 and 1959 and again from 1977 to 1981. In addition to numerous ALA committee assignments, Oboler was most active with the Intellectual Freedom Round Table (IFRT), including a stint as chair (1980-1981), and was a founding member of the Freedom to Read Foundation, its vice-president from 1979 to 1980, and a board member for two terms (1971-1975).

The workaholic image is confirmed by a look at his professional writings. He wrote seven books, over 200 articles, and more than 500 book reviews. He also served as editor of the *Idaho Librarian* (1950-1954 and 1957-1958), *Temple Topics* (1961-1962), and *PNLA Quarterly* (1958-1967). He received the 1964 ALA and H. W. Wilson library periodical award for his efforts on the latter. Oboler was also recognized by the 1976 Robert B. Downs Award for Intellectual Freedom and the posthumous creation of the Eli M. Oboler award by the IFRT.

The Downs and Oboler Awards point to Oboler's major thrust and key legacy to the profession—his persistent focus on the role of librarians in promoting intellectual freedom and Jeffersonian democracy. He was one of the first librarians to discuss openly a range of issues from segregation to feminism. He delighted in debate and controversy, as well as in his own erudition. Unfortunately, his pedantic penchant to play the devil's advocate clouded a full understanding of his personal philosophy for some contemporaries. In general, however, he appeared as a strict constructionist or "purist" for whom the ideal of intellectual freedom must dominate over any intervening social concerns. In his own words, "I cling to the obviously outdated and ridiculously old-fashioned notion that intellectual honesty is as important as, or perhaps more important than, timeliness."

It is difficult to capture the essence of an individual who delighted in the sobriquets "loyal gadfly" and "unconventional academic librarian." How can one characterize someone whom informants describe as both pest and prophet in the same sentence? But Oboler probably would have relished and perhaps even revelled in this biographer's dilemma. As an obituary recording his June 15, 1983, death in Idaho in the *Newsletter on Intellectual Freedom* stressed:

In his day, Eli Oboler rudely pricked more than a few forgetful consciences, ruffled the feathers of more than his share of smug politicians and complacent professionals. He could, at times, irritate his friends as much as he did his enemies, but that, after all, was what we loved and needed him for.

Biographical listings and obituaries—"Eli M. Oboler." *College & Research Libraries* 41:352 (December 1980); "Eli M. Oboler." *Newsletter on Intellectual Freedom* 25:105 (July 1976); [Obituary]. *ALA Yearbook 1983* (1984); [Obituary]. "Eli M. Oboler." *Library Journal* 108:1421 (August 1983); [Obituary]. "Eli M. Oboler." *Newsletter on Intellectual Freedom* 32:131, 170-1; *Who's Who in Library and Information Services* (1982). **Books and articles by the biographee**—*Defending Intellectual Freedom: The Library and the Censor.* Westport, Conn.: Greenwood Press, 1980; *The Fear of the Word: Censorship and Sex.* Metuchen, N.J.: Scarecrow Press, 1974; *Ideas and the University Library: Essays of an Unorthodox Academic Librarian.* Westport, Conn.: Greenwood Press, 1977; *To Free the Mind: Libraries, Technology, and Intellectual Freedom.* Foreword by Judith E. Krug. Littleton, Colo.: Libraries Unlimited, 1983. **Primary sources and archival materials**—Oboler's official papers are at Idaho State University in Pocatello, Idaho.

—FREDERICK J. STIELOW

POWELL, BENJAMIN EDWARD (1905-1981)

Benjamin Edward Powell, library administrator and teacher, was born to Willis Warren and Beatrice Franklin Powell on August 28, 1905, the first of their six children. His father was a lumberman, farmer, and county commissioner for many years in Gates County, North Carolina. The Powell family had settled in that eastern county nearly 200 years earlier.

Powell received most of his elementary education in nearby Sunbury and was graduated from Sunbury High School in 1922. That fall he entered Trinity College in Durham, North Carolina, with the hope of becoming a lawyer. He had no desire for the life of hard labor he had known since he was a child.

During his first two years at Trinity College, Powell waited on tables in a student boarding house for half of his board. He took a job in the college library as a student assistant in his junior year. In addition to working part-time during all of his four undergraduate years, he found time to play class baseball and football and earn a letter in track. He was a member of the Columbian Literary Society and the Sandfiddlers and "D" clubs.

Shortly after James Buchanan Duke gave millions of dollars to Trinity College on December 11, 1924, Trinity changed its name to Duke University. Thus Powell was graduated in 1926 from Duke University with a major in history. The Duke assistant librarian, Louis Tappe Ibbotsen, asked him to take a full-time position in the library during summer school that year, so he continued to work there for most of the summer.

In order to pay off his student loans, Powell became a teacher and coach of athletics at Bethel High School in Pitt County, North Carolina (1926-1927). He then accepted an invitation to return to a full-time position in the Duke University Library. Soon he became head of the circulation department, where he remained until 1929 when he went to Columbia University to study library science. While at Columbia he worked part-time in the reference department of the New York Public Library. He received his B.S. degree in library science in 1930 and returned to Duke to head both the circulation and reference departments.

Much later in life, Powell reflected on the reasons he had chosen librarianship as a career. He always had "an affinity for books," he said, "and liked to be around them." In his memoirs he also gave Ibbotsen some credit for his choosing the career he did. He said Ibbotsen had talked with him a great deal during the summer of 1926 about taking a degree in librarianship and becoming a librarian.

Powell's planning, organizational, and supervisory skills were all put to the test soon after his return to Duke in 1930. He was put in charge of moving the holdings from the library on the university's East Campus that were to go to the new General Library on its West Campus. According to one of his colleagues at that time, the move was a well-planned and orderly one.

Taking a leave of absence from the Duke University Library in 1934-1935, Powell attended the Graduate Library School at the University of Chicago. Returning to Duke in 1935, he remained there only two years before becoming acting librarian at the University of Missouri at age thirty-one. The following year he was appointed head librarian. On March 6, 1940, he married Betsy Graves of Scottsbluff, Nebraska. The couple had one daughter. After receiving a Ph.D. degree in library science from Chicago in 1946, Powell returned to Duke as university librarian, with professorial rank.

At Duke much of Powell's time and energy went into trying to provide adequate library accommodations and services for the university's students, faculty, and visiting scholars. He had fine rapport with the faculty, many of whom he counted among his friends. He encouraged them and alumni to participate in the development of the library's resources, and he was one of the staunchest supporters of the Friends of the Library. The atmosphere he nurtured within the library was one of goodwill and friendliness between it and all of its constituencies. He was aided in this endeavor by a stable, dedicated, and loyal staff.

During his administration, Powell succeeded in getting the libraries under his jurisdiction greatly expanded. The main library was enlarged twice, more than tripling the space of the original building. Major expansions were also made in the Divinity School Library and the departmental libraries. The staff more than tripled in number, and the holdings in volumes grew from around 875,000 in 1946 to nearly three million in 1975. The manuscript collection increased during that period from about 975,000 items to over 4.5 million items. A number of notable special collections were acquired, and several endowment funds were established to support the acquisition of research materials. At the time of Powell's retirement, the Library Endowment Fund, upon the recommendations of his staff, was renamed the Benjamin Edward Powell Library Endowment Fund. Powell also oversaw the establishment of the Duke University Archives in 1972.

Since he was a quiet, modest man, few subordinates fully comprehended how hard Powell worked on the daily operations of the libraries, on fund-raising, on building plans, and for his profession and community. With his staff he was formal and reserved, but he always strove to be fair minded, and was humane even when he had to be firm. He knew how to delegate authority, and trusted staff members to carry out their responsibilities without interference.

After integration became a university-wide policy in the late 1960s, Powell began to recruit blacks into the Perkins Library system. East Asians and Hispanics had been on its staff for many years. His advertisements of positions in library journals and his inquiries to library schools across the country in search of qualified black candidates stated that Duke was an equal-opportunity employer. It proved to be difficult, though, to find black professional librarians who were qualified to work in a university or college and who were willing to live in the South.

Powell inherited a predominantly female staff when he returned to Duke in 1946, and he made many promotions within the system. The majority of his staff, including heads of departments and branch libraries, continued to be women. His assistant university librarians, however, were men, except during the latter years of his administration, when there were two with that title, a woman and a man.

Most of Powell's career preceded the push by the academic library community for participative library management and for academic and/or faculty status. Although his style of management remained more hierarchical than collegial, he did support his staff in its successful effort to gain academic status in the university in 1973. He also supported the establishment of the Council of the Supporting Staff in 1971, and of the Librarians Assembly in 1973. An honest, kind, and friendly person who smiled easily, Powell was also a handsome and well-dressed man who radiated a sense of self-confidence but never arrogance.

A cautious, steady helmsman, operating within the confines of a tight budget, Powell did not rush to embrace automated national bibliographic networks. In 1966 he did, however, appoint a supervisor of library data processing applications. Two years later a study was made and goals were set in anticipation of the creation of a completely automated system. In addition, in 1968-1969 the computerization of serials, acquisition purchasing records, and the library's accounting system began. In 1974 the online ordering system became operational, and the next year a computerized microfiche of serials titles was produced. Although he recognized that library automation was here to stay, Powell remained primarily a bookman to the end.

He remained university librarian at Duke until he retired on August 31, 1975. For several semesters during those years he also taught a course in the theory of library administration in the School of Library Science at the nearby University of North Carolina at Chapel Hill. One of his students later wrote that his classroom demeanor was "relaxed, and the droll wit that his friends and colleagues knew so well came through time and again." As a practicing administrator, she said, he made theory come alive by conveying a "sense of the realities of library life," and added "special meaning and sparkle" to his lectures by telling his students how things were being done in the Duke and University of North Carolina libraries.

In addition to heading the libraries of two universities and teaching library administration, Powell made numerous other contributions to the library profession on local, state, and national boards and committees; as president of several library associations; as an author; and as a library consultant to college and university libraries and various agencies of the U.S. government.

While at the University of Missouri, Powell served as president of the Missouri Library Association (1938-1939). He was secretary of the Association of College and Research Libraries from 1940 to 1944, chair of its nomination committee, 1944-1945, director, 1946-1947, and president, 1948-1949. In 1947-1948 he chaired the Cooperative Committee on Library Building Plans, comprising librarians, architects, engineers, trustees, administrators, and faculty members. Fellow committee member Julian P. Boyd, librarian of Princeton, called Powell "a tower of strength and a voice of good common sense" during the working of that committee. Boyd added that the Committee had a profound influence on the construction of a number of post-World War II libraries erected at major universities, including the major addition to Duke's General Library. That addition was completed in 1969, and the library was renamed in honor of William Robertson Perkins, for many years the legal counselor of James B. Duke.

Powell served on the executive board of the Southeastern Library Association from 1950 to 1954 and was its acting chair in 1951-1952. He was a member of the executive board of the North Carolina Library Association from 1952 to 1954. Between 1950 and 1963 he chaired six committees of the American Library Association, was on its executive board from 1956 to 1961, and served as its president, 1959-1960. The title of his inaugural address, delivered on June 26, 1959 at the annual conference of ALA in Washington, D.C., was "A

Help and Ornament Thereunto." He spoke of the professional responsibilities of librarians, the attitudes they should have toward their work, and the challenges before them. The theme of ALA for 1959-1960, he announced, would be "Breaking Barriers."

During his presidency of ALA, Powell shared presiding duties in Montreal (June 19-24, 1960) with the president of the Canadian Library Association at the first joint meeting of the two organizations.

Writing did not come easy for Powell; neither was he noted as an innovative thinker. His published writings were limited to articles and lectures relating to librarianship. They appeared in twenty-four journals and other publications, including the *ALA Bulletin, College & Research Libraries, Missouri Library Association Quarterly, Southeastern Librarian, University of Tennessee Library Lectures, 1958-1960,* and *Louisiana State University Library Lectures, January 1971-March 1972.*

In 1963, Powell and thirteen other American librarians were invited to visit the Federal Republic of Germany for a four-week tour. The purpose of the trip, according to Powell, "was to afford them an opportunity to visit libraries, library schools, departments of education, antiquarian book dealers and publishers, and to discuss such topics as the acquisition, preservation, and use of books, professional and technical education, the responsibility of the state for libraries and the role of the school and city libraries in formal education." In September 1964, he and other members of the Board of Directors of the Association of Research Libraries attended a meeting in Hull, England, of the Standing Committee on National and University Libraries of Great Britain.

A civic-minded person, Powell's endeavors for his city and county, and his character and personality led to his becoming a highly esteemed citizen. He was a loyal Rotarian, serving as president of the Durham Rotary Club in 1953-1954, and he served on several civic boards. His most lasting contribution to Durham and Durham County was his service on the joint library board of trustees of those two governmental units from 1961 until his death in 1981, and as its chair from 1962 until he died. During those years the trustees, after two failures, succeeded in getting a bond issue passed in 1976 for the construction of a $3 million library within the city of Durham, to be called the Durham County Library. From the beginning Powell was involved in the planning of the building, as he had been in getting it funded. Although in failing health, he spoke at its dedication on October 5, 1980.

Also during Powell's tenure on the Durham City-County Library Board of Trustees, the county's separate white and black library systems and board were united. Moreover, for the first time the Durham County Board of Commissioners assumed all monetary and administrative responsibility for the library to serve both the city and county of Durham.

Two things that Powell never mastered were penmanship and public speaking. His handwriting was a challenge to his staff, and he communicated best to small groups such as meetings of his department heads and to individuals. He died of cancer at age 75 on March 11, 1981.

Biographical listings and obituaries—*ALA Bulletin* 53:685-8 (September 1959); *Biographical Directory of Librarians in the United States and Canada,* 5th ed.; Breedlove, Joseph Penn. *Duke University Library, 1840-1940.* Durham, N.C., The Friends of the Duke University Library, 1955; "In Memorium. Benjamin Edward Powell, 1905-1981." *Duke University Newsletter* 26 (April 1981); *Library Link. Duke University Libraries. In Honor of Benjamin Edward Powell, University Librarian, 1946-1975* (1975); [Obituary]. *College & Research Libraries News* 42:187 (June 1981); [Obituary]. *Durham Morning Herald* and *Durham Sun*, March 12-14, 1981; *Who's Who in Library Service*, 1st, 2nd, 3rd, 4th eds. **Books and articles by the biographee**—"Collection Development in Southeastern Libraries since 1948." *Southeastern Librarian* 24:59-67 (Winter 1975); "Growth of an Academic Library: Duke University." *North Carolina Libraries* 17:102-6 (Fall 1967); "Research, Resources and Librarianship in the Southeast." *North Carolina Libraries* 17:84-6ff (Spring 1959); "Southern University Libraries during the Civil War." *Wilson Library Bulletin* 31:250-4ff (November 1956). **Primary sources and archival materials**—Librarians Assembly Minutes, Duke University Archives, Durham, N.C. Minutes of the Board of Trustees of the Durham County Library, 1961-1981, Durham County Library, Durham, N.C. "Ben Powell's Memoirs" (n.d.), Biographical File, Duke University Archives. Benjamin Edward Powell Papers, Duke University Archives.

—MATTIE U. RUSSELL

PRICE, DEREK de SOLLA (1922-1983)

Derek de Solla Price was born Derek John Price on January 22, 1922, in Leyton, a suburb of London, England. In 1950, in response to his family's urging, he substituted "de Solla," his mother's maiden name, for John. His father, Philip, a tailor and outfitter, was descended from Ashkenazi Jews from what is now Poland; his mother, Fanny de Solla, a singer, was descended from Sephardic Jews from Spain.

Price's early education was in the local schools of Leyton and environs. His early inclinations toward mathematics and science were either the result or the cause of a youthful addiction to works of science fiction. In many respects his lifework was given to explorations of the role of imagination in the evolution of science and technology.

In 1938, at the age of 16, Price became a laboratory assistant in physics at the South West Essex Technical College under a work-study arrangement similar to the cooperative programs of Antioch and Northeastern Universities in the United States. He received an external (nonresident) bachelor's degree in physics and mathematics with first honors from the University of London in 1942, and was immediately recruited for wartime research in the optics of hot and molten metals at the South West Essex Technical College. Because of wartime personnel shortages, he was also pressed into service as a teacher of a variety of adult education evening courses and armed forces training programs. Learning science while (and by) teaching it, Price pursued thesis research and earned an external Ph.D. in experimental physics from the University of London in 1946.

Following a brief period of research in physics and mathematics (three published papers and a patent for an emissivity-correcting optical pyrometer), Price came to the United States in 1946 under a Commonwealth Fund fellowship. He worked for a year at Princeton University in theoretical physics, returning to Europe in 1947 and marrying Ellen Hjorth of Denmark, with whom he had two sons and a daughter.

In 1948, Price accepted a three-year appointment to teach applied mathematics at what is now the University of Singapore. Almost simultaneous with Price's arrival at the university was its acquisition of a complete set of the *Philosophical Transactions of the Royal Society*. Pending construction of a library to house these rare and valuable volumes, Price volunteered to house them in his living quarters. This circumstance had two extremely important results: first, by reading through the *Philosophical Transactions* from 1665 to 1850, he became keenly sensitive to the evolutionary nature and the historical aspects of science and technology; second, studying the numbers of papers in the various volumes of the *Transactions*, he found that they increased approximately exponentially. This gave rise to his theory of the exponential growth of scientific literature, which he submitted in a paper to the VIth International Congress on the History of Science in Amsterdam in 1950.

Also while at the University of Singapore, Price made the acquaintance of historian C. Northcote Parkinson, the postulator (or perpetrator) of Parkinson's Law. He tutored Parkinson in the significance and workings of the mathematics of exponential growth, upon which Parkinson leaned heavily in rationalizing his Law.

Upon finishing his three-year appointment in Singapore, Price returned to England in 1950, a convert to the research potential of the historical aspects of science and technology. After being turned down by the University of London, which apparently failed to see this research potential, he was accepted at Cambridge University as a candidate for a second doctorate, in the history of science. While at Cambridge pursuing his thesis topic, the history of instrumentation, he worked under Sir Lawrence Bragg in helping to reorganize the Archive and Museum of the renowned Cavendish Laboratory. Price also served as honorary curator of the Shipple Museum of Antique Scientific Instruments, which aided him in his thesis pursuits and fueled his long-held enthusiasm for scientific instrumentation and apparati. Related to this enthusiasm and his time in Singapore was his collaboration with Joseph Needham and Wang Ling in a book on the history of medieval Chinese clocks, entitled *Heavenly Clockwork: The Great Astronomical Clocks of China* (Cambridge: Cambridge University Press, 1960).

Further indication of Price's bibliophilic proclivities, or perhaps an impetus for them, was his chance discovery during his Cambridge period of a Middle English manuscript on a planetary calculating device, which he identified as a companion to Geoffrey Chaucer's 1391 *Treatise on the Astrolabe*. This manuscript proved to be the only existing sample of Chaucer's handwriting of significant length. Excited by this discovery, Price decided to make it the basis for his second thesis.

Completing his second doctorate in 1954, Price stayed on at Cambridge doing research in the history of science and technology until 1956. But despite growing fame as a physicist, mathematician, scientific and technical historian, and rare manuscript specialist, *inter alia*, he was unable to obtain a suitable permanent post. In 1957, he accepted a consultancy in the history of physics and astronomy at the Smithsonian Institution in the United States to help plan the American Museum of Natural History. This was followed by a two-year stint as a Donaldson Fellow of the Institute for Advanced Studies at Princeton University, where he pursued his interests in the history of science and technology, scientific instrumentation, and exponential-growth phenomena.

While at the Institute for Advanced Studies, Price studied and lectured on the Antikythera mechanism, dating from the first century B.C., which was credited as being the earliest known manmade instrument, but which could not be related to any specific writing or other instrumentation. In his next work location, at Yale University, he probed the Antikythera puzzle further by means of the newly available gamma-radiography, which helped establish the presence of gear wheels beneath the surface of the instrument. One of these wheels proved to be a differential gear, a mechanical development theretofore thought to be more recent than 1 B.C.

In 1959, upon completion of his two years at the Institute for Advanced Studies, Price was invited to lecture at Yale University; shortly thereafter he was appointed to a professorship in the history of science. In 1961, he was appointed chair of a new department which encompassed the histories of science, technology, and medicine. He was also named Avalon Professor of History of Science. His prospectus for the new department, and for his personal goals in the history of science, was published in 1961 as *Science since Babylon* (New Haven, Conn.: Yale University Press), a seminal work which helped to codify not only the progressivity of science and technology but also the causal relationships among scientific and technical disciplines and between pure and applied science.

Presented originally as five public lectures at the Sterling Memorial Library at Yale, the purposes of *Science since Babylon* were, in Price's words, "[to show] humanists that our new discipline might make an interesting neighbor of their own ..., to show scientists that we ought to be able to talk about science with as much scholarly right as other humanists receive ..., [and to show educators] that this subject was the missing bridge that would allow the good liberal education to include some mention of science [without] watering down science for humanistic babes or dishing up Greek sculpture in the hope of rearing cultivated scientists."

Perhaps most germane to an interested library community is the fifth chapter (and lecture) of *Science since Babylon*, "Diseases of Science." Here Price reviewed and enlarged upon the exponential growth of the literature of science and related it to the increase in the number of abstracting and indexing services. He also related exponential growth to his discovery of the reemergence of "invisible colleges," first postulated by Robert Boyle in the seventeenth century. Invisible colleges serve as interpersonal media for identifying and communicating with one's disciplinary and vocational peers to keep current, as sources of inspiration, and to cope with the increasing breadth and depth of scientific information sources.

Price also predicted or advanced the notion of relating fields of scholarly activity via interactive communication patterns. He suggested that, just as invisible colleges are products of common interests or common response to specific data and ideas, so kinds and strengths of relationships within and among disciplinary literatures can be identified and measured via their mode and degree of citation of one another. In a very strong sense, Price was the father (certainly *one* of the fathers) of what is now known and pursued as bibliometrics, which began as "reference-count" studies to help evaluate library holdings and to guide acquisition policies, and which are now used, among other purposes, for qualitative and quantitative analyses of intra- and interdisciplinary trends and relationships as planning and policy determinants. He discussed his ideas on the subject in an article entitled "A General Theory of Bibliometric and Other Cumulative Advantage Processes," which appeared in the September 1976 issue of the *Journal of the American Society for Information Science.*

The perception of Price as a prophet of bibliometrics is supported in the foreword to a posthumous and expanded version of a second book by him entitled *Little Science, Big Science ... and Beyond* (New York: Columbia University Press, 1986). In this foreword Robert K. Merton and

Eugene Garfield recognized Price as follows: "we can hardly doubt that with this book and the papers which followed it—nine included in this new edition—Derek John de Solla Price [sic] takes his place as the father of *Scientometrics*" (author's emphasis). Scientometrics may be defined as bibliometrics as applied to scientific literature.

Interestingly, as Price pointed out in the original *Little Science, Big Science* (1963) and its successor, the *Philosophical Transactions* and other scientific journals were instituted to help the casual but interested reader (the informed layperson of the day) to keep apprised without "the [theretofore mandatory] network of personal correspondence, private rumor, and browsing in Europe's bookstores." Ironically, the early journals were established to serve as substitutes for expensive and hard-to-come-by books and for invisible colleges, which were equally cumbersome, given the slowness of communication during the seventeenth century and until fairly recently. And these seminal journals did in fact serve their intended purposes laudably, until the second half of the twentieth century, when their sheer bulk and ubiquity again forced increasing reliance on invisible colleges, now traced and documented by Price and others via co-citation analysis, among other techniques.

The following chapter titles from *Little Science, Big Science ... and Beyond* provide important insights to Price's contributions: "Prologue to a Science of Science"; "Galton [a classical scientific measurer] Revisited"; "Invisible Colleges and the Affluent Scientific Commuter"; "Political Strategy for Big Scientists"; "Networks of Scientific Papers"; "Collaboration in an Invisible College"; "Measuring the Size of Science"; "Citation Measures of Hard Science, Soft Science, Technology, and Nonscience: Some Statistical Results of the Numbers of Authors in the States of the United States and the Nations of the World"; "Studies in Scientometrics, Part 1: Transcience and Continuance in Scientific Authorship"; "Studies in Scientometrics, Part 2: The Relation between Source Author and Cited Matter Populations"; "On Sealing Wax and String: A Philosophy of the Experimenter's Craft and Its Role in the Genesis of High Technology"; and "The Citation Cycle."

These chapter titles are indicative of the eclecticism of Price's work and thought processes, as well as his humor and humanity. The chapter (actually a paper) "Networks of Scientific Papers," is, according to Merton and Garfield, "probably his most important contribution to information science." A pioneering effort to characterize the world network of scientific literature, this work indicates that patterns of citation of the publications comprising that literature define the contents and perimeters of research fronts in science.

During the last decades of his life Price was very active in the International Council for Science Policy Studies, and devoted much of his research attention to the development of scientific instrumentation in history. He also remained closely associated with the Institute for Scientific Information and the *Science Citation Index*. He became seriously ill while traveling abroad in 1977, but over time recuperated fully, only to suffer a massive heart attack in 1983. He died in London on September 3, 1983.

In the final paragraph of his eulogy to Price, Belver Griffith summed up as follows: "Derek Price's understanding of the scientific literature has made major contributions to the management and evaluation of the world's major bibliographic resources and services and to our understanding of the role of recorded knowledge in science." Price also added measuring basis and understanding to the well-known but underappreciated Bradford's Law of Scattering, which demonstrated, among other things, that the most cited authors publish in the most cited journals, thus strengthening the notion and significance of co-citation and invisible colleges—formal and informal.

Biographical listings and obituaries—[Obituary]. *Bulletin of the Medical Library Association* 72:238-9 (April 1984); [Obituary]. Garfield, Eugene. *Information Today* 31 (January 1984). **Books and articles about the biographee**—Garfield, Eugene P. "A Tribute to Derek John de Solla Price—A Bold, Iconoclastic, Historian of Science." *Current Contents* 28:3-7 (July 9, 1984); Griffith, Belver. "Derek Price (1922-1983) and the Social Studies of Science." *Scientometrics* 6:5-7 (1984); Kochen, Manfred. "Toward a Paradigm for Information Science: The Influence of Derek de Solla Price." *Journal of the American Society of Information Science* 35:147-8 (May 1984); "The Leonardo da Vinci Medal." *Technology and Culture* 18:471-8 (July 1977). **Primary sources and archival materials**—The disposition of Price's papers is not known at this time.

—SAUL HERNER

REECE, ERNEST JAMES (1881-1976)

Ernest J. Reece was born in Cleveland, Ohio, in 1881. He attended Adelbert College of Western

Reserve University and received a bachelor's degree in 1903. He was a 1905 graduate of the first class of Western Reserve's library school, where he studied under Azariah Root, among others. Following his graduation, Reece spent one year working for the Cleveland Public Library and then two years studying at the Oberlin Theological Seminary. After his religious studies Reece reentered the field of librarianship in which he remained for the rest of his life.

In 1908 Reece journeyed to Hawaii where he became the first regular librarian of the Cooke Library of Oahu College in Honolulu. Here Reece gained almost all of his practical library experience. Cooke was a library in name only and Reece set out to organize a solid reference collection for the school. Having successfully completed the task, Reece left Hawaii to go to the University of Illinois, where he began his first teaching assignment. In a 1912 letter to Phineas Windsor, director of the University of Illinois Library and Library School, Reece gave an indication of the direction he would take during his next fifty years in library education: "... my interests lie in the social and cultural and 'humanity' side of library work, and that in case of my appointment I should probably be a little more successful in handling these than in dealing with the more purely technical." Throughout his career he would be a staunch advocate of the humanistic and social side of librarianship and continually warn of overemphasizing the trend of technical specialization.

Reece taught administration and education courses at Illinois from 1912 to 1917. He recalled many years later that perhaps he was not an inspiring teacher, but he considered himself well-organized and accessible. He took pride in the fact that during his years at Illinois the school became as professional as possible and even innovative. He felt Windsor was an effective director and attracted a quality faculty. In 1915, during his Illinois days, he married Sabra Elizabeth Stevens. They had one son.

Reece needed more challenge in his career, and in 1917 he left Illinois to become the principal of the Library School of the New York Public Library. Initially he had some professional hesitation about accepting the position. The New York Public Library School was not connected to an academic institution. It admitted students based on an entrance examination, and had its students do "practice work," laboring under the mistaken assumption that it was a training school mainly for the library itself. Always with a mind on the professionally qualified student, Reece thought that the bachelor's degree should be a prerequisite for library studies and that an examination was no substitute for this necessary preparatory education. "Practice work" evoked the idea of trade apprenticeship to him, and he felt it had no place in a professional curriculum. The attractions of the school—and New York City—however, overcame the drawbacks, and Reece came to the city where he stayed for the next thirty-two years.

In 1923 the Williamson Report on library education was published. Among its many recommendations for improving library training were the professionalization of library education and the affiliation of library schools with universities. At that time two of the main library schools in the state of New York, the State Library School in Albany and the New York Public Library School, lacked any academic attachment. The influence of the Williamson Report, along with the lack of legislative support for the Albany school and the limitations of the New York Public Library School, caused the merger of the two at Columbia University. Charles Williamson himself became the director of the new Columbia School of Library Service and recruited Reece as an associate professor. In 1938 when Columbia established the first endowed library school chair, Reece became the incumbent as the first Melvil Dewey Professor, and remained in that title until his retirement in 1948. From 1944 to 1947 he also served as associate dean of the school.

Reece made his major contributions to library education while at Columbia, where he concentrated on curriculum development. At Illinois he had the opportunity to put into practice the principles that guided his life and writings. Reece believed that library education should concentrate on content as well as form or the purely technical. He felt that librarians would continue to be classed with low status professions if they did not acquire subject expertise. One of Illinois's accomplishments, he stated, was that the school was able to raise the standards of library education from the practical to a theoretical plane and to integrate advanced subject study in the curriculum.

Reece's move to Columbia in 1926 permitted him to work more actively in curricular revision and to make his mark on library education. The new school at Columbia added the two-year master's degree program with a curriculum that afforded the opportunity for advanced training in all facets of librarianship. This type of curriculum was just what Reece had advocated.

Columbia's original curriculum underwent a review in 1936. Also in that year, Columbia published Reece's *The Curriculum in Library Schools*. In it Reece called for abandoning old ideals and practices and instead adapting methods of big business to reach out to the library's clientele. He thought librarians should be more aggressive and market their product to the widest possible public. He perceptively foresaw the information explosion in all media and formats and pointed to the need for more research-oriented librarians. He never lost sight, however, of the fact that the training of librarians was the main objective of library education. He also underlined the continuing problem of the librarian's low status and poor self-image.

Some reviewers of *The Curriculum in Library Schools* criticized Reece for not placing enough emphasis on the social aims of the curriculum. Although the social context of the profession was primary for him, he appeared conservative in relation to the social concerns and activism of the depression era. Columbia, however, combined in its new curriculum Reece's views on scholarship and subject expertise with the broader knowledge of the library's place and effectiveness in society.

Over the next decade Reece further developed and elaborated his ideas on library education. The views expounded in his 1943 book, *Programs for Library Schools* (New York: Columbia University Press), were so revolutionary for the profession that his book was almost completely overshadowed by Keyes Metcalf's *Program of Instruction in Library Schools* (Urbana: University of Illinois Press, 1943). Reece claimed the need for a complete change in library training, but it was a change that he had been advocating since his beginning days in the field. He believed that librarians were too conservative; he wanted to raise their level of education, break the old mold, and supply a new breed of practitioner. "The work of the librarian," he stated, " ... [demands] generous intellectual equipment, including conversance with an extensive body of professional knowledge, in the utilization of which the methods and devices once stressed in library schools are only means." Clerical workers could handle the means, or techniques, while the professionals could plan, administer, educate, and supply information and guidance in reading. In the elaboration of this view Reece foresaw the importance of information and its control in twentieth century American society.

Reece attempted in *Programs for Library Schools* to bring librarianship back on track by emphasizing the knowledge of books rather than concentrating on technique. He also believed that a more knowledgeable or intellectual librarian would surely raise the status of the profession. If librarians were to acquire merit outside of the profession, they had to study the literature of a particular subject. And it was the duty of the library school to provide such courses in its curriculum. Subject expertise, he said, is what the library's clientele appreciates the most.

In 1948-1949 Columbia once again revised its curriculum, a revision based partially on Reece's former work and on a study that he published in 1949 entitled *The Task and Training of Librarians* (New York: King's Crown Press). The school incorporated into its curriculum the view that library education was an intellectual discipline and not merely a technical apprenticeship. The new course of study revolved around four categories that included foundations, resources, readers and reading, and methods. Reece's continuing belief in interdisciplinary study was put into practice in the new program. Columbia also attempted to institutionalize the idea that a curriculum should embody a philosophy of librarianship, a view Reece advocated in his 1943 work and emphasized in the Metcalf Report.

Reece retired from Columbia in 1948, but he certainly did not become inactive. In 1950 he became assistant and then acting director of the Dayton and Montgomery County (Ohio) Public Library and then went back to the University of Illinois where he served as acting associate director of the Library School in 1952-1953. He also continued to turn out a steady stream of writings on library education. In most of his works he pushed for further changes in library training and never abandoned his emphasis on basic principles and knowledge. In 1961 he was still advocating a broad liberal arts requirement for librarians and once again warned of the overemphasis on the technical side of the profession. He never wavered from his belief that the librarian should have a broad background and a concentration on the principles and concepts of the profession. Subject expertise would allow further communication with patrons. In warning against the trend towards the technical side, perhaps he foresaw the day when library education, like many other disciplines, would tend to develop technical jargon, methodological virtuosity, and academic obscurantism.

Always professionally active, Reece was on the Council of the American Library Association for several years and chaired many of its committees. He was managing editor of *College & Research Libraries* in 1944-1945. Locally, he was on the council of the New York Library Club and served as its president in 1934-1935. In addition to his surveys of Columbia's School of Library Service, Reece also wrote reports on the Fisk University Library (1926), Decatur (Illinois) Public Library (1953-1954), and the curriculum of the University of Illinois Library School (1949), among others.

Reece's educational leadership was recognized early with his election to the presidency of the Association of American Library Schools in 1922-1923 and later with his receipt of the American Library Association's Beta Phi Mu Award in 1963 for achievement in library education.

The profession's view of Reece's long and distinguished career was summed up well in 1951 by Harry Lydenberg, a former director of the New York Public Library. Lydenberg had been asked to provide a reference required for Reece's forthcoming post as acting associate director of the University of Illinois Library School. He wrote to Reece, " ... I tried to say in diplomatic phrasing that the mere posing of such a question showed how ignorant and unknowing is the requirement. Anyone lucky enough to get Ernest Reece to help teach may count his blessings and then start over again."

Jack Dalton, dean of the Columbia School of Library Service, paid a fitting tribute to Reece when he wrote to him in 1968: "More alumni have spoken to me through the years about you and your friendship and what you and that friendship meant to them than about all the other members of this faculty combined." Reece died in Boulder, Colorado, on March 12, 1976, at the age of 94, leaving behind a rich legacy of service to the profession.

Biographical listings and obituaries—[Obituary]. *Library Journal* 101:1253 (June 1, 1976); *Who Was Who in America* VI (1974-1976); *Who's Who in Library Service*, 3rd ed. **Books and articles about the biographee**—Linderman, Winifred B. "Columbia University, School of Library Service." In *Encyclopedia of Library and Information Science*. New York: Marcel Dekker, 1971, vol. 5; Trautman, Ray. *A History of the School of Library Service, Columbia University, New York*. New York: Columbia University Press, 1954. **Primary sources and archival materials**—The Ernest J. Reece Papers are in the Rare Book and Manuscript Library, Columbia University. All quotations in this article are from this collection.

—LARRY E. SULLIVAN

REED, SARAH REBECCA (1914-1978)

The daughter of John W. and Ann Barber Reed, Sarah Rebecca Reed was born on February 8, 1914, in the tiny western Illinois town of Warren. She entered the local Community High School, never earned a grade below 90%, and was graduated in 1931, a year early and first in her class. That autumn, she enrolled at Cornell College, Iowa, from which she received an A.B. degree in 1936, with majors in English, music, history, and education. She later noted that paying for college was a "strain" and necessitated her employment "by five different people at a time." For two of those undergraduate years, one of the jobs she worked at was as a library assistant in the college library.

After college, Reed spent two years (1936-1938) as an intermediate English teacher in the public school of small Sac City, Iowa. She then moved on to Sioux Rapids, Iowa, Consolidated High School, where she seems to have had her first professional encounter with library work as teacher-librarian. In 1941, she moved to a similar position in the high school at Sandwich, Illinois, about 100 miles north of Urbana-Champaign, where, beginning in 1940, she spent three summers studying at the University of Illinois. She received a B.S. in library science in August 1942.

One year later, Reed left Sandwich and settled in Urbana to pursue an A.M.L.S. and work in the university library, first as circulation assistant (1943-1944), then as book stacks librarian (1944-1945). By the time she received her master's degree, she had already been accepted into the Ph.D. program at the University of Chicago's Graduate Library School (GLS). According to Illinois' library director, Robert Downs, she also had progressed rapidly on the job, receiving "several promotions in rank and salary" until she was supervising the work of "a considerable number of clerical and student assistants."

In 1945, she commenced her doctoral studies at Chicago and completed all of her course work twelve months later. Because of family concerns, she never completed the doctorate. She returned to work full time and accepted the position of librarian of the GLS library in 1946 and, in 1949, she added the title of supervisor of induction training. In this position she supervised the "laboratory" work done in the library by new students in connection with a core course. Lester Asheim, a student at GLS during the time, remembers his and his peers' fondness for Reed, describing her as an "old-fashioned librarian in the sense that nothing was too much, no effort was too great."

Reed's Chicago experience seems to have been deeply influential. Throughout her life, she emphasized the importance of faculty members' acquiring respected doctorates and carrying out research. Her reasons would have been at least partly political; she knew very well that these were emerging as requisites in prestigious institutions and that library schools would gain status if their faculty members were credible as scholars. But it also seems likely that she had internalized the strong intellectual values of the University of Chicago.

In her role as GLS librarian, Reed became involved in her first professional publication: *The Library in College Instruction: A Syllabus in the Improvement of College Instruction through Library Use* (New York: Wilson, 1951), which was co-authored by former GLS dean Louis Round Wilson, then teaching at the University of North Carolina-Chapel Hill, and Mildred Hawksworth Lowell, the former research assistant to Dean Wilson at Chicago (and later a professor at the Graduate Library School, Indiana University). Designed to facilitate the integration of instruction and library use in undergraduate education, the book was favorably reviewed and stands as a notable forerunner of related works in the library instruction movement. It was largely a bibliography, and Reed's selection of the books listed was a principal contribution.

In 1952, Reed began university teaching in summer session at the College of Librarianship, University of Denver. She enjoyed her students and, in a letter to Asheim, declared the experience "most satisfying and enriching"; she taught again in Denver the following summer.

Her first full-time faculty appointment came as assistant professor at the University of North Carolina (UNC)-Chapel Hill, beginning in autumn 1952 and ending with her departure three years later. She taught five courses: reference; social sciences literature; administration; research methods; and the selection and use of "book and non-book materials" for adults.

On the night of March 26, 1953, she and three other people were involved in a tragic automobile accident near Burlington, North Carolina, as they returned from a library building dedication. Dr. Pierce Butler, professor emeritus of the Graduate Library School of the University of Chicago and visiting professor at UNC, and George F. Bentley, assistant to the Director of Libraries, UNC, died as a result of the accident. Dorothy Long of the UNC Medical Library and Sarah Rebecca Reed were severely injured. This tragedy undoubtedly had a tremendous impact on her life.

By the end of 1954, she had begun to look around for another position. Her search led her to a five-year stint, beginning in 1955, as an assistant professor at the Library School at Florida State University, an experience capped by publication of her three-volume bibliography, co-edited by the school's famous dean, Louis Shores, entitled *Basic Materials for Florida Junior College Libraries* (Tallahassee, Fla.: State Department of Education, 1960). Quite possibly, Shores, who was the leading expositor and advocate of the "library-college" concept and later an inspiration to the progenitors of the library instruction movement, was attracted to Reed's fierce devotion to student service and the assumption underlying the book she had written with Wilson and Lowell. Reed continued to teach in the areas that had been her specialties at Chapel Hill: college library administration, reference, research methods, and bibliography (although in the humanities as well as the social sciences); to these she added a government publications course.

During these years, she resumed publishing. She wrote three articles in addition to the work with Shores. These are especially interesting because they are typical, in their nature and themes, of her later writing. One, a brief opinion piece, pointed out the need for research in the field and for the articulation of general principles, then presented a proposal for a conference to address this need. Reed's first publication reporting new data appeared in 1957 and set forth the findings of a survey of twenty-four urban public libraries regarding their reference services during the preceding decade.

By 1960, she had done essentially the same things in two different library schools at the same academic rank, for eight years. At this point, an opportunity opened that would exploit her administrative strengths and provide a far broader and more visible arena. For the next three years, she served as executive secretary of the American Library Association's (ALA) Library Education Division (LED) and secretary of the Committee on Accreditation (COA). She advocated sufficient flexibility in standards to permit the autonomous development of each library education program within the unique context of its parent institution. Without specifying examples, she criticized undergraduate programs in librarianship, which were then widespread and numerous, and inadequate teaching such as that caused by overreliance on practitioner-adjuncts. Then as later, a severe shortage of potential faculty members threatened the quality of library education. Reed spoke against this situation unceasingly and even at the end of her life still labeled it "the most critical problem we face."

Reed left ALA in 1963 to assume the newly created position of library education specialist within the Division of Library Services of the U.S. Office of Education (USOE). As a result, she became a mediator between the profession and Washington at a time when floods of funds (comparatively speaking) for education-related enterprises were pouring forth from the federal government. Summer 1964 saw publication of the first of her "Library Education Reports," a series that ran in the *Journal of Education for Librarianship* (*JEL*) through 1967 and comprised a dozen brief essays. Entitled "Good Intentions Are Not Enough," this article asserted that "national attention [is] focused on the recruitment and education of librarians" and posed five questions regarding division of responsibility for quality of "pre-service library education." The piece was earnest, determined, and goading. These same qualities marked the series as a whole. Throughout the crucial period of the first Johnson administration, Reed had a unique opportunity to speak to library educators through a regular column in their own journal.

A broad picture of her concerns during her USOE service can be drawn from the *JEL* articles in tandem with some short pieces written for the *ALA Bulletin*: The general mediocrity of much library education and the continued existence of hundreds of unaccredited programs, both graduate and undergraduate; the field's poor showing in terms of research and grant-winning; the small number of doctorates awarded by library schools; and, related to the last and preeminent, the undersupply of qualified faculty. A more general worry was the drastic shortage of trained librarians in the 1960s.

Frank L. Schick mentioned that Reed had initiated the idea of conducting a survey of library education programs while at ALA. "She had come to the conclusion there was no data to provide an overview about students, faculty, budgets, and the courses and programs which were offered across the land." Before she completed her survey, she had been hired by the U.S. Office of Education (1963-1967). She prepared the *Library Education Directory 1963-65*, and several other survey reports. Schick wrote that "the library education data which Sarah had collected and analyzed at such an opportune time served as the base for the development of two pieces of legislation which became Title II B of the Higher Education Act of 1965, P.L. 89-329. They are Library Research and Demonstration and Library Training."

While at the USOE, Reed also edited the proceedings of a 1965 institute on *Problems of Library School Administration* (Washington, D.C.: U.S. Office of Education, 1965). Conceived as an event of major importance, the conference attracted some notable speakers—among them Leon Carnovsky, Jesse Shera, and Raynard Swank. The other government publications with which Reed was explicitly associated were various directories.

In 1967, Reed moved to Edmonton, Alberta, Canada, to become the founding director of the Prairie Provinces' first post-baccalaureate library school at the University of Alberta. It opened a year later, on August 19, 1968. Although librarians from the three provinces had been planning such a school for several years, its final design surely reflected Reed's preferences. The one-year program, which led to a B.L.S., offered broad, general preparation and a substantial degree of prescription. Course work was required in reference, cataloging and classification, collection building, administration, "library in society," research methods, a type of library, and either the history of the books or library materials for a particular age group. Not in place at the time of Reed's departure, but being planned, was a sixth-year program to result in a M.L.S. Later, she remembered this "opportunity to develop a library school from scratch" as "tremendously exciting."

In the year following her arrival at Alberta (1968), Reed had won the Beta Phi Mu Award for "distinguished service to education for librarianship." During her Canadian years, she also retained high visibility through association work, chairing ALA's Committee on Library Education Statistics (1968-1971), LED Teachers' Section (1969-1979), and the Joseph W. Lippincott Award Jury (1970-1971). She also became involved in the Canadian Association of Library Schools, chairing its Committee to Establish Guidelines of Canadian Doctoral Programmes in 1969-1970 and serving as president the following year (1970-1971); and in the Canadian Library Association, for which she served a two-year term as chair of the Manpower Committee (1969-1971).

With the infant Alberta program on its feet and growing, Reed was again restless. Wishing to gain experience in a larger, better-established school with doctoral students, she accepted an associate deanship with the rank of professor at Indiana University's Graduate Library School. Among her duties was coordination of the doctoral program—a role that offered her special satisfaction, given her longstanding and vocal concern about the paucity of faculty members with doctorates and research inclinations. A year after Reed began work in Bloomington, D. Kathryn Weintraub joined the faculty. She remembered the associate dean as "going out of her way to be helpful" to students and could not recall ever conversing with her about a subject completely unrelated to librarianship. Reed impressed Weintraub as "very dedicated" to the profession and "domineering" but "effective" in her work on its behalf.

The pace of Reed's extramural activity slowed somewhat at Indiana, although she did serve a term as president of Beta Phi Mu (1972-1973). She also published two articles reporting informal surveys on library education and guest-edited the January 1974 *Library Trends* issue on "Evaluation of Library Services," a subject about which she had never written extensively, although her interest in it went back at least as far as the mid-1940s, when she had first proposed it as a subject for doctoral research.

Throughout her working career, which had begun when she was a teenager, Reed had never stayed in one job or one place for longer than seven years, with the more usual period being three to four years. In 1975, having spent four years in Bloomington and passing her sixtieth birthday, Reed moved on to what would be her last challenge, the library school of Emporia (Kansas) State College, soon to be renamed Emporia State University. After the school lost ALA accreditation in 1956, Reed had been among the consultants hired as it struggled to regain strength. In 1966, its faculty size more than doubled and new programs instituted, it was reaccredited. It seems likely, however, that the program remained in need of reform, for when Reed took over as director in 1975, she undertook considerable curriculum change, adding and eliminating courses and adjusting credit-hour allotments. During her three years at Kansas, she also planned continuing education activities and a sixth-year specialist program, and instituted three dual master's degrees. At the time of her death, she was working with the University of Kansas to develop a specialization in health sciences librarianship. Reed also published four articles overviewing various aspects of library education after she went to Kansas.

In Emporia, Reed won her usual reputation for industriousness, an indefatigably positive attitude, and deep, lively devotion to students. "She was a *figure* on campus," Professor Florence de Hart recalled. "She bordered on being a legendary personality." Determined to strengthen a comparatively weak program, Reed emphasized the importance of good teaching and constantly urged her faculty to carry out research and, if they lacked doctorates, to earn them—at good universities. She was "very warm on a personal level," according to de Hart (and others), but also "very forceful.... Nothing was going to sway her" in her determination to build a solid program. Reed successfully guided the school through a COA visit in the first spring after she arrived, and one former colleague believes that, had she remained at Emporia, the school probably would not have lost accreditation a second time in 1982. As it turned out, however, this time Reed's tenure was cut short not by her chronic search for new experience but by natural forces; she did not have enough time to effect large-scale change.

On July 17, 1978, Reed embarked on the Lake Pomona, Kansas, showboat named *Whippoorwill* for dinner and a theatrical presentation. She was accompanied by Emporia's Professor Zubaidah Isa and Muriel Fuller, professor emerita from the University of Wisconsin-Madison, who was teaching in summer session at Emporia. A relatively small tornado touched down on the lake and capsized the boat, killing Reed, her colleagues, and 12 others. She left no close relatives. Weintraub remarked on what a strange manner of death it seemed for a "take-charge" person like Reed—how odd it was to imagine her trapped, not in control.

Although in youth Sarah Rebecca Reed seems to have considered a career in some phase of music, her sense of connection to libraries was deep-rooted and very old; she described herself as "one for whom a small Carnegie Library served as a second childhood home." This connection, plus her passion for teaching, led her to library education; her desire to make a marked difference in the profession, to help build and develop training programs, led her to administration. Two schools stand in substantial part as her memorials, and the current state of library education—its problems, demands, and recent development—vindicate most of her plans and prophecies.

Biographical listings and obituaries—*ALA Yearbook 1978* (1979); Berry, John. "Sarah Rebecca Reed, 1914-1978." *Library Journal* 103:1325 (July 1978); *Biographical Dictionary of Librarians in the United States and Canada*, 5th ed. **Books and articles about the biographee**—Meder, Marylouise D. "Sarah Rebecca Reed: Teacher—Librarian—Administrator." *Library School Review* [Emporia State University] 18:4-7 (1979); "Sarah Rebecca Reed." In *Women View Librarianship: Nine Perspectives*. Ed. by Kathryn Renfro Lundy. Chicago: American Library Association, 1980; Schick, Frank L. "Sarah R. Reed and Library Education Programs." *Library School Review* 18:20-21 (1979). **Primary sources and archival materials**—Reed's official papers are scattered among the official archives of those institutions at which she was employed.

—MARY BIGGS

RICHARDS, JOHN STEWART (1892-1979)

In 1896, four-year-old John Richards and his parents arrived with plows, seeds, and treasured family books in the Pacific Northwest, an area of the United States still considered Indian territory by some Easterners. The boy had been christened John Stewart Richards after his birth on February 16, 1892, in Chicago. His mother, Minnie, who had emigrated from Canada, and his father, Milton, of Scotch, Welsh, and Irish descent, had farmed a small plot in Cook County on the outskirts of Chicago. In the year after John was born the couple visited the Pacific Northwest exhibit at the Columbian Exposition in Chicago and were captivated by the thought of moving West. Milton's brother had been a successful fruit grower in Washington's Yakima Valley, so John's parents decided that fruit farming there would be more profitable than in Illinois. But the Yakima Valley brought a meager income, nothing to compare with what they had anticipated. Everyone in the family read, so they frequented the small local Carnegie library. From an early age John became a reader, encouraged by his parents, aunts and uncles who were not well-educated but extremely well-read. John went to the local public elementary and high schools in Yakima Valley.

In 1912 Richards entered the University of Washington. In search of a part-time position to help defray expenses, he met university librarian William E. Henry, who hired him to shelve books. Henry had founded a library school at the university three years earlier—the first library school, Henry boasted, west of the University of Illinois. Through Henry, Richards developed an interest in librarianship and decided to major in library science. He became one of eleven students, the only male and the first alumnus to graduate with an A.B. degree in library science in 1916.

In 1916 Richards's first library job was as public librarian at Coos Bay (then Marshfield), Oregon, a town in which he capitalized on the intellectual receptivity of the youthful population. Coos Bay was the terminus of a newly constructed railroad. The burgeoning population was college educated and interested in all the intellectual avenues Richards opened to them. Sensing their openness, Richards brought in far more than the usual numbers of speakers from the University of Oregon Extension Division. Library discussion groups, something Richards always encouraged, gave a stimulating, intellectual dimension to an existence which was otherwise quite barren in the isolated coastal town. While serving in Coos Bay, Richards attended his first Pacific Northwest

Library Association (PNLA) meeting, a significant event because from that year on, Richards was one of the group's most supportive members. He served as its president in 1937-1938.

Richards was in Oregon when the War and Navy Departments, through the Commission on Training Camp Activities, asked the American Library Association to provide materials and urged librarians to help in the war effort. He served from February 1918 to August 1919 as an administrator of the army library at Camp Fremont (home to 60,000 soldiers) in Menlo Park, California. When the armistice was signed, he finished his service by selecting books and supervising shipments of materials to permanent army base libraries and to Siberia, where Americans continued to be involved in military activities after the Bolshevik revolution. Richards felt that the accessibility of materials to common soldiers in World War I was a turning point in American library history. The door had been opened for all who wished to obtain reading materials. As military men returned to their communities, Richards felt they would make use of their public libraries. No longer would public libraries serve only an elite clientele.

In 1919 he married Irene Fry, whom he had known at the University of Washington and by whom he had two sons. Because Richards felt he needed specialized work with larger libraries, he and Irene spent the first year of their married life in Albany, New York. There at the New York State Library School, Richards completed the two-year program in one year and received the special certificate awarded in those years. James Wyer, director of the school, informed Richards of many job openings in the New England area and was dumbfounded when Richards announced he was instead taking an academic library position in Idaho. Wyer had difficulty understanding why anyone would come East for additional training and not wish to remain.

After three years at what later became the Idaho State University in Pocatello, he accepted a better position at the Washington State Normal School at Ellensburg, where he served another three-year stint (1923-1926). But at the meeting of the PNLA in 1926, Dean Sydney B. Mitchell of the University of California, Berkeley Library School, encouraged Richards to apply for a position in Berkeley. He intimated that Harold L. Leupp, the university librarian, might be difficult to work with, but that the position would be a significant career move for Richards.

Leupp interviewed Richards, but offered only a temporary position. Richards knew a permanent position was available and insisted upon it. Leupp finally backed down and offered it. Richards accepted. Perhaps this confrontation partially explains their subsequently compatible relationship, something unusual for Leupp. Unlike others, Richards was even promoted. He came as superintendent of circulation, then became assistant librarian, but it is doubtful he was ever given full responsibility in either post. Leupp ran the library with an iron hand. In contrast, Richards was democratic with all subordinates. He delegated authority and encouraged creativity. These characteristics were part of the management style that made him a popular administrator throughout his career.

Richards took library science classes in his spare time at Berkeley, and in 1932, at the age of forty-two, he earned an M.A. in library science. His thesis evolved from an authentic library problem on which he was working—"Bibliographical Materials for a Literary History of Joaquin Miller," a model bibliographical essay. His scholarship and thoroughness are evident throughout the work. Richards became an authority on Miller, and in 1936 he was asked to edit and write the introduction for a volume on the author. The book was an outstanding example of fine printing, always an interest of Richards, and was published by Frank McCaffrey's Dogwood Press in Seattle under the title, *Joaquin Miller: His California Diary Beginning in 1855-1857* (1936).

In 1934, after eight years in Berkeley, Richards returned to Washington state, this time as executive assistant to Librarian Charles W. Smith at the University of Washington. It was in the middle of the Depression, and Richards, always interested in community activities, encouraged unemployed librarians to meet for discussions in the university library. Avant-garde in their ideas, the group called itself The Library Discussion Group of Seattle and sponsored an anti-war proposal at a time when the United States was becoming increasingly involved in the European war. Group members called for federal support of a national library program. They advocated the establishment of a new library publication that eventually became the *Quarterly* of the PNLA. Richards was the mentor of the group, and many of his ideas surfaced in the discussions, particularly the call for federal aid to libraries. Always interested in equality and democracy, Richards was responsible for drawing up classification and pay scales for librarians at the University of Washington.

Although Richards had not been involved with public library activities since his first job at Coos Bay, his interest had never flagged. In 1942, Josephine Quigley, chair of the Public Library Board of Seattle, asked him to submit an application for the head librarian position at the Seattle Public Library to succeed Judson Toll Jennings, who was retiring. Within a month the board unanimously approved his appointment, and for the next fifteen years he served as an indefatigable, respected, creative leader of the library world in Seattle.

Almost all of that time he was occupied with planning for a new central library, which he envisioned as a major resource center for the Pacific Northwest. The sixty-year-old Carnegie library was built of sandstone and reinforced with steel only in the roof. The building rocked ominously during earthquakes. Richards pleaded for a new stronger structure but failed to convince enough voters. From his first days in office, Richards had always urged better quarters for the staff and the collection. In 1951 after voters had turned down one of many bond issues, Richards blamed the defeat on an overcrowded ballot, a turn for the worse in the Korean War, but most of all on an uninformed citizenry. From then on he sought a strong "Friends of the Library" program. One earthquake in particular, however, loosened so many joints voters finally changed their minds. An act of nature sparked passage of a bond issue supporting new construction. The building program was finally getting underway just as Richards retired in 1957.

Richards considered the "Friends of the Library" group a major community accomplishment. Typical subjects for monthly discussions in 1944 included: "Inflation: What Is Your Money's Worth?," "Youth in Wartime Seattle," and "Socialized Medicine." Subjects were often nonacademic and timely, geared to community needs. Richards felt the library was not there to tell people what to think, but to present all sides of issues. It was kept as a free forum in the McCarthy years. He often fought off censorship attempts. When Richards noticed a list of "dangerous" books being passed around in the Seattle library, he stated that this "assault" must be recognized for "the gangsterism that it is and must be combatted." He also felt that the library was to serve the less educated and thus the "Freedom to Read" committee of the American Library Association always received his strong support.

Another major idea of his concerned cooperation. He urged all librarians and trustees not to guard their powers jealously, but to try to share with and help isolated rural communities. He organized the centralized purchase of books, cooperative publicity, interlibrary loan, use of TV and radio, and mobile units. He urged others in the profession from similar isolated "hinterlands" to follow PNLA's cooperative innovations, many of which he had created. Richards's cooperation knew no international boundaries; equally respected in British Columbia, he served as consultant there many times. In 1949 he did an in-depth study of the Vancouver library system.

The Seattle Public Library was honored in 1955-1956, when Richards was elected president of the American Library Association. An active member since 1920, a member of the executive board from 1945 to 1949, and a member of various committees through the years, he had always shown his interest and respect for the organization. During his term, Congress passed and President Dwight Eisenhower signed the Library Services Act, which gave the federal aid to libraries Richards had so long advocated. In fact, as president-elect in 1954-1955, Richards spent much time in Washington, D.C. representing the American Library Association in House and Senate committee hearings. His experience made him an ideal representative.

In Seattle, Richards was known as a joiner, a community-minded person especially in causes involving the library. He took particular interest in the organizations that aided the mentally retarded. Richards was urbane and cultivated, enjoyed opera, theater, fine printing, and bridge with a circle of friends. A noted conversationalist, his garrulousness and his sometimes high-pitched voice might have annoyed some, but there was always a sound message to what may have seemed like ramblings. Richards was always worth listening to.

He was known throughout the region as a doer, an able administrator. Never a great writer, his articles appeared sporadically in *Library Journal* and the *Quarterly* of the PNLA. He was recognized as a resource person for the entire Pacific Northwest, always valued as a consultant in California, Oregon, Idaho, and Washington, as well as in British Columbia.

By 1957 he had gained approval for the construction of a new library, was given permission to hire architects of his choice and had much to say about the plans. Just as the project was getting underway, however, he kept his promise to retire at sixty-five, and upon the advice of his doctor left his post. At the time the library was going through a period of infighting among the trustees, and Richards thought it best to turn the actual building over to his successor. With Irene, he left for a year's vacation in Europe in 1957. Upon his return Richards did some teaching in the University of Washington Library School, served on the Washington State Library Commission (1959-1964), and was sought after by many libraries needing his expertise. In 1964, he severed his remaining library obligations, and the couple retired outside Carmel, California. It was on a trip back to Seattle that Richards died on December 3, 1979.

Biographical listings and obituaries—*New York State Library School Report, 1887-1926*. New York: State Library School Association, Inc., 1959. 128-29; [Obituary]. *ALA Yearbook 1980* (1981); [Obituary]. "Former ALA President Dies." *American Libraries* 11:8 (January 1980); [Obituary]. *Wilson Library Bulletin* 54: 407 (February 1980). **Books and articles about the biographee**—Bevis, Dorothy. "John Stewart Richards." *PNLA Quarterly* 19:148-51 (July 1955); Corey, D. Steven. "Perspectives: An Interview with John S. Richards." *PNLA Quarterly* 36:20-25 (February 1972); "John S. Richards." *Utah Libraries* 6:11 (Spring 1963). **Primary sources and archival materials**—Richards's official correspondence can be found among records of the Library Board Meetings, 1942-1957, and the Northwest File at the Seattle Public Library, Seattle, Washington; and the American Library Association Archives, Executive Directors' Subject File, and Executive Board Meetings for 1955-1956, located at the University of Illinois Archives, Urbana, Illinois.

—MARION CASEY

ROLLINS, CHARLEMAE HILL (1897-1979)

Charlemae Rollins was born in Yazoo City, Mississippi, on June 20, 1897. The oldest child of Allen, a farmer, and Birdie Tucker Hill, a teacher and the granddaughter of a former slave, Rollins valued her heritage as a black American; she is remembered chiefly for her success in promoting a more accurate representation of blacks in children's books. When she was a young child, her family moved to the Oklahoma Territory because her father believed a black family could live in peace there. However, black children were not allowed to attend school with white children in the new town of Beggs. The Hill family established a school for black youngsters with Birdie Hill as teacher, which Charlemae Hill attended until she was thirteen years old.

As there was no high school for blacks in Oklahoma, young Charlemae was sent to black secondary schools in St. Louis, Missouri, and Holly Springs, Mississippi. She graduated from high school at Western University, a black boarding school in Quindaro, Kansas, in 1916. She returned to Beggs, Oklahoma, passed the teaching examination there, and taught for a short while before traveling to Washington, D.C. After a year at Howard University, she returned to Oklahoma to marry Joseph Walter Rollins on April 8, 1918.

Rollins remained in Oklahoma while her husband served in the U.S. Army in France during World War I. After his return in 1919, the couple moved to Chicago. Except for a brief period in 1920 when she returned to Oklahoma for the birth of her son, Rollins lived in Chicago for the rest of her life. In 1926, Rollins began her career as a children's librarian at the Chicago Public Library (CPL). She told an interviewer in 1972 that her childhood fondness for reading and her teaching experience had led to her decision to become a children's librarian. Making that decision was "the best thing I ever did," she said later. The Chicago Public Library provided funds for her training at the library schools at the University of Chicago and Columbia University, but Rollins never completed a college degree.

Beginning as a junior library assistant, Rollins worked for several years at the Hardin Square Branch, which served a multiethnic population of twenty-six different nationalities, but no blacks. When the George Cleveland Hall Branch opened in 1932, Rollins became the children's librarian and remained there until her retirement in 1963. The Hall Branch was the first branch established in Chicago's black community, and Rollins wanted to work with her own people. A wide spectrum of socioeconomic classes resided in the "black belt" at that time, and Hall Branch patrons included well-educated professionals as well as low-income families.

Rollins's tasks at the Hall Branch included the usual duties of children's librarians: book selection; storytelling; reference work with children, parents, teachers, and youth workers; visits to school classes; informing parents and teachers about children's books; and working with community organizations. Rollins also assisted branch librarian Vivian G. Harsh in building a collection of books by and about blacks.

Rollins soon noticed that there were very few nonfiction books for children about the contributions of blacks to society and few fiction titles or picture books with black protagonists. Many of the books that included black people portrayed them in negative, stereotyped ways or had illustrations that caricatured their faces and clothing. Images of the little black child with pigtails all over her head, wearing rags and going barefoot, were particularly offensive. Rollins knew black children who had been hurt and angered by such books; she had been hurt by similar books when she was a child.

Rollins began her work to change the image of blacks in children's books about 1938. The event that initially inspired her determination is not known. In her introductory essay to *We Build Together* (Champaign, Ill.: National Council of Teachers of English, 1941), her first major publication, Rollins noted that black poet Langston Hughes and others had pointed out the need for more adequate representation of blacks in children's books as early as 1932. Because the Works Progress Administration brought prominent black writers to the Hall Branch, Rollins came to know Langston Hughes, Richard Wright, and Arna Bontemps. She knew other black librarians, as well. It is most likely that a variety of factors, including a lifetime of experience and thinking, personal conviction, and encouragement from others, gave Rollins the impetus to challenge the status quo.

Rollins directed her first efforts at two institutions: publishing and the Chicago Public Library. Because of the lack of juvenile biographies about blacks, she wrote letters to publishers asking them to publish more books for children about prominent black people. Rollins collected magazine and newspaper articles about well-known individuals for children to use for homework assignments. Later, when she wrote collective biographies about black leaders and entertainers, these files provided valuable research material.

At the Chicago Public Library, Rollins tried to influence the purchase of books already published. In the 1930s staff at the headquarters of the CPL made lists of books recommended for branch library purchase. Rollins protested that some children's titles included in these lists did not reflect black life accurately. She did not prevail when she questioned *The Pickaninny Twins* by Lucy Fitch Perkins (1931). However, she succeeded in having *Ezekiel* by Elvira Garner (1937) removed from the buying list, even though it was a Junior Literary Guild selection.

Supervisor of Children's Services Agatha L. Shea asked Rollins to compile a bibliography of acceptable children's books about blacks. Rollins's mimeographed result was the beginning of *We Build Together*, published by the National Council of Teachers of English (NCTE) in 1941. Subtitled *A Reader's Guide to Negro Life and Literature for Elementary and High School Use*, the book consisted of an introductory essay and a classified, annotated bibliography. In the essay, Rollins discussed the criteria and considerations teachers should use in selecting classroom books about blacks. She suggested that her readers should look for books with accurate portraits of black people rather than caricatures, books in which black characters spoke as they do in real life rather than in a dialect invented by the author, books that avoided unnecessary use of derogatory terms for black people, and books with themes that did not stress socioeconomic class differences between white and black characters. She cautioned teachers to save the more violent and defeatist novels, such as Richard Wright's *Native Son*, for mature high school students, stressing the objectives of democracy and hope as most suitable for young people of any race. The essay gave examples of books containing deplorable attitudes towards blacks despite general critical regard for their literary value, and specifically mentioned Mark Twain's *Huckleberry Finn*.

We Build Together was a successful publication. The NCTE printed 15,000 copies initially, and the booklet was revised in 1948 and 1967. The officers of the NCTE invited Rollins to attend the 1941 annual convention as the association's guest and to appear at an intercultural luncheon (race relations were called intercultural relations at that time). However, the convention was held in Atlanta, Georgia, and various forms of segregation were still permitted. The luncheon was cancelled, but Rollins did attend the convention. On the train returning to Chicago, Rollins was refused Pullman car service because of her race, even though the NCTE had paid for her ticket. She was forced to sit in the Jim Crow car, where she was joined by John DeBoer, first vice-president of the NCTE, and four other members of the association. Rollins had not expected the segregation and was very disturbed by the experience.

The impact of *We Build Together* gave Rollins's career national scope. Awareness of racial prejudice was increasing, and Rollins was one of a number of people suggesting positive ways of changing attitudes. For the rest of her life, she was regarded as an expert in matters having to do with children's books about black people. Many opportunities to write, lecture, and teach opened up because of her publication. Children's book editors, such as Eunice Blake, Helen Hoke, and Helen Ferris, began sending manuscripts to her, requesting that she review them for their treatment of blacks. Children's authors requested her advice, as well, including Florence Crannell Means and Phyllis Whitney. She spoke at many conferences, workshops, and summer school sessions around the country, including southern colleges such as Fisk University, Morgan State College, and the University of Mississippi. In 1955 she estimated that she averaged two dozen speeches per year. She agreed to so many requests to address various groups that she sometimes had difficulty remembering them, and her son took on the responsibility for ensuring her timely arrival. Many of her speaking engagements were busman's holidays, undertaken during her vacations from the Chicago Public Library. At times she paid her own travel expenses, when the inviting group could not afford to reimburse her.

In 1946 Rollins began teaching children's literature at Roosevelt University in Chicago. The class was very popular with students, and by 1955 it had become a required course for education majors. After her retirement, the American Library Association honored Rollins by donating a collection of 2,000 children's books to Roosevelt University. The collection, part of the American exhibit at the 1962 Seattle World's Fair, was named the Charlemae Rollins Collection. The collection is still housed at Roosevelt University, but new books have not been added to it for several years.

The 1950s were a decade of very active participation for Rollins in the American Library Association (ALA). In 1950 she served on the Implementation of Division Goals Committee for the Division of Libraries for Children and Young People (DLCYP). Beginning in 1951, she served for four years on the ALA Council. Rollins was nominally the treasurer for the Children's Library Association (CLA, a section of the DLCYP) from 1954 to 1956, but her husband actually kept the books. During 1956, Rollins was elected vice-president/president-elect of the CLA, the first black to hold this office. As vice-president of the section, one of her duties was to chair the Newbery/Caldecott Committee. In 1957 the DLCYP separated into three divisions: the Children's Services Division (CSD), the American Association of School Librarians (AASL), and the Young Adult Services Division (YASD). Rollins presided over the CSD during 1957-1958, its second year as an independent entity.

An incident during Rollins's year as president of the CSD serves to illustrate her influence in the publishing of children's books. As president she was a member of the Newbery/Caldecott Committee (all CSD officers were part of the committee at that time). The 1958 Newbery Medal was awarded to *Rifles for Watie* by Harold Keith (1957). The first printing of the book contained some references to blacks which Rollins and other black librarians found offensive. Rollins contacted Elizabeth Riley, children's book editor at T. Y. Crowell and pointed out four objectionable phrases on two pages. Riley agreed to change three of them in the second printing of Keith's book.

But the struggle with the Newbery/Caldecott medalists was not over with the editing of *Rifles for Watie*. When Harold Keith was presented with the Newbery Medal at the summer 1958 ALA conference, he reportedly began his speech with racist jokes. Caldecott Medal winner Robert McCloskey refused to deliver his own speech, perhaps because Keith's speech was so long and perhaps because McCloskey believed he should not have received the Caldecott (his second). Most who attended this controversial meeting agreed that Rollins and Newbery/Caldecott chair Elizabeth Nesbitt managed the episode with grace.

Throughout her national career, Rollins continued working with children at the Hall Branch. She was especially noted for her storytelling. Some of her stories were tales she had heard her grandmother tell, others were folktales she learned from published sources, still others were accounts of the lives of famous blacks, derived from the clipping files she had compiled. Those familiar with her storytelling remember her performances as completely natural and compelling, no matter the age of the audience. Mothers were as eager to hear her stories as the children they brought. Rollins's storytelling ability was undoubtedly evident in her lectures; she established rapport easily with any audience.

Poetry was one of Rollins's favorite literary forms. As an adult, she and her siblings recited the works of Paul Lawrence Dunbar at family gatherings. During her year as president of the CSD, she suggested a Poetry Preconference, which was held prior to the 1958 ALA summer conference in San Francisco. Speakers included Annis Duff, Lawrence Ferlinghetti, May Hill Arbuthnot, Lillian Moore, and Arna Bontemps. Among the children she encouraged at the Hall Branch was Gwendolyn Brooks, winner of the 1950 Pulitzer Prize for poetry. Brooks, like Hughes and Bontemps, remained a lifelong friend.

In addition to *We Build Together*, Rollins contributed many articles to professional library and education journals. Most of these articles concerned children's books about blacks, but she also wrote about storytelling and cooperation with community organizations. Before her retirement from the CPL on August 29, 1963, Rollins had compiled her first two books for children, *Call of Adventure* (New York: Colliers, 1962) and *Christmas Gif'* (Chicago: Follett, 1963). The latter, a collection of stories, recollections, and poetry about black Christmas traditions in the United States, remains a valued title in the canon of children's literature. Retirement gave Rollins the time to write several biographical works on well-known blacks. Among these titles are *They Showed the Way: Forty American Negro Leaders* (New York: Crowell, 1964), *Famous Negro Poets* (New York: Dodd, 1965), and *Famous Negro Entertainers of Stage, Screen and TV* (New York: Dodd, 1967). Rollins wrote basal readers for Scott, Foresman, as well. One highly regarded work was *Black Troubadour: Langston Hughes* (Chicago: Rand McNally, 1970), for which she won the second Coretta Scott King Award in 1971. Rollins did not consider herself a writer in the artistic sense, but she wanted to continue writing biographies. Unfortunately, she began to experience memory loss about 1969 and was not able to continue her writing after the Hughes biography.

For a time during her retirement, Rollins maintained her lecturing and professional activities. Rollins's longest professional commitment was to the *Bulletin of the Center for Children's Books* (*BCCB*), published by the University of Chicago. She served on the advisory committee for the *BCCB* almost from its beginning in 1941 until 1977. During 1964-1965 she chaired the Jane Addams Book Award Committee for the Women's International League for Peace and Freedom. The award is given annually to the children's book that best promotes international peace. She traveled to Oslo, Norway, to present the award to Norwegian writer Aimee Sommerfelt, for *The Road to Agra*.

Rollins herself received many awards and honors. Awards from the library profession included the American Library Association Letter (1953), the Grolier Society Award (1955), the Children's Reading Round Table Award (1963), and life membership in the American Library Association (1972). She received a plaque from the Black Librarians' Caucus in 1976. Rollins was active in Chicago community affairs and was well known among educators. Some of her nonlibrary awards included the American Brotherhood Award from the National Council of Christians and Jews (1953), Zeta Phi Beta Woman of the Year (1956), honorary membership in Phi Delta Kappa (1959), the Good American Award from the Chicago Committee of 100 (1962), three Negro Centennial Awards (1963), the Constance Lindsay Skinner Award (1970), and the Torch Bearers Award of Alpha Kappa Alpha sorority (1972). In 1974, Columbia College in Chicago awarded Rollins an honorary doctorate of humane letters.

On November 19, 1977, the Chicago Public Library dedicated a room at the Carter G. Woodson Regional Library to Charlemae Rollins, and a portrait of her was unveiled. At that time her personal collection of books, including works autographed by black authors, was presented to the Vivian G. Harsh Collection of Afro-American History and Literature at the Woodson Regional Library. Although Rollins attended the ceremony, her health was failing, and the presentation was made by her son, Joseph Rollins, Jr. She died in Chicago on February 3, 1979, of pneumonia.

Two events memorialize Rollins's work for children's literature. One is the biennial Rollins Colloquium on black children's literature held at

North Carolina Central University's School of Library and Information Science in Durham, N.C. The second is the annual president's program of the Association for Library Service to Children, which carries her name and includes a short biographical sketch and Rollins's portrait in the program folder. The program is funded by donations made in her memory.

Those who knew Rollins remember her as a short, stout person, always well-dressed, with intelligence, a warm, vital personality, and an ever-present sense of humor. She encouraged and supported younger librarians both black and white. She had a firm religious faith and is recalled as a "good" person in the ethical sense of that word. When any acquaintance faced a personal problem, she would say, "Put it in the hands of the Lord, child." Despite her many painful experiences, she preferred to think positively of other people. She rarely discussed racial incidents in public and did not understand the black power movement of the 1960s and 1970s. She believed that people would lose their prejudices if they came to know each other, and she worked to bring people together.

During World War II, Ruth Tarbox, who was then a school librarian in River Forest, Illinois, invited Rollins to visit a sixth-grade class. The teacher had asked Tarbox to arrange a visit from a black librarian to talk to her class about intercultural relations. Rollins spoke candidly to the students and invited them to meet a class of black sixth-graders at the Hall Branch. The class did visit Hall Branch for stories and refreshments with the black children. After the white students had returned to their upper-middle-class suburb, one black youngster told Rollins that they were nice children, not like white children at all.

This venture in integration took place in 1944 or 1945, and Rollins apparently believed it successful since she came to see it as an important influence on her career. In a letter dated February 2, 1970, Rollins wrote to Tarbox, "you are really the person responsible for everything almost that happened in my career." Unfortunately for her biographer, however, she failed to specify why she was so indebted to Tarbox. Although Rollins had received national recognition for her bibliography of black children's books by that time, it may be that the event reinforced her belief that racial attitudes would change if people came to know members of other races. At the same time, the episode may have been confirmation that her methods were effective in promoting racial harmony. Charlemae Rollins dedicated more than forty years of her life to those ideals and methods.

Biographical listings and obituaries — Ethridge, James M., and Kopala, Barbara, eds. "Rollins, Charlemae Hill 1897- ." *Contemporary Authors* V:11-12 (1965); [Obituary]. *ALA Yearbook 1979* (1980); [Obituary]. "Charlemae Hill Rollins, 1897-1979." *School Library Journal* 25:78 (March 1979); *Who Was Who in America* V:7 (1977-1981). **Books and articles about the biographee** — "Charlemae Rollins — Librarian and Storyteller." *American Libraries* 5:413 (September 1974); Gagliardo, Ruth. "Charlemae Rollins Collection Established." *Top of the News* 20:275-8 (May 1964); Saunders, Doris. "Charlemae Rollins." *ALA Bulletin* 49:68-70 (February 1955); Shaw, Spencer. "Charlemae Hill Rollins, 1897-1979. In Tribute." *Public Libraries* 21:102-4 (Fall 1982); Thompson, Era Bell. "Crusader in Children's Books." *Negro Digest* 1:29-33 (August 1950); Wirth, Otto. "Roosevelt University Honors and 'Is Honored'." *Top of the News* 20:278-9 (May 1964). **Primary sources and archival materials** — Material by and about Charlemae Hill Rollins is held in the library of the School of Library and Information Science at North Carolina Central University in Durham, North Carolina; in the Special Collections Department of the Fisk University Library, Nashville, Tennessee; and in the Vivian G. Harsh Collection at the Carter G. Woodson Regional Library, a branch of the Chicago Public Library. In addition, many family records are in possession of Rollins's son, Joseph Rollins, Jr., of Freeport, Grand Bahama Island.

—HOLLY G. WILLETT

ROOS, JEAN CAROLYN (1891-1982)

Jean C. Roos was born on March 9, 1891, in Buffalo, New York. She attended grade and high schools in that city, then went on to the University of Buffalo, Cleveland School of Education, and Cleveland College, before receiving a certificate from Western Reserve School of Library Science in 1927. She began her professional career as a children's librarian in a branch of the Cleveland Public Library (CPL), a position she held from 1916 to 1918. From 1919 to 1922, she served as a school librarian (at the time school librarians were employees of the CPL). In 1925, the Robert Louis Stevenson Room of the CPL was founded to provide service and materials to 14-21-year-old youths, and Roos, then assistant to the head of the School Department at CPL, was chosen to be its director, a position she held until 1940.

Roos entered the field of what we now call young adult (YA) librarianship at its inception. Special collections of materials for young people had been set aside as early as 1906 in the Brooklyn Public Library, in public libraries in Buffalo in 1910, and in St. Louis in 1911. Another pioneer in YA service, Mabel Williams, had begun working directly with young people at the New York Public Library in 1916, where in 1919, she was appointed supervisor of work with schools—the first systematic service offered for young adults by a public library. When the Stevenson Room at the CPL was opened in 1925 to serve "intermediates" (who, CPL Director Linda Eastman said had been "clamoring" to get into the adult room), Roos was made the director of what she later called the "first room devoted entirely to work with youth with a trained staff and a collection of adult books selected with the interests of young people in mind" (*Library Trends* 3:132 [October 1954]).

In 1925, Roos described the room as "new and attractive ... for young people of high school age, whether in high school or not." She indicated that books would be chosen mainly for recreational purposes and 80 percent would be adult titles (only later did Roos allow that curriculum-related materials were also needed); there would be a close relationship between the young adults' room and the children's room and the adult departments of the library; and books from all departments would be available to the young people, parents, teachers, and to other adults serving youth. Roos stressed the importance of the librarian in making direct contact, being friendly, and knowing the reader well enough to be a vital and knowledgeable provider of reading guidance.

As soon as the Stevenson Room was operational, Roos set out on a campaign to reach out to *all* potential readers. "We hope," she wrote in the October 17, 1925 issue of *Publisher's Weekly*, "to reach the boys and girls who are continuing their education by their own efforts." She cited statistics in Cleveland (a city of many immigrants) in the 1920s—only 25 percent of high-school age youth were in school, of which 30 percent would not finish, and only 2 percent would go on to college. She firmly believed that librarians had "to start" with reluctant readers, the mischievous, youths in the gangs, who she once referred to as "the mechanically minded."

> We want this room to be used by the young people of high school age who are working in downtown offices and factories, and who are not using branch libraries, and who perhaps are occasional borrowers at the main library. (*Publisher's Weekly* 108:1413 [October 17, 1925]).

This was to be a room for "good readers, reluctant readers, and kids who had left high school and continued their education on their own."

Beginning in the mid-1920s, Roos arranged for all students who were leaving school to fill out forms with their names, addresses, the library they went to (if they used one), and the library where they might go if they did not have one. These forms were left with the school librarians, and the follow-up was done by the branch librarians. The library also sent to *all* young people under 17 who had been issued a work permit a form called a job card, which informed them of the services of their nearest branch library and invited them to use its facilities. In the 1930s, contacting young people individually via her own staff or school librarians became unfeasible, so Roos tried to get introductory cards to teenagers via fifty major employers of minors.

From the beginning of her career, Roos said that one vital aspect of librarianship for young people was maintaining relationships with other adults, especially those who worked with youths in other institutional settings. In the 1930s, Roos rechanneled her efforts to get out-of-school youth into the library by allying the library to other social institutions. In 1938, she deposited a collection of books in the offices of the National Youth Administration (NYA); adolescents who applied for NYA aid were invited to the Stevenson Room to make use of the collection and were told by NYA youth workers that the library's pamphlet files and vocational materials would be useful. In an aggressive effort to make other youth workers in the city familiar with the CPL's facilities and materials, Roos became active on many youth advocacy committees, serving on as many as twenty in the early 1940s. In 1949, at the height of this effort, Roos had contacted over 900 groups outside the library, of which over 500 actually visited the library.

Roos's Stevenson Room often co-sponsored joint programs with other youth agencies. Her most famous—"Roads to World Understanding"—lasted from 1945 to 1962 and was a cooperative effort to foster and develop world understanding. Each program centered on a different country (53 were covered in all) and might include films or slides, music or dancing from that country, or a guest speaker or a panel. Exhibits were borrowed from the Cleveland Art Museum; the CPL contributed books, maps, and magazines; and the 80,000 member Cleveland Press World Friends Club exhibited the letters that they had sent and received from children of other countries. "Roads to World Understanding" was a huge success, with a total attendance of 31,500. Its success was due in part to an active youth advisory committee that helped in the planning; also, it was a timely project, following so closely on the end of the war in which many of the students' fathers and brothers fought.

Roos also ran a very successful poetry group in the library from 1927 to 1942, in which young people wrote poetry and shared it with their peers. She also hosted book discussion groups from 1921 to 1956 and a book reviewing group, which, Roos wrote, produced surprisingly sophisticated criticism and was useful for librarians in their book selection. "All programs and activities," she wrote in the October 1954 issue of *Library Trends*, "are linked to young people's interests, all tie in with library materials, all provide valuable group experience, and an opportunity to relate personal interests to broader social and educational goals." In addition to the perennial summer reading clubs (begun as early as 1927), the Stevenson Room also sponsored two baseball clubs, a science club, and a Dr. DuBois Club.

In 1938, Charles Rush, then director of the CPL and a strong advocate of public library service to young adults, created a new department called the Office for Service to Youth (renamed the Youth Department in 1943) and named Jean Roos its supervisor in 1940. Though she was directly responsible to Rush, Roos was able to hire and train staff for the Stevenson Room and for branches, and to provide in-service training for the other librarians, which she began in 1941. Branch librarians, however, reported directly to their branch heads, so that Roos was not their direct supervisor. Although she did conduct weekly visits to branches and held monthly discussion meetings with the librarians, some library historians have suggested that work with the branches was not her strong point, and that the monthly meetings were deadly and static. There was apparently little discussion about books or services, and very little programming went on at the branch level.

Roos's writings indicate a strong avowal of reading guidance, which she defined as "the librarian's personal attention to a reader's needs." Over and over again, Roos stressed the need for the librarian to be well-read (*she* obviously was), to maintain a sustained interest in the reader, and to convey his/her own interests and enthusiasms. Personal contact, she wrote repeatedly, is the key to good service, working directly with young adults through conversation and discussion is the only way that the young adult librarian could keep up with their interests and reading habits.

Roos suggested that both the untrained librarian and the student would benefit from reader's notes, annotations of no longer than 35 words. These "teasers," which were used until 1957, were pasted in the book, kept in a card file, or in a notebook of annotations. Booklists were provided in all libraries, "not too long and always annotated."

Roos's training of librarians was much less sophisticated and rigorous than that of other heads of major young adult rooms or departments who were working contemporaneously. Nor was Roos very active in the schools, a problem that might have been exacerbated by the fact that Cleveland's school library service was, as previously noted, under the supervision of the public library from 1895 to 1968. Although Roos herself selected books for the school libraries at first, branch librarians did not make class visits or do many booktalks in the schools because Roos felt that the school librarians had enough professional standards and adequate literary backgrounds so that they could handle this task themselves.

Roos wrote throughout her entire professional career. Aside from describing the philosophy which informed the work in her beloved Stevenson Room, Roos also wrote about the importance of service to youth, especially reading guidance. She wrote with surprising compassion (though often idealistically) about the youth of her day, their needs and the ability of librarians to guide them.

> Youth longs for new things, old things are too commonplace; it is startled by new emotions and new ideals, and so experiments for itself. It will not accept, now, the law of its childhood but continually demands the why of things,

taking nothing for granted. Self-assertion often hides sensitiveness and self-consciousness. It craves companionship, sympathy, praise and approbation, and in all ways it is essentially honest. It needs a disciplinarian last, a comrade first ... contacts mean a great deal now, but there must be no superimposing of ideas, and guidance should be given indirectly. By continual stressing of the best, one can make possible a vigorous growth of the desirable, so that there will be little chance for the weeds to develop.

The librarian, then, in the role of an understanding comrade first, and a disciplinarian last, and as a custodian of a vast storehouse of books, can develop immeasurably the reading interests of this teen age group whose reading should be as broad as the sea and as high as the heavens.... (*Library Journal* 53:581 [July 1928]).

And in 1960, speaking at a conference on adolescents and their reading, she said that libraries would need to conform to the changing needs of youth. Because of the media, she said, young people are "exposed to social questions and issues beyond their experiences. Conflicting and changing concepts of life, changing values confuse them. The library, therefore, should become an important factor in their lives in their search for direction."

Roos prepared several bibliographies for young people based on the strongly held, often articulated, belief that they turn to fiction for truth. Books, she believed, should match teenagers' interests, but they should also expand and deepen these interests. Roos spoke and wrote often about the problem that occurs when young people get into a rut in their reading. She said people who read one type of story (e.g., westerns, romances) to the exclusion of everything else, are "merry-go-round" readers. Roos suggested, in her most famous book, *Patterns in Reading* (Chicago: American Library Association, 1954), that young adult librarians combat this problem by identifying subject areas ranging from Adventure and Mystery to World War II, using one central book to catch the youth's attention, and then supplementing easier-to-read books that the student might read before and more difficult ones that he or she might read after.

Roos's bibliographic work strongly enhanced her philosophy that a reader might be lured to excellence if a librarian is there to intercede and that "the purpose of work with young people is to stimulate and direct the reading interest of youth into adult reading on as high a reading level and into as many fields as possible." In her 1954 *Library Trends* state-of-the-art article on service to young adults, Roos wrote, "Every public library has the potential for special service for youth." She fervently believed that this could be accomplished with no special space (it just had to be reallocated; a corner would do), no new staff (train the most talented staff member), no special book collection (supplement the existing collection with a few new titles), and not even additional funds (although in her later years, she did suggest that service be allocated based on a percentage of adolescent usage).

Roos was an active member of ALA, serving on the Council, on the Nominating Committee, as a member of the Coordinating Committee on Standards for Librarians, as the chairperson for the ALA-National Education Association Joint Committee, and on the ALA Executive Board in 1954. Roos was president of ALA's Division of Libraries for Children and Young People in 1947-1948 and was instrumental in the organization of the Young People's Reading Round Table. In 1939-1940, she served as the librarian representative to the White House Conference on Children in a Democracy.

When she retired from CPL in 1959, Roos moved to Florida, where she worked as an acting librarian and with the Friends Group of the Martin County Public Library. She died on March 21, 1982, at the age of 91.

Jean Roos's strengths—her social awareness, her desire to serve the unserved, her commitment to high ideals for youth, her extraordinary energy—were immensely well-suited to the period in which she worked and wrote. She organized and created a viable library service for many young people who were, indeed, eager for what she and her staff of librarians had to offer. She shared with the other pioneers of early young adult service in those early years (notably Margaret Edwards of Enoch Pratt and Mabel Williams of the New York Public Library) a vitality, a strong sense of mission, and an ability to communicate with the potential clientele in the communities each served.

Biographical listings and obituaries—[Obituary]. *ALA Yearbook 1982* (1983); [Obituary]. *School Library Journal* 29:15 (January 1983); *Who's Who in Library Service*, 1st, 2nd, 3rd eds. **Books and articles about the biographee**—Atkinson, Joan. "Pioneers in Public Service to Young Adults." *Top of the News* 43:27-44 (Fall 1986); Braverman, Miriam. *Youth, Society, and the Public Library*. Chicago: American Library Association, 1979, 116-79. **Primary sources and archival materials**—The Cleveland Public Library holds materials on file about Jean Roos. Roos's annual reports are also available at the library.

—SUSAN STEINFIRST

SHERA, JESSE HAUK (1903-1982)

Jesse Hauk Shera was born December 8, 1903, in Oxford, Ohio, to Charles H. and Jessie Hauk Shera. He earned an A.B. with a major in English literature from Miami University in Oxford in 1925, an M.A. in English from Yale University in 1927, and a Ph.D. from the Graduate Library School of the University of Chicago (GLS) in 1944. He was married to Helen M. Bickham in 1928, with whom he had two children, Mary Helen and Edward Brookins.

Shera entered librarianship directly after receiving his master's degree in English at Yale. He found college teaching positions in English hard to come by and he accepted an appointment as an assistant cataloger in the library of his old college, Miami University. The next year, in 1928, he became a bibliographer at the Scripps Foundation for Population Research, also in his hometown. He kept that appointment until 1940, gaining experience as a special librarian that was to color much of his thought about libraries throughout his life. Between 1938 and 1940, however, he was on leave to study at the University of Chicago Graduate Library School, which did not require its candidates for advanced degrees to have a prior degree in library science.

After finishing his course work at the University of Chicago, Shera became chief of the library census project at the Library of Congress. From 1941 to 1944 he was assistant chief, Central Information Division of the Office of Strategic Services (OSS). Confronted at OSS not only with the task of supervising a conventional library and picture collection, he also had to organize reports from the various armed services and censorship intercepts. There he fell back on some of his experience at the Scripps Foundation and utilized tabulating machines, punched cards, and other new technology machines available to librarians at the time.

In Washington, Shera continued to work on his Ph.D. dissertation, which he completed in 1944, and he renewed his acquaintance with Ralph Beals, assistant director of the District of Columbia Public Library, whom he met as a student at GLS. Beals then returned to Chicago to direct the University of Chicago Library, and in 1944 he invited Shera to join his staff there. Going as a bibliographer in the social sciences, Shera soon became chief of preparations and then assistant director. Beals left Chicago in 1946 to become director of the New York Public Library. Shera, a man of strong loyalties as well as some strong dislikes, idolized Beals.

Shera, who had been thwarted by job scarcity from becoming a professor when he left Yale twenty years earlier, "backing," as he often said, "into the library profession," joined the faculty of the Chicago Graduate Library School in 1947 as an assistant professor, teaching courses in American library history, academic libraries, cataloging, library administration and the theory of classification. Advancing to the rank of associate professor and tenure in 1951, he left that position in 1952 to become dean of the School of Library Science (SLS) at Western Reserve University (WRU).

His career flowered at Western Reserve. He increased the size of the faculty, expanded the SLS graduate student population, and initiated a doctoral program in 1956, which served as a model for other library schools in its disciplinary approach. In 1953 he became editor of *American Documentation*, thus quickly identifying the SLS and WRU with scholarly research in documentation and special librarianship. From 1954 to 1959, he was editor of the Western Reserve University Press. He persuaded James Perry and Allen Kent from the Battelle Memorial Institute to join the faculty in 1955 and to establish the Center for Documentation and Communication Research (CDCR), which pioneered a curriculum and research agenda for the embryonic field of information retrieval. In 1956 the CDCR sponsored a Conference on the Practical Utilization of Recorded Knowledge (PURK), which brought together 700 representatives from industry, government, business, higher education, and librarianship to discuss common problems. The PURK Conference became the first in a series of interdisciplinary and international gatherings under CDCR auspices. Shera served as the center's director from 1960 to 1971. During that time, research and development in methods of information storage and retrieval gravitated towards government and private industry control, but Shera continued to work on an information curriculum of new courses and seminars.

In 1956 Shera received a grant from the Carnegie Corporation to undertake a three-year study of library education. From 1961 to 1968, he contributed a column, "Without Reserve," to *Wilson Library Bulletin*. After the merger of Western Reserve University with Case Institute of Technology in 1967, Shera remained as dean of the School of Library and Information Science. He retired as dean in 1970, but continued as a professor. In 1970-1971, he served as visiting professor at the University of Texas. In 1972 he became dean emeritus at Case Western Reserve, and continued writing and lecturing until his death.

Throughout his professional life, Shera was a prolific writer, and it was primarily as an author that he exercised an enduring influence on the library and information science profession. His first article appeared in *Library Journal* in 1931. When he died in 1982 he was in the process of preparing, with the help of his wife, a long biographical article, "Herman Howe Fussler," which appeared in the festschrift issue for the latter, published posthumously in *Library Quarterly* in July 1983. "A Bibliography of Jesse Hauk Shera," compiled by Gretchen M. Isard appears in Conrad H. Rawski, ed., *Toward a Theory of Librarianship: Papers in Honor of Jesse Hauk Shera* (Metuchen, N.J.: Scarecrow Press, 1973). It lists his publications through December 1971, including 11 books that he wrote, edited, or assisted in editing, 45 chapters in books, 10 reports, 108 periodical articles, 74 columns in *Wilson Library Bulletin*, 29 editorials in *American Documentation*, and 104 book reviews. Between 1972 and 1983, *Library Literature* recorded an additional 45 publications—some of them reprints and collections.

Jesse Shera wrote on a wide range of library topics. As Verner H. Clapp wrote in his tongue-in-cheek "Foreword: Toward a Theory of Jesse Shera" in the Shera festschrift, "... Jesse Shera has been too many for us; we could not keep up with him; and while we were heavily preparing to confront him on one front, he was gaily firing off on another."

Shera's writing was often eloquent and made frequent use of apposite quotations drawn from the great literature of our cultural history. This reflection of wide reading is all the more remarkable because he suffered visual handicaps that made reading somewhat difficult for him. He was afflicted with strabismus and in addition wore thick-lensed glasses. Confronting the problem of poor eyesight, he concentrated on compensating for it. He trained his memory to retain passages for recall at a useful time. In spite of his vision handicaps, Shera was a forceful figure at library meetings throughout the world. Helen, his wife, helped him control his manuscripts and other difficulties created by his vision problem.

The strabismus badly affected Shera's appearance, and he no doubt was aware of it. He was concerned about it as a student at Yale, and later wrote, "Tucker Brooks thinks impaired vision will not be a handicap to our securing a position on a college faculty." He was interested in sports and fondly remembered the Yale Bowl, as he told me once; but he could not participate in games demanding good vision. Perhaps the irascibility he sometimes displayed in personal relations and the provocativeness that often characterized his words were traits of compensation. Yet colleagues from his Chicago days have reported with admiration his refusal to yield to the physical restraints of his handicap. He ran unflinchingly up and down the six stone flights of Harper East Tower, and he identified people he could not see by mere hints of inflection in their voices.

His eyesight seemed to worsen as he grew older. In 1967 he was unable to visit India to deliver his lectures in the Ranganathan Lecture Series. He wrote to Dr. Ranganathan in part: "I must let you know that it will be necessary for me to cancel my proposed trip to India. The reasons for this are many, but the most important consideration and one that cannot be avoided is the state of my eyesight." (He added that he did not want to expose his wife to the worry that such a trip would cause her. The oral tapes of his lectures that he sent in lieu of his presence were published as *Sociological Foundations of Librarianship* [New York: Asia Publishing House, 1970]). When I last saw him in Chicago in 1981, he carried a white cane.

A recurring refrain in Shera's writings is the unity of the library with its sociological underpinnings. This appears in his studies of library history, on bibliographical organization, on library education, and in his more casual essays commenting on the library scene. His *Foundations of the Public Library: The Origins of the Public Library Movement in New England, 1629-1955* (Chicago: University of Chicago Press, 1949), a publication of his 1944 doctoral dissertation, illustrates the theme. In this study, he sought to find "those elements in American life which contributed directly or indirectly to the growth of the public library as a social agency." Institutions, in his view, were such basic organizations as the family and state, which determined the pattern of society. That social pattern, in turn, generated such social agencies as the school and the library.

Guided by his controlling assumption, his historical study of public library origins rests on an examination of the primary records of 1,085 social libraries established for community use in New England from 1733 to 1855. Using statistical tables, he analyzed their interests, goals, income, duration, book collections, and use. Mingled with the results of the primary research was his exposition of the contemporary life and culture in the region. Causal factors for the emergence of the public library that he identified included those that move society in many areas: economic ability; scholarship, historical research, and the urge for conservation; local pride; the social importance of universal public education; self-education and the lyceum movement; the vocational movement; and other lesser factors such as religion and the aims of the professional classes.

Shera's reputation as a library historian was established with this book. He was criticized by some for the contention that society shapes the library rather than the library shaping society, but he did not waver from his position. He continued his interest in library history after other interests and responsibilities led him elsewhere. He wrote on the nature and uses of library history and authored many reviews of historical monographs; but he never again undertook a library history comparable to *Foundations of the Public Library*. In fact, although he dealt with only one region of the U.S. and concluded the story with 1855, he thought he had written the definitive social history of the emergence of the form. His *Historians, Books, and Libraries* (Cleveland: Western Reserve University Press, 1953) was begun as a part of the syllabus for the core courses in the literature of the social sciences at Chicago. In the final decade of his life he served on the editorial board that produced the *Dictionary of American Library Biography* (Littleton, Colo.: Libraries Unlimited, 1978).

Shera's major writing on bibliographic organizations began in collaboration with Margaret Egan, a younger colleague at Chicago, whom he later invited to serve on the faculty at Western Reserve. In 1950 they led a conference on bibliographic organization at the Graduate Library School. The fourteen papers presented at the conference included contributions by the most eminent national and international scholars in the area, and were published with the title *Bibliographic Organization* by the University of Chicago Press in 1951. Shera's own paper dealt with classification. He began with a history of classification in general from Aristotle to Comte and then reviewed the history of library classification, reaching for a principle that "classification is basic to bibliographic organization." From that, he argued for divorcing classification from hierarchical order because such a single-faceted arrangement failed to account for multifarious relations in a book. He was one of the first American librarians to take note of classifications used outside libraries.

In 1952, Shera and Egan published "Foundations of a Theory of Bibliography" in an April 1952 issue of *Library Quarterly* (22:125-38). In it they called for "the analysis of the production and utilization of intellectual products" in much the same way that material products had been investigated. The idea had been adumbrated by others. Among library scholars, Douglas Waples and Pierce Butler and their students at Chicago had written about it, but Shera and Egan stated it as the integrating principle of bibliographical study. Fritz Machlup's economic study, *The Production and Distribution of Knowledge in the United States*, was not published until ten years later, but it hardly touched libraries. With the development of information science, the economic approach to knowledge was to become a major area of inquiry. Shera and Egan called it "social epistemology," a term Shera often repeated.

In 1956, Shera and Egan published *The Classified Catalog: Basic Principles and Practices* (Chicago: American Library Association). This was a report of a study, financed by a Rockefeller grant, of the classified catalog of the John Crerar Library of Chicago. Typically for these authors, it included a chapter on "The Nature and Functions of the Library Catalog" and another on "General Principles for the Construction of a Classification System." The two chapters were not remarkably original in their content, but they illustrate an insistence on a search for underlying principles. This intellectual collaboration of Shera and Egan ended with her tragic early death from an aneurysm in 1959, shortly before her fifty-fourth birthday.

Shera understood library periodicals and published a stream of articles throughout his career, attracting a wide following among readers. As editor (1953-1960) of *American Documentation*, the quarterly journal of the American Documentation Institute (of which he was a charter member), he was skillful in acquiring research manuscripts, and during his editorship the journal gained international stature, publishing articles by leading documentalists and information scientists in the United States and England.

As column editor of "Without Reserve" for *Wilson Library Bulletin*, he had an opportunity to express whatever was on his mind. He did so for seventy-four issues, giving each column its own issue title under the general one. Examples include "Yes, Virginia, There Is a Verner Clapp," "The Compleat Librarian," "Isis and the Librarian's Quest for Unity." With rhetorical polish, he drew on thinkers from the past and present, ranging from Aristotle and Milton to Henry Wriston Brown and Robert M. Hutchins, and leaning often on his library heroes, such as L. R. Wilson, Ralph Beals, and S. R. Ranganathan. Sometimes he also poked fun at people and ideas or held them up to scorn. About one proposed American Library Association action against censorship he protested: "The staunch Jeffersonian doctrine that every jackass has his constitutional right to bray, does not imply that we must amplify every insane bellow until it echoes and reverberates down the corridors of time" ("A Book for Burning," *Wilson Library Bulletin* 37:790 [May 1963]). He sometimes sought adversaries where there were none, as editor John Wakeman observed in a wry "sic" footnoting a column that presumed his editorial opposition to printing Shera's opinions.

By and large, "Without Reserve" hammered away at the issues that won its author a wide following. He defined "the true essence of librarianship" as "the maximization of the effective use of graphic records for any purpose that contributes to the dignity, beauty, and strength of human endeavor." Repetitively he deplored the resistance to the computer, the machine that he had blamed for the split between librarianship and documentation, and later information science. Over and again he asserted his thesis that the library must derive its goals and practices from the needs and goals of society, based on historical understanding of how our society came to be.

As his bibliography shows, much of Shera's writing was in the form of basic articles on various aspects of library and information science that were published in major general and subject encyclopedias, yearbooks, and annual reviews. All had a certain cohesiveness. Douglas Foskett, the English librarian and classificationist, edited a book of Shera essays entitled *Libraries and the Organization of Knowledge* (Hamden, Conn.: Archon Books, 1965). Foskett wrote in the introduction about new practices and needs reported in library literature. Then he said, "From time to time, a leading thinker makes a new synthesis by combining these explanations into a system, or theory, which gives a rational account of what is going on, and so prepares the way forward." Such a leader, he asserted, was Jesse Shera.

The word "foundations" appeared repeatedly in Shera's titles. *The Foundations of Education for Librarianship* (New York: Becker and Hayes, 1972) was the report of his Carnegie commission to study the needs of library education. Sixteen years in the making, the scope of his book was broadly cultural, as he explained in his preface: "We cannot pursue our limited calling with scarcely a thought for our place in the drama of human endeavor.... Francis Bacon was right in insisting that a subject should not be studied only within itself; the inquiry must be generalized."

His reference to our *limited* calling meant to him that librarianship is limited like any calling by special knowledge, practices, and goals. Pursuing his purpose of generalized inquiry, he started with a consideration of communication and the individual and spiraled in narrowing circles through fourteen chapters to the administration of library schools. Supported by readings in widely ranging disciplines in many periods of history as well as by his long concern with library problems and his long experience in library schools, this book rebuts criticism of its long period of gestation. It won the Scarecrow Press Award in 1974.

Written with Shera's mastery of rhetoric and style, the book conveys along with its theoretical message some aura of arrogance. Partly because of his backdoor entrance into librarianship and his early experience in unconventional libraries, and also by the keenness of his intellect, Shera considered himself a rebel in the profession. In the preface he rejected the main body of library literature, and in the epilogue he wrote: "One need be scarcely surprised that the restless youth of the profession, looking at its leadership and seeing mostly mediocrity, is in revolt."

Shera's rousing rhetoric, which characterized so much of his writing and inspired so many librarians, was well illustrated by John Berry in his *Library Journal* obituary column, "Shera's Rich Legacy." Berry quoted from an oral address presented by Shera to the students at the State University of New York School of Library Science at Geneseo. Shera began his final charge to the students with a quotation from *The Lantern-Bearer*, by Rosemary Suttcliff: " 'To keep something burning, to carry the light as best we can forward into the darkness and the wind': that, good friends, is the apotheosis of librarianship; that it is what librarianship is all about. To bring man and book together in a fruitful relationship for the individual, and through the individual to society, and to do so in an environment hospitable to serious meditation; that is our task."

Shera gathered many honors that librarians bestow. Chronologically listed they include: Beta Phi Mu Award, 1965; Melvil Dewey Medal, 1968; Distinguished Service Award (Drexel University), 1971; Lippincott Medal, 1973; Award of Merit (ASIS), 1973; Ohio Library Hall of Fame, 1973; Scarecrow Press Award, 1974; Kaula Gold Medal (India Library Association, 1976); Picken Award (Baldwin-Wallace College), 1976; Life Member, American Library Association, 1976; and the University of Chicago Alumni Award, 1977. Besides ALA, he belonged to Special Libraries Association, American Documentation Institute, Association of American Library Schools, Ohio Library Association, Mississippi Valley Historical Association (later Organization of American Historians), American Academy of Arts and Sciences, Phi Beta Kappa, Beta Phi Mu, and Phi Alpha Delta.

He served as a delegate to the UNESCO International Conference at Paris (1950), presenting the U.S. report, and he was a delegate to the International Conference on Bibliographic Classification, Dorking, England (1957). He was a member of the President's Commission on Employment of the Handicapped (1969-1980) and the President's Commission on Library Research and Education. He died in Cleveland, Ohio, on March 8, 1982.

Biographical listings and obituaries—*ALA Yearbook 1976* (1977); [Obituary]. *American Libraries* 13:320ff. (April 1982); [Obituary]. *College & Research Libraries News* 5:184 (May 1982); [Obituary]. *Current Biography* (1982); [Obituary]. *International Classification* 9:170 (Fall 1982); [Obituary]. *Journal of Library History* 17:518-20 (Fall 1982); [Obituary]. *Library Acquisitions* 6:246 (Fall 1982); [Obituary]. *Library Journal* 28:663 (April 1, 1982); [Obituary]. *Wilson Library Bulletin* 56:631 (April 1982). **Books and articles about the biographee**—Most of Shera's publications are listed in Isard, G. M., comp. "A Bibliography of Jesse Hauk Shera." In Conrad Rawski, ed. *Toward a Theory of Librarianship: Papers in Honor of Jesse Hauk Shera.* Metuchen, N.J.: Scarecrow Press, 1973; Wright, H. Curtis. "Shera as a Bridge between Librarianship and Information Science." *Journal of Library History* 10:137-56 (Spring 1985). **Primary sources and archival materials**—Shera's personal papers are housed in the Case Western Reserve University Archives, Cleveland, Ohio. They occupy 29 linear feet, 12 of which are publications, and 2 of office files.

—HOWARD W. WINGER

SHORES, LOUIS (1904-1981)

Louis Shores was born in Buffalo, New York, on September 14, 1904, to Paul and Ernestine Luttenberg Shores, the middle child of five. His parents were German immigrants who had settled in Cleveland, Ohio, in the late 1880s. The family's sojourn in Buffalo was a short one and its occasion unknown. The Shores returned to Cleveland almost immediately after Louis's birth.

Shores's father was an artist whose paintings won little popular approval; his mother was an excellent seamstress who maintained the family in genteel poverty. In 1918 she moved the children, without their father, to Toledo where she felt their educational opportunities were better. Through high school Louis contributed to the family income by his newspaper route and as a page in the Toledo Public Library.

After graduation from high school, Shores entered the University of Toledo where he majored in English. From his childhood, he wanted to be a writer and, at the university, he was encouraged in this aspiration by his younger brother Emmanuel, his close friend, Raphael Spiro, a violinist and fellow student, and Martin Ross, an older student who went on to become prominent in the early stages of educational television.

Writing poetry was Shores's first love, but he was practical enough to realize that this would not produce a remunerative career. Upon obtaining his B.A. in 1926, he and the remainder of the family (his mother, Emmanuel, and Helen, a younger sister) moved to New York City where opportunity for Emmanuel to study music was superior to Toledo and where Shores entered a graduate program in education at the City College of New York, finding employment as a page at the New York Public Library. He received a master's degree in 1927, but found that New York had no teaching jobs for an inexperienced high school English teacher and that rural areas presented few opportunities for a Jewish teacher attempting to gain the necessary experience to compete for a position in the city. Instead he decided to enter the newly opened School of Library Service at Columbia University, where he was awarded the B.S. in library science in 1928. Armed with these credentials, Shores was finally prepared to embark on his life's work.

His decision to accept an offer from Fisk University in Nashville, Tennessee, was applauded by his family. Ernestine Shores had raised her children in an atmosphere of racial and religious tolerance. The neighborhoods in which she could afford acceptable housing were invariably of mixed ethnic background and her own attitudes were reflected in the upbringing of the children. Although it is evident that his father, Paul, was of Jewish heritage, neither he nor the family followed that tradition. The children, from an early age, attended the churches of various friends. Usually these were Protestant, occasionally Roman Catholic.

In 1928 Fisk University was in turmoil. As part of a new president's program to raise the academic level of the university, the employment of a professionally trained librarian was necessary. Shores was undoubtedly recommended for the job by Ernest J. Reece, a member of the Columbia faculty. Reece had visited the Fisk Library as a consultant in August 1926, and the major need he cited in his unpublished report was that of a competent, trained librarian. Shores accepted the challenge and immediately began implementing the techniques he had learned at Columbia. His greatest triumph at Fisk, however, was organization of the Negro Library Conference held on November 20-23, 1931, in conjunction with the dedication of a new library building. Shores was criticized for excluding white southern librarians from the general invitation, but the meeting was judged a success. For the most part, in fact, papers reflected conservative mainstream positions on librarianship.

Shores had other, more personal, goals. He realized that success in academe depended on credentials as well as talent and, in 1929, after an aborted attempt to work toward the doctorate at Columbia's Teachers College, he entered the new doctoral program at the Graduate Library School at the University of Chicago. By 1930, he had reached the stage of collecting data for his dissertation on the reading interests of Fisk graduates, but a basic philosophical conflict with the director of his dissertation, Douglas Waples, forced him to abandon Chicago and enter the doctoral program at George Peabody College for Teachers in Nashville, where he was awarded the Ph.D. in 1934 for a dissertation on the development of libraries in the colonial colleges.

While at Fisk, he became a member of the Baptist Church and with the purchase of his first car developed his lifelong passion for long distance driving. Shores was also active in school and community affairs. He coached the Fisk debate team and was a regular participant in a weekly talk and news program on a local Nashville radio station. On November 19, 1931, he married Geraldine Urist, whom he had met while a student at the University of Chicago. For a year after their marriage, his wife remained in Chicago to teach school. But the financial advantages of maintaining two incomes was undermined by the fiscal uncertainty of the Chicago school system and she soon joined Shores in Nashville.

Early in his tenure at Fisk, Shores had suggested to Fisk President Thomas Jones that the university should consider establishing a library school. Jones was enthusiastic about any plan to advance the cause of black education in the South and to enhance Fisk's influence. Fisk was, at the time, the only black college offering a strong liberal arts education and seemed to many to be the best place at which education for librarians in the tradition approved by the American Library Association (ALA) could be realized. But, Shores's dream of establishing a school for black librarians at Fisk was doomed. Despite his persistence and the support of the Fisk administration, the school at the Hampton Institute preempted him.

In 1933, Shores accepted the deanship of the library school at George Peabody College for Teachers in Nashville. His challenge at Peabody was securing ALA accreditation for the school. ALA's Board of Education for Librarianship (BEL) was reluctant to offer full accreditation to any school not associated with a college or university and felt that Peabody, as a teacher's college, qualified as neither. The BEL would only approve its graduates for school library positions. The conflict with the BEL over "full" accreditation forged Shores's philosophy of educational librarianship. He argued that if a librarian's function was educational, then academic librarians with their educational responsibilities were properly prepared by the same schools that prepared other teachers. By the 1930s, the idea that librarians had an educational role was firmly established in the literature of public librarianship. Shores embraced the logical extension of his deeply held belief that libraries were educational institutions in his argument that teacher's colleges were also the appropriate place to train public librarians.

While members of the BEL felt that his rationale was self-serving, Shores was sincere. In high school, he came to believe that reference sources in libraries duplicated his teachers' lectures and that reference books offered information accessible to everyone. It was a realization that led directly to his first major contribution to the literature of reference services in 1937, *Basic Reference Books*. This book went through three editions and became a standard textbook in library schools well into the 1960s. Generations of librarians were trained not in an approach to reference work that addressed the titles one by one, but focused instead on prioritizing resources to employ the most productive possibilities.

Shores's tenure at Peabody was successful. He showed an innovative approach to library education and an ability to work productively with the Peabody administration. He attempted to establish his vision of librarianship as an educational enterprise and fought for the accreditation of the school. His intention at the outset was to address the interests of both schools and libraries in the Peabody curriculum. To further this, he offered courses for nonlibrarians and school administrators in the library's role in teaching. Under his deanship, the school offered the first regular course in the country in audiovisual materials. However, he was less than successful in obtaining acceptance of the Peabody program by the library community and the BEL.

Shores found the military an exciting third career when he tried to enlist in the Army Air Corps at the outbreak of World War II. Overage, undersized, and nearsighted, he was finally accepted for a special officers' candidate program in Miami and was assigned to the liberty ship, the *Penelope Barker*, as a security officer. The ship was part of a convoy delivering supplies to the Soviet Union and upon arrival he was assigned to a cryptographic unit in New Delhi in the Army Airways Communication System (AACS). After the war, Shores published his third book, a history of the AACS, royalties from which went to the Army Air Forces Aid Society.

His promotion to major in April 1945 acknowledged his contribution to the war effort. He was transferred back to the states in October 1944, as historical officer and chief of the Intelligence Analysis Division for the AACS, where he remained until demobilized in 1945. Using the techniques he had perfected while working on his doctoral dissertation, he collated historical information from all AACS units to compile a comprehensive picture of operations.

Shores remained active in the Air Force Reserves for a short time until he was ordered back to active duty as librarian for the new Air University at Maxwell Air Force Base in Alabama. Rather than accept this appointment, however, he resigned his commission, although he remained active as a consultant and lecturer at the Air University. In addition, he organized several workshops for military librarians at Florida State University.

Because Shores had been on leave from Peabody during the war, he faced a dilemma when he was demobilized. During his absence, a new administration had come to power which mandated that all faculty members teach four quarters a year rather than the customary three, at substantially the same salary. Shores refused to accept the new terms and actively sought other employment. For a while, he toyed with the idea of starting a business, with his wife as consultant, for people wishing to establish private libraries. He abandoned this notion in favor of a more stable job as editor-in-chief for *Collier's Encyclopedia*.

The arrangement was soon changed. In 1941, Doak Campbell, who had been dean of the Graduate School at Peabody when Shores was dean of the Library School, became president of Florida State College for Women. As part of his effort to turn the woman's college into a university, he determined to start a library school and turned to Shores as the appropriate person to head it. Campbell was so convinced that Shores was the man for the job that he offered him the choice between the deanship of the new school or the directorship of the library provided he organize the library school in his spare time. He allowed Shores to write his own contract. The latter responded by appointing himself dean of the School of Library Training and Service at Florida State University (FSU) and consulting editor for *Collier's*. His salary was divided between the university and the encyclopedia.

Collier's wanted to make Shores full-time editor-in-chief in 1946, but the lure of a deanship, even though it offered less financial rewards, proved too strong. In 1952 William Terry Couch became the senior editor instead. As an intellectual conservative, Couch brought new vision to the encyclopedia and his concept of the educational function of reference tools matched Shores's philosophy perfectly.

The extent of Shores's service to *Collier's* is difficult to assess. He participated in the decisions to include specific articles, in the design of the index, and especially in recruiting contributors. His ability to attract qualified scholars from the ranks of smaller academic institutions, his position as dean of an accredited library school, and the weight his name carried among reference librarians (most of whom had used his text in their reference courses in library schools across the country), were his essential contributions to the enterprise.

His career at *Collier's* culminated in the production of the 1962 revision of the encyclopedia. Because Colliers fired Couch in 1959, the early stages of the first major revision of the encyclopedia were left in a state of chaos. Shores was the only senior member of the editorial staff remaining in whom the company management had confidence. He gladly accepted the challenge of completing the groundwork laid by Couch and led the revision through to completion.

The years 1960 through 1962 saw him mostly in New York attending to editorial and production details of the encyclopedia. His involvement was so intense that he interested FSU president Robert Strozier and the president of Collier-Crowell in a scheme to move the encyclopedia to Tallahassee. He wanted to establish a relationship between *Collier's* and FSU similar to that between *Britannica* and the University of Chicago. The plan progressed to the point where the Tallahassee Chamber of Commerce had become active in the negotiations and a team from *Collier's* New York offices visited the city to inspect potential sites. But, Strozier's death and Shores's attack of better sense aborted the plot. While Strozier was enthusiastic, so was Shores. But he soon realized that the facilities at FSU and in Tallahassee were not adequate to support a major encyclopedia. Further, the idea generated great opposition by some influential members of the FSU library school faculty who felt that Shores intended to use them and the students of the school as a source of inexpensive labor for the encyclopedia.

Collier's retained his name on the title page as editor-in-chief after the 1962 edition, but Shores's main role turned to promotion. His much publicized tour of the world in 1964 was an attempt to introduce *Collier's* into an international market. As part of his responsibilities, Shores presented to the national libraries of countries he visited morocco-bound typescripts of the articles on the various countries covered in the 1962 revision. But the South African government refused to accept the gift and insisted that the article be rewritten to conform to its official position on apartheid or have the encyclopedia banned from the country. The controversy resulted in an overhaul of the article that ultimately satisfied South African officials.

By the early 1960s, Shores's neglect of FSU began to cause him trouble. When hired, he essentially brought the Peabody curriculum to Florida with the enthusiastic support of FSU president Doak Campbell. FSU assumed a prominent role in the introduction of audiovisual courses. The school itself, through most of the 1950s, provided basic audiovisual services to other university departments. Shores's commitment to service prompted him to offer a library use course required of all entering graduate students and a companion course offered at the freshman level. The faculty of the school also took over the task of reviewing theses and dissertations from all graduate departments on the campus to insure bibliographic integrity.

As he withdrew from an active participation in *Collier's*, Shores devoted increasing attention to the school. From its beginning, Robert Clapp, assistant dean, had largely been left in charge of the daily operations of the school. The situation had caused great dissatisfaction among members of the faculty and, frequently, among students. Further, when Campbell retired in 1957, new university administrators reevaluated Shores's nine month, part-time contract as dean. Then, when President Strozier died in 1960, they reopened the question of a part-time dean. Through it all, Shores insisted on retaining tight control over the application of policies that he alone formulated, even though he was more frequently away from campus on *Collier's* business.

In 1960, Shores brought a proposal for a doctoral program before the university administration. It was promptly rejected. Administrators were committed to turning FSU into a research institution, but they generally recognized that Shores had neither the faculty nor the facilities to support research on the doctoral level. Shores himself showed an extensive publication record, but his strength was in exhortation to action, not in research. He was an excellent teacher and public speaker, but he showed more concern with the educational functions of libraries than the forms of research regarded highly by university administrators.

Indeed, Shores had little sympathy for and little understanding of research methods and results. From an early age, he had maintained an active interest in parapsychology and a reliance on intuitive knowledge over what he viewed as the stylistic aridity of social science research. His inability to comprehend research as it had come to be practiced undoubtedly contributed to his leaving Chicago's Graduate Library School in 1931 and definitely was responsible for his failure to secure a doctoral program at FSU in the 1960s.

During his continuing battle with the FSU administration over a doctoral program, the reestablishment of the audiovisual courses and the media center in the school, which had been moved to the College of Education in 1959, and the reinstatement of the required library use service courses, Shores ultimately failed to convince his superiors that his vision of public service and education constituted the equivalent of research. Although his final retirement from the deanship in 1967 was not directly forced by the administration, he was not encouraged to remain. In 1968, Harold Goldstein, Shores's successor as dean of the school, produced a proposal for a doctoral program that the administration found acceptable.

At first, Shores's retirement was active and exciting. He was given a permanent office in the library, where he intended to organize his collection of books and papers. He became active in consulting and considered preliminary inquiries about heading other library schools and other jobs. He also took time out for teaching at the University of Colorado at Boulder and at the University of Montreal.

But grand plans for retirement failed to materialize. On his return from the Philippines on a 1964 *Collier's* tour, he suffered his first attack of vertigo. Through the 1960s he experienced numerous seizures of dizziness and blackouts which intensified after his retirement. As his health deteriorated, he was confined to his home in Tallahassee. He was forced to limit his activities. He had to abandon teaching Sunday School at the First Baptist Church, curtail support of Lions' Club activities in which he faithfully sold brooms door-to-door and operated the merry-go-round at fairs, and relinquish participation in the International Christian Leadership, a group that met weekly and which he frequently addressed on topics dealing with the Christian response to current events. As his illness progressed, he became increasingly isolated from his friends and the library community.

For Shores, the acme of his professional career was the recognition he received in winning the Isadora Gilbert Mudge Citation and the Beta Phi Mu award in 1967. As his hopes of greater professional achievement waned, he gathered his forces to push through publication of several anthologies of his writings and his autobiography. In some cases though, these activities proved an embarrassment to his friends.

In 1972, he published at his own expense, his only novel, *Looking Forward to 1999*. It is a political polemic that focused his fears of the campus unrest of the 1960s in a totalitarian solution. The book was noticed politely by the library press and ignored by the trade reviewing media. It was a novel that many thought reflected only the illness and confused state of mind of his last years, but it represented more than that. The style is wooden and stilted. It was derived almost directly from his friend and hero Philip Wylie's 1930 novel *Gladiator*. The idea of a supernatural savior of mankind was not a new one for Shores. As a child, in 1918, he began a history of the future of America that, with some accuracy, forecast World War II and also the eventual emergence of a Messianic figure who would save America and the world from dark forces. Throughout his life he maintained an almost compulsive faith in the infallibility of authority. His affirmation of the correctness of the American military in the Vietnam conflict and in the virtue of Richard Nixon after Watergate were not aberrations in his logical processes, but basic to his character.

His reaction to the relatively quiet student protests of the 1960s on the FSU campus was, at times, vitriolic. He viewed the student activists of the period as barbarians assaulting the foundations of civilization and librarians and libraries as the ultimate defenders of the faith in the liberalizing values of education. In a sense, he felt deeply that the anti-war movement was a betrayal of the values he held closest by the one group he considered his own constituency—the students.

Louis Shores was, above all, a kind man with a deep concern for people. He has been characterized by many who knew him well as the archetype of the southern gentleman—polite, gracious, and generous. His defense of the American military in Vietnam and the resulting political events confused many who expected him to be a liberal in all matters because of his established support of the civil rights movement in the South. But it was a position that was consistent with his deeply held faith in the values of order and stability over what he could only perceive as chaos.

Louis Shores died after a long illness on June 19, 1981. His intensifying interest in the occult and in the possibility of benign extraterrestrial civilizations led him to embrace the notion that he would be transported at the moment of death to another world where he would begin a new life. Characteristically, he began another, unfinished, novel on this theme.

Any assessment of his contribution to librarianship must include his devotion to library history. In 1946, he and Wayne Shirley founded the American Library History Round Table (ALHRT) of the ALA. In 1966, he began the *Journal of Library History* (*JLH*) at Florida State. For many years, the ALHRT was composed of a small group of his friends who shared the offices among themselves, presented papers, and avoided business meetings in favor of programs. He and John David Marshall pushed for the first library history seminar which was held in 1961. The *JLH*, the Library History Round Table, and the regular continuation of the library history seminars are persistent witnesses to Shores's influence on the development of library history as a subdiscipline in American librarianship.

But his greatest contributions to the profession derive from his vision of educational librarianship. Although he frequently claimed sole responsibility for the introduction of audiovisual materials into library collections, his role was to focus a growing trend toward multi-media collection development. Through his writings in library and education journals from the 1930s on, he urged, preached, and enthused over the cause of the audiovisual revolution.

His commitment to librarianship as one of the educational professions led him in the 1930s to develop the idea of the library-college in which the library became the true focal point of the educational effort at the undergraduate level. The idea became institutionalized in what has come to be called "The Library-College Movement," replete with its own journal (*Learning Today*), a series of conferences on the primary role of the library in higher education, and the experimental implementation of variations on the idea of independent study at several undergraduate institutions.

In Shores's concept of the library-college, librarians took active roles in the educational process. As it developed, the idea became an intrusion of independent study, an educational philosophy which had growing support among educators at the secondary level, into higher education. In his vision, the library was the heart of the college and the place where all learning took place. Consequently, as the library became the critical element in the learning process, librarians would gradually take the place of classroom teachers as the true "faculty" of the college. The idea enjoyed a burst of interest in the late 1960s and early 1970s, largely as a response to the student protest movements of the period. But, by the mid-1970s, the library-college was largely a minor issue in academic librarianship.

During his retirement, Shores often expressed disappointment that his contributions were not adequately recognized. *Learning Today* continued to carry his name on its masthead and, for awhile, he edited its "Innovations" column as the founder of the library-college movement. But the *Journal of Library History* dropped his name as editor emeritus when it moved to the University of Texas in 1977.

When Shores was Dean of the FSU library school, he dreamed of operating it in better facilities. During his tenure, the library school at first labored in the abandoned barracks in which it opened in 1947, and later in the basement of the university library. In 1985, however, four years after his death, FSU dedicated a new library school building, and named it after Louis Shores.

Biographical listings and obituaries—*Contemporary Authors*, V. 13-16R (1975); [Obituary]. *Learning Today* 14:16-18 (Summer 1981); *Who's Who in Library Service*, 1st, 2nd, 3rd, 4th, 5th eds. **Books and articles by the biographee**—*Around the Library World in 76 Days: An Essay in Comparative Librarianship*. Berkeley, Calif.: Peacock Press, 1967; *Audiovisual Librarianship*. Littleton, Colo.: Libraries Unlimited, 1973; *Basic Reference Books: An Introduction to the Evaluation, Study, and Use of Reference Materials, With Special Emphasis on Some 200 Titles*. Chicago: American Library Association, 1937; 2nd ed., 1939; subsequent edition entitled *Basic Reference Sources: An Introduction to Materials and Methods*. With a chapter on Science Reference Sources by Helen Focke. Chicago: American Library Association, 1954; *Library Education*. Littleton, Colo.: Libraries Unlimited, 1972; *Looking Forward to 1999*. Tallahassee, Fla.: South Pass Press, 1972; *Quiet World: A Librarian's Crusade for Destiny: The Professional Autobiography of Louis Shores*. Hamden, Conn.: Linnet Books, 1975. **Books and articles about the biographee**—Marshall, John David. *Louis Shores, Author-Librarian: A Bibliography*. Tallahassee, Fla.: Beta Phi Mu, Gamma Chapter, Florida State University, 1979. **Primary sources and archival materials**—Louis Shores Papers, Florida State University, School of Library and Information Studies; Louis Round Wilson Papers, University of North Carolina at Chapel Hill, Southern Historical Collection; William Terry Couch Papers, University of North Carolina at Chapel Hill, Southern Historical Collection. Shores carried on extensive correspondence with almost every major figure in librarianship from the 1930s to the early 1970s. Copies of most of this correspondence can be found in his papers at Florida State University from the mid-1950s on.

—LEE SHIFLETT

SPIVACKE, HAROLD (1904-1977)

Harold Spivacke was born on July 18, 1904, in New York City. His academic work at New York University led to a B.A. in 1923 and an M.A. in 1924. Thereafter he worked briefly in the business world and later concertized as a pianist, often with his first wife, violinist Carolyn Le Fevre, to whom he was married between 1927 and 1953. In 1929 he moved to Berlin, where he studied music with Eugene d'Albert and Hugo Leichtentritt and pursued academic work at the University of Berlin under the supervision of Curt Sachs, Arnold Schering, and Karl Erich Schumann. His dissertation, in the field of acoustics, is entitled "Ueber die objektive und subjektive Tonintensitat" ("On the Subjective and Objective Intensity of Musical Sound"). Returning to America on its completion and as Hitler rose to power in 1933, he served for a year as assistant to Olin Downes, music critic of the *New York Times*. There his celebrated achievement was to persuade the violinist Fritz Kreisler to publicly acknowledge that several works that Kreisler had implied were rediscoveries of forgotten eighteenth-century manuscripts were, in fact, Kreisler's own compositions.

In 1934 Spivacke joined the Library of Congress's prestigious Music Division. Following the awesome lineage of Oscar Sonneck (1902-1917) and Carl Engel (1922-1934), the Music Division was unsettled in its direction. Engel's successor, Oliver Strunk, was about to begin a distinguished career as a musicologist at Princeton University. When Spivacke was hired as assistant chief, he remained mostly in the background at first. But in 1937 he became acting chief, and in 1938 chief. Under his direction and during his long tenure (1938-1972) the Music Division moved boldly and efficaciously in several new directions. The reorganization of the library transferred all cataloging activities out of the Music Division in 1943 and into the newly established Processing Department, thus removing one of the division's major contacts with the world of librarianship. But Spivacke's activities more than made up for this loss as the division strengthened its ties to the communities of musical scholarship, performance, and composition.

Among the expanded programs was one devoted to American folk music, which came to flourish in the Spivacke era under the leadership of John Lomax and later Alan Lomax as the Archive of American Folk Song. Major music benefactions to the library involved two of the country's most respected music patronesses. Elizabeth Sprague Coolidge, champion of contemporary music and for whom the library's auditorium was named, was already established as a donor; Spivacke succeeded in sustaining her involvement. The patronage of Gertrude Clarke Whittall, on the other hand, was new and led to the library's acquisition of its Stradivarius violins, housed in the Whittall Pavilion adjacent to the auditorium, as well as a remarkable collection of autograph manuscripts of the master composers. The library's chamber music series flourished, through Coolidge concerts and festivals devoted significantly to newly commissioned works (among them Aaron Copland's *Appalachian Spring*, first performed at the Coolidge Festival of 1943) and through Whittall concerts on the Stradivarius instruments performed by the resident ensembles, the Budapest String Quartet (1938-1962), and thereafter by the Juilliard String Quartet.

Through Spivacke's efforts and the able assistance of Edward N. Waters, the library's collection was enhanced by an awesome succession of acquisitions of music holographs, personal papers, and other treasures. Most of the prominent musicians of the day were approached, and, remarkably, many responded: Samuel Barber, Leonard Bernstein, Geraldine Farrar, George Gershwin, Jascha Heifetz, Victor Herbert, Fritz Kreisler, Sergei Rachmaninoff, Richard Rodgers, Arnold Schoenberg, and William Schuman, among others. As a specialist in acoustics in Berlin, Spivacke had come to know the American physicist Dayton C. Miller, whose superb collection of flutes and materials relating to the flutes was bequeathed in 1941. Close ties within the Berkshire community helped persuade Serge Koussevitzky to set up a foundation at the library in 1949 for purposes of commissioning new works, the manuscripts of which were added to the collections. Last among the major new programs was the McKim Fund, established in 1969 for purposes of supporting the composition and performance of chamber music for violin and piano.

When Spivacke arrived at the library in 1934, sound recordings were collected only in the folk song archive or as gifts. One of his major achievements was to persuade recording companies, in the days before sound recordings could be copyrighted, to donate copies of their new releases. This practice was to prove munificent to the library collections as the LP record achieved wide acceptance, thereby laying the foundations for the major collection that emerged during the last decade of his incumbency. Spivacke's work with the Carnegie Corporation of New York made possible the establishment of a recording laboratory in 1940 (an operation set up largely by Jerome Wiesner, then recently graduated from college and later president of the Massachusetts Institute of Technology). No less important to the library world at large were Spivacke's efforts to subsidize the research that led to the landmark report by A. G. Pickett and M. M. Lemcoe on the *Preservation and Storage of Sound Recordings* (Washington, D.C.: Government Printing Office, 1959).

Equally important to Spivacke's success was the able staff he assembled, particularly in the early years of his administration. In addition to Waters, it included, perhaps most notably, Richard S. Hill, who without Spivacke's support could never have made the Music Library Association's journal, *Notes*, the remarkable source it was to become. William Lichtenwanger and Frank Campbell, the former in whom Spivacke identified a remarkable reference prowess, the latter a special sensitivity to a number of the more imaginative communities of performers and composers were also notable additions. Through this team Spivacke's library came to be recognized as a major center of the country's musical scholarship.

Working outside the immediate institution, Spivacke built strong ties during his early years with the Works Project Administration and the Pan American Union's music programs. Formally, his advisory work in and around Washington agencies included wartime assignments on the Joint Army and Navy Subcommittee on Music and later on the Fulbright Advisory Selection Committee and the Music Advisory Panel of the International Cultural Exchange Service. Informally, it extended throughout the music world as it impinged on the Washington political scene. Other activities included active and respected participation in the National Music Council, UNESCO (member of the U.S. National Commission, 1950-1956 and 1963-1967, and of the Executive Committee, 1954-1956), the music program of the Organization of American States, the American Musicological

Society, and the International Association of Music Libraries. An early leader of the Music Library Association and its president from 1951 to 1953, Spivacke nevertheless kept somewhat apart from the growing community in this field—except as it was served through its most valuable asset at this time, the quarterly journal *Notes*.

His later activities were strongly supported by his second wife, Rosemarie Grentzer Spivacke, who enjoyed a distinguished career as a music educator in her own right and to whom he was married in 1955. Among his awards were honorary doctorates from Baldwin-Wallace College (1947), the University of Rochester (1955), and the Cleveland Institute of Music (1969), as well as a Distinguished Service Award (1965) from the Library of Congress. He retired in 1972, and although hampered by further weakening of his poor eyesight, he continued to be active in professional activities to the time of his death in Washington, D.C., on May 9, 1977.

Harold Spivacke's published writings consist largely of descriptions of projects proposed or in progress—such as those of the American Office of the International Inventory of Musical Sources (RISM), which he helped establish. Others celebrate the wide range of valuable source materials that he was able to add to the library's collections, particularly those of European Romantic composers such as Paganini, Brahms, Chausson. These he described with impressive erudition, mostly in the Library's *Annual Reports*, later in the *Quarterly Journal of the Library of Congress*.

Spivacke's personality was essentially coterminous with his professional responsibilities. A jovial and lively raconteur, he delighted in relating his experiences. His anecdotes of the famous musicians of the day, seen by some as blatant name-dropping, were excused by others who recognized that Spivacke was not a household name, but rather one respected by political leaders behind the scenes in the national and international world of music. His manner was of an austere dignity and reserve, thanks further to his being a large person with a thin but deep and raspy voice, thick white hair, and a personal manner that conveyed at once both a quiet discipline and a hyperkinetic nervousness. It was obvious that he was a person with large objectives, although many of these probably developed as much out of dialogue with colleagues as out of any specific personal agenda, thereby reflecting a person whose delight was in working through others by way of reacting as much as acting. His personal life was extremely private. He was known to be an ardent and accomplished amateur photographer and rose gardener, for instance, but few persons could confirm that he did or did not ever touch the piano over the last 40 years of his life. His achievements remain evident in the imposing collections and imaginative programs of a single institution.

Biographical listings and obituaries—["Harold Spivacke."] *Fontes artis musicae* 24:190 (July 1977); ["Harold Spivacke."] *Newsletter* [American Musicological Society] 7:4 (Fall 1977); [Obituary]. *LC Information Bulletin* 36:333-4 (May 20, 1977). **Books and articles about the biographee**—Lichtenwanger, William. "Harold Spivacke." *Die Musik in Geschichte und Gegenwart* 12:1059 (1965); and *Supplementband 2* 16:1730 (1979). **Primary sources and archival materials**—A few personal papers are in the Library of Congress, where Spivacke's official papers also permeate the general correspondence files of the Music Division. Other papers, reflecting his career in music librarianship, are found in the archives of the Music Library Association at the University of Maryland.

—D. W. KRUMMEL

STEBBINS, KATHLEEN BROWN (1905-1962)

Kathleen Brown Stebbins was born in Rochester, New York, on September 18, 1905, daughter of Charles David and Stella DeLand Sanford Brown. She received an A.B. from Smith College in 1927. Her first library experience was at the Rochester Public Library, where she worked as assistant librarian from 1926 to 1931. She then went into newspaper work as assistant social editor of the Rochester *Times Union* and *Democrat and Chronicle*. In 1936 she received a B.S. in library science from Columbia University and became the first librarian and research editor at the Grolier Society in New York. A year later she moved to Crowell-Collier Publishing Company as a promotion writer. In 1940 she was appointed executive secretary of the Special Libraries Association (SLA).

During her term of office as executive secretary of the SLA (1940-1953), Stebbins helped to establish fourteen chapters (Washington, D.C., Toronto, Greater St. Louis, Minnesota, Western New York State, Washington State, Louisiana, Kansas City, Texas, Colorado, Georgia, Oak Ridge, and Alabama) and six new internal SLA groups, called divisions after a reorganization in

1951 (advertising, transportation, geography and map, hospital and nursing, publishing, and picture). In World War II, she sensed a chance to assist the war effort and extended the services of SLA to all libraries engaged in national defense. "She saw the opportunity for SLA to be of service and single-handed coped with calls," SLA President Elizabeth Ferguson recalled later. "She accomplished a lot because she was well organized and kept the red tape to a minimum." Stebbins also participated in the establishment of the U.S. Book Exchange, and arranged for SLA to join IFLA (International Federation of Library Associations, as it was called then) in 1947. During her term of office, SLA presented its first Professional Award to Edwin T. Coman, Jr., author of *Sources of Business Information*, and engaged its first full-time editor of *Special Libraries*, Dora Richman. The periodical itself gave implicit evidence of several of Stebbins's major contributions. "The record of ... new libraries and ... placements of personnel only appears in the rather laconic statistics in her reports," Ferguson notes, but adds, "I definitely feel ... that the effort had a great deal to do with getting special libraries much more widely known."

Stebbins was an effective administrator of a growing office, where she helped SLA gain financial stability. During her tenure as executive director, membership increased from 2,386 to 4,732. She built the reserve fund from $2,053 in 1940 to $46,000 in 1951, and increased SLA's annual income from just under $20,000 to over $83,000 in the same period. As advertising manager of *Special Libraries* she increased its advertising revenue in her first ten years from $1,311 to $7,202. She planned and prepared annual conferences with ever-increasing attendance and complexity and oversaw the publication of some thirty-six books and pamphlets from SLA headquarters. Publications included bibliographies and literature guides to specialized classification schemes and subject headings lists, directories, union lists, and handbooks. Stebbins also visited SLA chapters across the continent and talked to students and librarians wherever she went. In 1946, for example, she reported visiting nineteen libraries, six SLA chapters, and five library schools, often traveling by air, "rushing through space at better than 200 miles an hour" in a 48-passenger, four-motor plane. She ran an active placement service at SLA headquarters until members objected that it unfairly benefitted the New York Chapter. Placement services were later taken over by the chapters. In recognition of her contribution to SLA, she was elected posthumously to the SLA Hall of Fame in 1963.

Stebbins was always particularly interested in the human aspects of librarianship; she obtained her M.A. in guidance and personnel administration while working at SLA. In 1953 she left SLA to become personnel director of the Detroit Public Library. Here she introduced the idea of vocational guidance to the library profession. In 1958 her *Personnel Administration in Libraries* was published by Scarecrow Press. She was revising it at the time of her death and a second edition was finally prepared by Foster E. Mohrhardt and published in 1966. *Personnel Administration in Libraries* was a practical, common sense manual. It covered such subjects as managing a personnel department, the duties of a personnel officer, salary and wage administration, recruitment and selection, training, motivating, and communication, developing good work habits, executive development, and planning for retirement. It provided sample forms and summaries of the practices, classification plans, and salaries from public and county libraries. Stebbins quoted a good deal from the literature of library administration as well as from the field of personnel and industrial relations. Reviews in *Library Journal, Library Quarterly, The Library Association Record*, and *Special Libraries* all praised the book as a good summary of the theory and practice of personnel administration with a broad overview of the field. Several were critical of the quantity and quality of the literature quoted, and suggested that it was uneven and inadequate. One criticized it sharply for confining itself to public libraries. In general, however, critics agreed it was a useful book that filled a gap in the literature of librarianship.

In addition to her book, Stebbins wrote many articles, usually on some aspect of personnel administration in libraries. She was concerned about the low salaries offered to librarians, about the need for selling librarianship as a career to the most promising graduates and able people, about educating librarians, about recruitment, merit rating, and many other topics. She was a popular speaker at meetings of library associations and at library schools and conducted numerous workshops.

She was also active in many organizations. She worked for the New York and Michigan chapters of Special Libraries Association, chaired the Service Abroad and the International Relations round tables of the American Library Association and was president of its Library Education Division. She was a member of the Greater Detroit Chapter of the American Society of Training Directors and chaired the annual institute of the Michigan Training Council in February 1956, with the theme of "Changing and Developing Human Attitudes." She was active in the Detroit Employment Managers Club, Personnel Women of Detroit, and the New York City Librarians Club. She also served on the Civil Service Examination Board of Wayne County, Michigan. She died on July 23, 1962.

Kathleen Stebbins was an inspiring and dynamic librarian. During her tenure as executive secretary, the Special Libraries Association grew and developed into a major force in the library world in the United States and Canada. Her interest in people led her to a study of personnel administration resulting in her valued book. She was an inspiration to many young people, encouraging them to seek careers in librarianship and helping them to find jobs. Her innovative and forthright approach and the high standards she maintained for herself and others served librarianship well over many years.

Biographical listings and obituaries — *Library Journal* 78:1496 (September 15, 1953); [Obituary]. *Wilson Library Bulletin* 37:18 (September 1962); [Obituary]. *Special Libraries Association, Michigan Chapter Bulletin* 27:5 (August 1962); [Obituary]. Wessels, Helen E. "Kathleen Brown Stebbins: An Appreciation." *Special Libraries* 53:440 (September 1962); "SLA Hall of Fame 1963." *Special Libraries* 54:229-30 (April 1963); *Who's Who in Library Service*, 3rd ed. (1955). **Books and articles about the biographee** — Mitchell, Alma C. "Mrs. Stebbins, Executive Secretary, Resigns." *Special Libraries* 44:344 (October 1953); "Our Mrs. Stebbins: Some of Her Many Activities on Our Behalf." *Special Libraries Association. Michigan Chapter Bulletin* 27:7 (June 1956). **Primary sources and archival materials** — Letter to Miriam Tees from Elizabeth Ferguson, November 20, 1986. Stebbins's official papers are part of the Special Libraries Association Archives.

— MIRIAM TEES

TAUBER, MAURICE FALCOLM (1908-1980)

Maurice Falcolm Tauber was born in Norfolk, Virginia, on February 14, 1908 of parents who had emigrated from Europe. His father, Albert, owned a tailoring shop over which hung the sign "Tauber the Tailor." When Maurice was six years old, his father died, and his mother Leona began working as a seamstress in a women's fashion store and at home to earn money to raise her two boys and two girls. During his school years Maurice worked for a press that printed the *Virginia Pilot*, and he sold papers for the *Ledger Dispatch*. He also reported on high school sports for the *Pilot* and found time to play on his school's basketball team.

The family moved to Philadelphia in 1925; Tauber completed high school there. He received a four-year scholarship to Temple University. During his sophomore year at Temple he began working for the library as a student assistant and was later promoted to the night desk, where he answered reference questions and did other routine duties. He received his bachelor's degree in English and education from Temple University in 1930, but instead of becoming a teacher, he stayed on in the library at Temple and rose slowly through the ranks. While at Temple University, Tauber met Rose Begner, the fifteen-year-old sister of a classmate. Three years later, in 1932, they were married. They had two sons, Frederic and Robert. For a time Tauber served as librarian of the Teacher's College Library, then as head of the cataloging department in the Sullivan Memorial Library from 1935 to 1938. In the latter position, at the request of the Head Librarian, Edith Cheney, he reclassified the library's holdings from the Dewey Decimal Classification (DDC) to the Library of Congress Classification (LCC). Between 1930 and 1938 he found time to write a brief history of the library, compile a forty-page bibliography of Russell Herman Conwell, prepare an index to Temple University theses and dissertations, and collaborate with J. Periam Danton on a bibliography of Temple University graduate theses and dissertations. He also began to write crossword puzzles for publication in the daily newspapers.

In 1932 Tauber began commuting to New York to take courses at the School of Library Service at Columbia University, where he studied cataloging under Bertha Frick. He completed the bachelor's degree in library science in 1934. He also completed a master's degree in sociology at Temple in 1939. As he was finishing his master's degree he accepted a research assistantship and American Library Association fellowship at the University of Chicago for the 1938-1939 academic year. At Chicago Tauber came to know Louis Round Wilson, then dean of the Graduate Library School, who was to have a major influence on both Tauber's career and his publications. Tauber also forged close friendships with three students who later became leaders in the library profession—John M. Cory, Bernard Berelson, and Jesse Shera. The group became known as the Four Horsemen. Frances Henne, later a colleague at Columbia University, and Ralph Shaw were also classmates.

Tauber's dissertation, entitled "Reclassification and Recataloging in College and University Libraries," filled a 456-page volume. Parts of it were published in articles he wrote for *College & Research Libraries*. He wrote the dissertation from a historical and practical point of view, rather than from a theoretical one. This was to remain his library philosophy for the remainder of his career. As a result of this study, he concluded that the Library of Congress Classification was superior to the Dewey Decimal Classification, especially for large, research-oriented libraries; he never changed his opinion. During his long career, in which he surveyed scores of libraries, Tauber recommended to about sixty libraries that they switch to LCC. For libraries with fewer than 50,000 volumes, he recommended that they retain the Dewey Decimal Classification. His advocacy of LCC was always tempered by the size of the library's book collection. After Tauber completed his doctorate in 1941, he joined the University of Chicago Harper Library, first as Head Cataloger and later as chief of the preparations division. He was also appointed to the faculty of the Graduate Library School, serving as instructor from 1942 to 1944. In 1944 he was promoted to Assistant Professor.

Also in 1944, Tauber was lured back to Columbia University to begin his career there as Assistant Director of its library in charge of technical services. He was also appointed Assistant Professor in the School of Library Service. In the fall of 1947, he gave up his appointment in the library to become a full-time faculty member in the library school, with the rank of Associate Professor. He worked with Bertha Frick and other faculty members to develop new courses for the master's program, especially in the field of technical services. He was promoted to the rank of full professor three years later in 1949. In 1954 Tauber was appointed Melvil Dewey Professor. He remained at Columbia until June 24, 1976, the day he taught his last class. At that time he was named Melvil Dewey Professor Emeritus.

Tauber's many contributions to the library profession can be grouped under three topics: his teaching, his library survey work, and his publications.

Tauber taught for thirty-two years at Columbia University and influenced thousands of students. Many of them are now librarians, educators, deans of library schools, and library administrators throughout the world. Students remember him for his kindness, fairness, dedication, and sense of humor. Until his wife's death in 1964 he opened his home to many students, especially those from foreign lands.

Tauber's lecture style was low-keyed, relaxed, and anecdotal, and he often drew on his vast experience, especially his library surveys, to illustrate topics under discussion. A former student, Richard Hyman, noted that "his office was always accessible, though he was invariably occupied at the desk or typewriter or telephone."

Over his long career Tauber made scores of library surveys, including five national surveys; forty-five surveys of college, university, and research libraries; five of public and school libraries; eleven of special libraries; and nine of state libraries and library systems. His surveys of the University of South Carolina and Cornell University, and the Columbia University self-survey, are considered landmark studies. The latter survey was carried out by a subcommittee on the university libraries with Tauber as chair and C. Donald Cook and Richard H. Logsdon as members (*The Columbia University Libraries* [New York: Columbia University Press, 1958]). Many of the surveys were the results of collaborative efforts, involving teams of consultants. Tauber collaborated on these studies with a variety of people, including L. Quincy Mumford, Louis Round Wilson, Robert B. Downs, C. Donald Cook,

Richard H. Logsdon, and Foster E. Morhardt. In 1961 he spent several months in Australia as a Fulbright scholar. His visit was sponsored by the Australian Advisory Council on Bibliographical Services, and his task was to evaluate major library resources in the country. His forty-two page summary report (*Resources of Australian Libraries* [Canberra: Australian Advisory Council on Bibliographical Services]), was published by the Council in 1963.

Tauber traveled more than 10,000 miles across the continent and visited 162 libraries. He noted the nation's need for trained librarians, and pointed out the ramshackle state of library buildings, calling some of them fire traps. (Not much later one of the libraries in Perth burned to the ground.) He also visited libraries in Tokyo, Hong Kong, and Singapore. His survey work reinforced his interest in the planning and design of library buildings. (Tauber admitted later in his career to several misjudgments concerning his recommendations regarding classification systems in his university library surveys.)

Tauber's first publication in 1934 was a seventeen-page monograph, a history of the Temple University library. Two of his more substantial works are considered classics. *The University Library: Its Organization, Administration and Functions* (1945) was published by the University of Chicago Press in 1956 in a 2nd edition as *The University Library: The Organization, Administration, and Functions of Academic Libraries*. On both editions he collaborated with Louis Round Wilson. Wilson devoted his attention to administration, while Tauber concerned himself principally with technical services. Tauber's later, and equally influential, title *Technical Services in Libraries: Acquisitions, Cataloging, Classification, Binding, Photographic Reproduction, and Circulation Operations* (Columbia University Press, 1954), was written in collaboration with seven associates. This work argued strongly for the centralization of technical services.

A third major publication was less successful. Tauber's biography of his mentor (*Louis Round Wilson: Librarian and Administrator* [New York, Columbia University Press, 1967]) was generally well received, but two reviewers expressed some reservations about its objectivity. Recently published research has demonstrated that Tauber not only had Wilson's active collaboration, but Wilson also furnished him with a 340-page typescript of his memoirs, which came to form the backbone of Tauber's biography. After the first draft was finished in 1958, Wilson continued to offer his comments and suggestions, sometimes furnishing Tauber with completely rewritten passages. By the time the book was published, it was clear that the finished work was a collaboration between the two men. One scholar estimates that approximately 40 percent of the book is in Wilson's own words.

Tauber served as managing editor of *College & Research Libraries* from September 1945 (under the editorship of Carl White) until he was appointed the third editor-in-chief in 1948 at the midwinter meeting of the American Library Association. He served in that position until March 1962. Under his able direction *C&RL* reached maturity and became a valuable publication in its field. It expanded from a subscription journal to a membership journal, and grew from a quarterly to a bimonthly. In his final report to the Association of College and Research Libraries at the American Library Association midwinter meeting in 1962, Tauber paid tribute "to the many writers here and abroad who have provided the copy that makes a journal successful." During his incumbency as editor, Tauber had a readily available source for the publication of his own manuscripts, and he contributed eleven articles and thirty reviews to the journal. He also served on the editorial advisory boards of *Library Resources & Technical Services*, the *Journal of Cataloging and Classification*, *American Documentation*, and *Journal of Higher Education*, and others. He was chief editor for three issues of *Library Trends*.

He served the American Library Association in many capacities, including membership on the Council and on the Executive Board, although he was never elected president. In 1953 he received the Margaret Mann citation, given by the Resources and Technical Services Division "for outstanding professional achievement in the areas of cataloging or classification." In part, it served as an immediate acknowledgment of his significant accomplishment in organizing and directing the Institute on Subject Analysis of Library Materials during the week preceding the 1952 ALA conference under the joint sponsorship of the Division of Cataloging and Classification and Columbia University's School of Library Service.

He received the Melvil Dewey Medal in 1955. This award, established in 1952, is donated by

Forest Press "for recent creative professional achievement of a high order, particularly in those fields in which Melvil Dewey was actively interested." Tauber was president of Beta Phi Mu from 1967 to 1968, and founded the Mu Chapter at Columbia University in 1967. He was also a founding member of the American Society of Indexers. In 1968 Tauber received the Distinguished Service Award from the Findlay College Library in Ohio, where he was cited for his "outstanding contribution to higher education as a teacher, writer, librarian, critic, and leader in the science of library service." He also belonged to the New York Library Club, the Grolier Club, and the Archons of Colophon.

Carlyle Frarey, a long-time colleague, describes Tauber as informal in manner, unpretentious in appearance, and at home in any group, formal or informal. He was also patient, but with the ability to be blunt and direct, honest and natural. Most of all, he showed an inordinate capacity for work. Tauber died on September 21, 1980 at the age of 72.

In 1981 friends established the Maurice F. Tauber Foundation in New York. It sponsors an annual memorial lecture hosted by library schools throughout the United States, publications of scholarly works, and an annual award for excellence in library and information science.

Maurice Tauber epitomized the pragmatist in the annals of American librarianship. His knowledge of library practices and procedures, especially in technical services, was gained through his visits to and surveys of hundreds of libraries. He used this knowledge in his teaching and in his many publications. He was an ideal collaborator because he was able to work profitably with colleagues and students. This enhanced his publication record, but he always gave due credit to those who helped him. He served as a mentor to many students.

Biographical listings and obituaries — *ALA World Encyclopedia of Library and Information Services*, 2nd ed.; *Biographical Directory of Librarians in the United States and Canada*, 5th ed.; [Obituary]. *ALA Yearbook 1980* (1981); [Obituary]. "In Memoriam: Maurice F. Tauber, 1908-1980." *Library Resources & Technical Services* 25:8 (January/March 1981); [Obituary]. "Maurice F. Tauber." *College & Research Libraries News* 41:353 (December 1980). **Books and articles about the biographee** — Downs, Robert B. "Personnel: Maurice F. Tauber." *College & Research Libraries* 23:240-1 (May 1962); Frarey, Carlyle J. "Maurice F. Tauber." *Journal of Cataloging & Classification* 9:145-50 (September 1953); Lyle, Guy R. "Maurice F. Tauber." In *The Librarian Speaking: Interviews with University Librarians*. Athens, Ga.: University of Georgia Press, 1970, 163-71; Maier, Kurt S. "Maurice F. Tauber." In *Leaders in American Academic Librarianship: 1925-1975*. Edited by Wayne A. Wiegand. Pittsburgh: Beta Phi Mu, 1983, 318-45; Maier, Kurt S. " 'Maury' ." *American Libraries* 7:686-8 (December 1976); Martin, Robert Sidney. "Maurice F. Tauber's *Louis Round Wilson*: An Analysis of a Collaboration." *Journal of Library History* 19:373-89 (Summer 1984); Szigethy, Marion C. *Maurice Falcolm Tauber: A Biobibliography, 1934-1973*. Metuchen, N.J.: Scarecrow, 1974. This work includes a foreword by Jack Dalton, biographical appreciations by Louis Round Wilson, Carl M. White, Luther H. Evans, Theodore C. Hines, and Richard J. Hyman, and an essay by Tauber on the "Survey Approach to Library Problems." **Primary sources and archival materials** — The Maurice Falcolm Tauber Papers are held in the Rare Books and Manuscripts Library in Butler Library, Columbia University, New York. They consist of about 74,300 items covering the dates 1935-1978 and are housed in 230 boxes and on ten tape reels. The collection itself is divided into six series. The majority of the boxes are listed in a register of approximately 500 pages. Selected boxes have detailed inventories prepared by Tauber's archival seminar students. A brief description of the collection is available by writing to the Rare Books and Manuscripts Library.

—DORIS CRUGER DALE

ULRICH, CAROLYN FARQUHAR (1880-1969)

Carolyn Farquhar Ulrich was born in Oakland, California, on August 16, 1880, the daughter of Lina Linck Hartman and Rudolph Ulrich. Although little is known of her childhood, it is believed that she had a brother. At some point following her birth, the family moved east and settled in the state of New York. Ulrich entered Erasmus Hall School in Brooklyn, New York, in 1897 and received her diploma in 1901. While in high school, in addition to studying the regular curriculum, Ulrich showed interest in languages and studied French, German, and Latin. She also had a penchant for the arts and following high school graduation, she attended Pratt Art School for one year.

Ulrich's interest in librarianship became evident between the years 1901 and 1906, and it was in the latter year she began working as an assistant in the Brooklyn Public Library. At that time she had no formal library training and, undoubtedly sensing the need for this education, she attended the Albany Summer Library School in 1907. She remained an assistant at the Brooklyn Public Library until 1912; in 1913 she was promoted to first assistant, a position which she held until 1917. Ulrich was of scholarly disposition and interested in continuing and improving her education. During the years 1912 and 1914 she completed courses in literature and in Chinese and Japanese art at Columbia University and New York University.

Ulrich applied for admission to the certificate program in library science at Pratt Institute in April 1917, at the age of thirty-seven. Pratt Institute, which was founded in 1890, had a well-established program. When she applied, she was living in Brooklyn, and it is likely the institute's proximity affected her decision to attend that school. On the application for admission she was queried about previous library experience. She cited the Brooklyn Public Library, specifying "9 years—4½ as first assistant (Eligible for Branch Librarian)." Another question inquired about the character and extent of the applicant's reading habits. She answered: "Varied and extensive—Interested in Art, Philosophy and representative writing in all Literature." With her previous library experience, her year at Pratt Institute must have been exciting and augured well for her life as a student. A student information/evaluation form describes her dress as "absolutely correct in taste and style. Sport clothes types." Ulrich was also described as having a "good social manner," a "cultivated voice," "goodlooking presence," and as being in "excellent health." Other comments described Ulrich and her work as "gracious and very efficient, lots of enthusiasm and great energy, unfailing tact, unusual literary taste, and has good sense." Cataloging was apparently not one of her strengths, for in this area Ulrich was described as "a little careless but turns work off rapidly." The person completing the evaluation form could not recommend her for either cataloging or for work with children, but could recommend her for "executive work or organizing."

At the completion of the requirements for the library certificate program in 1918, Ulrich joined the Graduate Association of the institute. In June of that year she accepted a position as chief of the circulation department and branches (extension work) of the Bridgeport, Connecticut, Public Library, then under the direction of Henry N. Sanborn.

Ulrich quickly showed executive insight and organizational abilities in her new position. The 1919 annual report of the Bridgeport Public Library contains a section that reflects a flurry of activity in the library's circulation department, most of which was the result of Ulrich's forceful influence. This activity consisted of organizational changes, the establishment of traveling libraries in factories, and the establishment of Americanization classes for immigrants. The report also refers to binding of library materials. This latter task was particularly significant for Ulrich's future in serials librarianship. The 1920 annual report also notes that the circulation department was rearranged to give the public freer access to all the books on the shelves.

When Ulrich had applied for admission to the certificate program in library science at Pratt Institute in 1917, she was asked whether she would consider accepting a position, if qualified for it, anywhere in the United States. To this question Ulrich responded, "Yes, preferably in the vicinity of New York." In October 1920 she returned to New York and accepted a position as acting head of the central circulation branch of the New York Public Library (NYPL). It was a challenging position but one for which she was well prepared by her experience at the Bridgeport Public Library. She held this position for two years. In 1922 she was appointed chief of the Periodicals Division of the NYPL, a position she occupied until her retirement on April 30, 1946, and a position from which she built an international reputation in serials librarianship.

Ulrich was an active and participating member of the American Library Association (ALA), having joined that organization in 1916 while first assistant at the Brooklyn Public Library. Her name appears in the pages of the *ALA Bulletin* as early as 1920 when she was vice-chair of the ALA Lending Section. At the 1922 Detroit ALA conference she presented a short commentary on "Psychological Contacts" to the Lending Section and, in 1926, at the fiftieth anniversary conference of the association held in Atlantic City, she addressed members of the Periodical Round Table on the "Future of Periodical Work." Ulrich reiterated and expanded upon these remarks when she read a paper before a gathering of librarians of small libraries at the same conference. At the June 1927 Toronto conference, she spoke about "A Current Periodicals Room in a Metropolis" before the ALA Periodical Round Table, which she chaired in 1927 and 1928. In 1931, Ulrich served as acting chair of the ALA Periodicals Section and in 1935, she was chair of the Joint Committee on Standardization of Periodicals. In June 1941, Ulrich read a paper at the Boston ALA conference entitled "Some Problems Presented by Current Development in the Periodicals Field"; she was, at this time, chair of the ALA Serials Section and representative from the American Standards Association and the ALA to the International Standards Association Committee on Documentation.

Ulrich was also an author, and she published throughout most of her professional life. The papers she read at professional association meetings often appeared later in professional journals. Most of her writing concerned periodicals and serials management. Ulrich collaborated with others in writing two books. The first was *Books and Printing: A Selected List of Periodicals, 1800-1942* (Woodstock, Vt.: William E. Rudge, 1943), which she wrote with Karl Küp. This book developed from concern about the growth of journal literature devoted to printing and the book arts. The second collaboration, with Frederick J. Hoffman and Charles Allen, resulted in publication of *The Little Magazine: A History and a Bibliography* (Princeton, N.J.: Princeton University Press, 1946), a work whose completion was subsidized in part by a 1944 grant Ulrich received from the American Council of Learned Societies. Ulrich also wrote articles for business, publishing, and sociological journals like *Sales Management* and the *Journal of Social Hygiene*.

But it is for her work in producing the major periodical directory that bears her name that Carolyn Ulrich is known best. This popular and highly respected reference work first appeared in 1932, when Ulrich had been the chief of the Periodicals Division of the NYPL for ten years. The fifth edition, which appeared in 1947 and became known as the postwar edition, was the last she edited. *Ulrich's International Periodicals Directory*, now in its twenty-seventh edition (1988-1989), is available online, in microfiche, and on CD-ROM. Through the past fifty-six years, the work has grown to monumental proportions and is consulted in libraries and research centers all over the world.

With a demanding work schedule in her position at the NYPL, including serving upon and chairing several committees of that institution, her frequent and heavy involvement in the business of professional associations, and with her research and publication activities, Carolyn Ulrich was an extremely busy woman, and one deeply committed to her profession. Yet, she also had time to teach others that which she knew best—serials work. Beginning in 1920, and continuing to the year of her retirement, she served both as assistant instructor and lecturer in various library schools, principally the NYPL library school and the library school at Pratt Institute. Thus, her reputation as a scholar and as a librarian was firmly established through her research, her writings, her teaching, and her other professional contributions.

Little is known regarding the personal life of this dedicated librarian. Some evidence suggests she traveled to Spain and France during the summer of 1924. And she did have interests outside librarianship. She was a member of the Society for Japanese Studies and the Bibliographical Society of America. Following her retirement from the NYPL she settled in Winter Park, Florida, sharing her residence with a friend of many years, Marion Cutter. Carolyn Ulrich died at her home on November 22, 1969, at the age of 89.

Biographical listings and obituaries—[Obituary]. *AB Bookman's Weekly* 45:122 (January 19, 1970); [Obituary]. *American Libraries* 1:205 (March 1970); [Obituary]. *Library Journal* 95:625 (February 15, 1970); [Obituary]. *Orlando Sentinel*, 6 (D) (November 24, 1969); *Who's Who in America* 26 (1950-1951); *Who's Who in Library Service*, 1st, 2nd eds. **Books and articles by and about the biographee**—Patterson, Charles D. "Origins of Systematic Serials Control: Remembering Carolyn Ulrich." *Reference Services Review* 16:79-92 (Spring/Summer 1988). **Primary sources and archival materials**—Ulrich's papers are scattered among the official archives of her employers, including the Bridgeport, Connecticut Archives; New York Public Library Archives; and Pratt Institute Archives.

—CHARLES D. PATTERSON

ULVELING, RALPH ADRIAN (1902-1980)

Ralph Adrian Ulveling was born on May 9, 1902, in Adrian, Minnesota. He was the son of Frank, a merchant farmer, and Sara Dineen Ulveling. His father's ancestors came from Luxembourg and his mother's from Ireland. His mother, who died when Ralph was quite young, attended college, although it is not known whether she earned a degree. His father did not have any formal schooling, but was allegedly self-educated through wide reading and family education; he must have done quite well for himself as a merchant farmer, since Ralph attended a Catholic high school and a large portion of his college expenses were borne by his father.

After the elder Ulveling retired, the family moved to Chicago, where Ralph received his bachelor's degree at DePaul University in 1922. Upon graduation, he worked for one year for the Multi-Electric Manufacturing Co. and one year for Hart, Schaffner and Marx, both in Chicago. Like many people who entered the library field, librarianship was not his first choice of work. From 1924 to 1926 Ulveling worked as a reference assistant at the Newberry Library. This brief exposure to the library world must have influenced his ultimate decision to become a librarian. Still, he was uncertain about a vocation and went to Texas to work for a railroad as a clerk. The directorship of the Potter County (Amarillo) Public Library fell vacant and, at the urging of his friends, Ulveling applied for and was offered the position. After serving some months and thoroughly enjoying the work, he decided to make librarianship his life's work. He informed the library board that he would stay only one year and then enter Columbia University to receive professional library training. Because of his previous experience as an administrator, Ulveling was placed at Columbia in a special group which was subjected to keener competition. He told his peers that "since the faculty has set up perfection as the norm, it behooves us to exceed it." This quip would characterize the next forty years of his professional life.

Upon graduation from Columbia in 1928, Ulveling was offered a job as the chief of branches for the Detroit Public Library, an unusually responsible position for a recent library school graduate. Several reasons explain the offer. First, there was the fact that he was a man. Women in those days were seldom given positions of responsibility higher than a department head and certainly not when they were fresh out of library school. Second, there is the fact that he came highly recommended. When the library director, Adam Strohm, decided to fill the position, he turned to the American Library Association for recommendations. Hazel B. Timmerman, Assistant in the ALA personnel division, made the following observation about Ulveling:

> Another student at Columbia, who is especially interesting, is Ralph A. Ulveling, whom we are told will be in a few years one of the ablest men in the public library field. He has already had excellent experience and has the personal qualities which will make him an able executive.

Coupled with Ulveling's large, muscular physique was a sense of self-assurance that he seemed to wear easily. His confidence and "command-presence" prompted one colleague to remark that "he should have been in charge of something."

Ulveling was also polite, well mannered, and impeccably groomed, and possessed a keen political savvy. He expected these characteristics in his colleagues. As chief of branches, Ulveling was responsible for evaluating prospective heads of branches. Recurring phrases in his evaluations cited a candidate's tendency to be "impolitic" or the need for better grooming. Even the woman who was to become his wife was cited for her lack of political skills. It is important to note that Ulveling was not seeking out mediocre sartorial showpieces, but rather was convinced that only librarians who projected a professional image and who got along well with people could effectively relate books to the library's public. "Broad book knowledge" was another recurring phrase in the evaluations, but he tempered the importance of book knowledge by noting, "the acquisitive mind is frequently far less of an influence on our fellow-men than is that of another worker who may be less scholarly but who, recognizing each patron as an individual human detached from the mass, gives eagerly and graciously of his talents." Reading the evaluations sixty years later, one is impressed by his maturity and judgment of people.

In 1934, Ulveling was promoted to associate director, a position which afforded him the opportunity to further hone his political skills and to cultivate influential contacts in the library world. A memorandum from Ulveling to Strohm reporting on the controversy surrounding Archibald MacLeish's nomination for Librarian of Congress in 1939 underscores his political skills. Ulveling sympathized with those who favored a professional librarian, but he also believed that the library profession did not really have an alternative candidate and protested too much. He refused to sign a petition against MacLeish's nomination. Characteristically, many of his memorandums to Strohm began with a "chatty," even solicitous, tone before he launched into the matter at hand, which was but another indication of his ability to deal effectively with people. His position as associate director also cast him into the national limelight of librarianship. Beginning in 1934, he wrote the first of more than sixty-seven articles—a significant number for one who admitted that he did not like to write. He also became a featured speaker at state library association meetings in the Midwest and as far away as Louisiana.

In 1941, Ulveling was appointed director of the Detroit Public Library (DPL) upon Strohm's retirement. No national search was conducted for the vacancy, nor did he face any internal competition, as it was assumed that he was the heir apparent and had been groomed to succeed Strohm. His subsequent career can be analyzed on two levels: his achievements for the library profession and his accomplishments for the DPL.

Ralph A. Ulveling had one of the most successful careers of any twentieth-century public librarian. One reason for his success is that he had a social vision of what a public library should be. It would not be an exaggeration to characterize his thoughts as a "public philosophy" of librarianship. Ulveling believed that the chief purpose of the public library was to serve the educational needs of individuals, and so lead them to a higher level of educational attainment. Libraries, with the ultimate goal of becoming the "people's university," were one way of allowing individuals to gain the job skills or personal edification so that they could "travel on their own power." Ulveling had the acute ability to gauge the effects of change both on the individual and on society. This capacity for evaluating change and proposing a library response was a constant feature of his career.

Another important reason for Ulveling's success is that he had a coherent philosophy of librarianship, social harmony, which highlighted his leadership qualities. Ulveling's defense of blacks and Jews, and his pleas for tolerance clearly marked him as a leader. Social harmony had long been a mainstay of American liberal thought. However, it usually had a very conservative thrust because it sought, as one library historian has suggested, to "redress conflict and insure social order" by channeling "the interests of the American people towards the dominant culture." Ulveling's philosophy of social harmony was to change the existing culture along liberal and humane lines.

Thus he was a liberal on civil rights issues long before it was fashionable to be a liberal. In the wake of the disastrous Detroit race riot of 1943, Ulveling had the library assume a "positive role" by writing and distributing a brochure which preached the necessity of tolerance in a democratic polity. The brochure, widely requested across the country, was not intended to cool the tempers and passions of those prone to riot, but to influence the "self-respecting citizenry who would never deign to take part in such lawless outbursts but who ... delighted in spreading unfounded rumors which give tacit encouragement to the extremists." He believed that intolerance was the result of misunderstanding and must be combatted. He even publicly chided the ALA for requiring a religious preference question on its employment applications. Ulveling viewed public libraries as the perfect "medium" to effect this "widening of understanding" which would sensitize the various constituencies of American life to each other's problems, and so "broaden their horizons and think of social problems in national rather than local terms."

Ulveling never mentioned the role of women in his social harmony philosophy. He was not, however, unsympathetic to their professional aspirations. He recruited many able female "lieutenants," among them Katherine Harris, Head of the Main Library; Ruth Rutzen, Head of Branches; and Mable Conant, Head of Reference. Indeed, one contemporary has suggested that his best attribute was his ability to keep good female executives and thereby have the time "to make a name for himself in the larger world of librarianship."

Social harmony provided the philosophical foundation for Ulveling's second contribution to the library profession: the role of the library as an agent of adult education. Public libraries had been involved with adult education since the 1920s. Reader's advisors and the reading with a purpose (RWAP) "courses" were a common feature in several large municipal libraries in the 1930s. Neither, however, was completely successful, and thus they failed to be institutionalized on a continuing basis. The RWAP bibliographies were difficult to update and the role of the reader's advisors often was ill-defined. Ulveling's response to these problems was to reorganize libraries, physically and mentally, for adult education. Physically, the reorganization entailed a novel cataloging scheme that would "bring together in one place all material which links itself together to form one subject interest for readers regardless of form in which it is presented or nationality of the author." For example, the arts might include music appreciation, drama, poetry, and the fine arts; the world might encompass economics, fiction, travel, and selected biography. Ulveling's scheme was named the Readers' Interest Classification by adult education specialist John Chancellor. Beginning in 1949, it replaced the Dewey Decimal Classification in the branch libraries and it was also used in the "browsing" room of the Main Library. Reportedly, the plan was duplicated in other public libraries in the United States and other countries.

Equally as sweeping as the Readers' Interest Classification were his ideas on mentally reorganizing the library staff. Long before the reference interview became an aspect of academic interest, Ulveling had proposed that reference librarians take classes in psychology, so that they would be skilled in "opening conversations and drawing patrons out." Librarians also had an obligation to "guide" readers, so as to establish "right thinking." Less cataloging information on the catalog card and more annotations that pointed up the educational value of the book was one way of guiding the reader. Forsaking what he called "our time-honored neutrality" and taking a "positive approach" on issues that "threaten our security" was a prominent feature of his adult education philosophy. The overall thrust of his physical and mental reorganization, when coupled with strictures on recreational reading and film purchases, was to better position the library to focus on "the betterment of the individual" and the "development of people's minds and attitudes."

Ulveling's third contribution to the profession was his strong defense of intellectual freedom. In 1944, the Detroit Police Department banned Lillian Smith's *Strange Fruit* from the city's book stores. It was the practice in those days to invest the police with such broad power to regularly inspect the stock of bookstores. If the investigating officer suggested that a certain title be withdrawn, it was so done and all the other book dealers would then comply. The police wanted Smith's book removed from the library's shelves, but Ulveling adamantly refused, despite the fact that the police chief threatened to bring political, religious, social, and business pressures to bear that would force him to remove the book. Even the mayor threatened to fire him, but Ulveling did not relent. Not only did the book stay on the shelves, but the power of the police to routinely censor books was effectively broken. For his defense of intellectual freedom, Ulveling won the J. P. Lippincott Award in 1956.

The library's organizational structure and book selection policies also exhibit signs of Ulveling's commitment to intellectual freedom. Like the New York Public Library, the DPL was organized into a Reference-Research Service, consisting of 10 subject departments in the Main Library, and the Home Reading Services, which administered the branch libraries. Book selection policies for each service dictated that the Home Reading Services would provide books for nonspecialized readers, whereas the Reference-Research Services would provide "the obscure ... and even the socially, economically, religiously or politically unorthodox materials necessary for research, for freedom of inquiry." Writing at the height of the Red Scare in 1951, Ulveling noted that while sound factual information on communism could be found in both services, communist propaganda could be found in the Reference Services. It is unlikely that many library directors would have been bold enough to delineate their collection development policies in such a public manner.

Ulveling was quite as willing to oppose cheap and shoddy books as he was willing to defend the inclusion of titles that he felt were good. In the same vein, he was an opponent of loyalty oaths because they interfered with his ability to recruit qualified librarians. He also, however, had no intention of "allowing anyone with subversive tendencies to come into the staff." His handling of these volatile issues indicates a mastery of the local political scene and an unusual combination of idealism and realism.

In his 26 years as DPL director, Ulveling built a national reputation as a building consultant; founded the Friends of the Library, a Municipal Reference Library, a Browsing Library, and an Automotive History Collection; created a "self-charging" system (which expedited the checking-out of books); and recruited an excellent staff, many of whom went on to assume positions of responsibility in other libraries.

More important, he pioneered the introduction of legislation which broadened the library's tax base. In 1937, Ulveling drafted a bill which brought state aid to the library—$375,000 in 1938 but growing to over $1,000,000 by 1960. This was the first library equalization formula, and it was made available to other states through ALA. In 1948, he led the fight for an amendment to the city charter which permitted the city to supplement school district funds. City contributions to the library's treasury increased from $433,174 in 1950-1951 to $2,641,933 in 1967-1968.

Even more significant was his Detroit Metropolitan Library Project, a two-year experiment which opened the library's resources to residents of the six-county area. This project, paid for by the state and federal governments, was a response to what Ulveling viewed as a major problem for municipal libraries. Population shifts of people and industries from city to suburb crippled the tax base of the Detroit Public Library and stymied the research capabilities of transplanted companies, dependent as they were on large libraries. Two factors about the venture are significant. First, it was initiated in 1966, only one year before Ulveling's retirement, a testimonial to his continuing vision, energy, and ability to anticipate problems and to propose a library response. Moreover, he was able to enlist the support of Mayor Jerome Cavanaugh, who made speeches endorsing the plan, a tribute to Ulveling's ability to work the local political scene.

Taken together, the state aid, the amended city charter, and the Metropolitan Library Project improved the library's finances and paved the way for greater state assistance in the 1970s. By 1975, the library's resources were available to all state residents.

The years of Ulveling's tenure also witnessed the expansion of the library's branch system; ten new branches were built between 1949 and 1957 and six more were later expanded or built during the 1960s. The new branches were unique in two ways. The books were arranged according to the Readers' Interest Classification scheme. Although originally proposed by Ulveling in 1936, the idea was first tested in 1949 and gradually spread to all branches and the browsing collection in the Main Library. While Ulveling touted the plan in articles and speeches, one gets the impression that it was less than successful, especially in the branches. After his retirement, the branches returned to the Dewey Decimal Classification. The branches' functional architecture was another unique feature. Older branches costing about $4,000,000 were sometimes ornate, and built in accordance with Strohm's belief that "mean surroundings make mean people; things of beauty cleanse our heart." The new branches were plain buildings that cost only about $1,225,000. As the neighborhood populations shifted, the buildings could be abandoned and sold as commercial property. The new branches' plain style won plaudits from foreign observers and was copied in several library systems in the United States.

The reorganization and expansion of the Main Library was probably Ulveling's most visible accomplishment. Prior to 1941, subjects such as history, literature, and philosophy were what he called "one large undepartmentalized mess," which made book selection and staff specialization difficult. By 1950, ten departments had been organized, six of which were new. Ulveling was quick to point out that this departmentalization was a necessary prelude to the anticipated expansion of the Main Library. Compared to other cities of the same size, Detroit's Main Library did not fare well. Toledo, with one-sixth of the population, had a larger Main Library than did Detroit. Plans for an addition were made almost as soon as Ulveling assumed the directorship, but were placed in abeyance because of World War II. Opposition from Mayor Louis Miriani (1958-1962), who was reluctant to spend money on cultural projects, also served to slow the Main Library's expansion. The addition was completed in 1963, increasing the square footage from 180,000 to 452,000. Ulveling maintained a critical role in the expansion. During World War II, he acquired important parcels of land adjacent to the existing building, and after the war he constantly dramatized the need for more space, raising over $500,000 for the additions.

Earlier it was suggested that Ulveling had a successful career because his social vision and his social harmony philosophy marked him as a leader. His leadership in the library profession, however, also flowed from his membership on several boards and committees, and most important, his presidency of the American Library Association from 1945 to 1946. He was a member of the United States Committee for UNESCO, the Catholic Committee on Intellectual and Cultural Affairs, the Great Book Foundation, and the local Torch Club, of which he was the president from 1955-1956. He also served as a consultant for several public libraries, for the joint Army-Navy Committee on Welfare and Recreation, and the Kellogg Foundation. All of these memberships were ways of raising the visibility of libraries in the community, of linking the Detroit Public Library to the various constituencies of the community, and of "mingling" with the leaders of other professions who had the money to further Ulveling's goals. His activities for ALA were also varied. As early as 1930 he served on a Radio Broadcasting Committee. From 1943-1946, he was on the Demobilization and Post War Committee and from 1945-1946 he was involved in a Library Development Fund Campaign. He was in charge of local arrangements when the American Library Association met in Detroit in 1965 and also was a council member during the 1960s. From the inception of his career to its end, he worked in the "trenches" of ALA's committee structure.

Ulveling's weaknesses, such as they were, were few. Colleagues have recalled his "aloofness" from the staff, his never having "worked in the trenches" and his "impatience" with people who did not produce as they were supposed to. He also had a certain "distance" and stiffness which seemed to alienate some of the staff—a problem obviously compounded by his physical size. One colleague has commented that she had worked in the library for ten years before he knew that she was there. His broad smile and engaging charm probably made a better impression on people who did not work for him. His managerial style, at times, bordered on the authoritarian. Ulveling sought the advice of the staff, but did not believe that a large organization could be run on the basis of staff resolutions lest the library become "headless." And yet he was not an autocrat: he kept open the channels of communication. Staff members were also invited to present grievances "without fear of reprisal." "Teas" were held to introduce and welcome new staff members. Ulveling also sought the opinions of people he respected before he implemented ideas. His management style, when coupled with the personal characteristics noted above, indicate that he was clearly a man of his time—a director who was deeply respected by most and truly loved by some, but one who felt no need to be popular.

In 1967, Ralph Ulveling retired after 29 years of service to the Detroit Public Library. Retirement festivities feted, even lionized, his contributions to the Detroit Public Library. He received a citation from the Staff Association which was only one of many that he had acquired over the years. In 1954, he was cited by the St. Cyprians' Protestant Episcopal Church for his contributions to race relations; and in 1964 and 1967, he received citations from the Merrill-Palmer Institute and Michigan Library Association, respectively.

Following his retirement, Ulveling and his wife remained in the Detroit area until 1973, when they moved to Florida. Ulveling died on March 21, 1980, in Boynton Beach, Florida.

Biographical listings and obituaries—*Biographical Directory of Librarians in the United States and Canada*, 5th ed.; [Obituary]. *ALA Yearbook 1980* (1981); [Obituary]. *American Libraries* 4:306 (May 1980); [Obituary]. *Wilson Library Bulletin* 54:606 (May 1980); "Ralph A. Ulveling." *Library Journal* 87:4496-7 (December 15, 1962). **Books and articles by the biographee**—"Metropolitan Areas Growing and Under Stress: The Situation of the Detroit Public Library." *Library Trends* 14:76-82 (July 1965); "Organizing a Public Library for Adult Education." *Library Occurrent* 13:247-52 (January-March 1941); "Problems of Library Construction." *Library Quarterly* 33:91-101 (January 1963); "The Public Library—An Educational Institution." *Library Resources and Technical Services* 3:12-20 (Winter 1959); "The Public Library in a Large Community." In Leon Carnovsky and Lowell A. Martin, eds., *Library in the Community: Papers Presented before the Library Institute at the University of Chicago, August 23-28, 1943*. Chicago: University of Chicago Press, 1944, 23-37. **Primary sources and archival materials**—Material about Ralph A. Ulveling is held at the Detroit Public Library. These materials consist of 26 office file boxes. They have not yet been deposited with the Burton Historical Collection, but are available to researchers by special request. The Burton Room does, however, have other primary sources of a "ready reference" nature, including file folders labeled "Director Emeritus—Biographical Data," "Director Emeritus—Citations," "Director Emeritus—63-639," and a box entitled "E and M B U 47, Ulveling, Ralph. Miscellaneous Materials." These four items contain biographical clippings, news clippings, random memoranda, off-prints of his articles, pictures, and annual reports. Documents relating to his position as Chief of Branches are in the Director's Files, Box 59. The author is also in possession of transcripts of several interviews with Ulveling's contemporaries. The ALA Archives at the University of Illinois at Urbana-Champaign also contain a number of record series related to Ulveling, including 2/4/61—World War II Demobilization and Post-War File, 1943-1946; 30/59/5—Radio Broadcasting and Committee

Correspondence, 1930-1941; and 92/11/6 — Library Development Fund Campaign Subject File, 1945-1946.

—DANIEL RING

VITZ, CARL PETER PAUL (1883-1981)

Carl Peter Paul Vitz was born on June 3, 1883, in St. Paul, Minnesota, to Martin and Mary Engeler Vitz and was reared in the small western Ohio town of New Bremen. His French, German, and Swiss ancestors included a number of Calvinists as well as a grandfather who preached and established churches in northeastern Indiana. Vitz developed an appreciation for books in the home where his father, a minister in the Evangelical and Reformed Church, had assembled a fine personal library. Young Carl seemed almost fated for library work from his earliest days, having begun employment at the age of fourteen in the South Branch of the Cleveland Public Library. When as a college student he sought career guidance, an astute professor, cognizant of Vitz's eclectic interests, recommended librarianship. Vitz served at the Cleveland Public Library from 1898 to 1906 except for one year (1904-1905) when he was earning a certificate at the Western Reserve University Library School. He was also graduated from Adelbert College in 1904, having assisted in that institution's library during his senior year and his year at Western Reserve.

Vitz enjoyed success as a student, earning Phi Beta Kappa as an undergraduate, and he was the youngest member of his first library school class of seventeen women and three men. Moreover, his energy and enthusiasm favorably impressed his classmates at the New York State Library School (NYSLS) in Albany where he studied in 1906 and 1907, graduating with a bachelor's degree in library science. Breadth of knowledge and clarity of style were among his hallmarks; he had majored in the classics and would later take some pride in his familiarity with Greek and Latin as well as French and German.

After receiving his bachelor's degree from NYSLS in 1907, Vitz became assistant to George F. Bowerman, District of Columbia public librarian (a position considered by one of his Albany peers as the best in the class of 1907). Vitz also directed the newly established Useful Arts Department. He worked closely with Bowerman, who looked upon the library as an educational center. Bowerman's aggressive approach to public relations, extension programs, and children's services strongly influenced Vitz's attitude towards librarianship.

Vitz next served as assistant to the director of the New York State Library under James I. Wyer, beginning a three-year stint in 1909. It was during this time that he married Ruth Van Aernam, by whom he had three sons and two daughters. Vitz was on the scene during one of history's major library disasters, a fire that struck the state library (then the nation's seventh largest library) on March 29, 1911, destroying some 500,000 volumes and 300,000 manuscripts. He was part of a "small but courageous" corps of staff members and library supporters that repeatedly "entered the still smouldering Capitol ruins" to salvage what remained of the collection. As head of the Order Department, he assumed responsibility for a massive purchasing program facilitated by the state's book replacement appropriation of $1,250,000.

In 1912 Vitz returned to Cleveland and continued for the next decade to learn from more experienced colleagues. The Cleveland Public Library of that period bore the strong imprint of William H. Brett, its director from 1884 to 1918. Brett had championed open stacks, children's services, a subject divisional plan, and a large, fluid extension effort featuring book collections in branches, schools, factories, and various municipal and commercial outlets. Vitz matured professionally during the last years of the Brett administration and the first part of Linda Eastman's directorship; he served as second vice-librarian under Brett and vice-librarian under Eastman. He absorbed much of their professional spirit, a set of ideals that emphasized services dispersed widely throughout municipalities and among all age groups.

Vitz admired Brett in particular. He saw in Brett a leader of energy and vision, one whose sense of purpose inspired long hours of devoted service on the part of his staff. He saw a manager who made appointments with consumate care and who regarded his staff as human resources that should be developed to their highest potential. He also saw in Brett a director who drew great satisfaction in providing personal service to young and old. Vitz believed that Brett's creative genius lay in his adaptability, which the former defined as the ability to analyze a problem, to gather information from every available source, and then to devise a solution for improved services. Thus, a kind of practical flexibility combined with an unswerving commitment to better and stronger libraries were traits that Vitz appreciated and sought to internalize.

Having completed his apprenticeships, Vitz assumed the directorship of the Toledo Public Library, a post he held from 1922 to 1937. At Toledo, Vitz nurtured the skills that made him highly sought after as a member of the library community. He oversaw construction of four new branch buildings, designed the layout and equipment for five branches in school buildings, and initiated the planning for a new central library. Although he regarded the establishment of the Technology Department, specializing in business and industrial information, and the expansion from 8 to 14 branches as important accomplishments, his experience as a building planner and his growing reputation as a building consultant were of greater interest to him.

Architectural plans had first captured his imagination in Albany when he represented the state library in observing construction of the $5,000,000 New York State Education Building. He took blueprints of the new building, tacked them to the wall behind his desk, and spent hours poring over them. Here he began to develop his own concepts of library construction. Later in Cleveland he helped plan two branch buildings and assisted with preliminary plans for a new central building, but at Toledo his skills came to full maturity. The Toledo Public Library branch system exemplified his ideas. He eventually planned or consulted for more than 60 projects devoted to site selection, remodeling, or new construction for main or branch buildings in Atlanta; Boston; Cincinnati; Cleveland; Denver; Detroit; Minneapolis; St. Paul; Seattle; South Bend, Indiana; Tacoma, Washington; Ashland and Lexington, Kentucky; and at Marietta (Ohio) College.

In 1919, Vitz published *Loan Work*, which he later revised under the title *Circulation Work* (Chicago: American Library Association, 1927) for the ALA series "Manual of Library Economy." In these and later publications he wrote in a style that was spare and unadorned, straightforward, well organized, and closely reasoned. He considered the wide range of bureaucratic and economic variables that made up the library's environment, and he emphasized the need for thoroughly planning at all levels of the library enterprise.

Ruth Vitz died in 1932; on July 7, 1934, Carl married Alda Clayton, by whom he had four sons. Three years after his second marriage, Vitz left Toledo to direct the Minneapolis Public Library. He remained there until 1946. His interest in library buildings and consulting continued unabated, although he never had the opportunity to construct a new building for Minneapolis. He lamented the inadequacies of the obsolete central facility which had been in use for more than 50 years. He later recalled that "they never got around to doing anything, but the talk was live enough for me to fool around with plans all the time."

His Minneapolis period was not without accomplishments. Under his direction the library produced a brief history, *Minneapolis Public Library: Fifty Years of Service, 1889-1939* (1939), inaugurated bookmobile service, and established the temporary Vocational Information Service to assist veterans and domestic war workers in adjusting to peacetime employment. Vitz also directed a successful campaign to raise the local library tax by 50 percent. The special election held on June 11, 1945, resulted in a 65 percent favorable vote.

During the years of depression and war, while Vitz served at Toledo and Minneapolis, he emerged as an ardent spokesman on behalf of national planning for public library growth and federal aid to libraries. He edited a collection of papers, *Current Problems in Library Finance* (Chicago: ALA, 1933), regarded by reviewers as a tract for the times, especially clear in its explication of the relationships of libraries to other governmental agencies and to sources of public support. In cooperation with two American Library Association (ALA) committees, he wrote *A Federal Library Agency and Federal Library Aid* (Chicago: ALA, 1935), one of the more cogent arguments for an active federal role in library services. He also promoted the activities of the ALA Postwar Planning Committee, of which he was a member. In 1943, the Committee issued *Postwar Standards for Public Libraries* (Chicago: ALA), a tool for evaluating statewide and individual library development.

Naturally, then, Vitz opposed the withdrawal of federal funding for the Works Progress Administration (WPA). WPA workers had accomplished much at the Minneapolis Public Library. They completed construction at the Longfellow Branch (a replica of Craigie House, the home of American poet Henry Wadsworth Longfellow in Cambridge, Massachusetts). They developed education programs in the library's science museum, taught classes in photography, creative writing, first aid, and other subjects, and microfilmed and indexed the *Minneapolis Star Journal*. Vitz described their efforts as having become integral to the daily expectations of library patrons. Although state WPA officers commended Vitz highly for his planning abilities and for the cooperation he had given them, such praise could not erase the pain of personnel cutbacks and reduced services.

In 1946 Vitz became head of the Public Library of Cincinnati and Hamilton County. He made the move at age 62 (a time when most are planning retirement) amidst a barrage of criticism on the part of local citizens, who preferred younger blood. Chalmers Hadley, who opted for retirement following passage of a bond issue in 1944, had recommended Vitz as his successor on the basis of Vitz's expertise as a building consultant. The library board had committed itself to a new building project, and the bond issue had provided funds.

Vitz immediately saw Cincinnati's potential for a successful building. He observed that the central building for eighty years had been in a "downtown business location, on the most important business street in the city, with no setback and with the main entrance at street level"; these advantages were "definitely in line with present thinking and would, of course, be retained."

He identified three characteristics as essential to a building which would serve an active urban clientele. Foremost among these was easy access for the reading public, followed by a well-staffed ready reference and information service, and subject departmentation for the circulating collection. He emphasized accessibility, arguing that while the purpose of most buildings is to provide space, a "library should be a department store of knowledge."

The construction of the Cincinnati Public Library building did not go as planned. Vitz found the site to be less than desirable due to its proximity to some of the city's houses of prostitution. In addition, the failure of a supplementary bond issue forced him to reduce the final drawings to about 60 percent of the size that had originally been contemplated. Delays occurred due to a labor strike and to what initially appeared to be design flaws. Somewhat discouraged, Vitz attempted to resign in 1953 at age 70 while the building was still under construction. The library board asked him to remain until the task had been completed; he modestly offered to forego a salary increase that year.

Officially opened in 1955, the new building was constructed on the corner of Eighth and Vine, across from Garfield Park, one of the city's most picturesque memorials. It was designed by Frederick W. Garber and Associates in cooperation with Samuel Hannaford and Sons. On a site of 140 by 290 feet, the structure occupied a space of 140 by 180 feet and included a total square footage of 190,880. Three public floors and a bookstack contained a combined shelving capacity of 1,650,000 volumes. Vitz regarded the building as the crowning achievement of his career, since it represented the "thinking" of himself "and the architect very effectively."

The building was modular, designed for maximum flexibility, interior movements, and eventual expansion. Vitz described it as "clean" and "modern," not "cluttered up with unnecessary walls taking up essential floor space." It featured 19-foot stainless steel louvres designed to deflect the afternoon sun; at the time, they were the largest installed in any building in North America. Unfortunately, the louvres never functioned properly and were eventually removed. An abundance of space for the reading public was offset by inadequate workspace for the library staff. Similarly, the visual openness in public areas was not extended to work areas, where exterior glass had been painted a depressing green.

On the other hand, the building boasted more plate glass than that used in any structure of comparable size in the nation. Decorative features included a Venetian glass mosaic covering interior walls and columns, gold leaf tiles, and a graceful serpentine wall (adjacent to the garden) that had been copied from examples in the South but that was unique to the Midwest. It also housed A-frame shelving, popular enough to serve as a model for other libraries.

Despite setbacks, the building was, on the whole, successful. The aesthetic and functional unity of the structure, remodelled and greatly expanded in 1982, confirms the wisdom of Vitz's overall concepts. He emerged as the consummate planner, comparing himself to "a man who is putting his life savings in the construction of a new home. You would find him at the scene quite often seeing to it that everything is going as he wants it to." The building opened to the acclaim of the press, the reading public, and the library community. One reporter hailed Vitz as something of a modernist, describing the new building as up-to-date as the latest "jet fighter."

Contemporaries remember Vitz as affable, practical, hard working, and possessed of seemingly boundless energy. He stood about 5'8" and was quite trim, almost wiry. He had brown hair as a younger man but, during his Cincinnati years, appeared as a cotton-top in perpetual motion. Staff members regarded him as a no-nonsense taskmaster. One librarian who complained of too many responsibilities yet inadequate time and resources met with Vitz's admonition to simply perform her duties rather than talk about them. Yet his friendly manner ensured him a minimal number of enemies. He earned the Cincinnati staff's appreciation and respect for his success in raising salaries. On the other hand, he lost some of that political capital by appointing his wife to direct the library's education and religion section.

Vitz's stature as an association officer coincided naturally with his mounting reputation as a library administrator and building consultant. He presided over the Ohio Library Association (1920-1921, 1933-1934) and chaired its Legislative Committee (1921-1933, 1935-1936) and State Planning Committee (1933-1936). Similarly, he presided over ALA (1944-1945) and chaired its Public Documents Committee (1923-1926), Library Buildings Round Table, and the Librarians of Larger Libraries Round Table. In the latter capacity, he was instrumental in laying the groundwork for what eventually became known as the Public Library Association (PLA), an ALA division. He served on ALA's Board on Service to Children and Young People, ALA Council, Federal Relations Committee, Finance Committee, and Library Branches in Schools Committee. Vitz lectured in the library schools of the New York State Library, Western Reserve University and the University of Minnesota. He also received the J. B. Lippincott Award from ALA (1952), a Citation of Merit from PLA (1954), a citation from the U.S. Office of Education (1954), and honorary doctorates from Western Reserve (1954) and Marietta College (1962).

During his term as ALA president, Vitz emphasized a theme for which he had gained recognition nearly a decade earlier; international planning for library services. He regarded books as essential to American efforts in World War II. Similarly, books were necessary for a demobilized economy and for peaceful coexistence among civilized nations. Accordingly, Vitz promoted an ALA proposal that numerous war surplus collections be diverted to rural Americans (that one-third of the citizenry without access to library services in 1945). Such an ambitious effort should involve careful cooperation among levels of government, leadership by the U.S. Office of Education, and funding at public expense. The end result would be a first but vital step in the direction of a national solution to a persisting problem.

Vitz filled his leisure hours with gardening and reading. He particularly enjoyed biography and history. His activities included membership in the Ohio Historical Society, the Cincinnati Historical Society, the National Trust for Historic Preservation, and the Literary Club (Cincinnati). His earlier work in Toledo and Minneapolis had tended less toward historical and more toward benevolent or educational interests. His historical interests stimulated investigation into an early daguerreotype of the Cincinnati riverfront; he established the date as 1848, a significant discovery in the history of photography. Finally, he chaired the editorial committee of the Ohioana Library Association, sponsor of William Coyle's *Ohio Authors and Their Books* (1962). He died on January 8, 1981.

An overview of Vitz's library career necessitates mention of his ability to take full advantage of his various roles as understudy and then to rise, almost inexorably, to positions of higher management. His approachable manner and straightforward, communicative style made him a capable and trustworthy though not necessarily brilliant administrator. He deserved his national reputation as an advocate of library planning at local, state, and federal levels. His commitments to ease of access on behalf of the reading public characterize his expertise as a building consultant, leaving thousands of library users in his debt, especially in Toledo and Cincinnati.

Biographical listings and obituaries—*Biographical Directory of Librarians in the United States and Canada*, 5th ed. [Obituary]. *Cincinnati Enquirer*, January 9, 1981, 2-B; [Obituary]. *Cincinnati Post*, January 9, 1981, D-3; [Obituary]. *Sons and Daughters of Pioneer Rivermen Magazine* (March 1981); *Who's Who in*

Library Service, 1st, 2nd, 3rd eds. (1933, 1943, 1955). **Books and articles about the biographee**—Compton, Charles H. "Carl Vitz." *Bulletin of Bibliography* 21: 121-3 (January-April 1955); Hage, Hortense C. "Impressions of a Newcomer." *Minneapolis Athletic Club Gopher* 22: 13, 24 (July 1937); Swardson, Roger. "Vitz of the Library: His Thoughts on Planning and Modern Design Have Been Molded into Many Buildings." *Cincinnati Enquirer*, April 12, 1959, 1-J; Warnick, Charles. "There's No Dust: In Thinking of Carl Vitz, Chief Exponent of Modern Library." *Cincinnati Enquirer*, March 15, 1953, section 3, 1. **Primary sources and archival materials**—Material by and about Carl Vitz is held in the Archives, Cleveland Public Library; in Toledo Public Library Papers, Local History and Genealogy Department, Toledo-Lucas County Public Library; in the Minneapolis History Collection, Minneapolis Public Library and Information Center; and in the Rare Books Department, Public Library of Cincinnati and Hamilton County. The latter also holds reports to the Board of Trustees and publications of the Staff Association of the Public Library of Cincinnati and Hamilton County, especially useful in the Vitz period, 1946-1955.

—JOHN MARK TUCKER

WAPLES, DOUGLAS (1893-1978)

Douglas Waples was born on March 3, 1893 in Philadelphia, Pennsylvania, the only child of Rufus (1859-1940) and Christine Beach Isham Waples (1857-1898); his father remarried after the death of Douglas's mother, and by a second wife had two daughters, Dorothea and Evelyn. Waples grew up in Wayne, Pennsylvania, and attended nearby Haverford College, a Quaker school. Finishing "about second in the class" of 1914, he was elected to Phi Beta Kappa. In his autobiography, Waples reported that in his college years

> [I] won some literary prizes [and] did about as well in sports as I had in school. I won the all-round in inter-collegiate gymnastics and a bid to the 1914 Olympics which were never held.

In 1915 he received a Master of Arts degree in letters from Haverford, and in June 1917, an M.A. from Harvard. That same month he married Eleanor Jackson Cary, whom he had met three years earlier while working at a summer camp. Immediately the young couple were shipped to France "as the first two Quakers to be sent abroad by the now well-known 'Friends Service Committee'." While abroad, Waples completed a year of further study in educational psychology at the University of London. Upon their return to the United States in 1919, the Wapleses settled in Philadelphia, where he enrolled in the University of Pennsylvania; his doctorate was conferred the following June. His dissertation was entitled "An Approach to the Synthetic Study of Interest in Education."

Beginning in the fall of 1920, Waples held an assistant professorship at Tufts College near Boston. In 1923, the University of Pittsburgh offered him a challenge. He later described it as "trying to run three jobs at once: assistant dean of the graduate school, assistant professor of secondary education, and extension lecturer in the surrounding steel mill town." While at the university, he came under the influence of Werrett W. Charters, an authority in curriculum construction; when Charters joined the Education Department of the University of Chicago, Waples and his growing family, which eventually included three daughters, went along.

At the university, Waples taught several courses in the Education Department and continued his research activities, publishing *Problems in Classroom Method* (New York: Macmillan, 1927). Upon the establishment of the Graduate Library School, Dean George Works identified a major opportunity for research in the field of librarianship as "problems of method." He stated that "questions relating to the adaptability of library materials need much more critical evaluations than they have received." Seeking the most qualified candidate for such research, the Board of Trustees transferred Waples "from the College of Education and promoted [him] to a professorship of educational method in the Graduate Library School (GLS) on October 1, 1928." Once there, his research interests were expressed in such courses as "The Library and Education of Adults," "Adult Learning," "Methods of Book Distribution in Foreign Countries," "Methods of Investigation," and "Organization and Methods of Teaching Library Science." Bernard Berelson recalled later in *Library Quarterly*:

> As for Douglas Waples the person, the quality that impressed us most as students and colleagues was how untraditional, how independent he was in virtually every way. His talk was different: often hard to fathom, surprising in where it began and where it ended, seemingly beside the point, but always worth waiting for,

listening to, and pondering over—one felt one was overhearing an internal puzzlement being worked through aloud.

Waples also served as acting dean four times (for a total of one and one-half years) between 1929 and 1932. In this role, Waples continued to emphasize library science "primarily as a social enterprise"; for him, therefore, library administration was subordinated to the fulfillment of what he termed, "human needs." According to Richardson, Waples believed the GLS needed to show progress toward the following goals:

1. To establish librarianship as a legitimate field for graduate research in the opinion of competent scholars in related and contributory fields as well as in the opinion of the graduate faculty as a whole.

2. To clarify in the mind of the library profession at large the distinction between valid evidence and conventional assumptions regarding the present values and methods of library administration.

3. To identify or to train experienced librarians who are able to direct studies in the field of public library administration.

4. To increase the competence of instructors in library schools by developing candidates for such positions who are qualified to increase the professional content of the training courses as opposed to present content, which is largely clerical in character.

5. To identify and organize source material pertinent to library problems that now exist in various graduate departments, thus economizing and directing the efforts of future students in the field.

6. To produce, select, and publish significant investigations.

After Louis R. Wilson was appointed Dean in 1932, Waples continued to be a highly productive scholar. He wrote more than a dozen articles for the *Library Quarterly*, including an irregular column, "Graduate Theses Accepted by Library Schools," between 1933 and 1939. He published four works in the Studies in Library Science series, including *Investigating Library Problems* (Chicago: University of Chicago Press, 1939), which soon became the classic guide to relevant methodologies for library science and introduced more than one generation of researchers to the milieu of quantitative social science. Besides being a concrete apologia for the GLS's approach to problem solving, it challenged the status quo by moving away from personal opinion to ferreting out assumptions and sifting evidence in an attempt to create a "new set of values" and a more valid basis for knowledge.

In the other three monographs for the series, Waples applied his "nominalist" approach to the social aspects of reading in a stepwise fashion. *People and Print* (Chicago: University of Chicago Press, 1937) systematically explored what people do read, not what they should or could read. Unfortunately, it relied heavily upon charts, graphs, and statistical tables, leading Robert E. Park to argue in a review that it was "extraordinarily and unnecessarily hard to read." In *Libraries and Readers* (Chicago: University of Chicago Press, 1939), which he coauthored with Leon Carnovsky, Waples began to investigate the role of the state, specifically New York, in public education and reading. This study identified factors relating to the state's success in providing incentives for readers to read "better" publications. Notably, the authors concluded that stronger incentives could be provided by consolidating school districts, thereby maximizing support of school libraries and by redistricting public libraries. For his last major effort in the GLS, Waples edited volume six of the annual Library Institutes held at Chicago, entitled *Print, Radio, and Film in a Democracy* (Chicago: University of Chicago Press, 1942).

In December 1942, Waples joined the U.S. Army with the rank of Major. After various assignments at the Pentagon, in London, Paris, and Berlin, Waples and Helmut Lehmann-Haupt found themselves in Leipzig on V.E. Day, May 8, 1945,

one week before the Russians took Leipzig over from the U.S. Seventh Corps. We went down publishers' row in that city and picked some ten publishers whom we considered the best compromise between the most important pre-war German publishers and those most likely to be cleared by our own Intelligence Branch, which had a veto on all of our recommendations to license. Those we picked were moved out of Leipzig on the eve of the Russian occupation and across Germany by military convoy to Wiesbaden on the Rhine where they have prospered ever since.

Waples lived in Nuremberg until December 1948. When he returned to the United States, the University of Chicago reappointed him Professor of Researches in Reading in the Graduate Library School. However, he left the GLS in 1950 for the interdisciplinary Committee in Communication, becoming its chair in 1951 upon Bernard Berelson's resignation.

After retiring from the university in 1957, he settled down at his favorite retreat on Washington Island, Wisconsin, in Lake Michigan, with Dorothy Blake, whom he had married in October 1947; he had divorced his first wife earlier that year. Still active in teaching during his retirement, Waples was awarded a doctorate in literature from the University of St. Augustine in Peru while on a Fulbright Research Scholarship in 1958. In October 1960, Waples suffered a debilitating stroke that resulted in expressive aphasia; declining health eventually led to his death on April 25, 1978.

Waples stands as a scientific researcher par excellence in librarianship; his inquiring, analytical mind examined in particular the social effects of reading and adult education. As a consequence, much of his early work employed quantitative methods from the social and behavioral sciences, and for this his work was sharply criticized by C. Seymour Thompson at the 1931 American Library Institute as "bloodless and utterly de-personalized ... cold and unsympathetic ... [and] appreciative of nothing but minute facts." Nevertheless, other individuals supported his investigations; Henry Harap of Western Reserve University has said of Waples's *What People Want to Read About* (Chicago: American Library Association and University of Chicago Press, 1931), which he co-authored with Ralph W. Tyler:

> Their work is no ruthless invasion by myopic manipulators of slide rules, logarithmic tables, and correlation machines. The investigators are "little more than kin and less than kind" in relation to the library world and so apply their measuring instruments with courtesy, sensitivity, and with a respect for literary values. Measurers and calculators that they are, they never lose sight of the personal and cultural nature of the situation with which they are dealing.

Along with George Works, Waples significantly altered the library profession's definition of research away from bibliography and helped to imbue the formerly hollow phrase "library science" with real meaning. Waples attempted to clarify the "important distinction between research and *search* [which] is not apparent to many prominent librarians." Waples defined research in library science as

> extending the existing body of knowledge concerning the values and practices of libraries in their many aspects, and including the development of methods of investigation whereby significant data are obtained, tested, and applied.

His influence can clearly be seen in the work of students such as Amy Winslow, Bernard Berelson, Leon Carnovsky, Hester Hoffman, and Miriam Tompkins.

Waples never saw himself as a librarian, but rather as a professor of social science, in which library science was simply another human science. He characterized his GLS-era work as studies in "public communication." It was during this formative period in the history of library science that Waples brought his unique skills, training, and interests to bear upon library problems and issues he felt to be critical in the communication process. Borrowing the words he used to describe his own father, Waples "walked along the way, observing things curiously, as one who understands their purpose but finds no peace until he learns what each part does to make the whole."

Biographical listings and obituaries — [Obituary]. Berelson, Bernard. "Douglas Waples, 1893-1978." *Library Quarterly* 49:1-2 (January 1979); [Obituary]. *Chicago Sunday Times*, May 7, 1978, 110; [Obituary]. *Haverford Horizons* 76:29 (Autumn 1978); [Obituary]. *New York Times*, May 6, 1978, 26; [Obituary]. *Wilson Library Bulletin* 52:768 (June 1978); *American Men of Science: Social and Behavioral Sciences*, 9th, 10th eds. (1956, 1962); *Directory of American Scholars*, 1st, 2nd eds. (1942, 1951); *Leaders in Education*, 1st, 2nd, 3rd eds. (1932, 1941, 1948); *Who's Who in America*, 16th-30th eds. (1930-1958); *Who's Who in Library Service*, 1st, 2nd eds. (1933, 1943). **Books and articles about the biographee** — Karetzky, Stephen. *Reading Research and*

Librarianship: A History and Analysis. Westport, Conn.: Greenwood Press, 1982; Richardson, John V., Jr. *The Spirit of Inquiry: The Graduate Library School at Chicago, 1921-1951*. Foreword by Jesse H. Shera (Chicago: American Library Association, 1982); Richardson, John V., Jr. "The Gospel of Scholarship: Pierce Butler and American Librarianship, 1883-1953" (in progress). **Primary sources and archival materials** — Waples, Douglas, and Dorothy B. Waples. *On the March: A Short Autobiography for Friends and Family* [and] *Memories*. Washington Island, Wis.: privately printed, 1967. According to Waples's first wife, Eleanor, many of his GLS-era papers were destroyed in the 1961 Bel Air (Calif.) fire. A few personal papers are in the possession of Mrs. Dorothy Waples, in the archives of the University of Chicago Library's Department of Special Collections (President's Papers 1925-1945), and in the Graduate Library School.

— JOHN V. RICHARDSON, JR.

WARHEIT, ISRAEL ALBERT (1912-1973)

Israel Albert Warheit was born December 12, 1912, in Toronto, Ontario, Canada, the son of Nathan and Anna Gutzin Warheit. He had two younger brothers and a sister. His scholarship, knowledge, ability, and interest in learning enabled him to skip grades, and he was graduated from high school when he was 16. The family moved to Detroit in 1927. After finishing high school Warheit enrolled in Michigan State Normal College (now Eastern Michigan University), where he obtained his bachelor's degree in modern languages in 1933.

Warheit received a scholarship from the University of Michigan, where he received an M.A. in Germanic languages and literature in 1934. During that year he was also granted a fellowship to work on his Ph.D. The subsequent year he spent at the University of Zurich in Switzerland. He returned to the University of Michigan and became a naturalized citizen in 1936.

In 1939 Warheit married Elizabeth Limberg, who had obtained her library degree from the University of Michigan in 1935; in 1939 she was working as a cataloger in the Research Laboratory Library of General Motors. Her interest in library work influenced Warheit to enter the University of Michigan Library School while he was finishing his Ph.D. He received both his Ph.D. and his library degree in 1940.

Over the next three decades the library profession was heavily influenced by a variety of innovations, two of which directly affected Warheit's professional life. The first was the introduction of the scientific or technical report as an important, and in some cases, major portion of the literature collection of the technical and some governmental libraries. The second was the mechanization of library procedures.

Besides being heavily involved with both of these innovations, Warheit also engaged in a number of ancillary activities. From 1941 to 1946 he was librarian of the Allison Division of General Motors in Indianapolis, where he processed classified reports of government-sponsored research limited in distribution to those with a "need to know." The Allison Division Library received a large number of these reports in addition to a number of captured German documents, which Warheit translated.

In his first published library paper, Warheit recorded his Allison Library experiences. He found that no uniform policy existed to cover the format, classification, method of issuance, and distribution of the reports. If the publications were to be meaningfully used, they had to reach the proper people quickly and easily. He was impressed by Germany's central depository of aeronautical documents, which supplied reports to those who needed them. The librarian played an important role in this activity. This approach, Warheit believed, needed to be duplicated in the United States. "A centralized, coordinating bibliographic service or library," he concluded, "must be set up to provide the necessary coordination and information in order to insure a truly successful national research program."

Shortly after he published this article (and perhaps because of it) Warheit was invited to Oak Ridge, Tennessee, for an employment interview with the Atomic Energy Commission (AEC). He was offered and accepted the position of Chief, Library Section, Technical Information Branch, and served in it from 1946 to 1952.

Warheit described the Oak Ridge Library Section services in "The Atomic Energy Commission Library System," published in the January 1950 issue of *College & Research Libraries*. During the first three years he built the kind of library organization he had described in his first article. Although the Library Section had a small published literature collection, initially the primary resource was 18,000 classified and unclassified reports obtained from the various AEC and contractor installations. To accommodate the 800 inquiries received by the reference service group each month, the section maintained a stock of 75,000 copies of the reports. As many as 11,000 report copies were sold and 40,000 others distributed to government agencies, depository libraries, and research installations each month. The section's cataloging unit provided catalog cards on the technical reports to 68 libraries in the AEC complex. One installation eventually developed a catalog of 80,000 cards.

In September 1946 AEC formed a bibliographic unit. Initially it compiled and published title lists of declassified reports as they were issued and available to the public. In July 1948 the unit began compiling and publishing *Nuclear Science Abstracts*, motivated in part by the refusal of a major abstracting service to accept the unclassified AEC reports for abstracting in its journal.

During the 1940s and early 1950s, many ideas for the report literature were devised and tried by the library profession. Those preceding the mechanization of library procedures included the edge-punched card, the Batten or Peek-a-boo cards, uniterms or coordinate indexing, and facsimile transmission of copy.

Warheit followed these developments closely, and through his presentations and articles advised the library profession of their relative costs, benefits, and shortcomings. For example, he found that the edge-punched cards needed no filing, but files in excess of 5,000 cards took too long to sort. Also, uniterms broke down subject headings into approximately 6,000 terms rather than the many thousands used in Library of Congress cataloging, but the posting time took longer than the traditional card filing time. In addition, the combined uniterms produced many false citations and failed to locate items that traditional cataloging produced. Warheit's own innovation used unit record machines (keypunch, sorter, and printer) to produce the index to the first volume of *Nuclear Science Abstracts* in 1948. While he found the equipment satisfactory for duplicating cards, sorting them and making printed lists, it was not useful in more complex library procedures.

While at Oak Ridge, Warheit had the unique opportunity to accompany a group of AEC scientists to Bikini to witness a text explosion of an atomic bomb. From 1952 to 1956 he was head of the library department of the Argonne National Laboratory, a major unit of the AEC contractor research installations, which was located near Chicago. In September 1956, he returned to AEC headquarters in Washington, D.C., as Chief, Technical Library Branch.

The transition in data storage was made from punched cards to tape and then to disks in the 1950s. Large and very expensive machines did the searching. Warheit kept abreast of the machine developments and the esoteric applications for information retrieval. In 1957 he knew about RAMAC, the computer that could provide random access to data stored on disks, and he was aware that the National Bureau of Standards had tested the use of RAMAC to index steroids for the U.S. Patent Office.

In 1959 Warheit left AEC and joined IBM's Advanced Systems Development Division in Washington, and in 1961 he moved to San Jose, California. IBM did not consider libraries a potential market for the development of new machines. It did, however, have an interest in the application of existing equipment to information retrieval techniques and recognized that a knowledgeable library person who understood computers could make valuable contributions.

When Warheit joined IBM, his interest in information retrieval resulted in his development of a program called CFSS (Combined Files Search System) to be used with RAMAC. While the work may have been done initially for the library profession, its application was of interest to a number of professions. The San Jose edition of *IBM News* for February 25, 1966, reported that the Food and Drug Administration was using the program to speed the evaluation of drugs that might be dangerous to human health. IBM customers in chemistry, metals, and several other areas of engineering and industry were interested in using the program in their activities. For his work Warheit received IBM's Outstanding Achievement Award.

His ability to communicate with librarians resulted in so many queries to IBM field representatives, on topics such as machine-produced book catalogs, that Warheit was flooded with requests for help from the IBM sales staff. In self defense he prepared the *IBM Manual E20-0333, Library Automation—Computer Produced Book Catalogs* (1969). By that time the development of the computer had progressed to a level that would allow the cataloger to type the input for catalog cards on the terminal, and review and correct it from the display screen before it was recorded in the computer memory for subsequent printing. Warheit compiled other IBM manuals as they were needed by the sales force and the public. By 1970 library automation included the production of catalog cards, book catalogs, periodical check-in, serials holdings, circulation control systems, acquisition programs, and information retrieval. Initially these were separate, individually designed programs, but the systems developers began to integrate the programs into a single "total" system which was online on a time-sharing basis.

In his last major article, Warheit reported that while library productivity was falling and library costs had trebled during the preceding decade, there was hope for the future. Computer storage capacity was growing rapidly and data storage costs were dropping dramatically. For example, in 1956 the RAMAC storage capability was 20,000 titles, which cost $1.00 per character per year. In 1968 a contemporary computer had a storage capacity of twice that of the National Union Catalog, which carried 16 million titles, at a cost of $.08 per character.

Warheit's professional activities included participation in the American Library Association, the Special Libraries Association, the American Society of Information Science, and the International Federation for Documentation. He made frequent presentations at conferences in the United States and Europe. His articles appeared in *American Documentation, College & Research Libraries, Journal of Education for Librarianship, Journal of Library Automation, Library Quarterly, Library Research and Technical Services, Special Libraries,* and *Wilson Library Bulletin.*

Warheit made valuable contributions to the library profession in three areas. At AEC, Warheit's Library Section provided a model for other agency bibliographic units that issued, indexed, and abstracted technical reports. His contribution to library mechanization ranged from the 1948 index to *Nuclear Science Abstracts* to the 1966 Combined Files Searching System program. His journal articles, conference presentations, and company manuals presented his information and evaluation not only to the library profession, but also to IBM's sales staff and the purchasers of IBM products. He died on February 2, 1973, of a heart attack, survived by his wife, Betty, and two children.

Biographical listings and obituaries—[Obituary]. *Journal of the American Society for Information Science* 24:79 (March 1973); [Obituary]. *Special Libraries* 64:162 (March 1973); *Biographical Directory of Librarians in the United States and Canada,* 5th ed.; *Who's Who in Library Service,* 4th ed.; *Who Was Who in America* V (1969-1973). **Books and articles by the biographee**—"The Automation of Libraries." *Special Libraries* 63:1-7 (January 1972); "The Computer Produced Book Catalog." *Special Libraries* 60:573-9 (November 1969); "The Librarian and the National Research Program." *Library Journal* 70:119-21 (December 1, 1945); Fry, Bernard M., I. A. Warheit, and G. E. Randall. "The Atomic Energy Commission Library System: Its Origin and Development." *College & Research Libraries* 11:6-9 (January 1950). **Primary sources and archival materials**—Some private correspondence is in possession of the Warheit family. Mrs. I. A. Warheit (Elizabeth Limberg Warheit) reviewed a draft of this biographical sketch for additional information, deletions, and correction of data.

—GORDON E. RANDALL

WHITE, CARL MILTON (1903-1983)

Carl Milton White was born on August 12, 1903, in Burnet, Oklahoma, the son of a farmer. Apparently not attuned to a life in agriculture, White went off to college at Oklahoma Baptist University, where he graduated in 1925. Upon graduation he assumed the position of principal of a small high school in his home state. Feeling that life had more to offer him professionally, White left secondary education and entered graduate school at Mercer University, Macon, Georgia, where he received an M.A. in 1928. It was also the year when he married Ruth Bennett, in what became a fifty-five year companionship that produced two daughters and five grandchildren.

After Mercer University, White attended the University of Iowa at Ames in 1929-1930 and then matriculated in the Ph.D. program at Cornell University. In 1933 he received his Ph.D. in philosophy from Cornell. Believing that his future lay in librarianship, White then went to New York City where he attended Columbia University's School of Library Service. In 1934 he received his B.S. in L.S., and he was ready to begin his rapid rise in the field of library administration and education.

In the year of his graduation from library school, White accepted the position of librarian of

Fisk University in Nashville, Tennessee. White thus started his library career as a director. In 1934, however, Fisk was in no position to entice an experienced administrator of the first rank. What Fisk needed was someone to put a library in order, and White was the type of person to do the job. Young, eager, armed with newly learned knowledge and scholarship, he was ready to make his mark.

White quickly began building Fisk's library and within a few short years Fisk gained respectability, and White a reputation in the field of library administration. By 1937, after three years at Fisk, White was negotiating job prospects and offers.

Most notably, officials at Carleton College in Minnesota were looking for a new library director and felt White could fill the job. White's one drawback in these years was his limited experience. But experience stopped neither White nor Carleton, and White accepted the position for the 1938-1939 academic year.

Concurrent with these negotiations, Robert Downs, then library director at the University of North Carolina at Chapel Hill, was getting ready to assume the director's position at New York University. In January 1938 Carl Milam, American Library Association executive director, wrote to Downs recommending White for the Chapel Hill job even though he was relatively inexperienced. Downs and Louis Round Wilson, formerly of the University of North Carolina and then at the University of Chicago's Graduate School of Library Science, agreed that White was the person for the job. Although North Carolina was offering a lower salary than Carleton, White decided after corresponding with his colleagues, and at the urgings of Downs and others, that advancement in his career lay in the research library field that North Carolina represented rather than in the world of the small liberal arts college. White regretfully wrote Carleton's President Cowling of his decision and prepared to move to Chapel Hill. White had spent four years at Fisk and now began what would be a two-year stint as North Carolina's university librarian and head of the School of Library Science.

White's experience at the University of North Carolina indicates that his administrative and political skills were not particularly adept in the setting of a large, complex academic organization. In a 1939 letter to Louis Round Wilson, White complained that the library was being "shortchanged" compared to the rest of the university. In addition, North Carolina's president had remarked that "classes which have students in them come first." White also felt that the president relied more on the faculty's advice on the library than that of the librarians. Furthermore, White was unhappy about his complex relation to the library school. Although he was head of the school, he in fact had no real authority over its administration.

After one year in the job White was ready to leave. In June 1939 he was offered the post of director of libraries at the University of Illinois. Somewhat unsure of the propriety of leaving North Carolina so soon, he wrote Charles C. Williamson of Columbia University for advice. Williamson replied in a letter dated August 1, 1939, that it would be appropriate to leave especially since White believed North Carolina was not providing the proper financial support for the library. Williamson went on to state his concern that a professional librarian be at the helm at Illinois: " ... it would be disastrous for Illinois to give up its search for a professional person and appoint a professor. There is always danger that that may happen anywhere, but the results would be more calamitous at Illinois than at most universities."

White quickly took Williamson's advice and on August 18, 1939 he accepted the directorship of the University of Illinois libraries, effective the following year. He then went on to survey and write up a report on the University of North Carolina library. White's report reads like a compendium of many academic librarians' complaints about the place of the library in the university. He stated that the salaries were lower than those of professors; that the book budget was the last line in the university budget; that there was little recognition of the importance of the library for the life of the university; that the building was too small; that the library lacked centralization; that the library school should be directly administered by the chair; and that librarians were systematically excluded from the faculty. The latter point, the question of librarians' status, would concern White more than once in his later career.

In September 1940, White took up the directorship of both the library and library school at the University of Illinois. White's tenure at Illinois was also a short two-years' duration. Although the assistant director, E. W. McDiarmid mentioned several contributions White made during his stay, he was unsuccessful in his major goal of conveying the idea that "the modern trained librarian renders an auxiliary function to classroom instruction and research which makes him an independent actor in the academic scene."

White's greatest contribution to the field while at Illinois was in obtaining funds from the Carnegie Corporation to survey Illinois's library school on the occasion of its fiftieth anniversary. The report by Keyes Metcalf, Andrew D. Osborn, and John Dale Russell was published in 1943 and became a general survey of library education rather than a study restricted to Illinois. In that well-known report, Metcalf called for a theoretical foundation for library education, something he found lacking in the present curriculum. In noting the three objectives of the curriculum—principles, techniques, and professional standards—he stated that only the teaching of techniques was successful in library training and that the other two objectives lacked foundations in scholarship, especially in the history of libraries. In accepting the report, White did so not uncritically. He remarked that the authors were not educators but practitioners and took the short-sighted view that the history of libraries was not all that necessary for an understanding of librarianship. White, however, did not stay long enough in his post to use the Metcalf Report at Illinois.

In early 1942 White was offered the dual position of dean of the school of library service and director of libraries at Columbia University. He accepted the offer in 1943 under the assumption, as he wrote Columbia's provost Frank Fackenthal, that Columbia's library development would match that of Harvard's and Yale's and also have a strong library school faculty.

In preparing for his new life at Columbia and also in quest of the ideal of the university librarian, White wrote Princeton's Librarian, Julian Boyd, asking for his advice and opinion on the role of the academic librarian. Boyd wrote back on May 13, 1943, and concisely and succinctly focused on the problem of the librarian's status in relation to university faculty:

> The University Librarian is the one person next to the president in the academic community charged with responsibility of thinking of the whole institution rather than in terms of a department; he should regard himself as an educator rather than a custodian of books ... the librarian cannot meet individual scholars, committees, and officers of administration on their own terms, command their respect, and bring his voice to bear upon their problems, ... unless he is himself a scholar.

Boyd's statement lay at the heart of the problem of faculty status for librarians then as today. White's reaction to Boyd's letter is not known, but when he did move on to Columbia, his early years were marked by curricular revisions with an aim toward increased professionalism and research.

White, with the aid of Columbia colleagues Ernest Reece and Lowell Martin, began an intensive two-year study of the library school's curriculum. Building on Reece's previous studies, *The Curriculum of Library Schools* (New York: Columbia University Press, 1936) and *Programs for Library Schools* (New York: Columbia University Press, 1943), White, in his 1946 dean's report, called for the abandonment of the fifth-year Bachelor's program and the inauguration of a new program leading to the Master's degree. The aim was to emphasize librarianship as an intellectual discipline as opposed to a more practice-oriented profession.

The new curriculum as detailed in the 1946 report would comprise four parts: foundations, or the library as a social, educational, and historical institution; readers and reading, including readers needs and behavior; methods, which encompassed administration, programs, technical services, and bibliographic description; and resources, or information and its use.

The report also noted that librarianship had few qualified research scholars and that to rectify the matter Columbia should institute a Ph.D. program in the discipline. White reiterated his recommendation for this program in his 1947 report and also emphasized the library school's academic isolation in the university and urged a greater integration of disciplines.

In 1948 the university council adopted the library school's new curriculum to commence the following academic year (1948-1949), as well as a new Ph.D. program jointly administered with other academic departments.

The Ph.D. program lacked faculty support, however, and produced only two Ph.Ds. In 1951 it was abolished, and the professional Doctor of

Library Science degree, under the total control of the Library School, was substituted in its place. White was correct in bemoaning the lack of qualified research scholars in the field and took the loss of the Ph.D. as a personal failure.

By 1954 the curriculum warranted another intensive review which resulted in additional areas of study and allowed more flexibility in programming. The academic year 1953-1954 was also a turning point for White. In 1953 White's lack of administrative skills became glaring and the University decided that the dual directorship of University Librarian and Dean was too much for him; henceforth two discrete positions would exist. White relinquished the more responsible librarian position to Richard Logsdon and stayed on as dean of the Library School. At the end of 1954, political strife in the Library School made White's deanship untenable, and he resigned while remaining on as a professor.

While White was in library practice, he also served his profession in other capacities. He was a member of the ALA Executive Board from 1941 to 1945, served on the Advisory Committee of the Association for Research Libraries from 1941 to 1947, and was editor of *College & Research Libraries* (also 1941-1947). In 1961 he published his much cited *Origins of the American Library School* (New York: Scarecrow), then followed it with two editions of *Sources of Information in the Social Sciences* (Chicago: American Library Association, 1964, 1973) and *Bases of Modern Librarianship: A Study of Library Theory and Practice in Britain, Canada, Denmark, the Federal Republic of Germany and the United States* (New York: Macmillan, 1964).

The latter reflected an interest in international librarianship gained from his position as advisor to the U.S. Department of State on the organization of UNESCO in 1944-1945. In 1959, under the auspices of the Ford Foundation, he went to the University of Ankara in Turkey to direct the library school there, and on his return to the U.S. he resigned his post at Columbia. Thereafter he became program officer with the Ford Foundation (a position more suitable to his talents). From 1962 to 1964 he also served as library advisor to the Nigerian government. He retired to California in 1967, and until 1971 worked as a consultant developing the collection at the University of California at San Diego. He died at the age of eighty on November 8, 1983.

Biographical listings and obituaries—*College & Research Libraries* 23:160-1 (March 1962); [Obituary]. *New York Times*. November 11, 1983; [Obituary]. *American Libraries* 15:64 (January 1984); [Obituary]. *Wilson Library Bulletin* 58:376 (January 1984); *Who's Who in Library Service*, 4th ed. **Books and articles about the biographee**—Bonnell, Alice H. "Columbia University Libraries." In Allen Kent and Harold Lancour (eds.) *Encyclopedia of Library and Information Science*, Vol. 5. New York: Marcel Dekker, 1971, pp. 362-70; Carrol, C. Edward. *The Professionalization of Education for Librarianship*. Metuchen, NJ: Scarecrow Press, 1970; Columbia University. School of Library Service. *Annual Report of the Dean* (1946-1954); Linderman, Winifred B. "Columbia University School of Library Service." In Allen Kent and Harold Lancour (eds.) *Encyclopedia of Library and Information Science*, Vol. 5. New York: Marcel Dekker, 1971, pp. 370-90; Trautman, Ray. *A History of the School of Library Service, Columbia University*. New York: Columbia University Press, 1954. **Primary sources and archival materials**—Carl White Papers, Rare Books and Manuscript Library, Columbia University. All quotations from and references to correspondence in this article are from this collection.

—LARRY E. SULLIVAN

WILSON, LOUIS ROUND (1876-1979)

If one were to choose the single most important year in the history of American librarianship it would certainly have to be 1876. In that year the U.S. Bureau of Education published its monumental survey of *Libraries in the United States*, with its supplement, a slender pamphlet by Charles Ammi Cutter entitled *Rules for a Printed Dictionary Catalog*. Melvil Dewey issued the first edition of his *Decimal Classification*. Then, as the year drew to its close, the ALA was founded at the Centennial Exhibition in Philadelphia, and Louis Round Wilson was born. He, among all our contemporaries, most deserves to be ranked with those hardy pioneers who laid so well the foundations of the American library movement.

Louis Round Wilson was born at Lenoir, North Carolina, on December 27, 1876, the son of Jethro Ruben and Louise Jane Round Wilson. That he derives from true pioneer stock is evident

---

Prepared by the late Jesse H. Shera as a supplementary sketch to the *Dictionary of American Library Biography*, this first appeared in the *Journal of Library History* Vol. 17, No. 1, Winter 1982.

from his ancestry, which can be traced back to John Howland, who arrived on these shores on the *Mayflower*. His maternal grandfather was George Hopkins Round, a Methodist minister. Louis had four siblings, a sister and three brothers: Alice, who was graduated from MIT in 1900, and who taught at East Carolina University; Robert, who was a professor of chemistry at Duke University; Edwin, who was headmaster at Haverford School; and George, who was a 1901 graduate of the School of Law at Columbia University.

After graduation from high school at Lenoir, Wilson spent two years at the Lenoir Academy. He was a typesetter and "printer's devil," on the *Lenoir Topic*, from 1891-1894, during which period he continued his studies under the direction of J. D. Minnick. During this same period he began his library career by serving as librarian of the small library maintained by the Methodist church in Lenoir. After a year of study at Davenport College (a preparatory school), Wilson entered Haverford College in the autumn of 1895. At Haverford he received a prize for his outstanding work in Latin. After three years, he transferred to the University of North Carolina, where he received his baccalaureate degree in 1899. Upon graduation he was awarded the Hume Senior Essayist Medal. Following two years of teaching in private schools, he returned to Chapel Hill to serve as librarian and pursue graduate work. He received his M.A. in 1902, and the doctorate in 1905. His dissertation, on Chaucer's "Relative Constructions," appeared in the first issue of *Studies in Philology* (Chapel Hill, N.C.: University Press, 1906). Many years later, when this writer was in one of his classes at the University of Chicago, and reported unfavorably on Gray and Leary's *What Makes a Book Readable* (Chicago: University of Chicago Press, 1935), I concluded with the observation that perhaps it was no worse than counting the personal pronouns in *Beowulf*, to which Wilson replied, "Let's say, I got my doctorate by counting them in Chaucer." He supported my point of view, however, by observing that the Gray-Leary volume was "the most unreadable book I've ever encountered. I told the Press to print only 1,000 copies, for I knew once the word got around it wouldn't sell."

In 1909, he married Penelope Bryan Wright, who died in 1949. They had four children: Elizabeth, Penelope, Mary Louise (Mrs. Dean Stockett Edmonds, Jr.), and a son, Louis Round Wilson, Jr., who died prior to his second birthday.

Wilson was appointed librarian of the University of North Carolina in 1901, and for the first year he was not convinced that librarianship should be his chosen career; but by the end of that period he had reached a decision. During his 31-year tenure his library's collection grew from about 38,000 volumes to more than 235,000 volumes. From 1907 to 1915, he had but one assistant: by 1932 there were twenty-three professionals on his staff. At Chapel Hill he developed a collection of research materials on North Carolina history and culture numbering 47,000 items, which became a focal point for research workers throughout the South. In 1904, he inaugurated a collection on southern history that also added to the reputation of the university as a place of regional research.

His interest in library education began early. In 1904 he inaugurated a summer course in librarianship that was soon also offered during the regular academic year. Some two decades later he laid plans for a school of library science at the University, which was opened in 1931. In the beginning, the school was subsidized by a grant of $100,000 from the Carnegie Corporation.

But his interests at Chapel Hill were by no means confined to librarianship. Long interested in the university's extension program, he was appointed director of that program in 1913. In 1909 he worked on the *University Record*, and edited the *Alumni Review*. In 1922 the University Press was established with Wilson as its first director, a position which he held until 1932. Under his leadership the press published over one hundred titles and became prominent for social and cultural studies relating to the South. During this period he was the confidant of the University administration and advised them in many ways.

Wilson's library interests were far from being limited to the life of the University. In 1904 he worked actively for the establishment of the North Carolina Library Association, was its secretary-treasurer from 1904 to 1909, and in the last year was elected its president. He was to serve again as NCLA president in 1920-1921 and 1929-1930. In 1907 he worked on a draft for the establishment of the North Carolina Library Commission and in 1909 became its first chairman, a position that he held until 1916. He was active in the founding of the Southeastern Library Association and served as president of that organization from 1924 to 1926. He was also active in the Department of Libraries of the Southern Educational Association, becoming president of that department in 1911. From 1925 to 1932, he was a member of the Board of Education for Librarianship (BEL) of the ALA, and he was its chairman during 1930-1931. He was vice-president of ALA twice, 1930-1931 and 1933-1934, and president, 1935-1936. He also served actively in the Bibliographical Society of America and in the now long defunct American Library Institute. For the latter he never held a very high regard, considering it a collection of "stuffed shirts," who sought prestige rather than library promotion. He was, indeed, right, for it was not a group in which he could find much use for his talents.

In 1931, he was the official delegate to the annual conference of Library Association [United Kingdom]. He was also a delegate to the International Federation of Library Associations (IFLA) in Madrid in 1935. From 1930 to 1932, he was a member of the Advisory Committee on Liberal Arts College Libraries of the Carnegie Corporation of New York, and the Advisory Committee on Junior College Libraries in 1934-1937. He was long interested in the education of blacks and served on a special committee of the ALA to survey southern black colleges for the purpose of selecting one for the establishment of a library school. While he was dean at Chicago he provided a grant to Eliza Atkins Gleason to study library service to blacks in the South. The result of the study was published as a definitive statement of the problem.

In 1928, Wilson made his first library survey, that of the Union Theological Seminary library in Richmond, Virginia. Many more were to follow, some done alone, others with the assistance of former graduate students, of whom Maurice F. Tauber was the most prominent. It was through Wilson's influence and guidance that Tauber himself made something of a career as a library surveyor.

So one could go on enumerating the Wilson roster of activities, both library and nonlibrary oriented, until it could be said without much exaggeration that he represented a library and educational movement for almost the entire South. Though he left Chapel Hill for ten years at the University of Chicago, he did not lose touch with his native region, and his absence for a decade served only to expand his horizons and enrich his influence.

In 1932, just prior to his departure for Chicago, he established the Friends of the University of North Carolina Library, and secured a $30,000 grant from the General Education Board for the purchase of bibliographical reference materials. His interest in the Friends did not diminish. When he returned to Chapel Hill in 1942 he resumed active participation in the Friends organization, becoming chairman in 1945 and serving in that capacity until 1955.

Wilson's accomplishments were, by 1932, being recognized throughout the library world. He had received offers of important positions in other large libraries. Among these were offers from the University of Texas, and the New York State Library at Albany. Only the University of Chicago, however, was able to lure him from Chapel Hill, and even then the decision was made only after much careful weighing of advantages and disadvantages, and some hard bargaining with Robert Maynard Hutchins.

The Graduate Library School of the University of Chicago was born out of controversy, and most of its ten years under Wilson's direction were lived in that atmosphere. The argument began over whether librarianship needed a professional graduate library school at all, and if so what the curriculum would be at the level of the doctorate and the master's degrees.

But the acceptance by the University of Chicago of a grant of $225,000, from the Carnegie Corporation of New York, for the initiation of such a school, brought matters to a focus and raised the question of who should be its leader. All the disputation and negotiations that surrounded the eventual establishment of the school are set forth in John V. Richardson, Jr.'s admirable history of the GLS, and need not be described in the limited space available here.

In August 1926, Wilson was invited by a special faculty committee of the University of Chicago to discuss with them plans for the projected library school. As a result of that meeting he prepared a statement of the objectives and program of study as he perceived them. This statement was never published, but a copy is available in the Wilson papers at Chapel Hill. Wilson emphasized the need to consider the social science relationships of the library as a creation of society to meet particular needs. The sociological view,

Wilson believed, was especially important to the University of Chicago, which was then emphasizing the scientific study of society. The faculty committee had failed to take into account the need for specialized training for various types of libraries: academic, public, special, library agencies, extension services, work with children and youth, archival responsibilities, and similar specializations. Library administration as a field of instruction and research, he believed, had also been neglected by the committee. As a consequence of Wilson's observations, Max Mason, then the president of the University, offered Wilson the directorship of the projected school with the rank of professor.

But Wilson rejected the offer because of a variety of commitments back at Chapel Hill—the library at North Carolina was developing rapidly; he was director of the University Press and it had just received a foundation grant for an extensive program of publication; he was executive secretary of the group that was building the Graham Memorial; and he was preparing plans for a new library building. So the new library school at the University of Chicago was opened in 1928 with George A. Works, an educator but not a librarian, as its first dean.

By 1931, the situation both at Chapel Hill and on the Midway had changed. Early in that year, Robert Maynard Hutchins, then the president of the University of Chicago, came to Chapel Hill for a meeting of the American Association of Universities and arranged for a meeting with Wilson to consider again the possibility of going to Chicago. Works, after a short stint as dean of the library school, had become disillusioned with the lack of progress of the school and had resigned. After his departure, the school was being run on an interim basis by Douglas Waples and other members of the little faculty. The student body was small and Hutchins told Wilson that the school was "off the rails and bouncing along the cross-ties." He added, "Mr. Wilson, I'm going to get you to be director or dean of the Graduate Library School, or I'm going to give the endowment back to the Indians." To this Wilson replied, "Mr. President, you're the first university executive I've ever heard say he would turn loose any money he'd once gotten." Wilson, by his own admission, was charmed by this young and imaginative man and his reaction had much to do with his decision to go to the Midway.

Back at Chapel Hill, the university had already begun to feel the pinch of the Depression; the commitments that Wilson had made in 1926 had been largely fulfilled; the new library had been finished; the Graham Memorial was well under control; the University Press had published over one hundred volumes; both the assistant director and the assistant librarian were well qualified to take over new responsibilities; a grant of $30,000 for the development of a bibliographical collection had just been received from the General Education Board; and at the library school, Susan G. Akers, one of the first doctorates from Chicago, had been appointed to the faculty and could become acting director. By contrast, at Chicago the original Carnegie endowment had been accumulating and not all of the income had been spent, so there were reserves of about $100,000, which, in 1931, was no insignificant amount. So Wilson went to Chicago on September 1, 1932, but not until he had conducted some very shrewd and farsighted negotiations with President Hutchins over salary, academic rank, and tenure. His advice to his students, "Lay all your cards on the table before you accept, it will never be as easy again," is doubtless good advice, especially if one has the bargaining power of a Wilson.

Wilson and his family arrived in Chicago a month in advance of the beginning of his appointment. Though always a firm believer in academic freedom, from the beginning he left no doubt as to who was to be in control. William Randall recalls that prior to his arrival all decisions were made by the faculty sitting as a committee of the whole and concluded by a faculty vote. At the first meeting Wilson laid before the group a number of problems that were discussed fully. The group waited for the vote that never came. At the end there was only a "thank you gentlemen, that will be all for today."

The faculty was a strong one: Pierce Butler, who had taught the first class ever offered in the school, and who had been head of the Wing Collection at the Newberry Library, already had an established reputation in bibliography; Douglas Waples was an educator with a sound background in research methods; James Westfall Thompson was a leading medievalist of his day; William M. Randall had come from the University of Michigan Library, where he had been head of the cataloging department; and J. C. M. Hanson originally had come from the Library of Congress, where, with Charles Martell, he had developed the LC classification. Both Randall and Hanson had served on a committee to plan the cataloging of the Vatican library. No library school had ever begun with so much talent; all it lacked was direction, and that Wilson was ready and able to provide. He was, as Ralph A. Beals said, years later, "Just what the doctor ordered."

The courses that Wilson found already offered at Chicago were in such areas as bibliography; the history of books and libraries; technical services including acquisition, classification, and cataloging; and some specialization in library service to children and youth. He immediately perceived that there were a number of important areas that had been neglected: bases of library support; library legislation and its effectiveness; the place of the library in community life; the organization and administration of libraries of varying sizes and types; uniform cost accounting; costs of various library processes and the study of agencies through which the library could reach out to the public, such as school libraries and library services for young people. He also stressed, in his presentation to the faculty, the need for an increase in the number of formal courses (up to that time much of the work of the school had been done as directed instruction with individual students) and the value of other courses in the university to library school students. Throughout all of these areas he emphasized the importance of research, both for the students and the faculty. To the University administration he insisted upon the school's complete autonomy in matters of instructional program and finance. He also insisted upon the complete separation of the university library and the library school. The library was then under the direction of M. Llewellyn Raney, who had come from John Hopkins. Wilson and Raney left Chicago at the same time, and during those ten years they were seldom in agreement on anything relating to librarianship. Wilson made no pretense of hiding his contempt for the way the University library was run, and Raney said of his medical librarian that she was a good person until she took some courses in the GLS, which "ruined her forever." That Wilson was correct seems evident from the administrative chaos that Ralph Beals found as Raney's successor.

Wilson lost no time in implementing the plan for the school that he had set forth in 1926. To the limited offerings that he found when he arrived he soon added: librarianship as a field for research, and methods of investigating that field; school librarianship; studies in adult reading; publishing and book distribution in foreign countries; history and development of the printed book; principles of bibliography; the history of scholarship; history and techniques of the care of books; the administration and government of the public library; and the administration of college and university libraries. The following year, 1933, he introduced two courses that he developed and taught, one dealing with "library trends" and the other on the distribution of library resources, from which evolved his book *The Geography of Reading: A Study of the Distribution and Status of Librarians in the United States* (Chicago: University of Chicago Press, 1938).

Always a firm believer in the importance of adult and continuing education, in 1936 Wilson inaugurated a series of summer institutes, the first being on library trends, which he directed himself. Originally they were of two weeks' duration, supplemented by special readings and a relevant collection of books set apart for the use of the registrants. This extreme formality was, however, soon dropped and the period was reduced to one week with lectures and discussions. At the present time they are usually of only about four days' duration, but they still retain an important place among library conferences. Proceedings are always published, and some have remained as landmarks in library literature, notably Wilson's own *Library Trends* (Chicago: University of Chicago Press, 1937), Carleton Joeckel's *Current Issues in Library Administration* (Chicago: University of Chicago Press, 1939), and Douglas Waples's *Print, Radio, and Film in a Democracy* (Chicago: University of Chicago Press, 1942).

Notable additions to the faculty during the Wilson years were, among others, Carleton B. Joeckel in public library administration and government, Leon Carnovsky in foreign librarianship and the sociology of libraries, and Frances Henne in children's literature and school libraries. There were also adjunct faculty such as Herman Fussler in photographic processes, and Lucille Keck in special libraries.

In 1940, as he neared the end of his Chicago career, Wilson listed eight objectives of the school, which were, in effect, a summation of what he had been accomplishing during his regime.

1. The development of a theory, or philosophy of library science.

2. The extension of, and search for, guiding principles that may be applied to the various subdivisions of librarianship.

3. The training of students who would be competent to carry forward the appropriate library activities.

4. To instruct students in the various problems of librarianship as developed above.

5. To develop in the students a critical and experimental attitude.

6. To develop a strong publication program for both faculty and students.

7. To increase the effectiveness of the library in its various forms and for various clienteles.

8. To contribute to a better understanding of the means of communication throughout society.

Wilson was in a particularly strong position to advance the publication program of the school. His years of experience as director of the University of North Carolina Press gave him an easy entry to the publishing resources of its Chicago counterpart, he had ready access to funds from the Carnegie Corporation, and his faculty and students were well prepared and eager to produce publishable manuscripts. The *Library Quarterly*, which first appeared in 1930, was already well established when he arrived. Under his leadership, monographs rolled from the University of Chicago Press in unprecedented numbers—Pierce Butler's *Introduction to Library Science* (1933) today remains a classic. Waples and Tyler's *What People Want to Read About* (1931) marked the beginning of Waples's investigations into the social effects of reading, and was followed by his *People and Print* (1938) and *What Reading Does to People* (1940). James Westfall Thompson's *The Medieval Library* (1939) is a mine of information.

Carleton B. Joeckel's *Government of the American Public Library* (1935) still has value even though library legislation has changed drastically since it was written. The work of Randall and Goodrich on the administration of the college library is the most readable book on the subject that has yet appeared. There was also the series of volumes that came from the summer institutes, and Wilson's own *Geography of Reading* and (after his retirement) his *The University Library*, written with Maurice F. Tauber (Chicago: University of Chicago Press, 1945; 2nd ed. New York: Columbia University Press, 1956).

When Wilson arrived in Chicago in 1932 (the date is significant) the country was in the throes of the Great Depression, and the student body was small. Aided by Frederick Keppel, who had complete confidence in Wilson, and who was president of the Carnegie Corporation, money for fellowships was made available in substantial amounts, and Wilson invested the grants with the utmost shrewdness.

Publication was not restricted to the faculty. The students were active, too. Witness, among others, William C. Haygood's *Who Uses the Public Library* (1938), Gwladys Spencer's 1939 history of the Chicago Public Library, and Eliza Atkins Gleason's *Library Service to Negroes in the South* (1939), to name but a few. Many student publications that appeared after Wilson's retirement from Chicago were the results of work initiated under his direction. As an illustration of Wilson's support for research, it might be noted that, through Carnegie resources, he provided the present writer with a two-year fellowship to study for the doctorate, funds for a half-time research assistant for one year, and a travel subsidy for a four-month trip through New England to gather data for his *Foundations of the Public Library*. The listings here are very far from complete; suffice it to say that never before or since have so many influential volumes poured from a library school in so short a time.

Here it is possible to mention a few as a representative sample of those students who went on to positions of influence in librarianship and library education—John M. Cory, Ralph A. Beals, Lowell Martin, Frances Henne, Ralph Shaw, J. Periam Danton, Gwladys Spencer, Mildred Lowell, E. W. McDiarmid, Paul Howard, Esther Stallmann, Eliza Atkins Gleason, Arthur McAnally, and Richard Logsdon. There are many others whom one might mention with equal justification. Men, especially those interested in academic librarianship and library education, were numerically dominant, possibly because it was among them that the urge to acquire the doctorate was most keenly felt.

The student body was extremely homogeneous, held together not only by a common philosophy of the profession and a dedication to the importance of what they were doing, but also by the continuing antagonism toward the school of a major proportion of the library profession itself, which could see no need for the doctorate or for library research. Confronted by this continuing criticism the old school tie was particularly strong. Students and alumni were in every sense a fraternity, and Wilson was the guiding spirit.

The creation of that spirit was, perhaps, Wilson's greatest accomplishment at Chicago. He created an atmosphere of freedom of inquiry, a questioning attitude that was unique to a profession that had previously accepted unquestioningly the rules, opinions, and unchallenged dicta laid down since Dewey first initiated library training at Columbia. Chicago fostered the spirit of innovation. It was an exciting place during those ten years. They were, as Waples said, "Born and bred in the briar patch," secure in the knowledge that even their most sophomoric thoughts could be freely expressed without fear of reprisal. So solid was this spirit that it lived on despite Wilson's departure and the ravages to its student body and faculty of the Second World War. Today, only William Randall, now living in retirement in North Carolina, remains of that original faculty. But for those who were privileged to have been students during the Wilson years, there will always be something unique about the GLS and the tradition it created — "Go hang yourself, brave Crillon; we fought at Arques, and you were not there."

Shortly before retiring from Chicago, however, Wilson made what even his most loyal alumni considered to be a serious mistake. Prior to that time, all applicants for admission to the school were required to have the fifth-year bachelor's degree from an accredited library school. So far as the present writer knows there had been only rare exceptions to this quite rigid rule. Wilson had for some time wanted the BLS program at Chicago, too, so he instituted it during the last year of his tenure there. There appears to be no record of why this action seemed so important to him, but, as it proved, no great harm was done. Ralph Beals became dean of the school in 1945, and proceeded forthwith to abolish the program. By the close of the decade of the 1940s, most library schools had replaced the BLS with the MLS degree. From those who held the Chicago M.A. there had been required, in addition to the course of study, a knowledge of one foreign language and the writing of a master's thesis. These graduates believed, and quite rightly, that their M.A. degree represented something between the M.L.S. and the Ph.D., and that there was nothing to which their degrees could be equated. Their plight emphasizes the continuing need for some form of academic recognition, at the professional level, that exemplifies advanced study beyond the first degree but which is not necessarily oriented toward research. The change at Chicago may have been Wilson's attempt to meet the need, but time did not permit him to develop it to the full.

In August 1942, Wilson left Chicago to return to the University of North Carolina, though his library activities did not diminish in "retirement."

Upon leaving Chicago, at the age of 65, he could still look forward to more than thirty years of active professional life. He busied himself with writing the history of the University of North Carolina, made many library surveys, brought out, with Maurice Tauber, the first (1945) and second (1956) editions of his volume on *The University Library*, resumed his former position as advisor and confidant of the university president and others of the administration in planning both the physical plant and the academic program, and maintained throughout a lively correspondence with colleagues and former students. In 1956, the University named the 1929 building, expanded by an addition in 1952, the Louis Round Wilson Library. He officially retired from the university in 1959, but continued to retain an office in the library, which he visited daily, until 1975. He viewed with favor the inauguration of a doctoral program at the library school, the culmination of one of his dreams for the school he had founded almost fifty years before. When this writer visited him in the autumn of 1972, he was as keen and perceptive as ever and still retained his buoyant spirit and sense of humor.

Wilson was, of course, the recipient of many honors. He was an honorary life member of the ALA, the association's highest recognition. He was also given the Melvil Dewey medal and the Beta Phi Mu citation. At the dinner honoring his 100th birthday he was given a special citation by the American Association of University Presses.

In this, his finest hour, it is appropriate for us to slip unobtrusively away to acknowledge the magnitude of his contribution to our professional lives.

Louis Round Wilson died peacefully in his sleep on December 10, 1979, only seventeen days before his 103rd birthday. No doubt there are those who see in such longevity the reward for a lifetime of abstention from tobacco and alcohol. I would prefer to see it as the product of a joyous spirit, dedicated to the importance of what was being accomplished, and a genuine concern for the professional successes of his students.

But perhaps it is Wilson himself who has given us the most appropriate comment. When Ralph Beals, as a student at Chicago, expressed disbelief that he had passed the French and German doctoral exams on the morning and afternoon of the same day, Wilson advised the future director of the New York Public Library, "Don't question the ways of the Lord."

Biographical listings and obituaries — [Obituary]. *ALA Yearbook 1979* (1980); [Obituary]. *American Libraries* 11:6 (January 1980); [Obituary]. *College & Research Libraries News* 3:71 (March 1980); [Obituary]. *Library Journal* 105:147 (January 15, 1980); [Obituary]. *Wilson Library Bulletin* 54:282 (January 1980). **Books and articles about the biographee** — Martin, Robert Sidney. "Louis Round Wilson and the Library Standards of the Southeastern Association, 1926-1929." *Journal of Library History* 19:259-81 (Spring 1984); Martin, Robert Sidney. "Louis Round Wilson's *Geography of Reading*: An Inquiry into Its Origins, Development, and Impact." *Journal of Library History* 21:425-44 (Spring 1986); Martin, Robert Sidney. "Maurice F. Tauber's *Louis Round Wilson*: An Analysis of a Collaboration." *Journal of Library History* 19:373-89 (Summer 1984); Richardson, John V., Jr. *The Spirit of Inquiry: The Graduate Library School at Chicago, 1921-1951*. Chicago: American Library Association, 1982; Shera, Jesse H. " 'The Spirit Giveth Life': Louis Round Wilson and Chicago's Graduate Library School." *Journal of Library History* 14:77-83 (Winter 1979); Tauber, Maurice F. *Louis Round Wilson: Librarian and Administrator*. New York: Columbia University Press, 1967. **Primary sources and archival materials** — *Louis Round Wilson Bibliography: A Chronological List of Works and Editorial Activities* (Chapel Hill: University of North Carolina Library, 1976). This work includes a note on the Wilson Papers in the Southern Historical Collection at the University of North Carolina Library. Some papers from the University of Chicago period remain at the University of Chicago.

— JESSE H. SHERA

WINCHELL, CONSTANCE MABEL (1896-1983)

Constance Mabel Winchell was born on November 2, 1896, in Northampton, Massachusetts. Her family traced its ancestry back to the arrival in America of Robert Winchell in 1634 and included among its members a number of academics, primarily in the sciences. Constance Winchell's father, Joseph E. Winchell, who was treasurer of the Prophylactic Brush Company in Florence, a suburb of Northampton, died when she was five. Constance, her older brother Harold, and two younger brothers, Joseph Paul and E. Bliss, were raised by Inez Bliss Winchell, their extremely enterprising mother.

Because her mother rented rooms to Smith College instructors and because her paternal aunt, Mabel M. Winchell, was city librarian of Manchester, New Hampshire, Constance Winchell was exposed at an early age to the world of books and scholarship. She belonged to both of the libraries in her neighborhood (the Forbes and the Clark) and was an avid reader. She later commented that it had never occurred to her to be anything but a librarian.

After Winchell graduated in 1914 from the Capen School (a private institution for girls), her mother moved the whole family to Ann Arbor, Michigan, specifically to enable the Winchell children to attend the university inexpensively as residents of the state. Winchell's formal higher education began at the University of Michigan, which she attended from 1914 to 1918. She was a student in the College of Literature, Science, and Arts and a member of Kappa Alpha Theta sorority, which she joined, she said, because "I was a very shy, backward kind of girl and never could start anything myself." She intended to go to library school after graduation and as an undergraduate worked on the university's library catalog and served on the desks of the science and engineering department libraries. In the summer of 1917 she attended a library science course conducted by Dr. William Warner Bishop, who was to play an important role in furthering her career. After studying literature, history, and languages, she was graduated in 1918 with a bachelor's degree.

Winchell's career as a librarian began with a post at Central High School in Duluth, Minnesota, where she was also a teacher of ancient history. But she disliked the unruliness of the students and decided to follow William Warner Bishop's suggestion to enroll in the library school of New York Public Library (which later merged with the New York State Library School in Albany to become the Columbia University School of Library Service). While at the school, Winchell considered becoming a children's librarian and worked for a month in the children's room of the New York Public Library's Tompkins Square branch and for another two weeks in the children's room at the Forty-Second Street building.

Winchell did not have enough money to register for the library school's optional second year, and after taking her certificate in 1920, she accepted a job with the Lighthouse Division of the U.S. Merchant Marine. For five months she travelled up and down the eastern seacoast establishing libraries in lighthouses. She stocked them with books donated to the Merchant Marine Service by the American Library Association, which had collected the books for army camps during World War I. Then, in the fall of 1920, Winchell joined the staff of the University of Michigan. In her three years there, she served first as a reviser in the catalog department and then, in 1922, became a reference assistant.

The summer of 1923 brought another opportunity when a colleague, Eunice Weald, was offered a job at the American Library, which had been established in Paris for American servicemen stationed in Europe during World War I. Weald turned the offer down, but suggested that Winchell be hired instead. Winchell accepted when the American Library took Weald's suggestion. She arrived in Paris at the beginning of 1924, took up residence with a French family, and worked at the library as head cataloger until July 1925. While in Europe she quickly began indulging a passion for travel that was manifest until the end of her life. In 18 months she toured England, the Netherlands, and Belgium. In September 1925, Winchell returned to America to begin what would become her life's work in the Reference Department of the Columbia University library.

When Winchell showed up for work on September 15, 1925, she reported to Isadore Gilbert Mudge, head of Columbia's Reference Department and the formidable editor of the *Guide to Reference Books*. Mudge was as well known for her shrewdness in evaluating librarians as she was for her analysis of reference books. She was also a pioneer in systematizing interlibrary loans and worked in cooperation with the Library of Congress in what eventually became the *National Union Catalog*. Winchell watched Mudge work in all of these areas. One of her first assignments under Mudge's direction was to send a weekly list of wanted titles to a selected group of about one dozen libraries. She put the information about locations gleaned through this system on file cards, and as a result, created a substantial location catalog at Columbia decades before a printed national union catalog was available.

Working at Columbia also gave Winchell the opportunity to further her education. From 1928 to 1930 she was a student in the master's degree program at the university's School of Library Service. In 1930 she was granted a master's of science degree in library service on the basis of a thesis entitled "The Problem of Locating Books in American Libraries: A Study of Procedures and Sources of Information." Her thesis was published later that year by H. W. Wilson under the title *Locating Books for Interlibrary Loan*. Columbia acknowledged that expertise by putting Winchell in charge of interlibrary loan, where she performed admirably. In 1933 she was promoted to the rank of assistant reference librarian and participated in the Reference Department's 1934 move to roomier quarters in the newly constructed South Hall (now Butler Library). As assistant reference librarian, Winchell also responded to the changing nature of user queries by starting a serials catalog that today constitutes one of her most enduring contributions to Columbia's Reference Department. In 1941, when Mudge retired as head of reference, Constance Winchell succeeded her.

Winchell inherited more than an office and title from Mudge upon taking over the Reference Department; she also inherited the editorship of the *Guide*. Mudge herself had taken over the *Guide* from Alice Bertha Kroeger, who published the first edition in 1922. During the 1930s Winchell assisted Mudge with the supplements. The *Guide*, with its combination of careful scholarship and bibliographic practicality, has been of incalculable importance to the building of American research collections. Winchell's editorship coincided with the thirty years during which these collections expanded most rapidly. She edited the supplements to the sixth edition of the *Guide* that appeared in the 1940s, the seventh edition (1951) and its four supplements (1954, 1956, 1960, 1963), and the eighth edition (1967). The seventh edition, with its distinctive cover of royal blue (Winchell's favorite color), contained many more titles in the areas of psychology, fine arts, and history than the sixth. The eighth edition had 2,000 more titles than its predecessor; and instead of the thirteen subject divisions of the seventh, had five broad divisions. That Winchell's *Guide* exercised a strong influence on two generations of reference librarianship is beyond dispute.

Winchell's impact on reference librarianship was also felt through her teaching of reference, both formally, in classes at Columbia's library school, and on the job, in the university's reference department. Because she was herself of scholarly training and disposition, she demanded much of her students and trainees. In 1963 she criticized the trend among American library schools to abandon the master's thesis. She commented that "along with training in public speaking, librarians should be trained in writing ... [and] a certain amount of research work.... It makes a lot more sense to them when they are trying to help others if they have done some of it themselves." She insisted that new assistants on her staff have at least a college degree and a library science degree with a good academic record; she also demanded a knowledge of foreign languages and the ability to read the Cyrillic alphabet. Winchell also understood, along with a handful of her contemporaries, the essential role of interpersonal communication skills and public relations in reference librarianship. This perception underlay her insistence—which might not be acceptable in today's world of equal opportunity—that her employees be physically strong and attractive.

Outside her work at Columbia, Winchell was active in library association life and publishing. In 1951 she began to contribute articles semiannually for the January and July issues of *College & Research Libraries* and to annotate reference titles that appeared between *Guide* supplements. She served on the Council of the American Library Association and advised the H. W. Wilson Company on matters relating to indexing and the *Readers' Guide to Periodical Literature*. In 1960 the American Library Association's Reference Services Division awarded Winchell the Isadore Gilbert Mudge Citation for Distinguished Contributions to Reference Librarianship.

Winchell's official retirement from Columbia on June 30, 1962, followed a four-month leave of absence, during which she was able to go on an extensive tour to Asia. Between 1954 and 1962 she had also found time to travel to Mexico, Guatemala, India, Afghanistan, Hong Kong, Indonesia, Korea, and Japan. At the time of her retirement she was still at work on the fourth supplement to the seventh edition of the *Guide* with the assistance of John Waddel.

After leaving Columbia, Winchell not only finished the eighth edition of the *Guide*, but she also increased her participation in the "English in Action" conversation program for adult immigrants at Riverside Church, of which she was a member. After 1967 she resided primarily in New Paltz, New York, to care for her sick friend, Dollie Hepburn, former director of personnel at the Columbia University Library. In 1969 she gave up her Riverside Drive apartment. Winchell died at New Paltz on May 23, 1983, at the age of 86.

Constance Winchell's contributions to American librarianship were obviously influenced by Isadore Mudge, but Winchell pushed beyond those sturdy foundations. She faced new challenges forced by the rapidly expanding volume of published information. She also shouldered greater responsibilities internationally, with her leadership in reference coinciding not only with unprecedented collection expansion at home, but also with the period of American librarianship's greatest overseas influence. The integrity of Winchell's bibliographic scholarship, disseminated globally through the *Guide* and through the subsequent influence of her students and trainees at Columbia, established standards for professionals and their collections at a time when many emerging nations looked to America for guidance in building their domestic information infrastructures. Partially because of the sociopolitical environment in which she worked, Winchell may be seen as one of the most influential figures of mid-twentieth century librarianship.

Biographical listings and obituaries—*Contemporary Authors, Permanent Series, Vol. I* (1975); *Current Biography* (1967); [Obituary]. *Contemporary Authors* 108:531 (1983); [Obituary]. *New York Times Biographical Service* 4:632 (May 14, 1983); [Obituary]. "The Winchell Tradition." *Library Journal* 108:1186 (June 15, 1983); *Who Was Who in America* VIII (1985). **Books and articles about the biographee**—Whyte, Edith A. "Constance Winchell, Reference Librarian." (Master's thesis, Long Island University, 1971). **Primary sources and archival materials**—"Reminiscences of Constance Winchell." Columbia University Oral History Collection (1963).

—PAMELA SPENCE RICHARDS

WORKS, GEORGE ALAN (1877-1957)

Among librarians, George Works is best known as a surveyor of academic libraries and as the first dean of the Graduate Library School at the University of Chicago. His lasting influence on library science can be attributed to the publication of a landmark book, *College and University Library Problems* (1927), and his selection of the first faculty as well as the formulation of the curriculum for the Graduate Library School at Chicago.

George Works, the eldest of eleven children, was born in August, Wisconsin, on May 14, 1877, to Obadiah and Clarasia Perry Works. His father was a fairly typical Progressive dairy farmer. Works was graduated from River Falls Normal High School and attended the University of Wisconsin in Madison, where he received a bachelor's degree in 1904. He was elected to Phi Beta Kappa.

Later that same year, Works married Saidee B. Coerper of Hartford, Wisconsin. He continued to work in Wisconsin as a school superintendent until 1911. After a year of further study at his alma mater, Works received a master's degree and was appointed instructor in rural education. During this period, the University's School of Education was a center for the efficiency movement, one of those leaders was Professor Edward Elliott. Upon graduation, Works became an assistant professor at the University of Minnesota (1913-1914). In 1915 Cornell University lured him away with a full professorship and to head the rural education division.

At Cornell, Works continued to refine his skills in educational surveys and administration. Besides teaching, he directed the rural school survey of New York in 1921-1922 and the educational survey of Texas in 1923-1924. The latter effort formed the basis of his 1925 doctoral dissertation in education at Harvard, entitled "Distribution of State Aid in Texas." Because Works had become proficient in educational finance and scientific management, he was chosen in 1926 to become the first chair of the Division of Education at Cornell.

In the mid-1920s, The Commonwealth Fund's Committee on Administrative Units under the chair of Samuel P. Capen recommended to the Carnegie Corporation that a survey of academic libraries be conducted as part of its Ten Year Program in Library Service. Works's survey expertise and organizational abilities brought him to the attention of the Association of American Universities, which had received the grant to administer the project. Working closely with Works on this project was an advisory committee of influential librarians: W. W. Bishop at Michigan, Andrew Keogh at Yale, Sydney B. Mitchell at the University of California at Berkeley, Azariah S. Root at Oberlin, and Frank K. Walter at Minnesota. In the course of his study, Works visited fifteen university libraries as well as three college libraries across the United States, talking with librarians and each institution's financial officer. Thus he gained a firsthand knowledge of library problems nationally, as well as an understanding of the library's role and standing within the academic institution. Works's findings and conclusions were published as *College and University Library Problems: A Study of a Selected Group of Institutions Prepared for the Association of American Universities* (Chicago: American Library Association, 1927).

By adopting the social science research methodology he had honed earlier, in this survey Works identified conditions, trends, and problem areas in academic librarianship for the first time. He documented the increasingly important role of periodical literature in the production of knowledge. Nearly all of the libraries surveyed showed significant increases (some up to 1,400 percent between 1900 and 1925) in subscriptions. Works also discovered a constant relationship between university support of libraries and university expenditures on faculty salaries. His *College and University Library Problems*, though largely descriptive, was the first reliable study of this field and was well received by reviewers. It served as a guide for the Carnegie Corporation's philanthropic activities into the next decade and remained one of the frequently cited books in academic library administration literature for several decades thereafter.

Works's now-intimate knowledge of the workings of a wide variety of college and university libraries earned him a role on the College and University Subcommittee of the American Library Association's (ALA) Committee on Classification of Library Personnel beginning in 1927. The committee's task was to respond to the national interest in the classification of library positions, specifically embodied in the 1927 Telford Report from the Bureau of Public Personnel Administration of the Institute for Government Research.

The committee's published report of January 1929 was written by a subcommittee composed of George Works, Harold L. Leupp, and Charles Harvey Brown (the chair). The report borrowed from Works's Carnegie survey and offered library administrators a systematic scheme for classifying library personnel. Thus, by his completion of a successful national survey and his participation in a significant professional association committee, Works had gained good visibility within the library field.

When negotiations for the first deanship of the new Graduate Library School at the University of Chicago began, Works's name frequently surfaced along with such librarians and scholars as W. W. Bishop, Sydney B. Mitchell, Louis R. Wilson, William S. Learned, and Chauncey B. Tinker. After Wilson and Learned turned down the post, Works was asked, and he accepted the position. Chicago wanted a scholar from outside the field of librarianship and Works desired an appointment at one of the leading research universities of its time; it seemed like a happy situation.

Returning to the Midwest in the summer of 1927, he left behind an impressive reputation at Cornell. Francis Griffin, a Cornell student the following year, wrote: "I could well imagine I know him, so often was his name mentioned and his abilities extolled."

Drawing on both his background in educational administration and his recent experience surveying libraries, Works formulated the primary purpose of the GLS: "to organize and conduct investigations of problems confronting society in general or in particular fields of scholarship when such problems fall within the field of librarianship." Auxiliary objectives were to conduct service studies for the profession and to publish the results of significant investigations of library problems. Works saw a solid knowledge base as essential to the emerging discipline of library science. If faculty members were to be consulted by the profession, then they had to be on the research front "prosecuting studies of their own" and thereby leading the profession.

Works selected his new faculty to deal with the problems he thought needed scientific investigation. From the College of Education, he selected Douglas Waples, who was already studying the habits of reading; from the University of Chicago Library, he chose J. C. M. Hanson who, along with William M. Randall (hired from the Hartford Seminary in Connecticut), continued to investigate the principles of classification and cataloging. Works did not neglect library history, which, he said, "offers large opportunities for researchers." He asked Pierce Butler of the Newberry Library to join the faculty, initially on a part-time basis. To balance the academicians and nonlibrarians on the faculty, and to respond to some criticism by librarians and ALA Headquarters, Works appointed Harriet E. Howe, an officer of the ALA Board of Education for Librarianship, to the faculty.

The first students, all of whom had their professional degrees and at least one year's experience, included a large portion of exceptionally well-qualified women: Susan G. Akers, Amy Winslow, Eleanor Upton, and Margaret C. Taylor. The establishment of a fellowship program helped draw such individuals to Chicago.

For the curriculum, Works envisioned a strongly interdisciplinary program, for "the materials and methods necessary for the solution of problems in the field of librarianship refuse to be confined by the artificial boundaries of schools and colleges." When the school opened in October 1928 there were only three formal courses: Waples's "Methods of Investigation," Butler's "The Printed Book," and Howe's course on teaching library science. One other course offering was of primary importance; "410" offered the student individual research in eleven different areas. Thus, the emphasis of the school was on independent study and investigation—quite unlike the technical approach then in vogue in most other library schools.

Works's vision and enthusiasm for research were not shared by many "opinion leaders" in the profession. They were displeased that a nonlibrarian had been appointed to direct the first graduate school of librarians. There was a fundamental disagreement on the direction that the new Graduate Library School was to take. In his defense Works pointed out that when the ALA Board of Education for Librarianship defined *graduate* library school, it simply meant any school "requiring college graduation" for entrance. Many within the profession conceived such a school as largely vocational. At the University of Chicago, however, graduate meant research, and to Works and his associates that meant "the extension of the boundaries of knowledge." As a consequence, Works had organized the school's objectives, faculty, students, and curriculum around independent study and research. Regrettably, Works did not see fit to obtain the cooperation and, more important, the support of ALA Headquarters.

Within less than two years, Works's position became untenable and he resigned his post on April 12, 1929 because the profession, led by ALA Headquarters and Sarah Bogle in particular, continued to make "things disagreeable for him because he was not a member of that craft," in the words of Gordon Laing, Chicago's Dean of Arts and Sciences at that time. Works was made to feel like an outsider. Although he had assembled a highly talented faculty and put in place objectives which were largely unchanged by succeeding deans, Works was forced to let his successors, such as Louis R. Wilson, realize his ambitions for the school.

Although he possessed what others like Joseph Wheeler called "an unusual personality," he was a charismatic leader. In the summer of 1929 he left Chicago for the presidency of Connecticut Agricultural College in Storrs. After a brief, undistinguished stint of one year, he returned to the University of Chicago holding the position of professor of education, dean of students, and university examiner from 1931 to 1941. Works continued to advise Douglas Waples, the acting dean, on matters relating to the GLS until Louis R. Wilson was appointed in 1932. Works continued as a professor of higher education at Chicago until his retirement in 1942. Active in the scholarly world during this retirement, he served as Phi Beta Kappa National Association Secretary, and was also a member of Alpha Zeta, Delta Upsilon, and Phi Delta Kappa fraternities. He died in Ridgewood, New Jersey, on December 13, 1957, following a five-year bout with chronic cardiovascular disease. He was survived by his wife, two daughters, and two sons.

Building on his background and expertise in educational administration, Works made his initial contribution to librarianship with the publication of *College and University Library Problems* (1927). At Chicago, his choice of the initial faculty, the identification and selection of the school's objectives, and the research curriculum for the Graduate Library School were pioneering efforts in the emerging discipline of library science. His contributions left a narrow, but deep, impression upon librarianship.

Biographical listings and obituaries — *Leaders in Education*, 1st, 2nd, 3rd eds. (1932, 1941, 1948); [Obituary]. *Cornell Alumni News* (February 1958); [Obituary]. *The Ridgewood* (New Jersey) *Sunday News*, December 15, 1957, 108; *Who Was Who in America* III (1951-1960); *Who's Who in America* 30 (1958). **Books and articles about the biographee** — Coleman, Gould P. *Education and Agriculture: A History of the New York State College of Agriculture at Cornell University.* Ithaca, N.Y.: Cornell University Press, 1963, pp. 316, 319, 365, 384, 582; "Dean Made President." *Detroit Free Press*, April 11, 1929, 3; "Dr. Works Resigns from Graduate Library School." *Libraries* 34:317-9 (July 1929); Hamlin, Arthur T. *The University Library in the United States: Its Origins and Development.* Philadelphia: University of Pennsylvania Press, 1981, 125; "Prof. Works New Dean of U. of C. Library School." *Chicago Daily News*, July 5, 1927, 6; Richardson, John V., Jr. *The Spirit of Inquiry: The Graduate Library School at Chicago, 1921-1951.* Foreword by Jesse H. Shera. Chicago: American Library Association, 1982; Richardson, John V., Jr. "The Gospel of Scholarship: Pierce Butler and American Librarianship, 1883-1953" (in progress); Shiflett, Orvin Lee. *Origins of American Academic Librarianship.* Norwood, N.J.: Ablex Publishing Corporation, 1981, xix, 126, 155, 206, 229, 243; "University of Chicago." *Libraries* 32:382-3 (July 1927). **Primary sources and archival materials** — George Works's confidential University of Wisconsin student grade records are maintained in the Division of Archives. According to a university archivist, "Mr. Works' employment records at the UW are not extant." George Works, Jr., reports that his "father did not do a great deal of work at home." At the University of Connecticut (Storrs), there are 2 archival boxes, containing 41 folders, related solely to his presidency. According to Norman D. Stevens, "there is absolutely nothing from or to anyone at the University of Chicago." Consequently, most of Works's papers exist in the archives of the University of Chicago Library's Department of Special Collections (President's Papers 1925-1945) and in the Graduate Library School.

— JOHN V. RICHARDSON, JR.

WRIGHT, WYLLIS EATON (1903-1979)

Although Wyllis E. Wright was born in Jacksonville, Florida, on December 13, 1903, he considered himself a thoroughgoing New Englander. He began his library career at the age of 12 as a page in the Lowell (Massachusetts) Public Library and later in life proudly recalled that he worked his way through Williams College (Williamstown, Massachusetts), serving first as a student assistant and later, during his year of graduate work, as a library assistant in the Williams College Library. He was graduated in 1925 with a bachelor of arts degree in philosophy. A year later he was awarded the master's degree in philosophy.

Wright's obvious interest in library work led him naturally to New York City, where he obtained his first professional position as cataloger at the New York Public Library and enrolled as a student in the Columbia University School of Library Service. He completed his work in 1928, graduating with a bachelor of science in library science.

In 1929, Wright returned to Williamstown, where he married Helena Lawrence Kellogg, a Simmons College Library School graduate and librarian at Williams College Library. The next year, the Wrights went to Italy where he had a three-year contract as librarian for the American Academy in Rome. They lived in an apartment over the gatehouse at the Academy, where they had a spectacular view of the city. Their daughter, Barbara, was born in Rome on October 28, 1932.

Barbara Wright remembered her father as a person who seemed to know everything, who loved to recite nonsense verse and to sing Gilbert and Sullivan, as she put it, "with great enthusiasm, if not great musical accuracy," to her delight and that of her younger brother Lawrence, who was born on June 12, 1936. Wright also was a fine cellist and an avid chess player.

In 1933, Wright returned to New York City, where he accepted the position of chief classifier (1933-1936; chief cataloger, 1936-1945) at the New York Public Library. Benjamin A. Custer, who would later serve as editor of the Dewey Decimal Classification, and who was then a neophyte cataloger at the New York Public Library, remembers Wright as a "nice enough fellow, with a black mustache and crooked teeth and, to my Midwestern ears, an atrocious Yankee accent, which, for instance, had him always say 'lawr' to mean, I soon found out, 'law.' It didn't take too long, though, before I realized that the guy was really good and smart as a whip, and did not at all conform to my somewhat contemptuous provincial views of the proud New England aristocrat who looked down his nose at us poor saps who originated west of the Berkshires and the Hudson. In fact, we became good friends."

Custer came to appreciate Wright's generosity, not only in the matter of occasional small loans, but also as a supportive colleague. Both he and Wright were scheduled to speak on a program sponsored by a New York regional catalogers' group in the late 1930s. The youthful and inexperienced Custer was, as he put it, "scared witless." Wright sensed his friend's nervousness, and as Custer remembered, "Bill steered me into a cocktail lounge and plied me with at least two martinis, after which I gave a highly successful and much praised talk to the catalogers, which was said to be both informative and witty!"

The war years (1939-1945) were a period of great professional growth for Wright. As chief cataloger at New York Public Library he directed the cataloging of one of the greatest research collections in the United States. Increasingly he was called to professional commitments reflecting his deep knowledge of cataloging rules as well as his administrative ability. He taught cataloging as an associate teaching staff member at Columbia University School of Library Service. At the same time he began his lengthy tenure as chair (1939-1945, 1947-1954) and vice-chair (1958-1967) of the American Library Association (ALA) Union List of Serials Committee. The years 1942-1943 found him serving both as president of the New York Library Club and president of the ALA Division of Cataloging and Classification (later known as the Resources and Technical Services Division).

As his contribution to the war effort, Wright served as chair of the ALA Aid to Libraries in War Areas Committee (1944-1947) and secretary (1944-1948) of the American Book Center for War Devastated Libraries, an organization funded by the Rockefeller Foundation to purchase books and subscriptions to scholarly periodicals to be delivered after the war to libraries in war-torn areas of Europe. His work with the American Book Center and the Aid to Libraries Committee took him frequently to Washington, D.C., and gained him even greater professional stature. In 1945, he left the New York Public Library to accept the position of librarian of the United States Army Medical Library in Washington, D.C. (now the National Medical Library). Here he reorganized the cataloging program, arranging for the recataloging of the entire collection and introducing a number of innovations. However, this type of work was not where his chief professional interests lay, and when the opportunity presented itself in 1947, he accepted the position of librarian at his alma mater, Williams College. He remained at Williams College until his retirement in 1968.

Wright's years at Williams College proved to be the most fruitful of his long and productive career. His three-year tenure as librarian of the American Academy in Rome had brought him into contact with William Warner Bishop, J. C. M. Hanson, and Charles Martel, all members of the American mission to establish a new catalog of the printed books in the Vatican Library. After that he had taken a great interest in the Vatican Library *Norme*, which Bishop had called "perhaps the best of modern cataloging codes." Wright edited and indexed an English translation of the *Norme*, completed in 1940. It was published by the ALA in 1948.

The Vatican code is of interest to catalogers today chiefly as an intermediate statement of cataloging practice between the Anglo-American code of 1908 and the 1949 ALA *Cataloging Rules*. Dissatisfaction with the legalistic prescriptions for cataloging, which had grown by accretion since the publication of the 1908 code, climaxed in 1949 with the publication of the "new" ALA *Cataloging Rules*. Seymour Lubetzky's devastating critique of the 1949 rules (*Cataloging Rules and Principles*, 1953) made it obvious that a new cataloging code was in order. As chair of the ALA Division of Cataloging and Classification's Cataloging Policy and Research Board, Wyllis Wright assigned Lubetzky in 1954 to prepare such a code. That same year, Wright was named chair of the new ALA Catalog Code Revision Committee, a position which he was to hold until 1967, when the first edition of the *Anglo-American Cataloging Rules* appeared.

Wright's work as chair of the Catalog Code Revision Committee won accolades from highly respected peers. Seymour Lubetzky praised him for his "vast fund of knowledge and experience in librarianship in general and cataloging in particular, his scholarly attitude and approach to the business of the Committee, his impressive reputation of leadership and statesmanlike conduct in the deliberations and affairs of the Committee." Benjamin Custer recalled that "it was always a marvel to see how he could keep a committee with so many fractious heads in it running smoothly." His skill in synthesis, summary, and resolution of problems led to his being asked to serve as moderator at the 1958 Stanford University Institute on Catalog Code Revision, where, as Laura Colvin remembered, he "performed a tour de force acclaimed by all registrants at its close." In addition, he served as moderator at a similar institute held at McGill University in Montreal during the summer of 1960, and was the United States and ALA delegate to International Conference on Cataloging Principles held in Paris in October 1961. Of this important meeting and Wright's participation, Laura Colvin said that "the U.S. official delegate usually kept his own counsel, but when appropriate, spoke to the point; he thereby increased the respect of other national delegates for his statesmanship."

His invaluable contributions to the evolution of the *Anglo-American Cataloging Rules* were readily acknowledged when he received some of the most prestigious awards given by ALA. In 1957 he was the recipient of the Melvil Dewey Medal and cited for "creative professional achievement of a high order." In 1962 he was awarded the Margaret Mann Citation "for his devoted service in the field of cataloging culminating in his selfless and tenacious leadership ... in securing wide acceptance, both here and abroad, of cataloging principles which promise to advance the library profession as a whole." In 1968, on his retirement as Williams College librarian, he was honored with a reception by the Library Association in London.

Following retirement, Wright moved to Portola Valley, California. In September 1969 he began a new career as rare books cataloger at Stanford University Libraries, serving as chief of the Department of Special Collections, 1973-1974. He reduced his schedule to part-time in 1974 and continued to catalog on a part-time basis until shortly before his death. He died on October 2, 1979.

Wyllis Eaton Wright has been praised for his numerous articles, which as Laura Colvin said, "reveal his persistent concern over and penetrating knowledge of classification systems and lists of subject headings in special fields, codes of cataloging rules, problems of library catalogs, and cataloging standards and economies." But probably his most enduring contribution to the profession was that of moderator and committee chair, a role in which he played a significant part in the molding of the *Anglo-American Cataloging Rules*, the last great code of cataloging governing traditional library catalogs of the twentieth century.

Biographical listings and obituaries — [Obituary]. *AB Bookman's Weekly* 65:1003 (February 11, 1980); [Obituary]. *ALA Yearbook 1979* (1980); [Obituary]. *American Libraries* 10:674 (December 1979); [Obituary]. *College & Research Libraries News* 11:354 (December 1979); [Obituary]. *Library Journal* 104:2515 (December 1, 1979); [Obituary]. *Library Resources & Technical Services* 24:279 (Summer 1980); [Obituary]. *Wilson Library Bulletin* 54:264 (December 1979). **Books and articles by the biographee** — "The Anglo-American Cataloging Rules: A Historical Perspective." *Library Resources & Technical Services* 20:36-47 (Winter 1976); "Report of Progress on Catalog Code Revision in the United States." *Library Quarterly* 26:331-6 (October 1956); "Some Aspects of Technical Processes." *Library Trends* 1:73-82 (July 1952); (ed.) *Rules for the Cataloging of Printed Books*. Chicago: American Library Association, 1948. **Primary sources and archival materials** — The disposition of Wright's personal papers is unknown at this time. Some of his working correspondence can be found in the records of the New York Technical Services Librarians at the Columbia University Libraries in New York City and in the records of the Cataloging Code Revision Committee, Cataloging and Classification Section, American Library Association Archives, University of Illinois, Urbana, Illinois.

—MARGARET MAXWELL

174 / Name Index

Berelson, Bernard R., (S)12-15, 67, 252, 254, 423, (S)134, (S)148
Berelson, Elizabeth Duran, (S)14
Berelson, Rosalind Kean, (S)14
Berelson, Ruth Rappaport, (S)14
Berenson, Bernard, 217, (S)150
Bertram, James, 24-25, 71, 278, 446, 555
Beust, Nora, 306
Bigelow, Mary Eastman, 516
Billings, John Shaw, 25-31, 4, 9, 10, 48, 202, 234, 235, 329, 388, 431, 554, 585
Billington, Ray Allen, 389
Binkley, Robert C., 246
Biscoe, Walter Stanley, 32-33, 126, 128, 132, 173, 576
Bishop, William Warner, 33-36, 64, 122, 204, 206, 229, 274, 285, 286, 314, 322, 339, 340, 341, 342, 344, 363, 364, 423, 434, 445, 532, (S)52, (S)57, (S)163, (S)170
Bitner, Harry, 414, 415
Blackwell, Anna Marian, 24
Blackwell, Henry B., 507
Blair, James, 57
Blakely, Bertha, 323
Blatchford, E. W., 409
Bliss, Henry Evelyn, 36-39, 173
Bliven, Claire, 569
Blue, Thomas Fountain, 39-41
Blumenthal, Joseph, 358
Boardman, Mildred Adelaide, 310, 311, 313
Boaz, M., 362
Bogard, Travis, 94
Bogle, Sarah Comly Norris, 41-43, 180, 245, 253, 341, (S)8
Bolton, Charles Knowles, 43-44, 23
Bonk, Wallace J., 205
Bontemps, Arna Wendell, 44-47
Boring, William A., 516
Boromé, Joseph A., 49
Bostwick, Arthur Elmore, 47-50, 54, 92, 93, 104, 189, 209, 446
Bousfield, H. G., 64
Bowerman, George Franklin, 50-52, (S)144
Bowker, Richard Rogers, 52-55, 6, 127, 179, 224, 242, 299, 315, 316, 358, 359, 384, 463, 495, 525, 560
Bowles, Samuel, 117
Bowman, Isaiah, 459, 582
Boyd, Anne Morris, 55-56
Boyd, Julian, 83, 335, 426, (S)155
Boynton, Margaret Fursman, 561
Brace, Seth C., 157
Bradley, Margaret
  See Babb, Margaret Bradley
Bradley, William H., 409
Bradshaw, Frances, (S)13
Brandt, Cora, 367
Branscomb, B. Harvie, 35, 220
Bray, Elenor, 57
Bray, Thomas, 56-58

Breidinger, Anna, 417
Breman, Paul, 46
Brett, Alice Allen, 61
Brett, William Howard, 58-61, 14, 92, 138, 139, 153, 154, 178, 180, 244, 412, 413, 517, 522, 523, 538, 552, 553, 554, 576, (S)144
Briggs, Genevieve, 429
Brigham, Clarence Saunders, 61-63, 22, 164, 166, 529
Brigham, Harold F., 39, 252
Brigham, Herbert Olin, 61
Brigham, Johnson, 522
Brinley, George, 454
Brinton, Anna C., 323
Bristol, Roger P., 167
Broderick, Dorothy M., 13, 14, (S)40
Brodman, Estelle, (S)1
Brody, Leon, 19
Brokmeyer, Henry C., 230
Brooke, L. Leslie, 370
Brooks, Alice Rebecca
  See McGuire, Alice Rebecca Brooks
Brooks, Philip C., (S)29
Brown, Charles Harvey, 63-65, 80, 543
Brown, Helen Tracy, 285
Brown, John Carter, 568
Brown, John Nicholas, 149
Brown, Karl, 329, 439
Brown, Marcia, 417
Brown, Sophia Augusta, 568
Brown, Walter Lewis, 65-66, 160
Brubacher, Abram R., 416
Bruce, Dorothy, 484
Bruce, John Edward, 462
Bruckman, John, 542
Brunet, Jacques-Charles, 537
Bruntjen, Carol, 486
Bruntjen, Scott, 486
Bryan, Alice, 312
Bryan, Patricia L.
  See Knapp, Patricia L. Bryan
Bryant, Douglas, 94
Bryant, William Cullen, 55
Bryce, Lord James, 349
Buchanan, Scott, 18
Buck, Solon J., (S)29, (S)73
Bugbee, Sarah Tully, 230
Bull, Digby, 57
Burbank, Luther, 97
Burch, Benjamin, 544
Burger, Hans, 422
Burnett, Frances Hodgson, 493
Burnite, Caroline
  See Walker, Caroline Burnite
Burr, Aaron, 338
Burr, George Lincoln, 377
Burton, Ernest D., 229, 425, 426
Burton, Finie Murfee, 33
Butler, Elizabeth Shepard, 508
Butler, Nathaniel Lowe, 68
Butler, Nicholas Murray, 34, 377, 556, 563
Butler, Pierce, 66-67, 18, 56, 227, 275, 279, (S)159

Butler, Susan Dart, 68-69
Buturlin, Count Dimitri Petrovich, 356

Cadwallader, John L., 431
Caldwell, Otis William, 155
Calhoun, John C., 355
Calloway, Thomas J., 381
Campbell, Doak, (S)126
Campbell, Frank, (S)130
Campbell, James, 493
Canfield, James H., 131
Cannon, Joseph G., 586
Cannons, H. G. T., 374
Capen, Edward, 537
Carlson, Oliver, 225
Carlton, W. N. C., 361
Carnegie, Andrew, 69-73, 7, 8, 9, 10, 24, 29, 30, 39, 48, 51, 60, 102, 104, 105, 128, 134, 155, 202, 224, 264, 268, 276, 278, 291, 294, 305, 369, 445, 462, 514, 516, 523, 525, 528, 539, 552, 555, 580
Carnovsky, Leon, 73-74, 18, 275, 306, 442, 443, (S)43, (S)149, (S)150, (S)160
Carr, Henry James, 74-76
Carrére, John M., 29
Carsley, Josephine Donna Smith
  See Coolbrith, Ina Donna
Carsley, Robert, 96
Cartwright, Morse, 19, 181
Casey, Thomas L., 211
Cash, Ellen Buell, 155, 156
Castagna, Edwin, (S)15-19, 398
Castagna, Rachel Davida Dent, (S)15
Castañeda, Carlos E., 183
Cavanaugh, Eleanor, 460
Certain, Casper Carl, 76-77, 170, 226
Certain, Julia Lockwood, 77
Chamberlain, Mary Aims, 192
Chamberlain, Mellen, 218
Champlin, John D., 47
Chandler, J. A. C., 512
Charters, W. W., 180, 252
Chase, Harry, 563
Chase, Salmon P., 584
Chaves, Amado, 327
Cheney, Edith, (S)133
Cheney, John Vance, 361, 394, 449
Chesnutt, Ethel, 552
Chittenden, R. H., 202
Christern, F. W., 315
Christie, R. A., 439
Churchill, Winston, 22
Clapp, Robert, (S)127
Clapp, Verner Warren, 77-81, 19, 64, 86, 130, 376, 478, (S)24, (S)73
Clark, George T., 207
Clark, John B., 554
Clark, Kenneth, 462
Clark, Margery (pseud.), 421
Clark, Mary E., 422
Clark, Nettie M., 308

Clarke, Avis G., 62
Clarke, Edson L., 167
Clarke, Emma A., 573
Clatworthy, Linda M., 139
Clay, Henry, 545
Clayton, John, 20
Clemens, Samuel L., 584
Clement, Rufus E., (S)43
Clements, William L., 2, 291
Clemons, Harry, 81-83
Cleveland, Grover, 55, 584
Clift, David Horace, 83-87, 366, 557
Clift, David W., (S)4
Clisbe, Phoebe, 537
Cobb, Henry Ives, 410, 436
Cogswell, Joseph Green, 87-91, 382, 487
Cohen, Morris L., 415
Colburn, Evangeline, 320
Coldren, Fanny Alice, 208
Cole, George Watson, 91, 228, 361, 410
Coleman, Julia, 584
Colson, John, 258
Colvin, Laura, 341
Coman, Edwin T., Jr., 535
Compton, (Bishop) Henry, 57
Compton, Charles Herrick, 91-94, 49, 98, 223
Comstock, Alice Louise, 61
Coney, Donald, 94-95
Conner, Robert D. W., (S)29
Connor, Martha A., 475
Conover, Helen, 513
Conroy, Jack, 46
Cook, C. Donald, (S)134
Cook, Charlotte Augusta Langdon, 488
Cook, Dorothy E., 156
Coolbrith, Ina Donna, 95-97, 327
Coolidge, A. C., 301
Coolidge, Calvin, 63
Coolidge, Charles, 435
Coolidge, Elizabeth Sprague, (S)130
Cooper, Gayle, 486
Cooper, Mary K., 280
Copeland, Inez B., 482
Coplan, Kate, (S)18
Cordier, Henri, 151
Cornell, Ezra, 70
Corwin, E. B., 453
Cory, John Mackenzie, 85, 94, (S)134, (S)161
Coulehan, Catherine Placide, 424
Coulter, Edith Margaret, 97-98
Countryman, Gratia Alta, 98-100, 93, 251, 419
Coxe, Richard S., 355
Cramer, C. H., 191
Crandall, F. A., 234
Crane, Evan Jay, 100-102
Craver, Harrison Warwick, 102-103, 340, 476, 580
Crawford, Carolyn, 313
Crerar, John, 11, 410

Crissey, Lucy M., 313
Croll, Morris William, 83
Cronin, John, 399
Cross, Beulah, 98
Crunden, Frederick Morgan, 103-105, 48, 296, 399
Cuadra, Carlos, 325
Cullen, Countee, 44, 45, 46, 123
Culver, Essae Martha, 105-107, 170
Cunningham, Eileen Roach, 107-108
Cunningham, Mabel, 145
Cunningham, Robert Sydney, 107
Curry, Mary B., 537
Curti, Merle, 137, 138
Curtis, Florence Rising, 108-109, (S)43
Curtis, Josiah, 493
Custer, Benjamin A., 208, (S)169
Custer, E. L., 237
Cutler, Eliza A., 250
Cutler, Manasseh, 187
Cutler, Mary Salome
    See Fairchild, Mary Salome Cutler
Cutter, Annie Spencer, 539
Cutter, Charles Ammi, 109-115, 1, 38, 53, 126, 127, 128, 208, 216, 228, 231, 273, 296, 299, 302, 316, 343, 361, 384, 385, 386, 395, 407, 450, 454, 463, 464, 493, 495, 527, 533, 538, 570, 572, 576
Cutter, Louise, 255
Cutter, William Parker, 112, 328, 343

Daily, Jay E., (S)41
Dain, Phyllis, 234
Dale, Doris, 365
d'Alembert, Jean LeRond, 267
Dalton, Jack, 252, 313, (S)104
Dana, Charles, 120
Dana, John Cotton, 115-120, 92, 93, 144, 279, 328, 393, 517, 548, 566, 576, 580
Daniels, Joseph F., 328
Danton, Emily Miller, 253, 285, 451, 458, 460
Danton, J. Periam, 275, (S)133
Dart, Susan
    See Butler, Susan Dart
Daub, Albert, 478
Davenport, Henry J., 456
Davids, Mary Dow, 584
Davidson, Herbert, 5
Davis, Albert H., Sr., 171
Davis, Raymond Cazallis, 120-122, 75, 291
Dawe, Grosvenor, 125, 132
Day, Madeliene Rogers, 329
de Koster, Ellen, 36
De Wolf, Richard Crosby, 495
Deane, Charles, 237
Dee, Mathew F., 403

Deering, Charles, 292
Delaney, Rudicel A., 122
Delaney, Sadie Peterson, 122-124
Dell, Floyd, 190
Dennis, H. J., 493
Dent, Allie Beth
    See Martin, Allie Beth Dent
Dent, Rachel Davida
    See Castagna, Rachel Davida Dent
Deutsch, Babette, 330
Dewey, Annie Roberts Godfrey, 128
Dewey, Emily, 174
Dewey, George, 381
Dewey, Godfrey, 124, 131, 132, 174, 175, 176, 469
Dewey, John, 38, 155, 230
Dewey, Melvil, 124-134, 5, 6, 8, 11, 32, 48, 50, 53, 54, 59, 91, 92, 105, 110, 111, 120, 121, 163, 167, 168, 169, 173, 174, 175, 176, 178, 184, 202, 208, 215, 223, 231, 239, 243, 249, 265, 273, 278, 279, 296, 302, 315, 316, 317, 343, 361, 377, 382, 387, 392, 393, 399, 401, 404, 408, 419, 430, 434, 437, 450, 451, 463, 464, 468, 469, 470, 472, 493, 527, 533, 538, 572, 576, 579, 585
De Witt, Josephine, 280
Dickinson, Asa Don, 134-135
Dickinson, George Sherman, 135-137, 287, 288
Digby, Lord Simon, 57
Digby, William, 57
Ditzion, Sidney Herbert, 137-138, 304
Dix, Jane Griffin, (S)19
Dix, William Shepherd, (S)19-22
Doane, Gilbert H., 527
Dodd, William E., 425
Donahey, Victor A., 245
Doran, George H., 358, 369
Doren, Electra Collins, 138-139, 429
Dorf, A. Th., 229
Dorsey, Charles, 84, 87
Doubleday, Russell, 134
Doud, Margery, 48, 49
Douglas, Clarence DeWitt, 140
Douglas, Eva, 327
Douglas, Mary Teresa Peacock, 139-141, (S)37
Douglas, Paul, 305
Dow, George W., 222
Downes, Olin, 496
Downey, Mary Elizabeth, 460
Downs, Robert B., 84, 221, 264, 348, (S)51, (S)104, (S)154
Draper, Andrew Sloan, 129, 131, 471
Draper, Anna Palmer, 31
Draper, Eben S., 23
Draper, Lyman Copeland, 141-143, 514

176 / Name Index

Drury, Francis Keese Wynkoop, 143-145, 225, 328
Duane, William, 20, 21
Dudgeon, Matthew Simpson, 145-146, 504, 520
Dudley, Charles R., 328
Dufief, N. G., 188
Dunbar, Ralph McNeal, 146-147, 64
Duncan, Isadora, 96
Duncanson, William Mayne, 338
Dunham, William Huse, 389
Dunkin, Paul Shaner, 147-148, 486
Dunn, Jacob P., 5
Duran, Elizabeth
    See Berelson, Elizabeth Duran
Dwiggins, W. A., 358
Dyer, Margaret C., 328
Dyer, Mary, 559
Dyson, Malcolm, 325
Dziatzko, Karl, 401

Eames, Wilberforce, 148-153, 91, 329, 455, 529
Earle, Elinor S., 225
Early, Joe, 175
Eastman, George, 195
Eastman, Linda Anne, 153-155, 60, 61, 139, 180, 189, 446, 451, 524, (S)144
Eaton, Anne Thaxter, 155-156, (S)93
Eaton, John, 156-157, 127, 231, 393, 440, 463, 501
Eaton, Thelma, 175
Ebeling, C. D., 88
Eddy, Harriet G., 199
Eddy, Sarah S., 241
Edge, Sigrid A., 181, 520
Edison, Thomas A., 247, 388
Edmands, Abigail Lloyd, 158
Edmands, John, 157-158, 163, 265, 405, 533
Edmondson, Kate, 104
Edwards, Edward, 384
Egan, Margaret Elizabeth, 158-159, (S)121
Eisenhart, Ruth C., 395
Eisenhower, Dwight D., 182, 324
Eliot, Charles William, 488, 571
Eliot, Samuel, 162, 165
Ellinger, Werner Bruno, 375
Elliot, Charles W., 384
Elliot, Fannie, 414
Ellsworth, Ralph, 203, 270, 334, 532
Elmendorf, Henry Livingston, 65, 159
Elmendorf, Theresa Hubbell West, 159-160, 65, 469
Ely, Grace Duncan, 431
Ely, Richard T., 554
Embree, Edwin, 68
Emerson, Ralph Waldo, 499
Engberg, Lucia, 278
Engel, Carl, 498

Erler, Mabel J., 391
Ernst, Morris, 352
Ersted, Ruth, (S)37
Esterquest, Ralph Theodore, 160-161
Eunestus, Horst, 83
Evans, Anne Jane, 381
Evans, Charles, 162-167, 22, 178, 202, 407, 411, 478, 484
Evans, Helen Murphy, (S)23
Evans, Luther Harris, (S)22-26, 19, 78, 324, (S)32, (S)72
Everett, Edward, 87, 88, 273, 515
Everett, Emily, 1
Everson, Florence, 413

Fairchild, Edwin Milton, 168
Fairchild, Mary Salome Cutler, 167-170
Falkberget, Johan, 204, 205
Fall, John, 555
Farber, Sidney, 182
Fargo, Lucile F., 170-171, 42, 226, 227
Farmer, Frances, 415
Farquhar, Charlotte, 564
Farran, Don, 354
Fasquelle, Louis, 120
Faust, Clarence, 67
Faxon, Frederick Winthrop, 171-172, 160
Fay, Lucy, 156
Fellows, Jennie Dorcas, 173-174, 32, 322, 469
Fellows, Marguerite, 358
Fenger, Christian, 17
Fenwick, Sara, 352
Ferguson, Milton James, 174-176, 105, 200, 286, 364
Ferguson, Ruth B., 175
Field, Marshall, 178
Field, Rachel, 370
Field, Thomas W., 149
Finke, Grace, 138
Fiske, John, 126
Fitz, Carl, 98
Fitzgerald, John F., 218
Fitzpatrick, Rose, 584
Fleming, E. McClung, 52, 55
Fleming, Walter L., 22
Fletcher, Robert, 27, 30, 177
Fletcher, William Isaac, 176-179, 38, 244, 316, 343, 407, 408, 533
Flexner, Abraham, 155
Flexner, Jennie Maas, 179-182, 9
Flynn, Eleanore, 84
Fogarty, John E., 182-183, 521
Foik, Paul Joseph, 183-184
Folsom, Charles, 1, 406, 487
Folwell, William Watts, 540
Fontaine, Everett O., 43
Forbush, Gayle, (S)32
Force, Peter, 500
Ford, Paul Leicester, 149, 150
Forney, John W., 584

Forstall, Gertrude, 12
Foss, Sam, 517
Foster, William Eaton, 184-186, 127, 202, 482
Frankfurter, Felix, (S)60
Franklin, Benjamin, 186-188
Franklin, Deborah Read, 188
Franklin, William Temple, 188
Frarey, Carlyle, (S)135
Freehafer, Ed, 84
Freeman, Marilla Waite, 188-191, 410
Fremont, Jessie Benton, 327
Freneau, Philip, 20
Frick, Bertha Margaret, 191-192, 468, (S)134
Friedenwald, Herbert, 585
Friedenwald, Racie, 4
Froling, Barbara, (S)41
Frost, Robert, 358
Fuller, Melville W., 586
Funk, Isaac K., 47
Furth, Steve, 325
Fussler, Herman H., 203, 426

Gág, Wanda, 370
Gagliardo, Domenico, (S)27
Gagliardo, Ruth, (S)27-29
Gaine, Helen R., 100
Gardiner, John Sylvester, 515
Garfield, Eugene, 37
Garfield, James A., 584
Garland, Jennie P., 250
Garrigue, Augusta Harriet, 315
Garrison, Fielding, 25
Gaudet, Helen, S(13)
Gaver, Mary Virginia, 140
Gavit, Joseph, 577
Gay, Frank B., 454, 525
Gentry, Helen, 323
Gerould, James Thayer, 192-194, 35, 432, 433, 531, 540
Gerould, Winifred Gregory, 194-195, 193
    See also Gregory, Winifred
Getchell, Myron, 174
Gibbs, Josiah Willard, 533
Gibbs, Julia, 534
Gilbert, Cass, 104, 203
Gilbert, Christine, 466
Gilbert, Lou Mabel, 525
Gilbreth, Lillian, 422
Gilchrist, Donald Bean, 195-196
Gildersleeve, Basil L., 424
Gillespie, Edward R., 149
Gillett, Charles Ripley, 196-197
Gillis, James Louis, 197-200, 328
Gillis, Mabel Ray, 200, 197, 543
Gilman, Daniel Coit, 200-203, 383, 533
Gilman, John T., 87
Gilman, Mary F., 87
Gilpin, Brinca, 367
Ginn (brothers), 127

Githens, Alfred Morton, 203-204, 335, 517, 551
Gjelsness, Rudolph H., 204-205
Gleason, Eliza Atkins, (S)43, (S)158
Gleason, Fanny Maria, 406
Godet, Marcel, 35
Godfrey, Annie Roberts, 124, 127, 130
Godfrey, Grace, 437
Goepper, Adele Louise, 247
Goethe, Johann Wolfgang, 88
Goff, Frederick R., 167, 576
Goldhor, Herbert, 551, (S)51
Goode, G. Brown, 4
Goodman, Edward, 352
Goodrich, Francis Lee Dewey, 205-207, 35, 122, 293
Goodwin, John Edward, 207-208, 366
Goodwyn, Martha, 337
Gordy, Wilbur F., 242
Goudy, Frederic W., 352
Gould, Charles Henry, 208-210, 6
Gove, Aaron, 116
Gove, Frank Wadleigh, 115
Gowans, William, 149
Grabhorn, Edwin, 323, 358
Grabhorn, Robert, 323, 358
Graham, Bessie, 210-211
Graham, Clarence R., 85, 365, 449
Graham, Mae, 140, 141
Graham, Sarah Newcomb, 52
Grant, Arthur Hastings, 526
Grant, Claudius B., 120, 121
Grant, Mary Marie E., 100
Grant, Seth Hastings, 200, 383, 384, 526
Grant, Thirza, 246
Grant, Ulysses S., 55, 156, 157, 584
Gray, Asa, 89
Gray, William S., 13
Grech, Anthony P., 415
Greeley, Horace, 584
Green, Bernard Richardson, 211-212, 334, 500
Green, Duff, 355
Green, Elizabeth, 462
Green, James Albert, 247
Green, John, 213
Green, Samuel Swett, 212-216, 144, 173, 315, 316, 328
Greenaway, Emerson, (S)1
Greene, Belle da Costa, 216-218
Greene, Louis C., 358, 359
Gregory, Winifred, 192, 193
    See also Gerould, Winifred Gregory
Grenville, Sir Richard, 61
Griffin, Appleton Prentiss Clark, 218-220, 363
Griffin, Jane
    See Dix, Jane Griffin
Griggs, Alfred Flournoy, 220
Griggs, Lillian Baker, 220-221
Grove, Lee, 80

Grover, Esther Thomas, (S)29
Grover, Wayne Clayton, (S)29-32
Growell, Adolph, 151, 384, 455
Guild, Reuben Aldridge, 221-222, 163, 184, 274, 383, 384, 538
Guild, Thatcher Howland, 143
Gunsaulus, Frank W., 471
Gwynn, Stanley E., 290

Hadley, Arthur T., 284
Hadley, Chalmers, 222-223, 92, 98, 365, 525, 577, 580
Hadley, Morris, 18
Haft, Virginia G., 136
Haight, Charles, 203
Haines, Helen Elizabeth, 223-226, 143, 179, 474
Haines, Mildred Sellers, (S)72
Hale, Edward Everett, 54, 218, 393
Hall, Mary Evelyn, 226-227, 155, 170, 232, 320, 416
Halleck, Fitz-Greene, 90
Ham, Roswell Gray, 323
Hamer, Philip, (S)29
Hamill, Alfred, 390
Hamill, Harold, 313, 550
Hamilton, Alexander, 20
Hamlin, Talcot, 203
Hammond, Gladys, 147
Handy, Daniel Nash, (S)32-36
Handy, W. C., 46
Hanke, Karl David, 342
Hansbrough, Lilia Slaughter, 512
Hanson, James Christian Meinich, 227-230, 17, 34, 342, 343, 344, 411, 425, 495, 585, (S)52, (S)159, (S)170
Hargreaves, R. T., 170
Harper, William Rainey, 33, 425
Harrassowitz, Otto, 409
Harris, Addison C., 165
Harris, George William, 227
Harris, Joel Chandler, 14
Harris, Thaddeus William, 487
Harris, William Torrey, 230-232, 48, 126
Harrison, Alice Sinclair, 232-233
Harrison, Benjamin, 54, 230
Harrison, Evelyn, 221
Harrisse, Henry, 233-234, 455
Harsh, Vivian G., (S)112
Hart, Albert Bushnell, 24, 251
Harte, Bret, 96, 97
Hartranft, Chester D., 431
Hartzell, Mary Elizabeth, 583
Haskins, Rebecca Green, 271
Hasse, Adelaide Rosalie, 234-236, 328
Hastings, Charles H., 342
Hastings, Thomas, 29
Hatch, Gladys E., 276
Hatcher, Elizabeth, 462
Haussling, Jacob, 119
Haven, Samuel Foster, 236-237
Haycraft, Howard, 561

Hayden, Julia, 435
Haydon, Glen, 137
Hayes (Colonel), 445
Hayes, John Russell, 475
Hayes, Rutherford B., 445, 499
Haygood, William, 74
Haykin, David Judson, 237-238, 174
Hayward, Madlyn, 522
Hazeltine, Mary Emogene, 238-240, 460
Heartman, Charles F., 354
Heath, Anna Whiting, 248
Heath, D. C., 218
Heath, Julia W., 63
Hegel, George W. F., 230, 231
Hemingway, Ernest, (S)60
Henderson, Gladys S., 280
Hendrie, Edna Florence, 233
Henne, Frances Elizabeth, (S)36-40, (S)43, (S)160
Henry, Edward A., 196
Henry, Joseph, 272, 273, 383
Henry, Philip S., 392
Henry, William E., 322, (S)108
Herbert, Clara, 18, 52
Herrick, Edward C., 157, 201
Herrick, Francis H., 22
Hewins, Caroline, 240-243, 42, 265, 315, 358, 407
Heyne, Christian Gottlöb, 88
Hibben, John Grier, 432
Hicks, Frederick C., 414
Highsmith, J. Henry, 140
Hild, Frederick H., 328
Hill, F. J., 438
Hill, Frank Pierce, 243-244, 25, 117, 119, 160, 178, 255, 308, 316, 317, 566
Hill, May
    See Arbuthnot, May Hill
Hill, Richard S., (S)130
Hill, Robert W., 388
Hill, Samuel, 419
Hill, Thomas, 1
Hirshberg, Herbert Simon, 244-247, 170, 171
Hitchcock, Ada, (S)59
Hitchcock, H. Wiley, 498
Hodge, Genevieve Austen, 557
Hodges, Nathaniel Dana Carlile, 247-248
Hoe, Robert, 404
Hoffman, Hester, (S)150
Holden, Harley P., 484
Hollerith, Herman, 27
Holley, Edward G., 404
Holliday, John H., 165
Hollingsworth, Virginia, 139
Holt, Henry, 38, 53, 315
Homer, Dorothy, 447
Homes, Henry Augustus, 248-249, 129
Hopkins, Anderson, 33
Hopkins, Byron C., 181
Hopkins, John M., 132

178 / Name Index

Hopper, Franklin Ferguson, 249-250, 10, 181, 286
Hornback, Miriam L., 86
Hosmer, James Kendall, 250-251, 99
Hostetter, Anita Miller, 251-253
Houghton, Arthur Amory, Jr., 569
Howard, Annie T., 21
Howard, Frank T., 22
Howe, Harriet Emma, 253-255, 42, 173, 579, 580
Howes, Wright, 390
Howland, Anne W., 109
Hubbard, Gardiner G., 247
Hughes, Charles Evan, 388
Hughes, Langston, 44, 45, 46-47, 123, 447
Humboldt, Baron von, 21
Humphrey, Gertrude Priscilla, 291
Humphry, John A., 182
Hunt, Clara Whitehill, 255-256
Hunt, Everett, 474, 475
Hunt, Hannah, 256-257
Hunt, James, 283
Hunt, Jane Clifford, 222
Hunt, M. Louise, 34
Hunt, Mate Graye, 307
Hunt, Richard Morris, 435, 436
Huntington, Henry E., 62, 91
Hutchenson, David, 495
Hutchins, Anne, 488
Hutchins, Frank Avery, 257-259, 308, 396, 504
Hutchins, Margaret, 259-260
Hutchins, Robert Maynard, 18, 19, 311, 442, (S)158, (S)159
Hutchinson, Ann, 559
Hutchinson, Lura, 541
Hutchinson, Ruth, 531

Ibbotsen, Louis Tappe, (S)96
Icazbalceta, Garcia, 149
Ideson, Julia Bedford, 260-261
Immroth, John Phillip, (S)40-42
Irving, Washington, 90
Isom, Mary Frances, 261-263, 397
Ives, Brayton, 453

Jackson, Andrew, 355, 545
Jackson, Evalene Parsons, (S)9
Jackson, J. Arthur, 504
Jackson, Wallace Van, 109
Jacobs, John Hall, 263-264
Jahr, Torstein, 510
James, Hannah Packard, 264-266, 468
James, William, 230, 361, 437
James, Willis, 196
Jameson, James Franklin, 22, 349
Jamieson (Mr.), 467
Janowitz, Morris, (S)13
Jefferson, Thomas, 266-268, 20, 186, 187, 337, 338, 356, 544
Jenkins, Jeannie Cooper, 81

Jenkins, William S., 235
Jenkinson, Richard C., 117
Jennings, H. A., 453
Jennings, Judson Toll, 268-269, 92
Jesse, William Herman, 269-271
Jewett, Alice, 557
Jewett, Charles Coffin, 271-274, 1, 90, 221, 357, 383, 385, 537, 538, 570
Jewett, John N., 164
Joeckel, Carleton Bruns, 274-276, 18, 67, 73, 147, 281, 283, 362, 442, 483, (S)43, (S)160
Johnson, A. C., 531
Johnson, Alberta, 44
Johnson, Alvin S., 276-278, 259, 555
Johnson, Andrew, 584
Johnson, Annita Melville Ker, 344
Johnson, Charles S., 45
Johnson, Cornelia Phillips, 39
Johnson, Fenton, 46
Johnson, H. Earle, 288
Johnson, Harriette Amy, 441
Johnson, James Weldon, 44, 45
Johnson, Lyndon B., 361
Johnson, Sadie
    See Delaney, Sadie Peterson
Johnston, Edward, 231
Johnston, William Dawson, 377, 507
Jones, Edward Allen, (S)43
Jones, Hannah E., 492
Jones, Herschel V., 152
Jones, Katharine Edmonstone
    See Kuhlman, Katharine Edmonstone Jones
Jones, Leota, 175
Jones, Sarah, 140
Jones, Thomas, (S)124
Jones, Thomas Elsa, 45, 223
Jones, Virginia Lacy, (S)42-46
Jordan, David Starr, 207, 326, 327
Jordan, Robert T., 290
Josephson, Askel Gustav Salomon, 278-280
Joslyn, Dorothy, 473
Judd, Charles, 320
Juon, Paul, 135
Juul, Niels, 308

Kaessmann, Beta, 551
Kaiser, John Boynton, 280-282, 247
Kaiser, Virginia Conover, 282
Kaiser, Walter Herbert, 282-284
Kaun, Hugo, 135
Keally, Francis, 203
Kean, Rosalind
    See Berelson, Rosalind Kean
Kebabian, Paul, 255
Keenan, Stella, 574
Keep, Rosalind, 323
Keith, Effie, 292
Kellar, Herbert A., 354, 355
Kelley, Florence, 396

Kelly, Emma H., 276
Kelly, James, 444
Kelso, Tessa L., 234, 328
Kendall, Sergeant, 534
Kennedy, Charles E., 154
Kent, Allen, (S)52, (S)119
Kent, Henry Watson, 119, 173, 393
Kenyon, Sir Frederick, 217
Keogh, Andrew, 284-285, 33, 451
Keppel, Frederick Paul, 285-286, 17, 24, 35, 42, 314, 365, 556, 580, 581, (S)161
Kerman, Keith, 50
Kerr, Clark, 94, 95
Ketchum, Mary, 200
Kettlewell, John, 57
Kierkegaard, Preben, 74
Kight, A. C., 372, 373
Kildal, Arne, 92
Kilgour, Frederick G., 84, (S)4
Kimball, Ingalls, 352
King, Josias Wilson, 21
Kingsbury, Mary, 226
Kingsley, James L., 200
Kinkeldey, Otto, 286-289, 496
Kletsch, Ernest, 433
Knapp, Patricia L. Bryan, 289-290
Knapp, Robert Segrist, 289
Knight, Henry C., 121
Koch, Theodore Wesley, 290-294, 12, 122, 166, 206, 426, 535, (S)49
Koehler, Adele, 355
Koopman, Harry Lyman, 294-295, 531, 549
Koren, U. V., 227
Korty, Margaret, 187
Kossuth, Louis, 124
Krettek, Germaine, 182
Krieg, Amelia, 373
Kroch, Adolph, 442
Kroeger, Alice Bertha, 295-298, 169, 210, 377, 378, 531
Krug, Judith F., 86
Kubiek, Earl C., 340
Kuhlman, Augustus Frederick, (S)46-50, 425, 426
Kuhlman, Katharine Edmonstone Jones, (S)47
Kuhlman, Virginia Wood Walker, (S)48
Küp, Karl, 330

Labrouste, Henri, 435
Labrouste, Theodore, 435
Lacy, Dan, (S)26
Ladd, Dorothy Devereux, 78
Lafayette, Marquis de, 536
LaFollette, Robert M., 274, 350, 396, 514
La Fontaine, Henri, 469, 470
LaMontagne, Leo E., 343
Lancour, Harold Adlore, (S)50-52, (S)91

Lancour, Marie McClellan, (S)50
Lane, Henry S., 507
Lane, Rosamond
    See Lord, Rosamond Lane
Lane, William Coolidge, 298-301, 360, 361, 419, 495, (S)52
Lang, Paul Henry, 288
Langer, William Leonard, 459
Langley, Samuel P., 4
Langer, Mildred Crowe, 108
Lapham, Ruth, 66
Larned, Josephus Nelson, 301-305, 65, 225, 576
Larrabee, Charles H., 142
Lasker, Mary, 182
Law, Marie Hamilton, 336
Lawson, A. Venable, (S)9
Lazarsfeld, Paul, (S)13
Le Braz, Anatole, 22
Leacock, Stephen, 366
Learned, William Setchel, 305, 72, 278
Leavitt, Justina, 558
Ledyard, Lewis Cass, 10, 331
Lee, Edwin A., 381
Lee, George W., (S)34, (S)64
Lee, Mollie Huston, (S)45
LeFevre, Alice Louise, 306-307
Leff, Viola Susan, 476
Legge, James, 151
Legler, Henry Eduard, 307-310, 145, 442
Lehmann-Haupt, Helmut, (S)149
Leigh, Robert Devore, 310-313, 556
Lenz, Oliver, 291
Lepman, Jella, 306, 466
Lester, Robert MacDonald, 313-314, 24, 36, 365
Leupold, Jakob Friedrich Ferdinand, 314
Leupp, Harold L., 98, 328, (S)109
Leveridge, Robert, 217
Lewis, Edward, 56
Lewis, Lloyd, 390, 425
Lewis, Minerva Amanda
    See Sanders, Minerva Amanda Lewis
Leyh, Georg, 64
Leypoldt, Augusta H. Garrigue, 53, 54
Leypoldt, Frederick, 314-316, 53, 54, 127, 241, 408
Libby, Willard, (S)69
Lichenstein, Walter, 292
Lichtenwanger, William, (S)130
Liebenberg, Mary A., 361
Liebert, Herman W., 565, 566
Liepmannssohn, Leo, 287
Lincoln, Abraham, 357, 506, 507
Lincoln, Julia E., 212
Linderfelt, Klas August, 316-317, 159
Linderman, Winifred B., 129
Lindsay, Vachel, 358
Lippman, Walter, 459
Livermore, George, 1

Lloyd (Bishop), 57
Locke, Alain, 462
Locke, George Herbert, 317-319
Lodge, Henry Cabot, 494
Logan, James, 216, 492
Logasa, Hannah, 319-322
Logsdon, Richard H., (S)134, (S)156
Lohrer, Alice, (S)38
London, Jack, 96
Long, Harriet, 246
Long, Huey, 106
Lord, Isabel Ely, 169
Lord, Milton Edward, (S)52-56
Lord, Milton L., 34, 532
Lord, Rosamond Lane, (S)52
Lorenz, John G., 147
Louis, Marion, 170
Low, Edmon Horton, (S)56-59
Lowell, Mildred Hawksworth, (S)105
Low, Seth, 468
Lowe, Blanche, 244
Lowell, A. Lawrence, 300, 301
Lubetzky, Seymour, 147, 148, 208, (S)170
Luce, Henry, (S)60
Ludington, Flora Belle, 322-324
Luhn, Hans Peter, 324-326
Lummis, Charles Fletcher, 326-328, 144, 145
Lund, John J., 208
Lundy, Frank, 94, 208, 532
Luther, Flavel Sweeten, 242
Lydenberg, Harry Miller, 329-333, 10, 28, 30, 139, 149, 151, 152, 153, 250, 285, 286, 429, 430, (S)83
Lyle, Guy R., 425
Lyly, John, 83

MacAlister, James, 296, 298
MacArthur, Douglas, 64, 101
Macdonald, Angus Snead, 333-335, 203, 204, 424, 438, 517
MacDowell, Edward, 286
MacKillop, Dorothy Boyd, 484
Macky, Bessie R., 296
MacLeish, Archibald, (S)59-63, 78, 275, 332, 420, 421, 426, 427, 567, (S)23, (S)87
MacPherson, Harriet Dorothea, 336-337, 136
Madison, Dolley, 544
Madison, James, 20, 338, 544
Magruder, George, 338
Magruder, Patrick, 337-339, 544
Mahar, Mary Helen, 417
Malclès, Louise, 531
Malkin, Mary Ann, 487
Malkin, Sol, 487
Malone, Dumas, 83
Manakee, Harold, 551
Manley, Marion, 568
Mann, Horace, 142
Mann, Margaret, 339-342, 102, 471

Marcus, William Elder, Jr., 422
Marion, Guy Elwood, (S)63-66
Marke, Julius J., 415
Markham, Edwin, 327
Marr, Eleanor B., 101
Marsh, George Perkins, 294
Marshall, A. E., 100
Martel, Charles, 342-345, 34, 228, 411, (S)52, (S)160, (S)170
Martin, Adelaide Nevins, 102
Martin, Allie Beth Dent, 345-347
Martin, Lowell A., 74, 275, 456, 478, (S)155
Martin, Ralph F., 345
Marvin, Cornelia
    See Pierce, Cornelia Marvin
Marx, Alexander, 4
Masefield, John, 189
Mason, Edward G., 164
Mather, Samuel, 186
Mathews, Robert E., 403
Mathiews, Franklin K., 359, 369
Mayser, Helen Luise, 294
McAnally, Arthur Monroe, 347-349
McCabe, Margaret Bruce, 66
McCallum, A. N., 232
McCarthy, Charles A., 349-350, 258, 308
McCarthy, Joseph, 86, 390
McCarthy, Stephen A., 270
McClellan, Marie
    See Lancour, Marie McClellan
McClure, Alexander, 586
McClure, Bessie May, 135
McClure, S. S., 43
McConnel, Cecilia, 510
McCrea, Frances Anne Kemble, 301
McCrum, Blanche Prichard, (S)66-68
McCutcheon, Byron, 528
McDiarmid, E. W., (S)155
McDowell, Edward C., 84
McDowell, Mary, 396
McGeorge, Lucille, 347
McGiveran, Edmond, 264
McGuire, Alice Rebecca Brooks, 350-352, (S)37
McGuire, John Carson, 351
McKay, Claude, 123
McKean, Thomas, 20
McKelvey, Eleanor, 268
McKenna, Francis Eugene, (S)68-71
McKeon, Newton, 323
McKim, Charles Follen, 436-437, 203, 435, 516
McKinley, A. E., Jr., 321
McKinley, William, 4, 54, 299, 381, 419, 494, 585, 586
McLeod, Helen Florence, 455
McMichael, S. Ruth, 540
McMorris, Robert, 321
McMurtrie, Douglas Crawford, 352-355, 581
Mead, William, 436
Mearns, David C., (S)71-75, 219, 421, (S)24

180 / Name Index

Medina, José Toribio, 152
Medley, D. J., 391
Meehan, Charles Henry Wharton, 356
Meehan, John Silva, 355-357, 507
Meigs, Cornelia L., 156, (S)93
Melcher, Daniel, (S)75-78
Melcher, Frederic Gershom, 358-359, 242, 369, 422, (S)75
Melcher, Margaret Saul, (S)78
Melinat, Carl, 246
Mencken, H. L., 550
Meredith, Hugh, 186
Merrill, Julia Wright, 359-360
Merrill, William Stetson, 360-361, 228, 342, 411
Merritt, Helen Jean, 371
Merritt, LeRoy Charles, 361-363, (S)51
Mestechin, Natalie, 136
Metcalf, Anna May, 444
Metcalf, Elinor Gregory, (S)80
Metcalf, Ellen Elizabeth, 158
Metcalf, Keyes D., (S)78-84, 84, 212, 252, 270, 333, 429, 445, 446, 555, 557, (S)61
Metcalf, Martha Gerrish, (S)79
Meyer, Helen Harris Spalding, 364
Meyer, Herman H. B., 363-364
Michaels, Rose Frances, 366
Milam, Carl Hastings, 364-366, 34, 41, 43, 85, 92, 93, 170, 314, 360, 446, 580
Milam, Nell Robinson, 365
Milczewski, Marion, 94
Miller, Durand, 24
Miller, Edith, 270
Miller, Ernest, 283
Miller, Henry, 149
Miller, Joaquin, 96, 97, 327
Miller, Philip Lieson, 286, 287, 288
Millis, John Schoff, 18, 159
Mitchell, Alice, 54
Mitchell, Rose Francis Michaels, 367
Mitchell, S. Weir, 28, 30
Mitchell, Samuel L., 338
Mitchell, Sydney Bancroft, 366-367, 98, 169, 207, 208, 225, 580, (S)66
Möhlenbrock, S., 283
Mohrhardt, Foster, 34, 35, 485
Monington, Margaret Jones, 357
Monington, Rachel T., 357
Monroe, James, 20, 524
Montgomery, Thomas Lynch, 367-368, 265
Moon, Eric, 478
Mooney, James K., 167
Moore, Anne Carroll, 368-371, 9, 30, 49, 226, 242, 481
Moore, Ernest Carroll, 207
Moore, George Henry, 150
Moore, Grace Isabel, 318
Moore, John M., 474
Moreau, César, 536

Morgan, J. P., 70, 217
Morgan, Pierpont, 216, 217
Moriarty, John Helenbeck, 371-372
Morison, Samuel Eliot, 483
Morison, Stanley, 390
Morley, Christopher, 223, 359, 392
Morley, Linda Huckel, 372-373
Morris, Henry S., 559
Morris, Jack Cassius, (S)84-87
Morris, Lois Mae Lympus, (S)84
Morrisey, Marlene, 79, 81
Morsch, Lucile M., 373-377
Morse, James H., 419
Morton, Florrinell F., 141
Mudge, Isadore Gilbert, 377-379, 210, 260, 297, 340, 467, 531, (S)164
Mueller, Anne, 338
Mugridge, Donald H., (S)67
Muir, John, 326
Mulligan, Ethel Simes, 506
Mumford, Betsy Perrin Fox, (S)87
Mumford, L. Quincy, (S)87-91, 78, 79, 84, 324
Mumford, Permelia Catherine Stevens, (S)87
Munn, Ralph, 379-381, 203, 312, 387, 557, (S)93
Munroe, Charlotte Elizabeth, 419
Münsterberg, Hugo, 394
Munthe, Wilhelm, 67, 275, 334
Murphy, Helen
  See Evans, Helen Murphy
Murray, Anne Jane Evans, 382
Murray, Daniel Alexander Payne, 381-382
Murray, Nicholas, 424
Mussolini, Benito, 49
Myer, Elizabeth G., 182

Nash, John Henry, 322-323
Nelson, Charles Alexander, 382-383
Nelson, Emma Norris, 383
Nelson, Peter, 577
Nelson, Sarah, 228
Nesbitt, Elizabeth, (S)91-94, 380
Neugebauer, Otto, 531
Nevins, Allan, 55, 530, 547
Newberry, Walter Loomis, 409
Newell, Jonathan, 487
Newhall, Jannette, 395
Newton, A. Edward, 2
Nichol, Isabel, 254
Nicholson, Francis, 57
Nicholson, John Burton, Jr., (S)67
Nicholson, Meredith, 358
Nolan, Edward J., 328
Noonan, Michael, 453
Norden, William Van, 463
Norris, Emma, 382
Norton, Andrews, 88
Norton, Charles Benjamin, 383-384, 222, 273, 406
Norton, Charles Eliot, 291, 326

Norton, Margaret, 389
Notestein, Wallace, 193
Nourse, Mary Adelaide, 493
Noyes, Stephen Buttrick, 384-387, 463, 538
Noyes, Theodore, 51
Nutting, Mary Olivia, 323
Nyholm, Jens P., 208, 292
Nyhuus, Haakon, 411

Oberheim, Grace, 64
Oboler, Eli Martin, (S)94-95
Oboler, Marcia Lois Wolf, (S)94
O'Callaghan, Edmund Bailey, 149
Olcott, Frances Jenkins, 387-388, 490, 491, 539
Olinsky, Ivan G., 429
Orne, Jerrold, 348
Orr, Robert W., 64
Osgood, Emily Call, 218
Osler, Sir William, 27, 107
Osterhout, Isaac, 265
Otis, Harrison Gray, 326, 327
Otlet, Paul, 469
Ottemiller, John H., (S)4
Owen, Ethel Elliot, 361
Owen, Thomas M., (S)6

Page, John, 266
Palfrey, John Gorham, 237
Palmer, Bertha, 300
Paltsits, Victor Hugo, 388-389, 150, 152, 529
Pargellis, Stanley, 389-391
Parker, Francis W., 230
Parker, Ralph, 94
Parker, Theodore, 499
Parkins, Phyllis V., 574
Parkinson, William D., 115
Parrington, Vernon L., 322
Parsons, Arthur, 321
Parsons, Mary, 41
Partridge, Sarah, 499
Passos, John Dos, (S)60
Patterson, Austin M., 101
Patterson, Frank, 498
Payne, Daniel Alexander, 381
Peacock, Mary Teresa
  See Douglas, Mary Teresa Peacock
Peale, Charles Willson, 21
Pearce, James Alfred, 356, 357
Pearson, Edmund Lester, 392-393, 119, 328
Pease, Barbara, 575
Peckham, G. W., 328
Peckham, Howard H., 3
Peet, Creighton, 561
Peirce, Benjamin, 487
Peirce, Charles S., 230
Perkins, Frederick Beecher, 393-394, 128, 449
Perry, Everett, 542

Perry, James, 325, (S)119
Pershing, John, 424
Petersham, Maud, 370
Petersham, Miska, 370
Peterson, Edward Louis, 122
Peterson, Sadie Johnson
    See Delaney, Sadie Peterson
Petree, Kate, 197
Pettee, Julia, 394-395, 197
Pettit, Dorothy Bell, 94
Phelan, James D., 97
Phelps, William Lyon, 534
Phillips, P. Lee, 585
Pickett, William, 95
Pierce, Cornelia Marvin, 395-398, 258, 262, 263
Pierce, Walter M., 396, 397
Pierce, Watson, 423
Piercy, Esther June, 398-399, 148
Pilling, James Constantine, 149
Pimsleur, Meira G., 415
Pinchot, Amos, 349
Pinchot, Gifford, 349
Pincon, M., 440
Pius XI (Pope), 34
Plummer, Frances R., 7
Plummer, Hannah Ann Ballard, 7
Plummer, Jonathan Wright, 7
Plummer, Mary Wright, 399-402, 7, 10, 33, 42, 224, 226, 427, 446, 481, 542
Plunkett, Horace, 349
Poladian, Sirvart, 286
Poland, William Carey, 222
Pollack, Ervin Harold, 402-403, 415
Pollack, Lydia Weiss, 402
Pollard, Alfred W., 91, 151, 564, 565
Poole, Frances E. Haskins, 404
Poole, Franklin O., 573
Poole, Reuben Brooks, 404
Poole, William Frederick, 404-412, 1, 75, 91, 157, 162, 163, 164, 165, 172, 176, 179, 188, 202, 216, 227, 240, 247, 272, 273, 303, 317, 342, 360, 361, 385, 463, 493, 494, 527, 533, 572
Porter, George T., 165
Porter, John Addison, 585
Potter, Esther, 175
Potter, Marion E., 559
Powell, Benjamin Edward, (S)95-98
Powell, Betsy Graves, (S)96
Powell, Lawrence Clark, 95, 328, 367, 535, 536, 565, 582
Power, Effie Louise, 412-414, 170, 180
Pratt, Charles, 427
Pratt, Enoch, 70, 163
Predeek, Albert, 63, 64
Prescott, William, 87, 89
Price, Derek de Solla, (S)98-101
Price, Ellen Hjorth, (S)99
Price, Miles Oscar, 414-415, 403, 557, 558
Price, Sir Thomas, 57

Prince, Maria, 20
Pritchard, Martha Caroline, 415-417, 170
Probasco, Henry, 410
Pulling, Hazel, 321
Purdy, George Flint, 417-418
Putnam, George Herbert, 418-422, 16, 33, 51, 54, 78, 92, 98, 99, 104, 131, 135, 178, 219, 299, 308, 342, 343, 344, 363, 364, 381, 382, 432, 443, 494, 495, 496, 498, 499, 501, 508, 526, 579, 585, 586, (S)73
Putnam, George Palmer, 405, 443
Pyecroft, Henry (pseud.), 195
Pylodet, F. (pseud.), 315

Quigley, Margaret Closey, 422-423

Raleigh, Sir Walter, 61
Randall, William M., 34, 35, 206, (S)52, (S)159
Randolph, Edmund, 20
Randolph, Joseph, 337
Raney, Catherine, 426
Raney, McKendree Llewellyn, 423-427, (S)47, (S)160
Ranganathan, S. R., 74
Ranz, Jim, 273
Rappaport, Ruth
    See Berelson, Ruth Rappaport
Rathbone, Josephine Adams, 427-429, 261, 263, 484
Reagan, Agnes L., (S)9
Redgrave, G. R., 91, 564, 565
Redstone, Edward H., 24
Reece, Ernest James, (S)101-104, 108, 552, 557, (S)155
Reece, Sabra Elizabeth Stevens, (S)102
Reed, Sarah Rebecca, (S)104-108, 252
Reed, Walter, 107
Reese, Count Pio, 410
Regal, Ellen, 121
Reinhardt, Aurelia Henry, 323
Remington, Frederic, 326
Remsen, Ira, 424
Remsen, Lydia, 142
Remsen, Peter A., 142
Renan, Ernest, 233
Renner, J. G. E., 163
Rhees, Rush, 195
Rhodes, Dorothea, 326
Rhodes, Isabella, 170
Rice, Paul North, 429-430, 139, 333, 557, 561
Rich, Lora A., 441, 443
Richards, Charles, 452
Richards, Irene Fry, (S)109
Richards, John Stewart, (S)108-111
Richards, Samuel, 157
Richardson, Ernest Cushing, 430-435, 33, 38, 216

Richardson, Henry Hobson, 435-436, 21, 203
Richardson, Mary, (S)72
Rider, Arthur Fremont, 437-439, 98, 125, 175, 323, 429, 578
Riley, James Whitcomb, 223, 358
Rips, Rae Elizabeth, 56
Roach, Eileen
    See Cunningham, Eileen Roach
Robbins, Mary E., 296
Roberts, Clarinda, 158
Roberts, Ina, 190
Robinson, Nell, 364
Robinson, Otis Hall, 439-441, 195, 538
Robinson, Sarah E., 441
Rockefeller, John D., 427
Rockefeller, John D., Jr., 41
Rockwell, George T., 118
Rodell, Elizabeth, 399
Roden, Carl Bismark, 441-443, 12, 312
Roger, John M., 14
Rogers, Bruce, 358
Rogers, Frank B., (S)1
Rogers, James Gamble, 292
Rogers, Marie, 530
Rogers, Ruth, 92
Rogers, Rutherford, 376
Rollins, Charlemae Hill, (S)111-115, (S)45
Rollins, Joseph Walter, (S)111
Roorbach, Orville Augustus, 443-444, 486
Roorbach, Orville A., Jr., 443
Roos, Jean Carolyn, (S)115-119, 306
Roosevelt, Franklin D., 4, 5, 51, 426
Roosevelt, Theodore, 22, 130, 326, 350, 420, 436
Root, Azariah Smith, 444-446, (S)83, (S)102
Root, Sheldon L., 13
Rose, Ernestine, 447-448, 249
Rose, Helen Louise, 485
Rosenbach, A. S. W., 62, 565
Rosenberg, Betty, 367
Rothrock, Mary Utopia, 448-449
Rothschild, J., 73
Rothstein, Samuel, 578
Rourke, Constance, 306
Royall, Anne, 545
Royce, Josiah, 230
Rudolph, Alexander Joseph, 449-450, 164
Rufsvold, Margaret, 252
Rugg, Arthur P., 216
Rush, Benjamin, 21
Rush, Charles Everett, 450-452, 191, 286, (S)117
Rush, James, 493
Russell, Charlie, 326
Russell, John M., 286
Rutan, Charles, 435
Ryan, Arthur, 324
Ryerson, Edward, 526

Sabin, Joseph, 452-455, 110, 150, 331, 529
Sabine, Edward, 116
Sacconi-Ricci, (Signora), 402
St. John, Francis Regis, 455-456, 175, 550
Salisbury, Edward E., 533
Salisbury, Stephen, 215
Salvator, Ludwig, 494
Sand, George, 233
Sandburg, Carl, 358, 425
Sanders, Minerva Amanda Lewis, 456-458
Sanders, Samuel, 456
Sands, Charlotte, 203
Sangren, Paul, 306
Sargent-Smith, Bessie, 523
Satterthwaite, Marian, 74
Savage, Susan Keim, 367
Savord, Catherine Ruth, 458-460
Sawyer, Lucy, 47
Sawyer, Ruth, 481
Sayers, Berwick, 37
Sayers, Frances Clarke, 155, 370
Schenk, Rachel Katherine, 460-461
Schick, Frank L., (S)106
Schirmer, Rudolph, 497
Schomburg, Arthur Alphonso, 461-463, 9, 45, 123, 447
Schreiber, Lucile, 349
Schurz, Carl, 55
Schwab, John C., 284
Schwartz, Jacob, Jr., 463-465, 128
Schwartz, Mortimer D., 415
Schwartzman, Bernice, 512
Schwegmann, George, 433
Scoggin, Margaret Clara, 465-467, 306
Scott, Edith, 228
Scott, Thomas, 69
Scroggs, W. O., 459
Scudder, Wallace, 118
Sealock, Richard, 550
Sears, Anna, 118
Sears, Minnie Earl, 467-468, 192, 340, 377, 560
Seaver, W. M., 525
Seelye (Professor), 126
Seligman, Edwin R., 554
Sellers, Mary Jane (Sally), 392
Serra, Junípero, 328
Sewell, Helen, 370
Seymour, May, 468-470, 32, 132, 173
Seymour, Whitney North, 79
Shank, Russell, 94
Shanley, Maria, 544
Sharp, Katherine Lucinda, 470-473, 132, 168, 169, 253, 254, 255, 296, 339, 340, 377, 469, 522
Shasta, Calle, 96
Shaw, Charles Bunsen, 473-476, 35
Shaw, Dorothy R., 341
Shaw, George Bernard, 495

Shaw, Ralph Robert, 476-481, 64, 159, 353, 485, 486
Shaw, Robert K., 173, 215, 216, 573
Shea, Agatha L., (S)112
Shearer, Augustus H., 65, 304, 371
Shedlock, Marie L., 481-482, 369, 370
Shepard, Anne, 379
Shepardson, Whitney Hunt, 459
Shepley, George, 435
Shera, Helen M. Bickham, (S)119
Shera, Jesse, (S)119-123, (S)38, (S)134
Sherman, Clarence Edgar, 482-483, 184, 185
Sherman, P. D., 295
Shipton, Clifford Kenyon, 483-484, 44, 62, 166, 167, 388, 486, 488
Shirley, William Wayne, 484-485, 429
Shoemaker, Richard Heston, 485-487, 353, 479
Shores, Geraldine Urist, (S)124
Shores, Louis, (S)123-129, 45, 289, 290, (S)105
Showers, Victor C., 491
Sibley, John Langdon, 487-489, 1, 382, 483, 571
Silliman, Benjamin, 89, 201
Simnett, W. E., 143
Sims, William S., 424
Sisler, Della J., 98
Skelton, Martha, 266
Slade, William Adams, 363
Sleeper, Grace J., 146
Small, A. J., 573
Small, William, 266
Smalley, George W., 584
Smith, Caleb B., 507
Smith, Carleton, 286
Smith, Charles Wesley, 489-490, 268, (S)109
Smith, Charlotte McMahon, 305
Smith, Elva Sophronia, 490-491, 387, 388, 458
Smith, Eugene Ferry, 542
Smith, G. W. V., 116
Smith, George E. P., Jr., 490, 491
Smith, Joseph, 95
Smith, Josephine Donna
  See Coolbrith, Ina Donna
Smith, Lillian, 319
Smith, Lloyd Pearsall, 491-493, 216, 408
Smith, Mildred C., 358
Smith, Samuel H., 57, 267
Smith, Walter McMynn, 228
Snider, Denton J., 230
Snyder, Franklyn, 293
Solberg, Thorvald, 493-495, 54, 342, 343, 562, 585, 586
Sonneck, Oscar George Theodore, 495-499
Sorber, James, 475
Soule, Charles C., 494

Spain, Frances L., 156
Spalding, Charlotte, 582
Sparks, Jared, 89
Spear, Dorothea N., 62, 63
Spiller, Helen Newbold, 2
Spivacke, Carolyn Le Fevre, (S)129
Spivacke, Harold, (S)129-131
Spivacke, Rosemarie Grentzer, (S)131
Spofford, Ainsworth Rand, 499-501, 219, 228, 357, 363, 381, 384, 419, 493, 506, 537, 585
Sprogle, Howard O., 308
Sproul, Robert Gordon, 95
Stallman, Esther Laverne, 501-503
Stamps, Frances, 263
Standen, Anthony, 101
Stanley, Henry M., 584
Stanwood, Ethel, 44
Starks, Samuel W., 503-504
Stearns, Lutie Eugenia, 504-505, 258
Stebbins, Kathleen Brown, (S)131-133
Stefansson, S. T., 342
Steiner, Bernard Christian, 505-506
Steiner, Lewis H., 163
Steinke, Eleanor, 107
Stephens, Marion, 250
Stephens (Mr.), 320
Stephenson, John Gould, 506-508, 357, 499
Stephenson, Reuben H., 499
Stevens, B. F., 409
Stevens, Edward F., 427
Stevens, George, 200
Stevens, Henry N., 405, 568
Stevens, Hestor Lockhart, 26
Stevens, Katherine Mary, 26
Stevens, M. E., 41
Stevenson, Adlai, 390, 399
Stevenson, Burton Egbert, 508-510, 263
Stevenson, Grace, 87, 346
Stewart, Mildred, 476
Stillwell, Margaret Bingham, 185, 569
Stoddard, Charles Warren, 96, 97, 327
Stokes, I. N. Phelps, 388, 577
Stokes, Katharine, 307
Stone, Alice B., 17
Storms, Jeanette Boynton, 208
Story, Joseph, 515
Stout, James, 258
Strang, Ruth, 466
Streeter, Thomas W., 62, 353
Strohm, Adam Julius, 510-511, 42, 269, 283, 555, (S)139
Strong, George F., 553
Strout, Ruth French, 74
Strunk, Oliver, 136
Studebaker, John, 93
Sturgis, Russell, 517
Suhl, Louise, 547
Sullivan, Louis, 436
Sullivan, Peggy, 74

Sutherland, Zena, 13, 14
Swank, Raynard C., 536
Swem, Earl Gregg, 511-512
Swift, Gertrude I., 280
Symonds, John Addington, 219

Talmadge, Robert L., 398
Tarkington, Booth, 358
Tate, Allen, (S)61
Taube, Mortimer, 512-513, 208
Tauber, Maurice Falcolm, (S)133-136, 260, 270, 426, 513, (S)43, (S)158, (S)162
Tauber, Rose Begner, (S)133
Taylor, Archer, 390
Taylor, Elizabeth Morrow, 462
Taylor, Frederick Winslow, 189
Taylor, Kanardy, 16
Taylor, Margaret C., (S)167
Taylor, Mark, 13
Taylor, Oliver A., 272
Ten Brook, Andrew, 121
Terry, J. S., 19
Thomas, Douglas, 424
Thomas, Esther
    See Grover, Esther Thomas
Thomas, Isaiah, 62
Thomas, Martha Carey, 554
Thompson, Adeleine True, 171
Thompson, Lawrence S., 17
Thompson, William Hale, 441
Thorndike, Israel, 88
Thumm, Janice Lovaine, 573
Thurston, Ada, 216
Thwaites, Reuben Gold, 513-515, 22, 142
Thwing, Charles Franklin, 246, 523, 553
Ticknor, George, 515-516, 87, 88, 89, 90, 273
Tilden, Samuel J., 55
Tilton, Edward Lippincott, 516-517, 203, 204
Tinker, Edward Laroque, 23
Tisdel, K. S., 362
Tisserant, Eugène, 34
Titcomb, Mary Lemist, 518-519
Titley, Joan
    See Adams, Joan Titley
Titzell, Josiah, 370
Tobitt, Edith, 320
Tolman, Frank, 577
Tompkins, Miriam Downing, 519-521, 286, (S)150
Toomer, Jean, 44, 45
Torrey, Bertha Louise, 554
Treadwell, Daniel G., 149
Trelease, William, 17
Trost, Herminie Frances, 286
Trowbridge, Ella, 195
Truman, Elizabeth D., 499
Truman, Harry S., (S)30
Truman, William T., 499
Trumbull, James H., 179, 454

Tucker, Harold Walton, 521-522
Turner, Frederick Jackson, 207, 349, 515
Turner, Sallie, 337
Turville, Jessie Inwood, 514
Twain, Mark, 301
Tyler, Alice Sarah, 522-525, 459, 579
Tyler, Anna Cogswell, 481
Tyler, John, 524
Tyler, Moses Coit, 227
Tyler, Ralph W., 520, (S)150

Ulrich, Carolyn Farquhar, (S)136-138
Ulveling, Ralph Adrian, (S)138-144, 306
Upton, Eleanor, (S)167
Upton, William Treat, 497
Usher, Robert J., 22
Utley, George Burwell, 525-527, 12, 361, 365, 384, 390
Utley, Henry Munson, 527-529

Vail, Robert William Glenroie, 529-530, 150, 152, 455
Van Heusen, Neil, 45
Van Hoesen, Henry Bartlett, 530-532, 82, 270, 541
Van Doren, Mark, (S)59
Van Kirk, Kate, 196
Van Laer, A. J. F., 577
Van Loon, Hendrik Willem, 370
Van Name, Addison, 532-534, 201, 284
Van Patten, Nathan, 535-536, 426
Van Vliet, Jessica Sherman, 284
Van Zandt, Nicholas, 337, 338
Vann, Sarah, 41, 279, 556
Varner, Velma, (S)39
Vattemare, Hippolyte, 536
Vattemare, Nicolas-Marie-Alexandre, 536-537, 357
Vermuelen, C. H., 283
VerNooy, Winifred, 426
Victor Emmanuel III (King of Spain), 526
Vignaud, Henry, 233
Viguers, Ruth Hill, (S)93
Vinson, Robert E., 245
Vinton, Frederic, 537-538, 384
Vitz, Alda Clayton, (S)145
Vitz, Carl Peter Paul, (S)144-148, 281, 360, 541, 577
Vitz, Ruth Van Aernam, (S)144
Voight, Melvin, 94
Vormelker, Rose, 154

Wadlin, Horace G., 23
Waggener, Adine Rowena, 116
Wagman, Frederick H., 81
Wagnalls, Adam W., 47
Waldstein, Charles, 517

Walker, Caroline Burnite, 538-540
Walker, Martha Blanche, 143
Walker, Robert Rastall, 539
Walker, Virginia Wood
    See Kuhlman, Virginia Wood Walker
Wallace, Malcolm W., 319
Wallbridge, D. Edith, 75
Waller, Theodore, 86
Walraven, Margaret, (S)37
Walter, Frank Keller, 540-542, 531
Waples, Dorothy Blake, (S)150
Waples, Douglas, (S)148-151, 19, 143, 144, 520, (S)13, (S)159
Waples, Eleanor Jackson Cary, (S)148
Ward, Charles F., 346
Ward, Samuel, 89
Warheit, Elizabeth Limberg, (S)151
Warheit, Israel Albert, (S)151-153
Warner, Frances, 64
Warren, Althea Hester, 542-543, 239
Washington, George, 266
Wasson, Donald, 459
Waters, Edward N., (S)130
Watson, Dorothy E., 160
Watterson, Henry, 586
Watterson, George, 543-546, 355
Wayland, Francis, 272
Weaver, Ruth Elizabeth, 204
Webster, Daniel, 515
Webster, Joy Louise, 52
Weintraub, Benjamin, 486
Weitenkampf, Frank, 546-547
Welch, d'Alté A., 62, 63
Welch, William, 26
Wellman, Hiller Crowell, 547-548, 516, 517
Wells, James M., 390
Welsh, Charles, 491
Wenzel, Evelyn, 13-14
West, Dorothy Herbert, 156
West, Theresa Hubbell
    See Elmendorf, Theresa Hubbell West
Westby, Barbara M., 467
Westcott, Mary Ann, 394
Whaley, Margaret M., 280
Wheeler, Benjamin I., 97
Wheeler, Joseph Lewis, 549-552, 86, 92, 170, 203, 204, 259, 282, 334, 335, 374, 456, 517, 526, 577
Wheeler, Mabel, 551
Whiston, Emily Andem, 548
White, Andrew Dickson, 201, 228
White, Carl Milton, (S)153-156, 45, 312
White, Frank Linstow (pseud.), 546
White, Horace, 55
White, John G., 60, 61
White, Llewellyn, 311
White, Paul Dudley, 182
White, Richard Grant, 455
White, Ruth Bennett, (S)153

White, Stanford, 435, 436, 437
White, William Allen, 349, (S)27
Whitehill, Walter Muir, 569
Whitfield, Louise, 70
Whitman, Walt, 586
Whittall, Gertrude Clarke, (S)130
Whittlesey, Julia M., 523
Widener, Harry Elkins, 300
Widener, (Mrs.) George D., 300, 301
Wiggin, Kate Douglas, 369
Wight, E. A., 73
Williams, Edward Christopher, 552-553
Williams, Evelyn Blanche, 305
Williams, Harold Workman (pseud.), 561
Williams, J. J., 257
Williams, M. S., 259
Williams, Mabel, 465
Williams, Roger, 559
Williams, Samuel Wells, 533
Williamson, Charles Clarence, 553-558, 10, 42, 72, 84, 225, 278, 279, 285, 333, 380, 428, 446, (S)102, (S)154
Wilson, Eugene H., 64
Wilson, Halsey William, 558-561, 172, 579
Wilson, Irene Atwood, 237
Wilson, James Grant, 546
Wilson, Justina, 561
Wilson, Leslie, 574
Wilson, Louis Round, (S)156-163, 18, 42, 67, 94, 146, 220, 275, 426, 474, 556, (S)36, (S)105, (S)134, (S)135, (S)149
Wilson, Martha, 170, 171, 226, 227, 416

Wilson, Penelope Bryan, (S)159
Wilson, Woodrow, 82, 431, 432
Winchell, Constance M., (S)163-165, 378
Windsor, John Alexander, 562
Windsor, Phineas Lawrence, 561-564, 108, 259, 541, (S)49, (S)102
Wing, Donald Goddard, 564-566
Winger, Howard, 74
Winn, Barbara
    See Adams, Barbara Winn
Winser, Beatrice, 566-568, 117, 281
Winship, George Parker, 568-570, 2, 62, 185, 327, 328, 575
Winslow, Amy, 275, 451, 550, (S)150, (S)167
Winslow, Helen, 135
Winsor, Justin, 570-572, 126, 127, 184, 202, 216, 298, 299, 300, 303, 317, 384, 385, 393, 408, 419, 440, 463, 488, 493, 501, 527, 538, 568
Winterborn, (Mr.), 452
Wire, George Edwin, 572-573, 33, 228
Wittcoff, Ray, 93
Wolf, Edwin, II, 487
Wood, Annie M., 243
Wood, Sarah B., 213
Woods, Bill Milton, 573-575
Woodward, Charles L., 149
Woodworth, Florence, 576
Woolley, Mary Emma, 323
Woolsey, Elizabeth Dwight, 200
Woolsey, Theodore Dwight, 201
Works, George A., (S)166-168, 67, 580, (S)148, (S)159

Works, Saidee B. Coerper, (S)166
Wormer, Grace, 374
Wright, Frank Lloyd, 436
Wright, Helena Lawrence Kellogg, (S)169
Wright, John Kirtland, 583
Wright, Purd B., 328
Wright, Wyllis Eaton, (S)168-171
Wright, Zoe, 306
Wriston, Henry M., 531
Wroth, Lawrence Counselman, 575-576, 151, 152, 153, 162, 165, 167, 217
Wyche, Benjamin, 260
Wyer, James Ingersoll, 576-579, 49, 92, 108, 252, 322, 379, (S)144
Wyer, Malcolm Glenn, 579-582, 237, 253, 254, 576
Wylie, Susan Wilson, 385
Wynar, Bohdan S., (S)41
Wynkoop, Asa, 392
Wythe, George, 266

Yarmolinsky, Avrahm, 330
Yonge, Ena Laura, 582-584
Young, James, 585
Young, John Russell, 584-586, 219, 228, 299, 343, 381, 419, 494, 499
Young, Lena, 163, 166
Yust, William F., 179, 554

Zeitlin, Jake, 536
Zimmerman, Carma, 313